PEASANTS IN THE MIDDLE AGES

To Bärbel, Anne and Benno

PEASANTS
IN THE
MIDDLE AGES

Werner Rösener

*Translated and with foreword and glossary
by Alexander Stützer*

University of Illinois Press
Urbana and Chicago

Illini Books edition, 1992
© C. H. Beck'sche Verlagsbuchhandlung (Oscar Beck), 1985
First published in Germany as *Bauern im Mittelalter*
This English translation © Polity Press, 1992

Manufactured in Great Britain
P   5   4   3   2

This book is printed on acid-free paper.

ISBN 0–252–06289–2

Contents

Part VI   The Upheavals of the Late Middle Ages

Illustrations

Translator's Foreword

Sparked by interest in the German Peasants' War of 1525, an increasing number of books and articles on agrarian society in central Europe during the Early Modern Period have recently appeared in English. This welcome change has, however, scarcely generated a corresponding increase in publications for the Middle Ages. In order to learn more about medieval agrarian society in central Europe, the English-speaking reader must still turn to the pages of the *Cambridge Economic History*, which only reflect the state of scholarship in the 1930s, or to George Duby's important survey, itself now nearly thirty years old and really only suggestive of developments peculiar to central Europe. More recent works on medieval agrarian history, such as those by R. Fossier and R. H. Hilton, focus on France and England. Now, however, this translation of Werner Rösener's *Peasants in the Middle Ages* offers a survey on the principal problems affecting the medieval peasantry of central Europe. For the English-speaking reader this book has a twofold importance. On the one hand it places developments particular to the Germanic and Slavic regions within a general European context, and on the other, it presents the reader with a brief introduction to the methods and subject-matter of German scholarship on agrarian history. This latter point is of particular importance where the issues raised by German scholars have diverged from those raised in France and Britain.

It is worth pointing out that both the unique character of historical developments and the diverging historical tradition presented here raise problems for a translation. Numerous terms have no English equivalents or ones that are at best ambiguous. However, loading the text with too many German terms would be cumbersome and reduce the text's readability. Hence the use of German terminology has been restricted to those cases where there could be misunderstandings or to where it would have been necessary to repeat phrases in English when a single word in German would suffice. These German words are clarified in the text, and most are also included in the Glossary at the end of the book. In addition, where possible, bibliographical suggestions have been added for English-speaking readers, but as much of the subject-matter concerning central Europe has received recent treatment only in German, an extensive English bibliography is premature.

Finally, for their assistance with the translation, I would like to thank Clif Hubby, Bob Scribner, and Martin Vinsome.

Alexander Stützer
Freiburg im Breisgau

PART I

MEDIEVAL PEASANTRY:

Origins and Development

INTRODUCTION

When one considers how rural life and peasant existence have long been reputed to be backward and primitive, it is surprising to witness the popularity which it has attained in the last few years. City-dwellers, who had previously regarded village life with contempt, now try to escape 'the inhospitability of our cities' (Alexander Mitscherlich) and look to the country in search of self-identity, healthier surroundings and closeness to nature. Everywhere we find an interest in village life and forms of peasant existence. Books like J. Seymour's *Complete Book of Self Sufficiency* are best sellers,[1] and pictures romanticizing the peasant world decorate the walls of modern city buildings. Not only a fashionable nostalgia but also the ecological movement, the new awareness of environmental issues and the concern for the preservation of a humane society have contributed to this development.[2] The political motives and origins of this newly awakened interest in the world of the peasant are in fact quite diverse, ranging from the well-known disenchantment with civilization and the anticipation of a healthier life-style to the prospect of discovering genuine social ties within the more easily grasped limits of a village. The pleasure of trips to the country and fond memories of previous holidays feed these expectations unintentionally, by emphasizing the contrast with the modern city.

This new appreciation of nature, landscape and the world of the peasant is ultimately founded on a desire for identity and security which many people find pointedly missing in the highly specialized working world of modern industrial society and in the monotony of daily life in the anonymous residential areas of big cities. By contrast, the apparent wholeness of peasant existence represents a world in which the status of each is clearly defined, and personal fulfilment appears less impaired. How far does this view of peasant life correspond with reality past and present? Has this ideal of peasant life ever existed as far as the family, village or nature are concerned?

It is no longer a secret that the village has changed, and that the contemporary working world of farmers is dominated by machines and specialized production. Although there may be a handful of villages and distant regions with old-fashioned farms – with horse-drawn vehicles, diversified forms of cultivation and virtual self-sufficiency – modern farms in central and western Europe conform on the whole to EC standards. Many operations have been mechanized: machines such as tractors, combine harvesters and milking machines dominate, replacing human labour with capital-intensive equipment. Specialized production has restricted the contemporary farmer, making him even more dependent upon the fluctuations of the market. He has turned into a market-orientated producer of agricultural goods who, like any other producer, is constrained by the rules of that market. The structure of agriculture has been changing drastically for a long time now, resulting in particular in a reduction of employment in the agrarian sector. In 1800 more than 60 per cent of the German population worked in agriculture. This proportion was reduced in West Germany to 25 per cent by 1950 and to as little as 6 per cent by 1980.[3] Such radical changes in the social structure were only possible because of a significant increase in productivity and because ever fewer peasants produced ever more agricultural commodities until over-production finally became a major problem on the European market.

There has been a fundamental structural transformation of the village parallel to the changes on the farms themselves. Many villages have lost their former function,[4] at the same time losing their schools, town halls, shops and jobs. As a result, modern farmers and commuters have to cover long distances to get to work, or to reach schools, municipal authorities or shopping centres, thereby contributing to the ever increasing density of traffic. The writer Walter Kempowski comments on the contemporary situation of the villages:

> For years, townspeople have been fumbling with structures which have been taken for granted for centuries. I am talking about small, well-balanced communities where, on the whole, nothing was amiss. They have taken the schools away from them, and with them the teacher who felt responsible for all cultural and educational matters . . . Then they started what they thought was a necessary simplification of administration. Village authorities were consolidated, with the single result that costs increased outrageously. But worse than that, the old names were abolished. Today there are villages in Lower Saxony just called NBI. All this was brought about by mindless townspeople. And now they come here and want to recuperate in surroundings they have despised and destroyed.[5]

In the German-speaking world, agrarian Romanticism and a tendency to idealize the peasantry and rural life can be traced back to the nineteenth century. W. H. Riehl (1823–1897), the pioneer of German folklore studies, should be specially mentioned in this context for his utopian view of the patriarchal peasant family and of rural life in general.[6] His interest in past social conditions, and especially social structures before the turning-point brought about by the French Revolution and the rise of industrial capitalism, was predicated upon a conservative critique of contemporary society. He thought that the political and social crisis of the 1850s consequent on the social, economic and political changes of the first half of the nineteenth century could be overcome by a restoration of traditional values and communal forms. The focus of his efforts for restoration was the peasantry. He idealized peasant life into a model of all things good by contrast with the apparent decadence of urban industrial centres; indeed he held that it was solely as a result of the stubbornly conservative attitude of the peasant that the German aristocracy survived the revolution of 1848–9:

> At the heart of the German nation is an insuperable conservative power, a steadfast core resistant to all change, and it is embodied in our peasants . . . The peasant has more political influence in this country than peasants in other countries of Europe; the future of the German nation is the peasant. The life of the German people is constantly being invigorated and restored to youth by the peasants.[7]

Riehl described the harmonious companionship of the peasant household with great sympathy, comparing the relationship between master and servant with that between father and child, thereby glorifying the 'good old days' of the authoritarian, patriarchal family and household. Social inequality seemed a law of nature as far as he was concerned. He claimed that the medieval peasant's bondage had been no evil but 'a true blessing', and that it had even helped 'to prevent peasant vagrancy' and had laid the foundations for what would become the main characteristic of the peasantry, namely perseverance.[8] Accordingly, the weight of feudal tyranny bearing upon the German peasantry in the Middle Ages was actually a 'schooling for life',[9] and the peasant had it to thank for one of his most precious virtues, his boundless tenacity. In his own time, Riehl found true moral values represented only in the traditional peasantry: 'Where religion, national feeling, social and family life are still simply instinctual and customary, there is the German peasant.'[10] Riehl's views and formulations were appreciated by many contemporaries influenced by Romanticism and traditional Teutonic views, and were echoed in later decades. His splendidly written books and other writings sold well and were read and reread with interest not only by students of folklore but also by a broad middle-class audience. It was not only Riehl who contrasted healthy peasant life with urban decadence. The spectre of the modern city had already been invented by the literature of the nineteenth century and contrasted to the idyllic and wholesome world of the village and the peasant.[11] Such attitudes were furthered and developed, if in modified form, in the emerging social sciences and in conservative cultural criticism. The study of how far these different currents of thought influenced National Socialism's 'ideology of the peasant' is an important subject which, for obvious reasons, cannot be treated in this book.[12]

As early as the 1850s, the reality of peasant life was rather different from the picture painted by Riehl and other contemporary advocates of agrarian Romanticism. The same is true of rural social and material life in the Middle Ages and in the centuries before the profound changes of the nineteenth century, as recent scholarship in agricultural history and historical ethnography has shown. We must always keep the 'otherness' of the pre-industrial peasantry firmly in mind if we are to arrive at a proper understanding of a rural world so alien to us in all its manifold economic, social and cultural relationships. What, for instance, did it mean to live in huts without electricity, glazed windows and running water, with only an open fireplace producing inadequate heating during the cold winter months? How did people live together when several generations had to occupy the same working, living, eating and sleeping spaces along with the servants? What happened when harsh winters and rainy summers caused crop failures? Or when supplies ran out too quickly and led to death – all part of the harsh reality of the so-called 'good old days'?

The sublime historical events and deeds which fill the pages of weighty historical books had only marginal significance for the peasant viewing them from the perspective of the village. The introduction of the three-field system, the clearance of forestland and the harnessing of horsepower mattered more to the development of the medieval village than Otto the Great, Pope Innocent III or any other emperor and pope. Similarly, the Concordat of Worms, the Golden Bull or the Battle of Bouvines were relatively unimportant for the peasants compared to bad harvests, floods or catastrophic epidemics such as the plagues. The demands of life, its cares and worries, its joys and pains, determined the daily and annual rhythm of peasant existence. Injustice, inequality and oppression were accepted as divinely ordained and unavoidable, although they were sometimes resisted with great determination. Unremitting toil from dawn to dusk set its stamp on the daily round of peasant work in the home, in the farmyard, in the fields or meadows. The hard labour of peasants cannot be adequately recaptured by the painstaking study of archival sources or learned tomes, but must be experienced in living contact with the reality of farming life. The harsh world in which the traditional peasantry worked has been characterized by U. Jeggle, an ethnographer, as follows:

Little change affected the implements of agrarian production; peasant life was almost completely restricted to providing for material existence . . . The farming body was not familiar with luxury of any kind: it only knew work. Likewise, wife and children were merely means of production. Socialization meant nothing other than getting used to work. Work determined the rhythm of the day, the seasons, and the phases of life. Cows, goats or roosters got the peasant out of bed in the mornings, and his mealtimes depended on the time of year and its activities. There was much more time for sleep and social activities in winter when the peasant household gathered around pine-torch and distaff in the evening. But leisure-time as such did not exist because working and living were closely connected with each other.[13]

Fear was a basic experience of peasant life, operating on a day-to-day basis and shaping all its threatening aspects.[14] The peasant existence was ruled by uncertainty and disease, natural catastrophe, misfortune and war, as well as oppression by feudal lords. Especially in the Middle Ages, peasants (90 per cent of the entire population), suffered from the consequences of brutal wars, manorial encroachments and the capriciousness of the forces of nature. Despite occasional peaceful interludes interspersed between major acts of war, feuding knights and mercenary gangs eager for prey still constantly threatened farms and villages, fire-raising and looting, terrorizing an already tormented rural population. Yet for the peasants in the Middle Ages, the forces of nature were worse than acts of war because they had to cope with them in summer as well as in winter, in hot and in cold weather, in rainy and in dry periods. With little available technical aid and low productivity, the peasant economy of that time depended even more on climate and weather. The same capriciousness of nature which produced cereals and fruit, vegetables and raw materials of all kinds could literally reclaim all of this in times of disaster, devastating crops with hail, hay with great drought, or cattle with diseases. The law of nature, being at the same time provision and denial, shaped the life of the peasant family. Nothing was secure or predictable for any length of time; the dependence on nature and environment was ubiquitous in every aspect of peasant life.

Yet another powerful factor of peasant existence in medieval feudal society was the bondage to the manor. Until German peasants were liberated in the nineteenth century, the majority of them depended on feudal lords who were entitled to various tributes and services. The manorial lords let land to the peasants on certain conditions, claiming taxes or farm produce in return. A wide range of services was due to the lords of the manor, personal lords and judicial lords at certain times of the year, or at certain points in the peasant's life. Taxes had to be paid upon marriage and death, on St George's and on St Martin's Day, in spring and in autumn. Pathetically little remained for the peasants in years of bad harvests, and even in normal years the remaining supplies only allowed for a modest livelihood.

With rare exceptions over the last few decades, West German historians have neglected the social history of the peasant as well as the conditions of peasant existence in medieval society. Further works in the excellent tradition of K. Lamprecht, A. Dopsch, R. Kötzschke and others on the economic, social, agrarian and settlement history of rural areas are to be hoped for in historical research on peasant life.[15] Most works on peasant and agrarian history focused on those aspects which related to the history of law and constitution in regard to the free and the bonded status of the peasant, the structure of rural authority and the development of the village.[16] The only notable exception to this trend is W. Abel with his works on the history of medieval agriculture, agrarian crises, agrarian economy, and on the increase of deserted settlements in the late Middle Ages.[17] Recent discussions on the forms of peasant resistance and peasant wars have indeed come out with some interesting studies of the late Middle Ages, yet most of them have dealt primarily with the peasant of early modern times.[18]

Traditional West German research on the Middle Ages was still primarily concerned with themes related to the development of the papacy, royal authority and problems connected with the church, the Holy Roman Empire and the nobility. As a consequence of this H. Dannenbauer, whose investigations on the structure of medieval authority and the development of the nobility have had a decisive impact on recent contributions to the study of constitutional history, explicitly contrasted the power of the nobility with the insignificance of the peasant in medieval society:

> The medieval world was an aristocratic world; both state and society were ruled by the nobility. A number of influential families . . . had command over the country and its people. The good and the evil doings of this ecclesiastical and secular aristocracy have shaped the history of those centuries, filling the pages of the chronicles of that time. About other people there is nothing to be said. The rural folk were mostly in bondage, in various conditions of dependence. They were to obey, work, and pay their taxes; they had no political voice. In fact, they had no history at all.[19]

This attitude towards the peasantry was almost identical with Leopold von Ranke's notorious view of the 1525 peasant war which he called 'the outstanding natural phenomenon' in German history,[20] thus assigning the peasants to the sphere of elementary powers of nature. Even K. Bosl, exceptional among medievalists in his treatment of the role of rural lower classes, denied in a widely read textbook that the peasants had a 'real' history:

> As far as constitutional history was concerned, they [the aristocracy] were, in addition to the king, 'the people of the state and of the [German] Empire.' Since other social groups were neither influential in a political sense nor of historical significance, only their activities have been recorded in the chronicles; actually, countryfolk did not have a history.[21]

In contrast to German medievalists, French and British scholars have studied the medieval peasantry intensively over the last few decades. Among the French social historians who have dealt especially frequently with the conditions of peasant life in the Middle Ages, M. Bloch, G. Duby, G. Fourquin, E. Le Roy Ladurie and R. Fossier deserve special mention.[22] The most inspiring of the British and American contributions have been the studies by R. Hilton and A. J. Raftis.[23] After World War II, the impetus for research on the social history of the peasants was given by social and cultural anthropology. Especially stimulating among these contributions were 'community studies' and investigations into the 'peasant societies' in Africa, Latin America and European countries, which, according to their specific structural characteristics, allowed for a distinction between 'peasant, tribal and industrial societies'.[24]

T. Shanin, R. Redfield and above all E. R. Wolf have studied the characteristics of peasant societies in detail.[25] According to Wolf, the historical relevance of peasant societies as we find them today, mainly in Third World countries, consists in the fact that they form the basis of modern industrial societies. In such pre-industrial societies, peasants are in fact an integral part of the body politic, in which non-peasant members make demands upon them. If necessary, they are even in a position to enforce sanctions against them. The peasant farm and household form a single unit of production and consumption, encompassing all of its members. As opposed to the medieval peasant, the modern farmer works as an entrepreneur whose workers are no longer members of his household. One can see from the anthropological works mentioned above how far modern research on the social history of the peasantry has been influenced by the study of the economic, social and political situation in Third World countries.[26] In countries such as India, Cameroon or Mexico, the fact that peasants form the largest group of the population clearly reveals the numerous structural problems of peasant agrarian societies. The overwhelming majority of the population in most parts of the world today are peasants engaged in agriculture or stock-raising, dependent on weather, climate and frequently enough hovering on the brink of mere subsistence. Not only historical and anthropological research but in addition some related disciplines have added to our knowledge of the medieval peasantry and its forms of existence. The archaeology of the Middle Ages has taken a considerable step forward and has provided rich material for the study of peasant life drawn from numerous excavations of medieval settlements.[27] The study of popular culture (U. Bentzien, K. S. Kramer, G. Wiegelmann) has also contributed remarkably to the understanding of peasant mentality and the material culture of the medieval peasantry.[28] In this context, special heed has to be paid to the interdisciplinary study of medieval material culture which has set out to study both material culture and daily life and, as far as possible, to locate peasant material culture within its overall framework.[29] At this stage of research on the social history of the peasant, it would be rash to aim for a comprehensive study of the structure and development of the medieval peasantry. Much more work on the economic, social, cultural and political situation of the peasant population at the various stages of medieval history must be undertaken before we can come to final conclusions. Hence the following analysis focuses on the main aspects of the living conditions of peasants according to our present knowledge. Special emphasis will be placed on the basic economic, social and legal conditions of peasant life in the high and late Middle Ages. As far as the geographical scope of this analysis is concerned, peasant living conditions and processes of change in western and central Europe will be discussed and, to a lesser degree, developments in the neighbouring regions. Although by no means complete, this analysis is intended to illustrate a world which for many reasons has become alien to us in urban and industrial society, but which may attract a particular interest precisely because of its otherness.

1

THE FOUNDATIONS OF MEDIEVAL PEASANTRY

The problem of defining 'warriors' and 'peasants'

It is a common presupposition that medieval society was divided into the two estates of peasants and knights (or nobles). These two estates of peasantry and the knights were regarded throughout the entire Middle Ages as hereditary orders constituting the basis of a 'society of orders' which first broke down in the wake of the French Revolution. Does historical evidence support this common picture of the medieval social order? Did a peasantry and a nobility actually exist from the earliest days of the Middle Ages? The image of the timeless peasant, since ancient times tilling his farm eternally from generation to generation in the same manner, in the face of the assaults of nature, seems to accord with this picture of the medieval peasantry. Oswald Spengler, who propagated this idea of an eternally unchanging peasantry in *The Decline of the West* (1922), portrayed the peasant as an organic, rather than historical figure.[1] He summed up his views as follows:

> The peasant is without history. The village stands outside world-history, and all evolution from the 'Trojan' to the Mithridatic War, from the Saxon emperors to the World War of 1914, passes by these little points on the landscape, occasionally destroying them and wasting their blood, but never in the least touching their inwardness. The peasant is the eternal man, independent of every culture that ensconces itself in the cities. He precedes it, he outlives it, a dumb creature propagating himself from generation to generation, limited to soil-bound callings and attitudes, a mystical soul, a dry, shrewd understanding that sticks to practical matters, the origin and the ever-flowing source of the blood that makes world-history in the cities.[2]

The view of medieval society as a 'society of orders' goes back in large part to the social theories of medieval thinkers. They understood contemporary society as a social system determined by the three orders of the clergy, the knights and the peasantry.[3] Thus a chronicle reports that in 1030 Bishop Gerhard of Cambrai taught that the human race was from the beginning divided into the three estates of those who pray, those who labour and those who fight: '*Genus humanum ab initio trifarium divisum esse monstravit, in oratoribus, agricultoribus, pugnatoribus.*'[4] About the same time Aldabero of Laon distinguished between those who pray (*oratores*) those who fight (*pugnatores*) and those who labour (*laboratores*); all three estates were mutually interdependent, and so were assured a harmonious coexistence and guaranteed the divinely ordained order in society.[5] The 'theory of the three orders' of these and other medieval authors can be found for the most part in theological works, sermons on the estates and certain legal sources, but less so in charters and written documents concerning daily life.

Remarkably, the medieval peasantry appears as an 'estate' only from the eleventh and twelfth centuries.[6] The early Middle Ages had no concept corresponding to what we call a peasant, in the sense of a farmer, describing the mass of the population engaged in agriculture. Before the eleventh century the Old High German word *gebure* referred primarily to the other occupants of the house (*bur*), to fellow settlers or to those belonging to a 'neighbourhood' (*burschap*).[7] When early medieval sources mention the groups within the rural populations, they do not speak of *geburen*, *agricolae* or *rustici*, but use words such as *liberi*, *liti* and *servi*, meaning free, half-free and servile. All those engaged in agricultural and pastoral activity were subject to the general law of the early Middle Ages, as recorded in folk laws (*leges*).[8] Freemen were allowed to attend common assemblies and enjoyed the full legal rights and usually owned the land and the farm on which they worked. Bondsmen and bondswomen by contrast, did not have property of their own. They were liable to dues and services, and were subject to manorial lords who were also their personal overlords.

The peasant in the legal sense, therefore, was not an ancient figure unaffected by history but rather a historical figure that emerged in the high Middle Ages. Evidence reveals that the word 'peasant' did not appear before those engaged in agriculture became legally distinguishable from professional warriors, and, like knights and burghers, were classed together in a social division of their own.[9] From the eleventh century, *milites*, *cives* and *rustici* became increasingly standard words in legal texts, and the traditional distinction between *liberi* and *servi* disappeared. But why did the peasantry as an estate appear from the eleventh and twelfth centuries onwards? What factors determined these surprising historical developments? Clearly, the rather superficial reply which contended that all of mankind were originally peasants, and that for this reason the peasantry required no special attention, does not suffice as an explanation. What follows is an outline of the principal developments useful for an understanding of the complex history of the peasant in the early Middle Ages.

There can be no doubt that differentiation into a 'society of orders' was decisively quickened by the formation of a professional class of mounted warriors who were supported by fiefs, large-scale holdings and bondsmen, while the free armed yeomen were gradually forced out of military service. As a result, the mounted warriors and those prepared to join them excluded themselves more and more from the peasant population. The extensive and time-consuming military campaigns of the Frankish kings made it increasingly difficult for yeomen to take part in them. Hence, before long, the army turned into an elite, professional cavalry.[10] Two factors contributed to the social distinction between peasants and warriors, and to the further differentiation of their social roles: first, the special protection of the peasant in the peace settlements (*Landfrieden*, *Gottesfrieden*) of the eleventh and twelfth centuries, and second the introduction of special prohibitions which forbade peasants the possesion of arms.[11] Furthermore, with the spread of feudal tenures and the manorial system in Carolingian times, free persons became increasingly subject to feudal and manorial lords. Eventually free peasants were able to survive in backward areas only as fringe groups in society. In addition to political, manorial and military developments, special heed must also be paid to the changes in agriculture and the peasant economy.

Max Weber saw the main reason for peasant estrangement from military service in the intensification of farming. A fine example is the increased production of cereals in the high Middle Ages: 'Since the needs of farming required the continous presence of the peasant, male peasants were no longer available for raids and military campaigns. The less opportunity the peasant had for this kind of income, the more he clung, as it were, to the soil, and thus became relatively unwarlike.'[12] Compared with the early Middle Ages, the activities of the rural population in the high Middle Ages concentrated much more exclusively on agriculture. Otto Brunner has remarked that as the 'peasant warrior' turned into a 'husbandman',[13] the crucial political and military tasks were taken over by the noble manorial lords.

The interesting fact that the formation of the peasant order was not completed before the eleventh century must not be confused with the birth of the peasant as such. In purely economic terms, of course, peasants existed earlier as cultivators and stock-breeders, decisively shaping Europe's agricultural society in the early Middle Ages. However, with the emergence of a new peasant type in the high Middle Ages a new form of peasant life mingled with the traditional one, making it almost justifiable to restrict the word 'peasant' to use only after the emergence of a fully-fledged peasant order.[14] The peasantry of the high Middle Ages may be characterized by dependence to a manorial lord, the farming of individual or family lands and bondage to the soil in addition to a life-style and attitudes peculiar to peasants, such as being conservative, sedentary, placid and unwarlike. These peasant characteristics are quite similar to those which modern cultural anthropologists have found outside Europe. For cultural anthropologists as well as for ethnosociologists, peasants are the predominant group within a society based on a division of labour which does not need all of its members for the production of foodstuffs.[15] Peasants in these complex societies have in fact developed intensive farming methods, enabling them to produce in excess of subsistence in order to provide for non-agricultural members of society, that is for artisans, merchants and priests. The peasants within these societies are ruled by powerful non-peasants, have traditional attitudes and are tied to local social customs.

What striking changes and developments in the early Middle Ages had a lasting impact on the peasants of the time and their mentality? Although by no means complete, the following description seeks to point out some of the factors determining the life-style and social condition of the early medieval peasantry with special emphasis on economic, military, social and political aspects, as well as settlement patterns. Regional differences in environment, agrarian structures, legal relations and economic development can, of course, only be touched upon briefly.

New tendencies in the agrarian economy

First of all, special mention must be made of some of the changes in the agrarian economy.[16] On the threshold from the early to the high Middle Ages, land use was intensified, which resulted not only from the application of the three-field system and from an increase in grain production, but also from the employment of more efficient ploughs. The extra effort put into agriculture meant more work for the peasant at sowing and harvest times, making him less available for political and social tasks. The reshaping of the agrarian economy was most apparent when the conditions of the eleventh century are contrasted with those of earlier centuries. A less efficient use of land prevailed in most parts of Europe during the early Middle Ages: the methods of cultivation provided low yields, and primitive forms of crop rotation (*Urwechselwirtschaft*) as well as extensive grazing of meadow lands were common almost everywhere. There had been little change in farming methods since antiquity, nor were revolutionary changes in cultivation introduced in Carolingian times. The agricultural population possessed nothing more than primitive farming implements, generally wooden ones. Most of the soil was cultivated with hook-ploughs, the types of which varied in shape and quality. Since the soil was inadequately manured in the Middle Ages, the soil was soon exhausted and had to be left fallow for one or even two years before the land could be sowed again. Owing to the old method of crop rotation, with its long fallow periods and low yields, large tracts of land were necessary to produce the basic supply of grains and vegetables; on the whole, however, large pastures prevailed, as livestock contributed significantly to feeding the population.

Changes in settlement structures

Unlike during the high Middle Ages, settlement in the early medieval period was subject to marked fluctuations.[17] The inhabitants of such common settlement forms as single farms, groups of farmsteads and hamlets were forced from time to time to resettle on account of war or natural disasters. Resettlement was not difficult, since most houses, huts and working quarters were primitive constructions made out of wood, clay and straw. Over the past few decades, archaeological excavations of settlements and farms from the early Middle Ages have demonstrated that in many regions settlements existed for only a few centuries at a time and that the construction materials were relatively impermanent. Often only the old cemeteries outside the settlement centres survived. The density of settlement varied: conglomerations of densely settled areas alternated with large woodlands, swamps and thinly populated regions. With the use of sturdier construction materials, the gradual improvement of cultivation methods and the intensification of grain production, peasant settlements became more permanent. The proverbial sedentary character and rootedness of the peasantry in the high Middle Ages was the result of a long process and should not be taken as characteristic of peasant life at all times.

Another dynamic element in the history of the early Middle Ages was extensive expansion of settlement, which progressed, though with varying intensity, in almost every country and region, thereby enlarging the living space for an ever growing population. Colonization was carried out all over Europe, progressing particularly in the densely populated parts of the Frankish Empire where it was systematically promoted by the king as well as ecclesiastical and secular lords. The clearing of land started in Merovingian times, and may be studied in its various phases only through regional research. While peasants in the former provinces of the Roman Empire often simply recultivated lands long left fallow, some regions in central and northern Europe, mostly uninhabited or thinly populated woodlands and swamps, could only be developed with great effort. In Carolingian times, settlement was frequently advanced by systematic clearing under royal orders, but was often interrupted by the invasions of Vikings, Saracens and Magyars. These early attempts at colonization in the tenth and eleventh centuries thus paved the way towards those of the high Middle Ages, the zenith of the medieval colonization movement.

The development and consolidation of the manorial system

Developing and spreading out over a period of centuries, the manorial system became extremely important for every aspect of peasant life.[18] In its various forms, it was doubtlessly a central element of agrarian conditions in the early Middle Ages. Throughout the Middle Ages it provided the economic foundation for the secular and ecclesiastical elite, for lordship and courtly culture. While absorbing the majority of peasants in the course of its development, it left its imprint on their entire social, economic and political position. The modern terms 'manorial system' or 'seigniorial system' refer to one of the basic forms of medieval lordship: to 'the domination (*Herrschaft*) over land and peasants, that is over those who live and work on the land' (Otto Brunner).[19] The medieval peasant was not a tenant in the modern sense; rather he was dependent on or subject to his lord in a variety of ways.

In the manorial system rights over the soil were divided: the manorial lord held the direct ownership of the soil (*dominum directum*) while the peasant held the rights of usage (*dominum utile*). Among the important variants of the medieval manorial system was the early medieval *Fronhof*-system, also referred to by medievalists as the *Villikation*-system or the 'classical' demesne system. Another was a system based on the collection of rents and dues (*Rentengrundherrschaft*). The medieval manorial system must, however, be distinguished from the eastern European manorial system in early modern times, which can be characterized as the concentration of seigniorial rights within a limited area (*Gutsherrschaft*).

To avoid a confusion of terms, it is necessary to comment briefly on the relationship between the manorial and feudal systems. Historians and social scientists employ the word feudalism in a variety of ways.[20] The broad use of the term feudalism virtually equates manorialism and feudalism. As a rule, one meets this view in Marxist research which regards feudalism as the historical stage between a slave-based economy in antiquity and modern capitalism. Moreover, this view is also held by some social historians like Marc Bloch who, in his well-known work *Feudal Society*, has analysed the feudal system of the high Middle Ages and the condition of the peasant under manorial rule.[21] According to this view, feudalism refers not merely to legal relations in the feudal hierarchy from the king, through his great vassals, to the lowly *Einschildritter* – it included the economic and social order of the dependent peasant population. The structure and development of the manorial system, then, are seen in close correspondence to the growth of medieval feudal society in its various phases.

The formation of the early medieval manorial system fell into two main periods: the first, the birth and development of the manorial system from the sixth to the ninth centuries;[22] and the second, a period of expansion and consolidation from the ninth to the eleventh centuries. First it will be necessary to outline the conditions which led to the development of the manorial system. The origins of the west European manor can be found in the conditions of agrarian society in the later Roman Empire with its particular forms of peasant bondage, such as the colonate system, and in the structure of Germanic lordship and society. Although some historians contend that the medieval manorial system derived exclusively from the economic and social structure of the later Roman Empire, one must take into account that the seigniorial system of the early Middle Ages only inherited certain aspects of later Roman agriculture which by themselves were not identical with the manorial system of the early Middle Ages. Forms of personal bondage primarily characteristic of Germanic lordship, and Roman forms of property-holding were the two roots of the early medieval manorial system which, particularly in the Frankish Empire, developed a political and economic structure of its own.

The *Fronhof* system

The early medieval or 'classical' manorial system (*Villikation, Fronhof* system) was characterized by the demesne farm (*villa* or *curtis dominica*) in the centre, which was cultivated under the lord's management with the assistance of the domestic slaves and the tenants of dependent *mansi* or *Hufe*, known as *Hufebauern*. A *Hufe* (English 'hide', Latin *mansus*) was in effect a peasant holding including land and usage rights which in turn were subject to the demesne farm itself. The *Hufebauern*, that is the occupiers of a holding, were required to perform certain services and to pay rent.[23] The fully-developed manorial system consisted, therefore, of the demesne land (*Salland*) and the various holdings (*Hufen*) held by the peasants. The manors of the larger estates tended to be more systematically organized. Hence certain manors acted as central farms in charge of several main and subsidiary farms, which were in turn the nucleus of the individual manors with their peasant holdings. The conglomerate of manors with its numerous branches was organized in districts, each with a manor at its centre which was directed by an official called the *villicus* or bailiff. The proportion of the demesne land (*Salland*) to the individual holdings often varied from manor to manor, determining the quantity of peasant labour services, and hence the economic and social position of the peasants settled on the holdings. Even at the heart of the manorial estate, the greater part of the land was left to the peasants who, with the domestic slaves of the demesne farms, formed the association of lordly dependants known as the *familia*.

An established economic and legal system for the dependent peasant population came only with the development of the seigniorial system in Carolingian times. Royal, ecclesiastical and noble manors were unevenly spread all over the Carolingian Empire. These usually large estates derived from former Roman lands as well as through the occupation and bestowal of land. In addition to farming, the economy of the great manors depended on its workshops; consequently, the individual manors had a more or less self-sufficient economy which, for its own needs, depended little on the market.

No doubt there were also manors which served primarily to collect peasant dues, relying less on the production of demesne agriculture. However, the twofold system of demesne land and dependent peasant tenures, especially as it emerged at the core of the Carolingian Empire between the Rhine and the Loire, continues to be a significant factor in early medieval history.

The research of A. Verhulst confirms the assumption that this 'classical' form of the manorial system had its origin in the extraordinarily productive grain-growing areas of the seventh and eighth centuries in northern France and in the Paris area, spreading from there into the neighbouring regions.[24] Further, it would be utterly misleading to think that the Frankish Empire was covered by an extensive network of large manors under the management of a single centre. On the contrary, it was the relatively small peasant holding which, on the whole, determined the inner and outer relations of the manors. This applied to dependent peasants with holdings of their own as well as to those peasants who, although free, could not escape manorial rule altogether.

The detailed records of the Carolingian era provide more information on the conditions of manorial relations at the time. The *capitulare de villis* (*Landgüterordnung*), probably drawn up during the reign of Charlemagne, contains detailed information on the administration and cultivation of the royal demesnes.[25] Charlemagne gave express instructions to keep lists of the large-scale holdings of the crown and the churches. Indeed, in the ninth century registers on the ownership and revenues (polyptychs; in German *Urbare*) of the large ecclesiastical manors were drawn up which provide insight into the overall conditions of the dependent peasantry. Probably the best-known polyptych is that of Irminon, Abbot of Saint-Germain-des-Prés near Paris at the beginning of the ninth century. It was an extremely thorough record of the structure of a large ecclesiastical estate including all of its manors and holdings.[26] This 'land register' is invaluable in illustrating the conditions of peasant existence and gives a good idea of the size of peasant holdings as well as providing valuable information on revenues and the extent of labour service.

The period of the expansion and consolidation of the manorial system, between the ninth and the eleventh centuries, saw the fuller development of the rudimentary tendencies of the previous period. The substantial enlargement of the estates of royal, ecclesiastical and lay lords was produced by and likewise stimulated the rise of Carolingian kingship and the development of enfeoffment. There were three ways in which an increasing number of peasants were subjected to this growing manorial regime. The first was voluntary surrender of free peasants into bondage to the lord of the manor; the second was the violent oppression and enslavement of free peasants; and the third was the spreading of the manor through land clearance. During the troubled ninth and tenth centuries, peasants could not rely on the crown for protection. Hence many of them commended themselves to the authority of powerful lay and ecclesiastical lords in the region or even asked for their protection because the latter had usurped military, judicial and political authority. Quite a few lords enlarged their landed holdings, and hence their authority, by means of land-clearing, for which they enjoyed the advantage of having the necessary implements at their disposal. They were capable of organizing and conducting both clearing and settlement much more effectively than the peasants on their own.

The tenth and eleventh centuries brought about notable changes in the structure of the manorial system which also affected the position of the peasants. Immunities (*banalités*, *Bannbezirke*) were gradually developed which served on the one hand to consolidate the manorial rights and on the other to augment feudal revenues.[27] The exercise of the immunity rights allowed the manorial lords to establish and profit from monopoly enterprises, which included particularly mills, inns, wine-presses and baking-ovens. Decisive, however, was the judicial immunity, which was of greatest importance for the development of immunity districts by forcing the local peasants to attend the lord's court. The judicial immunity reached its fullest effect on those manors which were independent, that is in districts where neither the king nor his representatives exercised authority and the lords of the manor held the functions of authority in their place.

The decline of freemen

In the wake of the development of manorial rule between the ninth and the tenth centuries, a great number of previously free peasants were reduced to dependence on manorial lords. The aristocratic element of early medieval society was especially reinforced in the post-Carolingian centuries when the upper level of feudal society strengthened its economic and legal position, increasingly emphasizing its distinction from non-noble yeomen and gradually developing into a noble estate.[28] None the less, the sources of the period reveal that the number of free peasants in the empire of Charlemagne was far from negligible. In any case, the opinion must be rejected that aristocratic rule over dependent peasants was very widespread and that freemen were only a minority in early medieval society. Another hypothesis raised in recent historical debates should be regarded with great scepticism. Some researchers have maintained that the majority of free peasants in the Frankish Empire, the so-called *Königsfreie* (royal freemen), were granted the privilege of free status by the king or powerful lords for their services as military settlers in strategically important regions or for their efforts as colonists in woodlands or swamps.[29] On the contrary, the originally numerous freemen only became a minority in most parts of western Europe with the progression of the feudalization of state and society between the eighth and the eleventh centuries. Although there is evidence that relatively large groups of free peasants continued to exist in some parts of France, Italy or Scandinavia, their influence on the social structure of these countries in this period was negligible. There was almost no connection between them and the *Freibauern* (free peasants) of the high Middle Ages, for these were, as a rule, a new class of peasants whose duty it was to clear land (*Rodungsbauern*).

The rights and disabilities associated with freedom and bondage were for the most part determined by the structure of the manor and the degree of manorial dependence. In Italy, for example, free tenants survived throughout the Middle Ages next to servile peasants; their respective economic situations, nevertheless, were almost identical because rent played a greater role in the Italian manorial system than labour services.[30] Insofar as the peasant's obligation to serve the lord was gradually reduced in favour of rent, the distinctions between bonded and free tenants became less apparent. The bonded peasant with a large holding was often better off than a free peasant with little land or a tenant of a poor farmstead. In order to arrive at an accurate view of the situation in the Middle Ages, one must discriminate between the economic and the legal aspects of peasant life.

Changes in medieval warfare

Overall, the proportion of freemen among the peasantry decreased as a consequence of the changes in warfare and the military structure in Carolingian and post-Carolingian times. With the emergence of an army of mounted warriors endowed with fiefs and manorial property, a strong knightly nobility emerged, which furthered the process of differentiation between peasants and warriors until it was completed in the eleventh and twelfth centuries.[31] The growing strategic importance of the cavalry caused military expenses to rise, and this forced the peasants out of military service. Only with difficulty could an average farm supply the expensive armament for mounted warriors. When the Frankish Empire transformed its army into a cavalry, the average peasant, who was in possession of one or two holdings, was unable to take part in the military campaigns. He could not afford to leave his farm for weeks on end, especially during sowing and harvesting times, making it impossible, for example, to join the extensive campaigns of Charlemagne. Charlemagne took this into account, and with the reform of the military in 807 he decreed that only those peasants who held at least three holdings or a fief were required for military service. A year later, the minimum was raised to four holdings. The poorer freemen were then ordered to form groups combining property holdings and to choose from among themselves someone to represent them in military service.[32] In the years that followed, fief holders rather then peasants were recruited. Consequently it was generally left to the vassals to take part in the military campaigns of the tenth and eleventh centuries.[33] The system of fiefs and the rise of professional mounted warriors changed the military drastically. Those formerly involved in campaigns, including the previously independent peasants, were replaced by an army of noble vassals ideally represented by the mounted warrior in heavy armour. In comparison to the swiftness and mobility of the cavalry, peasant troops were slow and inefficient, as a result of which they were only rarely levied.

Of all these developments it was the emergence and expansion of the manorial system which had the most lasting impact upon the life of the rural population. Essentially the early medieval manorial system developed a strong tendency towards the levelling of the various peasant groups within its reach. On the other hand, the condition of the slaves and domestic dependants of earlier centuries improved as they were settled on individual farms and holdings by their lords; the condition of the majority of free peasants, on the other hand, worsened as they were forced into the fold of the manorial system. As a result the differences between free and bonded peasants became almost indistinguishable.[34] Before long the various social groups on the manor – the bonded domestics of the lord's own farm, the serfs settled on *Hufen* and rent-paying tenants – amalgamated into an internally differentiated, yet much more homogeneous peasantry. The old hereditary distinction between *liber* and *servus* slowly disappeared until the eleventh century, when it was replaced by the new functional distinction between *rusticus* (peasant) and *miles* (knight). The two estates, the knighthood and the peasantry, joined by the rising burghers of the towns, would shape the society, the economy and the culture of the high Middle Ages.

2

TRANSFORMATIONS IN
THE HIGH MIDDLE AGES

Origins and main aspects of the changes in the high Middle Ages

After a period in which little progress was made in colonization and clearance, and the growth of the economy and population stagnated, Europe experienced a unique period of social, economic and cultural development from the eleventh to the thirteenth centuries. In the opinion of Marc Bloch, a 'second feudal age', characterized by fundamental changes in the economy, began with the eleventh century. 'Produced, no doubt, or made possible by the cessation of the last invasions, but first manifesting themselves some generations later, a series of very profound and very widespread changes occurred towards the middle of the eleventh century.'[1] Bloch thought that the breathtaking speed at which Europe changed in the high Middle Ages was largely due to a driving movement towards colonization, including settlement in the thinly populated Iberian highlands and in the lands east of the Elbe, as well as inner colonization through the clearance of woodlands and swamps:

> the intensive movement of repopulation . . . from approximately 1050 to 1250 transformed the face of Europe . . . in the heart of the old territories, the incessant gnawing of the plough at forest and wasteland; in the glades opened amid the trees or the brushwood, completely new villages clutching at the virgin soil; elsewhere, round sites inhabited for centuries, the extension of the agricultural lands through the stages of the process.[2]

The enormous increase in population, progress in agriculture, trade and productivity in the high Middle Ages paved the way for the development of European cities and the emerging division of labour between town and country. Thus the rise of the town and of the urban economy made itself felt in rural areas, and for this reason the high Middle Ages have rightly been described as the turning point between the era of the relatively closed, autarkic household economy and that of an exchange economy based on the division of labour.[3] The fundamental economic, social and political transformations of this era[4] obviously left their imprint on the daily life of the peasant population and altered in particular its social and economic situation. The present chapter examines some of the principal changes in the high Middle Ages essential for an understanding of peasant life and peasant society. For indeed it is only against the background of the social and economic conditions of the high Middle Ages that the daily life of the peasantry can be understood.

Seen against the background of long-term economic development, the eleventh to thirteenth centuries constituted a period of pre-eminent expansion of the agrarian economy in comparison to the period of stagnation and depression in the fourteenth and fifteenth centuries.[5] A dramatic increase in population, massive land clearance, the extension of arable and, insofar as can be ascertained, a steady long-term rise of grain prices were the characteristics of the economic expansion in the high Middle Ages. The most striking of these, the rise in population, can for lack of records only be estimated.[6] It is clear, however, that from the eleventh century the population increased tremendously nearly everywhere in Europe, doubling and even tripling in most countries until finally slowing down at the beginning of the fourteenth century. This population growth manifested itself especially in colonization and clearance activities and the opening up of new farmland for the production of cereals.[7] The large-scale land clearance in the high Middle Ages dramatically altered the natural and cultural landscape in Europe for centuries to come. Indeed, many regions retained their new form until well into the nineteenth century. As has been mentioned, there had been earlier attempts at clearing land and increasing the extent of arable. This process, none the less, entered a new stage with the high Middle Ages as colonization advanced not only on an unprecedented scale but also much more systematically. Often enough even today, place-names and certain geographical characteristics serve as reminders of the extensive colonization which began in the eleventh century. The expansion of arable land was simultaneously carried out in the older areas of settlement as well as in thinly or totally uninhabited areas, such as the lands east of the Elbe and in northern Scandinavia. Moreover, the growth in population necessitated the extension of agricultural land in areas which had long been settled, transforming single farms into hamlets and hamlets into villages. Tidal and alluvial marshes were drained, and mountainous areas systematically cleared, all in order to satisfy the peasants' hunger for farmland.

In short, there was a strong correlation between population growth, land clearance, and progress in agricultural production. Is it therefore possible to say that the population increase of the eleventh century was indeed the decisive cause for the momentous changes in the twelfth century? Obviously, population expansion was closely related to progress in agriculture, and in particular to the increase in agricultural production. Likewise, the marked enlargement of arable was affected by the rise in population.[8] Hence both population growth and agricultural progress must be seen as mutually dependent. A better supply of foodstuffs permitted increase in population, just as the latter stimulated both the expansion and the intensification of agricultural production. However, population growth and the rising prices for primary produce were not the only causes for the upsurge in agriculture. Equally important were technological progress, changes in agrarian structures and the transformation of agricultural production. In addition to the extension of arable, increased yield ratios and a greater variety of cultivation methods, as well as types of foodstuffs, have to be taken into account.

A variety of decisive technical improvements merit attention. Peasants were gradually supplied with much more effective farming implements, such as carts, larger ploughs, and handtools. In addition, the use of water-power increased with a much expanded water-mill system,[9] and better harnesses for horse or ox-drawn vehicles also helped to raise productivity and yield ratios. Similarly, the utilization of the available farmland became much more efficient with the widespread application of the three-field system during the course of the twelfth and thirteenth centuries; as a consequence of this, older methods, such as the much more primitive two-field systems, were generally abandoned.[10] The increase in yield ratios, which is for the most part attributable to the transition to the three-field system, permitted a reduction in the proportion of farmland used for grain production. Hence more vegetables, fruits and particularly wine-grapes could be grown – a trend which helped to improve the diet of the entire medieval population in terms of quality and variety alike. J. Le Goff has even gone so far as to say that 'the increasing application of the three-field system and the progress in the production of protein-rich vegetables provided the basis for Christianization, clearance, urbanization, the crusades and the construction of the medieval cathedrals.'[11]

The rise of the urban economy

A more complex trade network, the growth of towns and a money economy contributed to, and was in turn stimulated by, the growth in agriculture and population, causing fundamental changes in the economic and social structure of the high Middle Ages. In a similar manner, the concentration of craft production and trade in the expanding urban communities gave a new impetus for a division of labour between town and country; consequently towns were supplied with grains and livestock in return for a variety of urban manufactured and commercial goods. Such division of labour quickly reached its limits, wherever the peasant economy had weak marketing links and peasant farms supplied for themselves their basic needs for work tools and manufactured goods. In sum, the forces of the intensifying market relationships and the development of urban networks radically altered medieval feudal society, reshaping the agrarian economy in ways that did not leave the condition of the peasantry untouched.

The traces of the population growth from the eleventh to the thirteenth centuries can be seen not only in colonized areas, but also in the towns. Although the revival of urban life began earlier than the eleventh century, it reached a new velocity in the high Middle Ages.[12] Most towns in the lands north of the Alps, which had largely been untouched by the urban culture of the Romans, were founded during the period of rapid urbanization in the twelfth and thirteenth centuries. European society changed to such an extent that towards the end of the phase of economic expansion roughly 10 per cent of the entire population lived in towns. The process of medieval urbanization included both the founding of new towns and the further expansion of the previously existing towns. With some of the new foundations it was at times difficult to distinguish between towns proper and large villages or markets, which by and large retained their rural character. This is in itself a sufficient reminder of the basic similarity between the foundation of towns and villages. One of the origins of urbanization was undoubtedly the increase in the division of labour between town and country from the twelfth and thirteenth centuries in which craft production removed itself from the countryside. Hence the town and its market became the focal point of the high medieval economy and created the basis for an increasing specialization of manufacture and commerce. A new drive towards building and construction caught hold in urban areas, manifesting itself in the well-fortified town walls and in the regular, ring or grid-like street pattern within them. Urban and rural development were twin aspects of the economic expansion in the high Middle Ages and cannot be studied in isolation from each other. The innovations in the towns of the high Middle Ages received much of their impulse from the countryside; yet they also revolutionized life and economy in rural areas – a development which in turn caused further economic and social change. Differences between town and country emerged especially in the organization of government and justice. It should be noted, however, that this does not mean that towns ruled the country, but rather that they became economic centres whose influence extended over large territories. Through the separation of town and country, the town developed into a distinctive legal entity and an autonomous community governed by bodies elected by its citizens. Townsmen craved for autonomy and corporative self-determination, especially in the twelfth and thirteenth centuries, and they had their greatest successes in northern Italy. The principle *Stadtluft macht frei*, whereby a serf became a freeman if he stayed in a town for a year and a day, incidentally corresponded to the motto among German peasants that 'land clearing sets you free' (*Rodung macht frei*). This is yet another illustration of both the mutual dependence and similarity of urban and rural history in the high Middle Ages.[13] The economic upswing provided the growing population with more jobs, and for this reason more and more people moved into the towns. Above all Flanders and Lombardy witnessed the emergence of a dense urban network during the high Middle Ages, but in other regions some large towns arose side by side with medium and small-sized towns. Hence the urban communities were indeed a common phenomenon. Although it is true that there was a certain continuity between the cities of antiquity and those of the Middle Ages, it must be stressed that the restoration of urban communities and the growth of the early bourgeoisie during the high Middle Ages marked a new era in medieval history. Urban economy and a civic mentality were new elements within the structure of medieval feudalism.

The interdependence of the forces of change in the high Middle Ages

In examining the causes for the economic boom, Henri Pirenne stressed the importance of trade as a catalyst for the changes which characterized the high Middle Ages.[14] He emphasized that especially the re-establishment of long-distance trade in the eleventh century stimulated the rise of western Europe. Trade gave a vigorous impetus towards economic expansion and urban development as well as the dissolution of the narrow constraints of the autarkic economy which Pirenne believed had characterized the manorial system. However, critics of his arguments have attacked just this – the overrating of outside influences such as long-distance trade.[15] Other historians have tended to put more stress on the importance of population growth for the astounding prosperity in the high Middle Ages as well as for later developments.[16] Marxist scholars, on the other hand, are convinced that the overall transformation in this period was in the last resort caused by the dynamic elements of feudal production.[17] They argue that economic progress and the refinement of feudal production were the result of the struggle between feudal lords and dependent peasants for the greatest possible share of production. The dynamics of the feudal system are usually considered to be the driving force for the growth of manufactures and the process of urbanization in the high Middle Ages.

A critical evaluation of all of these factors suggests that the transformation of agrarian production and the manorial system were particularly important as driving forces for the economic upswing in the high Middle Ages. The expansion of arable, better methods of cultivation, increased grain production and the growing productivity of peasant labour were the decisive factors stimulating overall economic development. The extraordinary increase in agrarian output enabled an ever growing population to be adequately fed, especially in the towns. G. Duby has analysed early medieval economic growth, outlining the relationship between the demands of the feudal lords and the success of peasant production particularly in the eleventh and twelfth centuries.[18] In his view, the pressure of the lords on their dependent peasants was the decisive factor for the increase in agrarian productivity which stimulated overall economic growth. 'It stemmed largely from pressure by lords anxious to see the surplus product from the labour of their personal dependants, tenants and other subjects grow, so that they might appropriate it for themselves.'[19] It seems that the increase in population which began earlier facilitated these efforts of the lords.

The analysis of the causes and main aspects of the socio-economic changes in the high Middle Ages should take into account the interdependence of various factors within feudal society. Population growth, the development of agricultural land, colonization and a continously increasing agrarian productivity, as well as the upswing in trade, formed the basis for the rise of towns and flourishing manufactures. Also one must emphasize the manorial system itself, which had a dynamism of its own which caused and stimulated a considerable number of changes. Indeed the study of the transformation of the manorial regime and the dissolution of the manorial system is particularly important because the changes in the manor also had a substantial influence on the social condition of the peasantry.

The dissolution of the *Fronhof* system

The existing manorial structures and the organization of the demesnes began to crumble under the changing economic and social conditions in the high Middle Ages. Although the course of this development varied from region to region, it is generally agreed that it began in the eleventh century, continued in the twelfth century and was almost complete by the late thirteenth century.[20] In northern France, however, the dissolution of the manorial system began as early as the late tenth century.[21] It took two basic forms. First, the entire demesne of a manor could be divided either into newly created independent holdings or divided equally among the local peasants already in possession of land. Or secondly quite often the lord retained a considerable portion of the demesne while leasing a part of it to a single peasant. In many instances these leasehold-farms (the German term was either *Meierhof* or *Dinghof*) served as collecting points for those goods and rents which the peasants were required to deliver to their lords, or they were the seat of the court for the *familia*, the association of dependants living within the bounds of the manor. In other cases, however, the manor (*Villikation, Fronhof*) continued to be farmed under the direction of the lord himself or a reliable administrator, and it was here that the traditional autarkic economy survived.

Despite a number of regional variations, the dissolution of the manorial system in the twelfth and thirteenth centuries generally was marked by a notable reduction of demesne lands and peasant labour services, as well as in a considerable relaxation of personal bondage to the manor. In numerous regions peasants enjoyed greater freedom as their legal status as well as the conditions of landholding improved. The abandonment of labour services in favour of rents, which were often fixed, increased the independence of the peasant household economy and even worked to make peasant labour more profitable. From this time on peasants supplied most of the produce to the growing markets of the towns. Even in those areas where the manorial system had been less common, its dissolution consolidated the economic position of the peasant landholder and enabled him, in the wake of development of market relations, to profit from rising grain prices. On the whole, the legal status of the peasant became much less important than the extent of his payments in rents and dues.

The structural changes in the manorial system were closely related to other changes in the late medieval structures of domination. From the eleventh century onwards the basic forms of domination in the high medieval feudal state were gradually superseded by local and territorial structures of domination. The development of legal immunities and of special jurisdiction within castle precincts (*Bannrecht, banalité*), constituted a new form of domination with more effective political and administrative control.[22] Moreover, the beginnings of territorial sovereignty affected both the striving of the crown for authority and the territorial aspirations of secular and ecclesiastical lords. Colonization, land clearance, the siting of castles, the endowment of monasteries and the founding of towns were the seminal elements of a process of territorial acquisition, in the wake of which a new type of government, the institutionally used territorial state, began slowly to emerge.[23] These emergent territories were characterized by new forms of legal and administrative organization which included both modern forms of local administration and new forms of central government. The political changes that crystallized from the twelfth century onwards were to be of fundamental significance for the political structures of Europe in the course of the following centuries. Powerful monarchies arose in France and England, while Germany took the road towards a state based on a 'society of orders', founded on the dominance of territorial princes.

Chivalric life-style and peasant culture

Towards the end of the high Middle Ages, the feudal lords were faced with a peasantry whose social position had notably improved because of the boom in agriculture and the complex constitutional trends of the time.[24] Social solidarity and a sense of communality had developed within the peasantry, and as the manorial system dissolved,[25] the centre of social and economic life shifted for the dependent peasantry to the village, and this process resulted in the consolidation of the village community. Thus, a social and political, as well as a cultural rift opened up between the nobility and the peasantry. In the twelfth and thirteenth centuries, the chivalric life-style of the elite, so splendidly represented in the poetry, the architecture and the artistic and social activities of this period,[26] had little in common with the popular culture of the peasants. For the rural population, as will be shown later, had a mentality and material culture of its own.[27] The courtly culture of the high Middle Ages, on the other hand, was the first lay culture in Europe. Its life-style and mentality were very influential, in particular among the urban populations. With the rise of the courtly society towards the end of the high Middle Ages, the distinction between the elite and the rest of society increased.

And finally to conclude this chapter it is worth looking at the economic position of the peasantry. The majority of scholars have viewed this position in a positive light. According to A. Dopsch, the twelfth and thirteenth centuries were 'the golden age of the German peasantry'.[28] He argued that a growing number of peasants must have been wealthy because they managed to attain better property rights on their manorial holdings. 'The golden age of the German peasantry', however, was contemporaneous with the courtly culture of feudal lords which could only develop on the basis of peasant prosperity in the first place.[29] F. Lütge followed this argument in stating that the twelfth, thirteenth and fourteenth centuries were in fact the apogee in the history of the peasantry: 'Its economic and social position had never been better, and would never be better thereafter.'[30] A different view is proposed, however, by W. Abel who argued that in economic terms the peasants 'were hanging in the balance' during the high Middle Ages,[31] which is of course a considerable qualification of the more favourable views on peasant conditions. However, instead of simply offering a general answer to the question of the position of the peasantry in the high Middle Ages it will be better to discuss a variety of aspects of peasant life from the eleventh to the fourteenth centuries. Such an approach provides a better understanding of the varied and unique character of the daily life of the peasantry in the Middle Ages.

PART II

PATTERNS OF PEASANT SETTLEMENT AND DWELLING, 1000–1400

3

NATURE AND ENVIRONMENT, CLEARANCE AND SETTLEMENT

The increase of population in the high Middle Ages

A concern for the environment that has long been the preserve of romantic enthusiasts and local conservation groups has recently entered the consciousness of the general public. The dramatic side of the ecological dilemma, such as the destruction of trees by acid rain, the deterioration of soil by overintensive cultivation in the industrial countries and the massive deforestation and hunger in developing countries, has again illustrated how closely the economy, population growth and the environment depended upon one other.[1] Although there can be no real question about the relevance of the ecological movement today, it must be stressed that ecological damage has a historical dimension as well and that human activities have always left their marks on the environment.[2] Alarming symptoms such as overpopulation, famine, deforestation and soil contamination face many Third World countries.[3] They also troubled the societies of early Europe: population density, inadequate nourishment and the overstraining of natural resources became particularly problematic with the end of the boom in economic and population growth at the beginning of the fourteenth century.

During two hundred years of large-scale clearings, eager peasants constantly uprooted wide stretches of woodland and drained marshes to increase grain production in order to feed the ever growing population. The ecological consequences of land clearance and spreading settlements have been neglected in traditional scholarship. At the beginning of the fourteenth century in many parts of Europe, overpopulation and the ruthless exploitation of natural resources culminated in a near-devastation of the ecological equilibrium. Then the less productive soils were coming under the plough, while deforestation was increasingly followed by erosion, making it even more difficult to avoid bad harvests and famines.[4]

It was above all western and central Europe that suffered from these problems towards the end of the expansion of the high Middle Ages. The population of these countries tripled between the eleventh and the fourteenth centuries to a total of about 40 million. By 1300, England had a population of about 4.5 million, France had 21 million and Germany 14 million.[5] Considering the economic, social and technical limitations and the other constraints of medieval agrarian society, these figures were extremely high. Had it not been for the famines, epidemics, wars and migrations in later centuries, the growth of the population at the annual rate of this time, which was about 0.5 per cent, would have resulted in a total population of 1.13 billion by 1970 compared with the actual figure of 190 million in 1985. This estimate clearly illustrates how dramatic the increase in population and the demand for arable land must have been. Faced with a low level of technology and slow economic growth, the peasants depended even more on favourable environmental conditions. Disregarding the fact that climate and soil conditions have always determined the productivity of farming, it is safe to say that the medieval peasant was involved in a constant struggle with nature. Droughts and floods, extremes of hot and cold weather, and storms could diminish yield ratios, which were already low due to poor and badly manured soils. A three- or fourfold return on seed sown was about average. Despite the technical improvements of the last centuries, contemporary agriculture is far from being independent of the assaults of nature; farming in the Middle Ages was even less so. In short, the climate and soil conditions of a given region and the damage to the environment, such as deforestation or the exhaustion of soil, had an immediate effect on the life and work of the medieval peasantry.

The question remains as to which factors led up to the conditions of crisis at the beginning of the fourteenth century. And what were the regional variations in the processes of growth and differentiation in respect to the colonization and settlement of Europe in the high Middle Ages? The expansion of agricultural land under the pressure of constant population growth helped for quite some time to prevent famines and was accompanied by various improvements in agricultural technology. Land clearance during this period changed the landscape of central Europe very rapidly. This was a unique and drastic change with only the Industrial Revolution of the nineteenth and twentieth centuries approaching comparison. G. Duby has called it 'the most spectacular and most decisive economic event' of the period.[6]

Land clearance in old Germany

The rise in population in the high Middle Ages was accompanied by an ever denser concentration of settlements both in Germany and in other parts of Europe. The insistent and relentless drive of colonization and settlement in this period is mirrored by the fact that the density of German settlement had actually reached its historical peak prior to the abandonment of settlements in the later decades of the fourteenth century. It should not be forgotten, however, that many of these settlements were rather small, consisting as a rule of fewer households and inhabitants than in later centuries. The settlement movement was part of the economic expansion of the high Middle Ages and it worked to transform central Europe, a landscape with older scattered settlements, vast woodlands and marshes, into farmland. In the early Middle Ages there had already been clearances, which had helped to develop the arable land, particularly between the seventh and the ninth centuries.[7] At that time, population too had risen, especially in valleys and plains, and clearing had started either spontaneously in a second wave of land acquisition, or under manorial guidance. Engaged in this clearance movement were both secular and ecclesiastical lords of such foundations as the monastery of St Gallen on Lake Constance or the abbey of Lorsch in Odenwald which by clearing woods and draining marshes sought to raise their revenues.

Agricultural land was extended not just in the old settlements, but also on their fringes by the establishment of entirely new farms and settlements nearby. In fact, quite a few hamlets and villages today can trace their origin back as far as Carolingian times. Despite the problems of interpreting settlement names, it is safe to say that the endings *-ingen* and *-heim* indicate settlements dating to the migration period. Similarly, place-names ending *-dorf* or *-hausen* point to settlement at an early stage, while those ending *-hof* or *-hofen*, on the other hand, are evidence for settlement in either Frankish or Carolingian times. The same holds true for endings which hint primarily at the local geography, such as *-berg*, *-bach*, or *-wald*. In comparison with later periods, clearance and settlement in the early Middle Ages was far less systematic: farms were set up one after the other along streams or in valleys as new settlers or families appeared. Access to fields was easy because they were laid out in the vicinity of the farmhouses. As a consequence there was less cause for dispute among neighbours in the new settlements than among those in the older settlements. These pioneering peasants also enjoyed larger holdings and often favoured livestock-raising, which was more profitable in woodlands and mountainous regions.

Nevertheless, the extent of early medieval land clearance should not be overrated since, as pointed out earlier, this was only the beginning of the clearing and settlement movement. It should be kept in mind that apart from the fringes and valleys of large mountainous areas such as the Black Forest, the Odenwald and the Harz, and just a few places in the woods and marshes of the plains, most of Europe remained unsettled until the high Middle Ages.[8] Clearing activities increased in many regions of

Europe with the remarkable growth in population between the tenth and
the thirteenth centuries, providing the peasantry with arable lands
especially within the vast tracts east of the Elbe and within older
settlement areas in general. Colonization and settlement certainly had
much more influence on central and eastern Europe where more land was
available for clearing and for the application of new cultivation methods
than in the more developed parts of western Europe, where clearing
usually reduced the commons and the traditional open grazing lands in
favour of grain production.

In most cases land clearances in old settlements have not been recorded,
as a consequence of which research relies on the study of the forms of
fields and villages and on the study of place-names. The actual work of
clearing, which was mostly the heavy burden of the peasants and not that
of the lords, varied according to the nature of the land. Dikes were
erected along the coast of Flanders and further north along the North Sea
coast to protect the land against the floods and storm-tides in spring and
autumn.[9] In the interior, great efforts were made to drain the moors and
the marshes along rivers. Clearing woodlands was even more laborious,
the only tools available at that time being axes, saws, hoes and spades.
Especially in the mountains, timber served as construction material for
peasant houses and working quarters, and the remaining wood and scrub
were consumed as firewood.

In the old settlements, the peasants apportioned the land to be cleared
amongst themselves. Clearances for entirely new settlements were

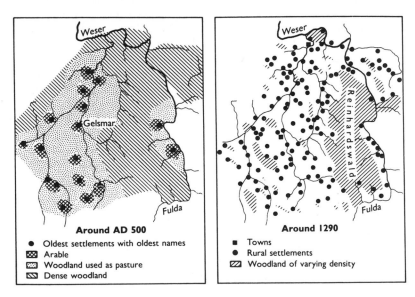

Figure 1 Changes in settlement structure in the Diemel area (after H. Jäger)

conducted mostly in the vicinity of neighbouring villages. They were often encouraged and supported by lords who had a great interest in the enlargement of their arable land because this also expanded their territories and increased their revenues. With their sponsorship, enterprising settlers founded many new farms, hamlets and villages which even today can be identified by their name and shape. Villages and towns in German-speaking areas whose names end with *-hagen*, *-hurst*, *-wald*, *-rode*, or *-reuth* indicate settlements from the high Middle Ages, just like the *villes neuves* in the north of France, the *bastides* south of the Loire and the *poblaciones* in the Spanish provinces which were reconquered from the Moors. It should not be forgotten, however, that the clearing movement varied in Europe both temporally and geographically: dike building and land reclamation started as early as the eleventh century in Flanders – but only in the twelfth century in northern Germany. The clearing of the Île de France reached its peak around 1200, at a time when large-scale German colonization of the thinly populated Slavic lands in the east had only just begun and would continue for at least another hundred years.

Planned settlements

Planned settlements were created in many areas, especially in the eastern colonization regions, but also in the older settled parts of Germany.[10] In addition to the already existing forms of single farms, hamlets and nucleated villages (*Haufendorf*, an irregularly patterned, dense type of village), there were other types of settlements, such as street villages (*Strassendörfer*), small rounded villages with a central common (*Rundling*) as well as village settlements arranged in a straight line with strips of farmland extending behind each house (*Hufendorf*; see figure 2). Most of the new villages were laid out along roads, so that the bulk of farmhouses formed a row along a single road. In other cases, a square or a village green remained vacant in the village centre for either a church or the village pond (*Angerdorf*). On either side of the Rivers Elbe and Saale *Rundlinge* were discovered which might have been defensive settlements in the border areas between Germanic and Slavic peoples. The farms were grouped around a central area which served to protect farms and livestock in times of war. *Hufendörfer* were arranged along a road like street villages (*Strassendörfer*), but with strips of land always stretching immediately behind each house. In certain areas these strips could reach far into the wooded mountain slopes. Hence access to, use of and expansion of the land were easier because there was no interference from the owners of neighbouring plots. The same held true for the *Hufendörfer* in northern Germany, especially in the marshes near sea coasts and along riverbanks. A *Hufen* (English 'hide' or 'holding', Latin *mansus*), a fenced-off measure of land sufficient to maintain an average peasant family, was also designed for individual use, being directly attached to the farmhouses and stretching in long, narrow strips far into the marshland. In these villages a canal often ran parallel to the main street and served to drain the soil nearest to the village.

The development of a number of *Hufendörfer* in the marshes of the River Weser has been recorded in 1106 in a contract between Dutch peasants from Utrecht and Frederick, the Archbishop of Bremen. The list of conditions under which Frederick assigned holdings to the settlers provides interesting information on their legal and social status:

> We think that our contract with certain Dutchmen should be known to all men. These people have come to His Grace the Archbishop imploring us to assign to them for cultivation the barren marshland of our Archdiocese, which has been useless for our subjects. We have agreed upon the following terms: A penny per year shall be paid for each holding of the aforesaid land. To avoid future dispute among our subjects, a holding shall be 720 King's rods (*Königsruten*) in length and 30 in breadth, and shall include the streams that run therein. We do think it is necessary to note this concession also. In return, they shall give the eleventh sheaf of crops, and every tenth head of sheep, goats, pigs and geese. Likewise, a tithe shall be given of honey and flax . . . They have agreed to pay 2 marks annually per hundred holdings, that

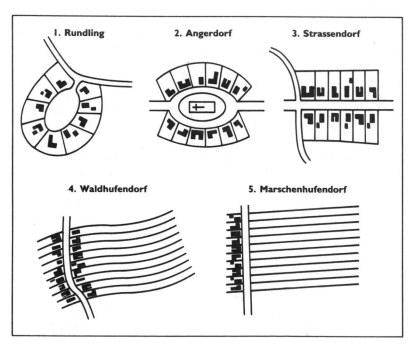

Figure 2 Types of planned rural settlement in medieval Germany

they shall not suffer from strangers and the verdicts of secular courts and are in the position to settle disputes amongst themselves. However, if there are matters they can not decide themselves, they should consult the Archbishop for legal advice. They must support him from their own property as long as he is with them, and he is to receive a third of the fines in legal disputes.[11]

The extraordinary size of these farms served as compensation for the difficulties of land reclamation and drainage. The farmhouses were built on stilts, and the land was divided into long, rectangular holdings. Favourable property rights, low rents, and a far-reaching autonomy were for the most part sufficient means to attract an adequate number of volunteers for colonization and settlement.

The conditions granted to the settlers of the *Hagen* settlements were even better.[12] The communal privileges granted with the *Hagenrecht* were also meant as a reward for the hardships of settlement, and consisted of the right to inherit the farm, a great degree of personal independence and considerable autonomy in local matters. Settlements of this type, with their characteristic arrangement of farms which were lined up in a row, were founded in the twelfth century, particularly in the eastern regions of Westphalia and in the Weserbergland.

Clearing and settlement continued in southern Germany even after the twelfth- and thirteenth-century expansion when particularly the Black Forest, the Odenwald and the Bavarian Forest were settled on a larger scale. In Swabia, the systematic founding of villages, in particular the *Angerdorf* village with the village square or the village pond at its centre, even extended until well into the fourteenth century. Some of the settlements in Swabia have been recorded in great detail,[13] so we know that both secular and ecclesiastical lords initiated the clearances by appointing a bailiff, known as the *Reutmeister*, to recruit peasants and also supervise the actual clearing and the planning of the settlement. These planned settlements consisted essentially of fifteen holdings surrounding either a church or a village pond, with a broad street running through their centres and immediate access to the common. Settlers enjoyed inheritance rights to their farms, and had their own village court as well as the concession of fixed rents and dues. Most of the farms were roughly 25 hectares in size. The *Reutmeister*, a man of high status in the village, possessed more land than the other peasants, presided over the court of low justice and mediated between the manor and the village community.

Next to these organized clearings, there were also numerous rather random settlements in 'Old Germany'. There was a notable growth in the number of single farms, loosely grouped farms and hamlets. Random development of this kind was far more frequent and more important than organized colonization in Europe, except in the lands east of the Rivers Elbe and Saale, where systematic clearance and settlements prevailed.

German settlement in the east

The German colonization of these territories was a complex process involving the development of political rule, Christianization, peasant settlement and the dissemination of the constitutional forms and cultural influences of western Europe. This section provides a description of this colonization movement and examines the types of settlements prevalent in the eastern parts of Germany.[14] First of all it must be stressed that we are concerned with a gradual process, and that the colonization of the territories in eastern Germany coincided with the extension of the arable land in the older German territories in the twelfth, thirteenth and fourteenth centuries. The movement began slowly along the marches (*Grenzmarken*), border areas of the Empire which had been established in the tenth century. These marches formed a broad belt of land from the Baltic to the Fichtel Mountain ranges between the German regions to the west and the Polish territories in the east. At this point, however, the thinly populated marches were not the immediate focus of large-scale settlement. This changed in the course of the twelfth century, when the colonization movement really got under way. The process of settlement took two basic forms: either the founding of villages by peasant settlers from the German-speaking territories or the Low Countries, or the founding of towns and the remodelling of existing Slavic settlements according to Germanic law. Colonization in this region, none the less, did not occur in a land without political and social structures of its own. On the contrary, the archaeology of the Slavic settlements has revealed a level of cultural achievement far more developed than had been assumed in the past. In addition it can no longer be maintained that the Slavic population was generally ousted from these territories, for over the years colonists usually became integrated with the indigenous population.

Most clearings and settlements were initiated by powerful lay and ecclesiastical lords who in turn endowed their vassals with landed property and manorial rights, thereby creating a sizeable local estate of knightly manorial lords. With the swelling stream of peasant settlers, many villages were founded without a manor. Their development was directed by a settlement planner called a *Lokator*, who was entitled to assign standard-size holdings to a set number of settlers on behalf of the lord. They also recruited the peasant settlers and surveyed the construction works within the villages as well as clearing and drainage. Settlement planners were often granted hereditary rights to the post of the village mayor (*Erbschulze*). In addition their farms were far bigger than the farms of peasant settlers and they were granted reductions on dues and taxes.

The majority of settlers in the eastern regions came from the densely inhabited north-western lands of the Empire, particularly the Low

Countries, Westphalia, and eastern Saxony. They were lured by the prospect of larger holdings and greater personal freedom, lower dues and an end to labour services. The new villages in the east of Germany took as their model the legal rights of an independent peasantry which had been established in assarted areas west of the Elbe and in particular in the Dutch settlements along the marshes of the North Sea and its rivers. The strong participation of Flemish and Dutch peasants in the stream of east German settlement, especially in the Altmark, Mark Brandenburg and Saxony, meant that the legal rights of the settlers were determined by the long-standing experience of these groups, and in some places there was even explicit mention of a *ius flandricum*. The legal position of many of these settlers was characterized by minimal ties to the manor, better property rights and fewer feudal obligations than was the case elsewhere. Considering the size of the eastern territories, the scarceness of settlers and the difficulties presented by clearing, the improvement of the legal and social position of peasant volunteers was an effective stimulus for the settlement of these lands. The better legal position of the settlers eventually improved the condition of the indigenous population too: many Slavic villages came under German law (*ius theutonicum*), as a result of which peasants were granted better property rights and adopted new agricultural techniques. Whereas Slavic peasants traditionally practised only extensive farming, the introduction of German law often led to the modernization of cultivation too, particularly the introduction of the three-field system.

The shape of the new settlements and cropping methods were usually identical with those of established settlements and incorporated the experience learned from earlier clearings. The division of arable land into holdings, so instrumental for further settlement, was introduced by the first wave of colonization east of the Rivers Elbe and Saale. The standard farm in the north-east consisted of two 'hides' or holdings, approximately 33 hectares – the basis of calculation being in this case the Flemish hide, equalling 16.8 hectares. *Waldhufendörfer, Strassendörfer* and *Angerdörfer*, as already described, were the most common types of rural settlements in the eastern territories. The rather large *Angerdorf* villages in Mark Brandenburg probably resulted from a concentration of small-size German and Slavic settlements. *Waldhufendorf* villages prevailed in the western and central parts of the Erzgebirge Mountain range, and it is clear from their shape that the Frankish hide, which equals 24 hectares, was used in the apportioning of the land. As lay and ecclesiastical lords increasingly promoted the systematic planning of settlements in the course of the twelfth and thirteenth centuries, villages and holdings in the lands even further east were much more regular in shape than settlements in the west.

Against the older view that the German colonization movement in the thinly populated Slavic territories was a unique and isolated process it must be objected that it was part of the larger colonization movement which was being conducted almost everywhere in Europe; it was part of the general movement towards the development of arable land for an ever increasing population.[15] In overemphasizing the achievements of German settlers in eastern Europe, nationalist historians in Germany have sketched a misleading picture of German colonization in the lands east of the Elbe and Saale. Clearings and the founding of villages were not only carried out here, but also in the neighbouring Polish, Bohemian and Hungarian countries.[16] Many Polish villages adopted German law (*ius theutonicum*) on the day of their foundation, yet this does not necessarily imply the presence of German settlers. Often settlers merely adopted the favourable legal terms for peasants in western Europe, in this case Germany. In order to develop their land and increase agrarian production, the eastern European nobility made great efforts to recruit experienced settlers from the west and the middle of Europe. The kings of Bohemia, Poland and Hungary also made their own peasantry develop the border regions of their kingdoms. After the conquest of Transylvania in the eleventh century, for example, the Hungarian kings promoted the systematic settlement of their country – first with the help of their own peasants, and later by recruiting German settlers.

Land development in England, France and Spain

Turning to look at other parts of Europe, we find that a new stage in land clearance and settlement in England arrived after the Norman Conquest in 1066.[17] The appearance of the English landscape changed fundamentally after the second half of the eleventh century, with the draining of marshes and moors and the clearance of woodlands which followed an enormous rise in population. As historians such as M. Bloch, G. Duby, C. Higounet and R. Fossier have shown in detail, there is evidence for similar trends and forms of land development in medieval France.[18]

The Iberian Peninsula provides another fine illustration for considerable migration and large-scale settlement. The gradual reconquest of the Islamic territories in Spain by the Christian nobility went hand in hand with substantial immigration into these areas. Depopulated and deserted by the Moors, these flat, unprotected lands were only recolonized in the thirteenth century when the *reconquista* managed to put an end to Moorish attacks. The arable was then assigned to peasants on favourable legal and leasehold terms, a practice typical for most clearing enterprises in medieval Europe.[19]

The looming crisis in the early Middle Ages

At the close of this era of land reclamation the proportion of land under the plough had risen to an extent unattained for a long time to come; in fact most of the available land in the densely inhabited regions was under cultivation by the beginning of the fourteenth century – including soils unsuitable for permanent cultivation. Even in comparison with the nineteenth and twentieth centuries, much more land at high altitudes, particularly in the Alps, was used for agriculture, and many of the newly founded places in high and low mountain ranges together with arid regions were deserted after a short time. In such places the soil was exhausted relatively quickly, leaving the peasants with insufficient yields from the land they had cleared only a few decades before. Some of the settlements along rivers were also given up because they had been built on terrain which was far too low, and for this reason these places had often experienced severe flooding. Sometimes landslides covered the villages and fields under steep mountain slopes, and droughts and poor sandy soils drove settlers out of arid regions, especially after overcropping.

A. Dopsch stated that

> the enormous demand for agricultural land which gave so much momentum to settlement in the twelfth and thirteenth centuries blinded the peasants to the essential preconditions for successful cultivation. The soil in many places proved to be unsuitable for permanent cultivation, or it could only be sustained at costs that were too high. As soon as the natural nitrogen reserves of the soil were depleted, the inadequate manuring typical of the age was unable to correct this deficiency, so that the soil was no longer productive. In some cases, the land became deserted and trees began to reclaim the fields.[20]

It would be inaccurate to regard these failures in settlement as the principal cause for the desertion of lands and villages in the late Middle Ages,[21] yet it is necessary, nevertheless, to emphasize that the extent of land development in the high Middle Ages had serious consequences for the environment. The deforestation of huge areas sometimes caused a dangerous fall of the water table, leading to dehydration of the soil and finally to bad harvests, especially in hot summers. The newly settled places in particular had difficulties in producing crops at a reasonable cost, and many of the new settlements were threatened by decline, for example those which had moved furthest into woodlands, arid regions, mountainous areas or extremely flat plains. The names of deserted settlements prove that it was mostly late foundations that were given up, for many of them ended with either *-rode*, *-hagen*, or *-feld*.[22]

The constant demand for grain from the ever growing population was the ultimate reason why the land reclamation movement in the newly colonized regions spread to unprofitable soils, and meadows and woods were brought under the plough in older settlements. This resulted in a serious reduction of the commons, especially the common woodlands – which were usually used for grazing livestock.[23] Hence there was a marked decrease in livestock-raising. Moreover, the subsequent deterioration of peasant nutrition was further worsened by the shortage of animal manure which accompanied the reduction of cattle and pig stocks. Finally, grain production stagnated or declined, so closing the vicious circle of a nutritional crisis at the end of the high Middle Ages. Deforestation even further threatened the peasant economy because the common woods supplied the rural population with other essential foodstuffs, such as fruit, berries, mushrooms and herbs, as well as supplying firewood and timber for building.[24] With the reduction of the woods, essential nutrients were gradually washed out of the soil and the water table fell. In response to the shortage of grazing lands, lords and village authorities restricted the public use of the commons and the droving of cattle to mountain pastures. Depending on either their legal position or the size of their holdings and stables, peasants were no longer allowed to keep more than a certain number of stock. In addition strict regulations were introduced for the utilization of woods.[25]

Yet the population continued to grow in many places in spite of the shortage of arable at the beginning of the fourteenth century. Less space was available for the population, and grain prices increased incessantly. Particularly in the densely populated regions there were now many peasants with too little land to live off. Most of the peasantry was affected by a nutrition crisis which worsened with the rise in population.[26] Severe famines, epidemics and finally a decrease in population after the mid-fourteenth century were the consequences of this crisis. Already in the first half of the fourteenth century bad harvests and cattle diseases became more frequent, causing famines and shortages of all kinds. The famine of 1315–17, for instance, was caused by a series of bad harvests which shook many regions of Europe far more severely and longer than any previous crisis. Cereal prices rose dramatically, leaving the starving population to subsist on insufficient food and substitutes unfit for consumption such as diseased animals, so that many people died of infectious diseases and malnutrition.[27]

Heavy feudal dues and high rents contributed to the deterioration of peasant living standards, in particular as regards nutrition. Because yields were low, rents and feudal dues turned into an unbearable burden for many peasants – particularly those of secular and ecclesiastical lords. Hence it is above all how the feudal system caused peasant impoverishment which must be at the centre of the analysis of the crisis of the late Middle Ages. The last chapter of this study will examine this problem in detail.

4

CHANGES IN THE VILLAGE

Characteristics of the village

Now that city life has slid into perplexity many people recall what country
life used to be like. Provincial life, scorned so long, has acquired new
attractions for bored city-dwellers: 'Village' sounds like 'Adam and Eve', and
smacks of eternal renewal, good health and authenticity, that is of everything
the alienated pine for.[1]

This is how Walter Kempowski has characterized the nostalgic return to
country life and the village. After a long period of contempt for village
life, there is today a new interest in the village and its natural
environment.[2] Those who have observed this trend, however, have found
out to their regret that the village of 'the good old days' is gone. In fact,
the contemporary village is in a serious crisis owing to the loss of many of
its former functions. In some cases municipal authorities have even set
themselves the task of restoring the independent village. Conspicuous as
it is, the transformation of the village is not an isolated phenomenon. It is
part of an overall transformation of society which even the country has
not escaped. At this point the historian is frequently asked what a village
is and what its essential characteristics are; it is a question about the
village's past. In what circumstances and from what elements did villages
arise? Certainly, the village in its fully developed form has not always
been there. As in the case of the town, the village is the product of a long
historical process, in the course of which it emerged as a unique social,
economic and legal entity. This chapter is limited to the period between
the eleventh and the fourteenth centuries, which was the decisive phase of
this development.

How, then, can the village be defined, and what are its principal
characteristics? The word 'village', as used in daily speech and in academic
discourse, is just as difficult a concept to define as the word 'town', if we

are looking for a definition both uncontroversial and with universal validity. Geographers and researchers on land settlement have long discussed just when a rural settlement could be called a village. The criterion of attaining a minimum size[3] has now been displaced by emphasis on certain qualitative and functional aspects of particular settlement types. The village is no longer merely regarded as little more than a cluster of farms; rather, 'it is the relationships reaching beyond the individual farm' which constitute a village in the eyes of modern scholarship.[4] Since farms are connected by a system of communal facilities such as village ponds, wells and paths, these elements are now considered to be as important as other aspects of the village,[5] such as the legal and economic arrangements of the community. For this reason, K. S. Bader has defined the village as 'a more or less self-contained group of homes, forming a unit of settlement, which is recognized as such by its inhabitants, that is as a social and economic community'.[6]

The nuclear village (*Haufendorf*) with open fields and common lands was the most common type of village in the late Middle Ages (see figure 3).[7] The centre of the village was reserved for housing, and often it was merely a random assemblage of peasant homes and working quarters connected by a network of paths and lanes. Fenced-in gardens lay directly beside fenced-in farmhouses. These were farmed independently by the peasant family as they were their private property (see circle I, figure 3). The arable lay outside the village centre; it was split up into a number of large open fields (*Gewanne*) which were subdivided into small strips (see circle II, figure 3). As a rule, each peasant held at least one strip in each open field, and because some strips were in the middle of these fields – where there were no paths – access was possible only by crossing neighbouring strips. Provided that the arable land was farmed with the three-field rotation system, which was the case in most villages, the arable was portioned into three large open fields (*Zelgen* or *Schläge*), each rotating between fallow, winter and summer crops.

The land was partly farmed by each peasant on his own, partly by the community. In most villages, cultivation was strictly regulated: the village co-operative (*Dorfgenossenschaft*) or village leader scheduled sowing and harvesting times, as well as the installation of fences to protect the crops, or their removal after harvesting so that livestock could graze on the stubble-fields of all members of the community. Peasants who missed the deadline for harvesting had to be prepared to find their cornfields destroyed by other peasants' grazing stock. What tied the individual peasant to the agricultural arrangements of the community was the extent to which the arable was fragmented into strips held by different peasants (*Gemengelage*), as a consequence of which the farming of some strips had to be co-ordinated with that of neighbouring fields for the lack of direct access. The meadow was laid out either parallel to streams, on low ground between the open fields, or near the commons. It was farmed individually by each peasant. The common (*Allmende*), the third sphere within the bounds of the village, was even further removed from the village centre, and usually consisted of pasture and woodland (see circle III, figure 3). The common, also called 'common mark' (*gemeine Mark*), was used collectively by all members of the community: the pastureland served as a common meadow whilst the common woodland – forest or brushwood interspersed with pasture – was open to all peasants who used it as a place to graze pigs or to get whatever timber, firewood, foliage, berries, and honey they needed.

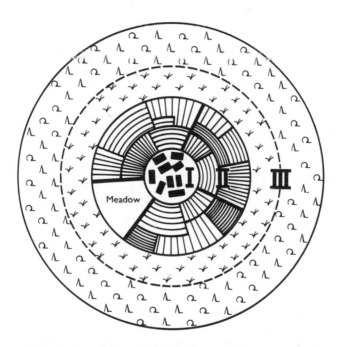

Figure 3 Model of nucleated village using the three-field system
Ring I: Living quarters including farmsteads and gardens;
Ring II: Arable with three main fields and pasture;
Ring III: Common with pasture and woodland

The emergence of the village in the high Middle Ages

The complex topography of the traditional nuclear village which, as has been shown above, consisted of individual farmsteads, parcels of meadow and arable land, and sundry usufructs of meadows and woodland, has never ceased to raise interest among historians, particularly as to its origin, development and function. As opposed to the traditional view which had survived in some textbooks, villages operating on the basis of the three-field system and this complex division of the land were not an ancient phenomenon. The three-field system with its characteristic open-field structure was the result of a complicated set of mutual restrictions which were worked out by the village communities in times of population growth and land shortage. In fact, 'it was achieved by striving towards the intensification of farming over several centuries',[8] which finally put an end to older methods of cultivation like the two-field system. Although even the three-field system eventually became obsolete with the technical improvements of the agrarian revolution in the eighteenth and nineteenth centuries, it is safe to say that it was by far the most successful farming method in the high and late Middle Ages. 'Even in the early modern period, the three-field system determined the forms of economic organization within the village. Given the condition of fragmented holdings and strip-farming, it achieved the optimum exploitation of the available arable by not wasting any land for access paths.'[9]

The impact can hardly be overestimated of villages in which the open-field system was combined with the three-field-cropping methods. The effects can be seen in the history of Europe from the early Middle Ages to the Industrial Revolution in the eighteenth, nineteenth and twentieth centuries. According to Otto Brunner, the landholding structure (division into holdings called hides), the three-field system and village farming based on collective usage characterized the conditions and structures of agrarian life in western and central Europe and had a lasting impact on the peasantry of Old Regime Europe; on the other hand agriculture in eastern Europe, especially in Russia, was radically different in economic organization and settlement patterns.[10] The three-field system, the landholding structure and the feudal system itself were extremely progressive elements in the history of the Middle Ages in engendering the unique dynamism of European society and economy – for both the expansion of the three-field system and the extension of arable during the high Middle Ages which provided the basis for urbanization and economic progress in Europe.

Nineteenth-century legal and constitutional historians and historical geographers such as A. Meitzen have argued that nuclear villages with their common-field economy had their origin in early Germanic society, especially in the alleged grouping of freemen into mark communities (*Markgenossenschaften*).[11] They argued that villages with collectively organized farming of the arable land were the remnants of the collective effort of the peasantry in occupying and apportioning newly colonized land. They assumed that the first settlers actually sat down and worked out a plan for how the land could best be divided into farms, arable and pasture land, assigning the strips of the open fields to the individual families and kindreds of the village. This would imply that mixed crops, and even the fragmentation of the land into open fields for periodic crop rotation, originated from the days of land acquisition by Germanic tribes. Consequently what was originally collective property must have later been turned into private property, a tendency towards privatization which started with the farms and gradually affected the arable and pasture land too. The fact that the common meadow and the common woodlands continued to be farmed collectively in the Middle Ages was regarded as proof for this hypothesis. Similarly, the compulsory and predetermined division and use of collectively held land (*Flurzwang*) and the rights of escheat (*Heimfallrechte*) were also believed to corroborate the supposition that there must have been such arrangements.

Recent research in the history of rural settlement has shattered this theory by showing in great detail that nuclear villages with their open-field system developed only during the high Middle Ages and that they were preceeded by smaller settlement types in the early Middle Ages.[12] Archaeology, too, has demonstrated through numerous excavations that agrarian conditions of the early Middle Ages were characterized by a remarkable variety of small-sized settlements from single farms and hamlets to small villages. In addition to this, economic historians have supplied evidence that only in the high Middle Ages did peasants form mark communities as a means of coping with the consequences of the increasing density of settlement. The development of the village was thus determined by a number of fundamental changes in the nature of settlements, the economy, lordship and society during this period.

Rural settlement in the early Middle Ages

In particular the much higher density of settlement marked the difference in topography between the early and the late Middle Ages. As shown above, recent studies of the development of rural settlement and the topographic organization of farming together with village excavations have confirmed that the majority of settlements in the early Middle Ages were single farms, groups of farms, and hamlets. The prototype of German villages in the north-west for example, was a loose group of farms called a *Drubbel*, which was surrounded by a narrow belt of strips, or squares, of grain fields and the nearby woods.[13] Around the inner ring was a wider, denser girdle of forest, used for summer pasture, hunting grounds, or timber-felling areas. Obviously the forests in the vicinity of the fields were not sharply divided from the huge areas of virgin woods beyond the villages. The example of south-west Germany, whose nuclear villages have long been regarded as the best illustration for the origin of communal farming methods in the early Middle Ages, must also be reassessed: it can be shown that a considerable number of villages evolved from single farms and hamlets dating back to the period of Alemanic settlement. Cultivation must have been far less systematic and only temporary at that time. The villages were surrounded by small grain fields which reverted rather haphazardly to fallow grassland used as pasture – a cultivation method which some historians call ley-farming.[14]

However, in spite of the prevalence of smaller settlement types in the early Middle Ages, there is evidence for more densely populated areas as early as Carolingian times. Indeed, a close look at the total number of farms in some regions strongly suggests that villages were already in existence. The analysis of land registers (*urbaria*) and books in the west and south-west of Germany has revealed that, from the ninth century, some of the villages consisted of as many as twenty, thirty, or even forty farms.[15] The village of Menzingen, for example, had thirty to thirty-five farms, that is a population of 100 to 200 inhabitants. Hence, as far as size was concerned, Menzingen must have been a village – leaving aside communal institutions and arrangements as the decisive criteron for a fully-fledged village. However, it was the size in particular which suggested that life in Menzingen was surely arranged in some way or the other; and some of these arrangements could well have been the historic origin of the more developed regulations of social and economic life in late medieval villages. Furthermore, it would be misleading to underrate the impact of the manorial system on the transformation of the village.[16] In particular the period of the enlargement of the manorial property of the crown, the church, and the nobility saw the manorial system leaving its imprint on rural society and economy, mainly through the demesne farms and their dependent holdings. Moreover, it has already been mentioned that the expansion and consolidation of manorial organization reduced the number of free peasants and small proprietors.

Innovations in the high Middle Ages: the communal three-field system

The movement from the hamlet, as the prevailing settlement type in the early Middle Ages, to the nuclear village of the high and late Middle Ages, that is the emergence of the village as the prevailing settlement type (*Verdorfung*), essentially followed the expansion of the arable; as the number of farms grew, strips of land had to be extended and new ones created.[17] Names and shapes of villages, as well as their topographical features, are often helpful in distinguishing the open fields of the Middle Ages from those of later centuries. A long, rectangular shape, for instance, usually indicates a field which was originally laid out in the Middle Ages. Likewise, the division of clearances into arable reveals, even today, that the development of land within village bounds and the advance of individual farms into the commons were often the joint work of the village community. In the course of the high Middle Ages, however, the development of the arable and the intensive use of pastures and common lands reached their limits. At this point a new cultivation method allowed a more efficient use of the available land: the individual land parcels were organized into three large fields (*Zelgen, Schläge*) with a co-ordinated system of triennial crop rotation; the transition to the fully-fledged three-field system was complete.

This innovation was extremely important for every aspect of the agrarian economy in the high Middle Ages, particularly for the development of the village.[18] From now on, the village community farmed as an economic co-operative, and this co-operative predetermined the division and use of collectively held land (*Flurzwang* and *Feldgemeinschaft*) and the rotation of crops, the arrangements of the co-operative being mandatory for every peasant in the village. What contributed to the tendency towards cropping in three alternating fields was the fact that the difficulties in the actual tilling increased in proportion to the progression in land fragmentation. It had become more and more difficult to agree on access rights through neighbouring fields, on the rotation of crops, or the installation of fences to protect cornfields from grazing stock. Nevertheless, the main cause for the increasing fragmentation of the land, especially the existing parcels, was the rise in population on the one hand and the intensification of cultivation on the other. With the growth in population, pressure towards partible inheritance (*Realteilung*) increased. Consequently land was often divided according to the number of heirs. This, of course, entailed an often unprofitable fragmentation of the arable land due to the rising number of farms. The introduction of the common-field system forced the peasants of a village to co-operate in arranging the collective use of the fallow as pasture, which meant that herdsmen had to be appointed and further steps had to be taken to guarantee the smooth working of the village economy. Especially since the eleventh century the new methods of crop rotation contributed to the formation of the village as an economic co-operative. The repercussions on peasant mentality of the altered modes of life and work engendered a communal spirit among the village inhabitants and put an end to privileged use of farmland. For although the individual parcels remained the property of each peasant, individual farming was increasingly subject to communal regulation.

It was not until after the twelfth century that the majority of villages introduced the three-field system, both in the older settled regions of Germany and in the newly founded ones in the clearances east of the Elbe.[19] In these eastern areas, where most villages had communal fields from the time of their foundation (*Gewanndörfer*), peasants received shares of the communal main fields of equal productive value according to soil quality and location. In the western regions of the Holy Roman Empire, however, the transition to the three-field system was much more difficult. Fields had to be newly laid out, and this was only possible with the permission and support of the manorial lords. For there can be no question that manorial lords, whose demesne farms comprised a substantial portion of the larger holdings, were strongly in favour of the introduction of the more efficient cultivation systems.

The transition to the open-field system and triennial crop rotation (*Dreizelgenwirtschaft*), it is important to note, was more rapid in some regions than others, being particularly rapid where stimulated by rising demand, higher prices and increasing trade. These were regions which were closest to the centres of urbanization and to large consumer groups, especially the Rhine valley between Alsace and the Black Forest, the Moselle area, other regions in the south-west of Germany, and the fertile basins of the low mountain ranges.[20] The transformation of medieval farming, which took several centuries, had its origin in these centres. Its progression was determined by the level of economic and demographic development in the neighbouring regions.

Even today, experts on rural settlement have difficulty determining exactly when individual villages reorganized the cultivation of their land. None the less, evidence suggests that certain regions in the north of France and in the south-west of Germany were the first to introduce the open-field system in the eleventh century. It is almost certain that these areas served as models for neighbouring regions.[21] By the end of the thirteenth century, most of the villages in the centre of western Germany were farmed with the open-field system and advanced crop rotation (*Gewannflursied-lungen*), although there were still areas using older cultivation methods and less efficient forms of field division. The German settlers colonizing the lands east of the Elbe and Saale also applied the new agricultural techniques and introduced the new village type; indeed most of the foundations in the eastern regions were nuclear villages – the only exception being the forest villages in the low mountain ranges, where farms were arranged in a straight line with strips of farmland extending behind each house (*Waldhufendörfer*). Lacking large open fields, these farms were more distinct from each other, at most bordering on each other or forming very small groups of single farms, as in the marshes in the north-west of Germany. Similar, in this regard, are the *Hagen*-settlements with their characteristic long strip farms as well as settlements in other areas with poor soil. Moreover, some villages in the north-west of Germany continued to be farmed on a one-field system with soil manuring (*Plaggendüngung*) which permitted the uninterrupted cultivation of rye.[22]

Origins and development of the village

Which factors, then, led to the development of villages with open fields and advanced crop rotation in the high Middle Ages? As mentioned before, the formation of the European village depended on a number of radical changes in the social, political as well as economic sphere; changes which were contingent on one another. The rise in population, for example, led to the development of arable land and to the introduction of more efficient growing methods. These, in turn, increased the production of cereals at the expense of livestock-breeding, particularly in the regions of longest settlement. The first to introduce the three-field system were the grain-producing areas of western and central Europe, as opposed to wine-growing areas which went over to the two-field system.[23] In spite of low yields cereal production supplied far more food for the ever increasing population than had livestock production. Consequently meat was gradually replaced by grains and vegetables in the peasant diet.

In addition the formation of the village was stimulated considerably by the transformation of the manorial system and the subsequent relaxation of peasant dependence. The manorial system, the 'classical' form of the manor in the early Middle Ages, was characterized by the demesne farm (*Fronhof*), which was farmed by dependent peasants performing labour services under the direction of the lord who was also entitled to substantial peasant dues.[24] The king and other lay and ecclesiastical magnates possessed several manors each consisting of an entire network of dependent farms. The *Fronhof*, the centre of the manor, was also the residence of either the lord himself or of one of his administrators, who appear as a *villicus* or *Meier* in the records. They co-ordinated the work on the demesne farm itself which was carried out primarily by the dependent domestics of the lord.

The farms of the dependent peasants which were part of the manor were located either nearby or in groups or hamlets further away. Here lived the peasants who performed labour services for the manor or supplied dues in kind which served substantially to provide for the lord and his servants. The amount of work which had to be done by the dependent peasant was in turn dependent upon the size of the demesne farm and on the size of its household. The peasants had to supply their own tools, draught-animals and ploughs. Land registers (*urbaria*) illustrate the nature and extent of labour services and other peasant duties: peasants were obliged to perform a wide range of services, such as ploughing, sowing, mowing, harvesting, threshing, corn-grinding and baking. In addition, peasants had to look after the stock of the manor, or they had to build fences, to supply firewood or timber, to drive carts and to run errands. Moreover, their wives and daughters had to do the spinning, weaving and laundry for the demesne farm.

With the dissolution of the manorial system the extent of demesne farming as well as labour services in general were greatly reduced if not completely abolished.[25] These obligations were replaced by dues in money and kind, which ameliorated the condition of the peasants by making them more independent, and by giving them more time for collective farming and their life in the village. Most lords abolished the manorial system during the twelfth and thirteenth centuries; this process was completed by the end of the thirteenth century.

In those regions where the manorial system had been the dominant mode of feudal organization, the transition to money rents and leasehold farming changed peasant life considerably. Little attention, however, has been paid to the question of whether the manors were actually the dominant mode of production in the various lands of Europe, and to what extent the peasants were really involved in them. By comparison with the east Frankish region between the Rivers Rhine and Loire, where the 'classical manor' had its origins, the Frankish lands east of the Rhine had a less developed manorial system.

In addition to classical manors there were a number of manors in these areas whose revenues derived from peasant dues rather than from production on the demesne farm itself. Generally, however, the fragmentation of the demesne, the founding of new farms on what had been the lords' home farm, or even the undivided holding of the old manor either by peasants or by the lords' officials (see n. 26) had decisive repercussions on the entire structure of agrarian society – including the peasantry and the formation of the village, especially in areas where manors with large demesne farms had predominated. But this transition also affected estates with an advanced system of collecting rents and dues: now that peasant dues were increasingly fixed and property rights improved, peasants gained more independence from manorial intervention.[26] In many regions land-leases became more flexible and the personal dependence on the feudal lords was loosened considerably. Peasants formerly engaged in time-consuming labour services were increasingly able to spend more time on their own holdings, as a result of which their labour yielded greater profits, with more time to produce for their own benefit and sell surpluses in the growing number of urban markets.

As the dissolution of the manorial, or *Fronhof*-system, and the transition to rent payments reduced the importance of these traditional centres of peasant life and economy, social life gradually shifted to the village. By the beginning of the fourteenth century, villages using compulsory cultivation systems and common lands and with more developed village co-operation had become the most successful type of settlement. Nevertheless, the transition from the old manor-centred community to the village community was by no means abrupt. The *Fronhof* continued to be important in many areas as a legal centre – in particular for the court sessions of the former members of the *familia*, and they were also used as centre for the collection of peasant dues. Even the economy of the village continued to be at least partly directed from the old demesne farms, which were now held by bailiffs, mayors (*Meier* or *Schultheiss*) and rich peasants, who retained the privilege of the first crop at harvest-time. Yet these otherwise privileged village members also had duties such as the keeping of breeding animals.[27]

In the course of the high and late Middle Ages, these changes in settlement, economy, manorial organization and so forth caused the rise

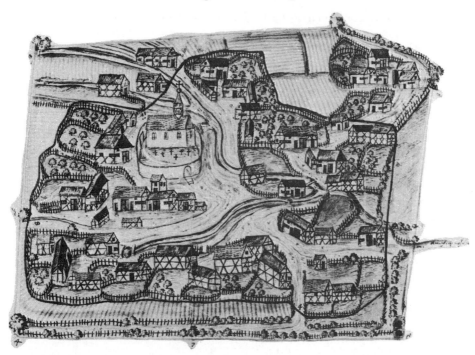

Figure 4 The village of Heudorf near Constance in 1576. The living quarters of the village, including church, farmsteads and gardens, are surrounded by a village fence (*Etter*)

of village communities with their own competences and authority. This process, however, will be examined in detail in a subsequent chapter.[78] Furthermore, regional and temporal differences accompanied the emergence of the village and the village community. The socio-political and economic changes in the high Middle Ages, none the less, encumbered the village with a number of tasks which called for new administrative bodies both in the villages themselves and in rural districts in general. The decreasing influence of the manor on local farming, the organization of peasant holdings and the development of commons with advanced crop rotation created economic, legal and administrative problems for the villages which increased in proportion to their growth and to changes in settlement structure, particularly in densely populated regions.

In this context it is important to realize that the village community had manorial as well as co-operative origins, which determined its development. The legacy of the manorial system manifested itself, for the most part, in the overall structure of the village in the high and late Middle Ages. Cultivation under the supervision of a bailiff or other manorial agents was now taken over by the village community itself. Similarly, the village court continued to be held in the old manorial centre with the former manorial official becoming an important official within the village community. Furthermore some of the old manorial laws left their traces in the village laws of the high and late Middle Ages, and there was also a certain continuity from the manorial to the village court.

Another important aspect was that social solidarity among peasants grew not merely as a result of political and economic changes, but also due to the levelling of the social and legal differences between the various strata within the peasantry.[29] The close ties of bonded peasants to their lords were gradually loosened as peasants gained greater room for manoeuvre in economic and social affairs. The membership of various manorial bodies was gradually replaced by the community of all residents of the village. The differences in estate between free, partly free and dependent peasants gave way to an assimilation of all those resident within the confines of the village to a uniform legal status. Other factors contributed to this levelling tendency, such as the legal equality of settlers in clearance areas, as well as the privileges bestowed on villages, modelled on the Beaumont law code, which encouraged the founding of a number of 'liberated' villages with unitary village laws in northern France and western Germany.[30]

As a result of the rise in population, the increasing settlement density and the land shortage in the high Middle Ages, latecomers received less land in clearance areas, and this is why they often were among the lower strata in the social hierarchy of the village. From the thirteenth century, greater numbers of cottagers (*Seldner, Schupposer*) as well as day-labourers began to appear in previously settled regions, especially in southern Germany. Recent studies of historical settlements in eastern Swabia have shown that cottagers played an important part in the formation of the village.[31] In addition to such general trends as the tendency to produce grain rather than livestock, the increase in partible inheritance systems, the introduction of open fields and the growing settlement density, another social factor must be mentioned which stimulated the development of nuclear villages: the rising number of cottagers apparent from the thirteenth century on. The houses and working quarters of cottagers, which often stood in separate rows within the village, filled the gaps within the villages in eastern Swabia, and this turned many settlements which had been hamlets into densely populated villages. The emergence of a larger lower stratum among the peasantry in other regions must have had a similar effect on the growth and development of the village.

It is interesting to note that in the high Middle Ages there were obvious parallels between the development of the village and that of the town – apart from general similarities between urban and rural communes which will be discussed at a later stage.[32] Villages in wine-growing areas, for example, replaced their fences with moats, walls or palisades, an observation which illustrates that cities had a considerable influence on the village, especially in terms of its topographical development. Urban elements permeated the countryside in many regions of Germany, particularly in Alsace and the Rhineland. This is why even today's traveller in these regions has difficulty telling town from village at first glance. Many villages, just like towns, were not only heavily built up but also surrounded by walls. The study of settlement topography and forms of economic organization has revealed further similarities between town and village. In the late Middle Ages, the residential areas in towns and villages had similar types of landholding structures with only the proprietors of such holdings enjoying full rights to the commons in either towns or villages. Moreover, both the fenced village centre and the fortified town had legal immunities, although this was much more apparent in the town with its codified laws. It should be kept in mind, however, that there were considerable differences in terms of legal status between villagers and townspeople.

Archaeological evidence on the development of the village

The archaeology of the Middle Ages has contributed to the understanding of the development of the village, and it has had a considerable influence on the study of peasant conditions and the medieval village. For instance, when P. Grimm carried out his large-scale excavation of Hohenrode – a clearance settlement from the high Middle Ages – he drew on archaeological evidence from a number of settlement excavations in England and Denmark.[33] However, historians in these countries already had a long tradition of research into the archaeology of medieval rural settlement. Since the end of World War II, rich finds from medieval settlements were produced in a number of extensive excavations almost everywhere in central Europe.[34] The excavation of a Saxon settlement near Warendorf, inhabited from the seventh to the ninth centuries, revealed one of the finest examples of a Carolingian village.[35] The village consisted of a grouping of four to five farms of considerable size; and four distinct phases of settlement can be distinguished. Each farm had its rectangular farmhouse and fourteen to fifteen farm buildings such as barns, sundry storehouses, stables and weaving rooms. There is evidence for both livestock and grain production in the village. The pattern of construction was specially designed to meet a variety of economic needs, with individual buildings designed for specific uses – an observation which also applies to many other settlements of that time.

The archaeology of the high and late Middle Ages, on the other hand, has illustrated to what extent the villages of those centuries differed from early medieval settlements like the one near Warendorf. In Langendorf near Aachen, for example, excavations have unearthed the remains of a village from the high Middle Ages: the find includes houses, cellars and stoves.[36] What surprised archaeologists most was the fact that the ground-plan of Langendorf in the eleventh century was radically different from its present day structure. In the high Middle Ages, it resembled a nuclear village and was only later developed into a two-row linear village. This confirms the evidence from other excavations which also suggests that settlements were subject to radical transformations over the centuries. Apparently the layout of medieval villages was particularly unstable because of dynamic changes in agrarian conditions which constantly worked towards altering settlement patterns.

The excavation of Hohenrode, the settlement mentioned above, sheds light on two distinct settlement phases: a period of Slavic settlement from the tenth to the twelfth centuries followed by German settlement from the twelfth to the fourteenth centuries.[37] Wooden houses built on stilts or in pits (*Pfahlhäuser* and *Grubenhäuser*) were found in the Slavic village – as opposed to houses and farm buildings on stone foundations supported by crossbeams which characterized the German phase. The latter were half-timber constructions, and the fact that most of the residential buildings had several rooms indicates that peasant houses met differentiated dwelling requirements. Even storehouses were constructed as multi-storey buildings. Wells, ovens and sunken paths were also found in this settlement, which resembled a hamlet rather than a village, owing to its loose cluster of farmhouses and adjacent buildings surrounding a stream coming from the well which was the main water supply for humans and animals. Soil analysis reveals that local clay was used to produce the pottery of the community. And the iron artefacts from Hohenrode were surprisingly similar to the sketches of peasant tools in the Saxon Code. Thus their authenticity now seems to be confirmed by archaeological evidence. Nevertheless it remains unclear why Hohenrode was deserted in the fourteenth century.

Königshagen, the excavation of which provides researchers with one of their finest examples of the archaeology of the high Middle Ages, is a good illustration of a forest clearance settlement.[38] Situated on the foot of the Harz, a low mountain range in northern Germany, Königshagen was founded around 1130 by local lords who held the royal mandate to administer the crown land of the region. Some 300 years later, in 1420, the village was destroyed by a fire set during the course of a feud. The main components of the village were a modest castle which was later remodelled into a church, thirteen farms and a circular fortification which served to protect the group of small houses surrounding the castle tower and the church. A variety of artefacts, mostly pottery and iron tools such as spades, shovels and other farming implements, throw light on the material aspect of rural culture in the Middle Ages. As its suffix indicates, Königshagen was founded in the wake of the great clearings of the high Middle Ages. After the clearing of the land which was to become

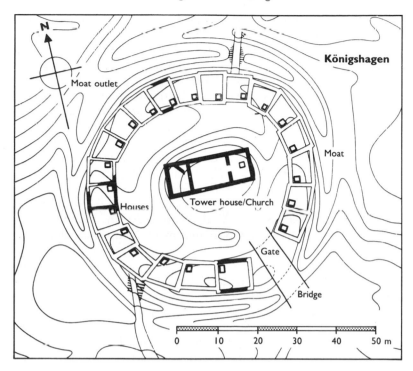

Figure 5 The centre of Königshagen, a deserted village near Barbis in the southern part of the Harz Mountains, a circular type of planned settlement from the high Middle Ages (after W. Janssen)

Königshagen in the twelfth century, the first settlers reinforced their fields on mountainous slopes with terraces to avoid erosion of the soil. Hence it must be assumed that the peasants of Königshagen depended at least partly on the cultivation of unprofitable farmland. Some of these terraced fields were overgrown by brushwood after the desertion of the village, while others were taken over by peasants from a neighbouring village. All of them, however, can be detected even today in the terraced layout of the landscape.

Most peasant villages had an almost exclusively agrarian economy. Farming and the breeding of livestock dominated their everyday life, as in the case of Hohenrode, where there is no evidence for any commercial production whatsoever. It appears that the village subsisted entirely on agriculture. It should, however, be taken into account that archaeological evidence alone does not suffice to determine the extent of animal-raising, because some of the buildings which might have been stables have not been identified yet in terms of their function. Nevertheless, what is clear so far is that grain production was quite important in Hohenrode, as several grain stores and ovens have been found close to the centre of the settlement. Yet many of the settlements from the high Middle Ages that have been excavated so far had not only agricultural but also artisan and commercial production. In the area of Königshagen, for example, a small pottery workshop has been discovered; but as it is rather small, it has been argued that its sole purpose was production to meet the requirements of the villagers, for the bulk of the earthenware excavated in the houses of the place had been made in that workshop.[39]

On the basis of present archaeological research two main groups of settlement forms can be distinguished in the Middle Ages. There are settlements without a discernible layout; most of the excavated settlements from the early and high Middle Ages can be characterized thus. The unsystematic grouping of farms and adjacent buildings is characteristic of the older medieval settlements. As their ground-plans bear no trace of deliberate planning, it would appear that many of them developed over longer periods, rather than arising from a single act of foundation. On the other hand there are a number of systematic forms among the group of planned settlements, such as circular, linear, or nuclear villages. There are hundreds of such villages, all of them founded in the phase of massive colonization and settlement in the high Middle Ages. Rows of houses with fenced-in fields laid out along streams were typical of the settlements in Lower Saxony and Westphalia, as well as the colonized territories on the eastern fringes of medieval Germany. There were also planned settlements surrounding an open village square, mainly in the Margravate of Brandenburg.[40]

One of the most important results from excavations in central Europe has been a better insight into the continuity of settlement in the Middle Ages. Settlements changed with time, and some of them quite drastically, particularly under the impact of wars or other catastrophes. Others disappeared after long periods of development, such as the villages which were deserted towards the end of the high Middle Ages or in the course of the late Middle Ages. A close look at the archaeological evidence shows, however, that almost none of the villages existed for just one settlement period. Most excavations have uncovered various distinct strata in the course of their soil analysis, which point, of course, to different phases of settlement. This is why W. Janssen assumed that hardly any of the settlements excavated until now existed without interruption: 'There were considerable gaps and breaks in the development of many settlements, and they can be reconstructed by scrutinizing the various layers with the help of soil analysis. Moreover, there are instances in which the entire layout of the village was changed.'[41]

In England, where archaeologists have studied rural settlements for more than a century now, particularly the excavation of village centres has produced a better understanding of village history. A fine example is the excavation of Wharram Percy, a village in eastern Yorkshire. There, rich finds have been made on the development of farms, the village church, and the manor.[42] The ground-plan of Wharram Percy provides a unique illustration of the growth and change of a rural settlement between the early and the late Middle Ages. In its beginnings the village was inhabited by Anglo-Saxons, who were the architects of a wooden church which was later replaced by one constructed in stone. The village was situated in the bottom of a valley where very little space was available, so that it was relatively small. In the course of the twelfth century, the village grew pretty much at random, reaching higher ground in the west. By 1200 the construction of the lord's manor was complete. In the thirteenth century, a large proportion of the commons was incorporated into the actual settlement centre by splitting the land into individual holdings. Hence what was an unevenly laid out village from the ninth to the twelfth centuries was now supplemented by a two-row extension along the river which was probably initiated by the lord of the manor.

At least until the thirteenth century, farmhouses were usually constructed out of wood; the various construction phases suggest that they had to be rebuilt with each generation. As a consequence, many houses were shifted to new sites or were completely revised in their ground-plan. Even the manor and the church were subject to drastic topographical and architectural alterations in the high and late Middle Ages. The church, which was originally a small half-timber building, was later replaced by a single-nave stone construction which was furnished with numerous extensions. The remodelling of the church paralleled the transformation of the village itself, which reached its greatest physical extent in the thirteenth century. The economic decline of the settlement, which eventually led to its desertion around 1500, was also reflected in the decreasing size of the church, although its core was preserved. What was surprising in the case of Wharram Percy and other settlements was the extent to which the layout changed. The general impression from these settlements is that the shapes of peasant holdings and the overall layout of English villages changed profoundly in the Middle Ages.[43] All in all, however, the considerable fluctuation of settlement structures discovered by archaeological investigation has only rarely been confirmed by the study of written sources.

Settlement excavations in Moravia have added to the evidence on medieval settlements already gathered in England and Germany.[44] It is above all the extensive excavation of Pfaffenschlag, a clearance settlement from the high Middle Ages near Slavonice, which must be mentioned in this context.[45] In the eleventh and twelfth centuries, the settlement could scarcely have had more than fifty to sixty inhabitants who lived in seven small huts similar to pit-houses along a stream. After an interruption of about one hundred years it was resettled. Colonists built a new village with a regular ground-plan on both sides of the same stream. This consisted of eleven or twelve farms with a total of twenty buildings. Because of its topography, Pfaffenschlag has been classified as a two-row village, a settlement type widely used by German colonists in the lands on the eastern frontier.

In contrast to the wooden houses of the older settlements, the houses of the colonists were built on stone foundations which supported half-timber or even massive stonework buildings. Indeed we find peasant life and economy mirrored in buildings which served the peasantry in a variety of functions: there were residential buildings with living-rooms and bedrooms, as well as stables, stores, ovens, stone floors, cellars and fences. During its brief existence between the thirteenth and the fifteenth centuries, Pfaffenschlag was a medium-size village with 100 to 120 inhabitants. The social position of the villagers can be gauged from the size and the furnishings of their houses. After the desertion of the village, which may have been caused by passing bands of Hussites, the peasants, who had moved into the neighbouring village of Slavonice, continued to farm the old commons for some time. Studies on the landed area of Pfaffenschlag have revealed that it had about 123 hectares of arable. Since the village apparently consisted of eleven farms, the size of each of them must have been about 10 hectares, in addition to meadows and other pasture land of about the same size. The three-field system was used to farm the arable and the open fields were subdivided into long strips.

The study of Pfaffenschlag and other Moravian villages has brought archaeologists and historians to the conclusion that the layout of these settlements 'was characterized by a much greater stability in the thirteenth century'.[46] This tendency was also true for the forms of Moravian farmhouses, settlement structures and the field distribution in the centuries thereafter. By the end of the thirteenth century, the development of Pfaffenschlag came to a halt, largely because the holdings were of sufficient size by then, and because of the satisfactory use of the three-field system and other agricultural innovations. The Moravian evidence has turned out to be surprisingly similar to village development in Germany, which also reached its peak in the high Middle Ages.

5

PEASANT HOUSE AND HOLDING

Problems in peasant house research

Many studies, both older and more recent, of the age of chivalry have
affirmed the unique character of courtly culture by expatiating on the
diversity of clothing and knightly armour as well as the changes in the
construction of castles and other noble residences. This splendour is all
too often contrasted to what appeared to be the wretchedness of peasant
conditions. Does this widespread view of the unchanging quality of
peasant material culture correspond with the reality in the high and late
Middle Ages? Were neither peasant house nor holding subject to change
over the centuries? This chapter proposes to examine the transformation
which affected peasant farms and the overall living conditions of the
peasantry without diminishing the undisputed magnificence of chivalrous
culture. As it is, some major innovations which will be discussed in more
detail were, for the most part, introduced in the high Middle Ages and
continued to have an influence on the life and work of the rural
population for centuries to come.[1] The present preference for traditional
building styles, the dislike of concrete, and the meticulous restoration of
half-timber and other traditional buildings in villages and even big cities
have aroused a new interest in the singular character and worth of the
popular culture of our ancestors. Nevertheless, nostalgic trends such as
the enjoyment of open fireplaces should not distort the view of the actual
living conditions, particularly the uncomfortable housing of the peasantry
in the Middle Ages.

Moreover, regional differences in medieval Europe, especially the
various environmental and economic conditions, hinder any serious
attempt to generalize about the structure and development of house and
farm buildings. Notwithstanding these difficulties, the present chapter
tries to give at least a general idea of the relationship between the housing
and work of peasants in central Europe during the Middle Ages. What

are, then, the basis and sources for the study of peasant housing, which has recently become a special field of study, with international congresses and research institutes all of its own? In addition to the traditional study of ethnology and popular culture,[2] recent advances by archaeologists have led to the gathering and analysis of relevant material on the development of peasant housing. Despite a number of unresolved questions, some interesting conclusions on medieval housing can be drawn from what has been excavated so far.[3] The study of popular culture, which is studied in a separate *Volkskunde* department in German universities, has long dealt with buildings of the fifteenth and sixteenth century with the aim of tracing the regional types of peasant houses back into the early Middle Ages; yet results have been far too speculative. Consequently, ethnographers have recently returned to the empirical study of peasant houses and date wooden building material with the help of dendrochronology.[4] This and careful analyses of written evidence have led to much sounder conclusions on the history of peasant housing and construction in the high and late Middle Ages.

Are there, in any case, grounds for making a distinction between 'peasant houses' as opposed to the houses of artisans, merchants, city-dwellers, or the nobility? And which historical factors have to be accounted for in making such distinctions? These questions turn out to be much more problematic than they seem at first glance. In the first place the concept of the peasant is itself ambiguous,[5] and in the second place social and economic conditions within the medieval village were changing constantly. In addition types of farmhouse also changed, generally evolving according to the types of produce of a given region; hence they had to suit the needs of either grain, vegetable, wine, or stock production. The forms and facilities of peasant houses were also determined by the social position of their inhabitants. Scholarship has long been aware of the complex differentiation of the nineteenth- and twentieth-century peasantry, and the same applies to the various strata within medieval peasantry, which included a wealthy upper layer with fine farmhouses of their own and poor cottagers and day-labourers who lived in much humbler lodgings.[6]

The variety and regional diversity of farmhouses as well as their origin have been closely examined by ethnologists and specialists in popular culture. Unfortunately, however, ethnically biased scholars who thought that certain farmhouse types were characteristic of certain tribes influenced this research for decades.[7] Some ethnologists claimed, for example, that the authentic building material of the early Germanic tribes was timber as opposed to the stone of Roman architecture. Furthermore, the longhouse (*Hallenhaus*) which is characteristic of northern Germany was considered typical for the old Saxon tribe; consequently a distinction was made between what is known as the Franconian farmyard and the genuine Saxon farmhouse.

With the decline of such 'folk ideology', which had its greatest triumphs in the Third Reich, research on farm buildings has been conducted much more in terms of the social and economic reality of their occupants rather than in terms of primitive tribal traditions. This new functional approach examines types of farmhouse with respect to the geographical as well as the economic conditions of a given region. Comparisons were made, for example, between the farmhouses of cattle-breeders, wine-makers and grain producers.[8] The environment has played a prominent role in such studies because it is clear that the peasant, rather than being in control of nature and cultural influences, essentially depended on them. Moreover, not only the nature of agricultural production but the available building material contributed to the emergence of different types of farm buildings. Timber was, not surprisingly, characteristic of most construction in northern Europe, and stone in the south, whereas in central Europe, where both timber and stone were available, both materials were used in construction.

Two principal reasons make a close look at the design and development of farm buildings important for the analysis of peasant conditions in the Middle Ages. First, because the daily life of the peasantry was immediately affected by the structure of peasant house and peasant farm alike, and secondly because their architectural transformations reflect the changes in the work conditions of the peasantry. The following section, then, summarizes the main aspects of each farmhouse type by surveying its formation within the context of the social and economic position of the peasants, which, in turn, will be seen against the background of the overall economic, social and cultural change in the high and late Middle Ages. In addition the transformation of farm buildings cannot be isolated from the development of building in general which, particularly in the high and late Middle Ages, was markedly affected by the thriving culture of the towns on the one hand and by architectural achievements such as churches, monasteries and the residences of the nobility on the other. The longhouse of northern Germany, for example, was decisively influenced by urban culture and the typical characteristics of urban building. This has been proved by a detailed study of urban and rural construction in the Weser area.[9]

The innovations of the high Middle Ages in particular marked a new era in the history of farm buildings as basic forms were developed which have left their imprint on the appearance of rural settlements until the present. With the exception of the *Gulfhaus* in Frisia and the *Engadinerhaus* in Switzerland the basic structures of the farmhouses were already attained by the sixteenth century. The high and late Middle Ages, especially the radical changes of the twelfth and thirteenth centuries, were in fact years of innovation and advancement which affected virtually every aspect of peasants' existence, including their homes and farms.[10] Finally, this process cannot be separated from the general transformation of agrarian

Figure 6 View of a village centre in northern Switzerland (Gossau near St
Gallen), with church and half-timbered houses, around 1490; from the
illustrated chronicle by Diepold Schilling at Lucerne (1513)

conditions including the unprecedented development of land used for
grain production, the more efficient agricultural techniques, the increasing
application of the three-field system, and the intensification of agrarian
production by means of special crops.

One of the most influential changes in building in the high Middle Ages was the transition from post to frame constructions. The wooden load-bearing supports of farm buildings were no longer sunk into the ground, but placed on stone foundations and sills which made them much more durable. In comparison with the traditionial post constructions which only rarely outlasted the lifespan of one generation, the new constructions could survive for centuries. They required, however, additional stabilizing elements such as squares, nogging pieces and long braces, with the result that peasants depended more than previously on the professional skill of the carpenter familiar with half-timbering. Prior to the eleventh century peasants tended to build their houses, working quarters and huts themselves, although they could rely on active help from their neighbours. Frame construction with its firmer foundations even allowed the construction of two-storey buildings, providing a much more effective division and allocation of interior spaces and the possibility of a loft. Eventually this transition to more permanent buildings must have resulted in the development of standard peasant houses, such as the famous *Hallenhaus* of northern, or the *Schwarzwaldhaus* of southern Germany – to name only two types.

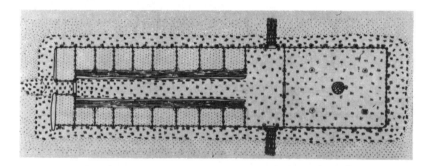

Figure 7 Ground plan of a cattle-stall farmhouse in Feddersen-Wierde (near Bremerhaven) and its division into peasant lodgings, working quarters and stables (third century)

Peasant holdings in the early Middle Ages

The farm of the early Middle Ages, which will be briefly discussed now to illustrate the scope of innovation in the high Middle Ages, was in fact an assembly of several buildings. The excavations at Warendorf in Westphalia and Merdingen near Freiburg as well as customary law codes (*Weistümer*), have confirmed that early medieval farms consisted of several separate houses and working quarters.[11] As they were somewhat spread out, they had to be surrounded by fences for protection against wild animals and intruders. Farms contained various functional buildings including barns, sheds and stores, in addition to smaller adjacent buildings such as bakeries, kitchens, bathhouses etc. Not all of the buildings on the farms of the early Middle Ages were constructions at ground level. It seems that pit-houses (*Grubenhäuser*) were still in use, although not for housing. Most of them served as stores or for craft activities such as weaving. The walls of early medieval farm buildings, which were almost exclusively one-storey, consisted of a row of posts sunk upright into the ground or of wattle-and-daub structures. Straw was used to thatch the high, steep roofs covering an undivided loft space. Prior to the high Middle Ages hanging roofs predominated with roof-ridges and roof-joists covering walls and ridge-posts which supported the entire roof (*Rofendächer*, see figure 8). By contrast, the rafter constructions which were introduced in the high Middle Ages were composed of a rack of double rafters firmly joined to both the walls and the studs upon which it rested.

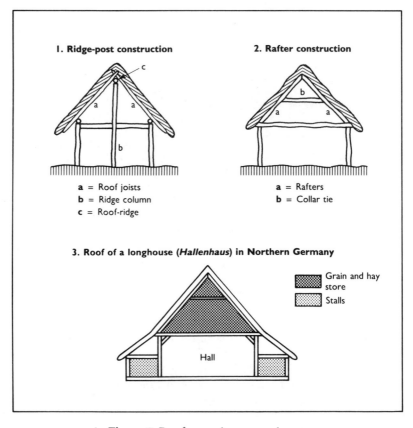

Figure 8 Roof types in peasant houses

Housing in the one- or two-storey peasant homes of the early Middle Ages suffered from the lack of a flue for smoke coming from the hearth fire. Without chimneys, smoke rose to the roof, where it escaped only through little openings or skylights. Hence these houses built without internal ceilings were almost always filled with smoke; as a result the rooms were rather sparsely furnished and were lit only by the light from the hearth fire or pine-torches.

Not all of the early medieval farms in central Europe had separate buildings for humans, animals and the storage of agricultural implements, produce and so forth. Large three-part farmhouses are known to have existed on the North Sea coast and in Scandinavia which contained both stables and a hearth room which was the centre of family life.[12] Although these early medieval cattle-stall farmhouses might have served as a model for the development of the longhouse in northern Germany,[13] most farmyards in central Europe apparently consisted of several separate buildings. This observation has shattered the assumption of traditional scholarship which had claimed that the standard farm types of the early modern era were the descendants of former Germanic, Roman or Slavic farms. Likewise, the view that there were distinct Germanic, Romanesque, Saxon, Slavic, Alemannian or Franconian farmyard types must be rejected, since in the early Middle Ages farms in the various regions of Europe were relatively similar.

As a consequence of the simple design of early medieval farm buildings, and above all owing to the rapid rotting of the wooden posts on which they rested, buildings often lasted for only fifty years before replacement or major repair became unavoidable. Excavations of early medieval settlements have confirmed that for this reason entire farmhouses, even villages, were shifted to new sites for reconstruction. Archaeological studies in England and the north-west of Germany have shown that, in addition to the decay of the buildings themselves, the shifting of settlements in the early Middle Ages was also caused by water seepage, floods and fires.[14] We can also compare early medieval buildings with peasant huts and villages in India and other Third World countries. The received stereotype of the medieval peasant as immobile and tied to the soil can hardly be sustained in the light of such modern archaeological evidence.

Innovations in the peasant house of the high Middle Ages

In the high and late Middle Ages, stud-frame structures were also frequently shifted, especially since dismantling and reassembling such half-timber constructions was easy. Consequently it was customary when buildings were torn down to save the well preserved wooden building parts for future use.[15] Moreover, sometimes in medieval law, houses and working quarters were not even regarded as immovables. Instead they were sometimes classified as movable property which would be taken away by a departing tenant. According to the thirteenth-century Saxon Code (*Sachsenspiegel*), a peasant on leaving his holding was obliged to offer his fences, house and muck-heap to his lord for sale. If the lord was not interested, the peasant had the right to take them with him.[16]

As mentioned before, one of the most important innovations of the high Middle Ages was the longhouse (*Hallenhaus*) of northern Germany, a milestone in the history of the farmhouse.[17] Even today, a few specimens of this type of farmhouse can be seen in villages in northern Germany, and their size and overall layout are still highly impressive. Justus Möser, the conservative philosopher of the late eighteenth century, assessed the advantages of the *Hallenhaus* from the perspective of the peasant's wife:

> The house of the common peasant is so perfect in its floor-plan that it can hardly be improved and can be taken as a model. The hearth is situated almost in the centre of the house, and is so placed that the peasant's wife, who spends most of her time sitting and working there, can see everything at once. No other type of building has such an ideal and yet comfortable vantage point. Without having to get up from her chair, she can overlook three doors, greet people entering the house, offer them a seat, while keeping an eye on her children, servants, horses and cows, tending cellars and bedrooms, and get on with her spinning or cooking. Her bed is just behind the hearth, and from there she can exercise the same supervision, watching her servants getting up for work or going to bed, listening to her cattle feeding and keeping an eye on the cellar and other rooms. Each task is linked in a chain with the others.[18]

Types of peasant house in Germany

Like the early medieval *Hallenhaus* of the North Sea coast and Scandinavia, the longhouse of the high Middle Ages had a framework (see figure 9) made of two rows of posts or studs which divided the inside into three sections to provide enough room for humans and animals to live under a common roof. Grain was stored above a loft ceiling of thick boards just above the central section (see figure 8). To allow loaded wagons to drive into the hall, the gabled roof had to be furnished with a huge gate at the front of the house. Moreover, the central section, which had always been used to feed the animals from the inside when necessary, was now built much larger to make room for a threshing floor. The rear of the central section was also used as the residential space for the peasant's family, which gathered around the open hearth fire, especially on cold days, and which used this area, the *Fleet*, for working, eating and sleeping.

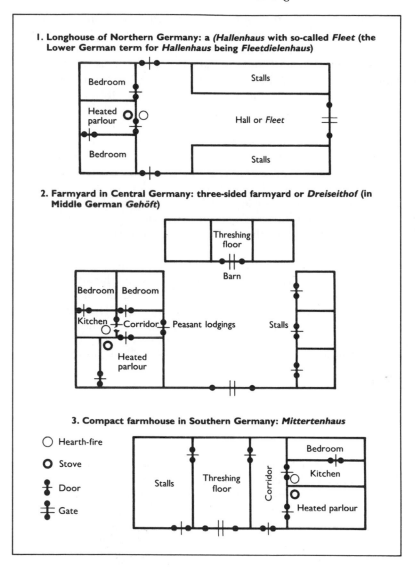

Figure 9 Farmhouse types in Germany

The storing of harvested grains under the enlarged roof of the fully-fledged *Hallenhaus* developed as a result of the agricultural upswing of the high Middle Ages. In the wake of the increasing demand for foodstuffs which was caused by the rise in population, the size and proportion of the farmland which served for the production of cereals was considerably expanded. More storage room was needed in addition to the existing barns to hold the harvested grain, and because the dampness from the North Sea and the frequent rains in that region often caused grain to become damp, the enlarged roof of the new longhouse proved to be ideal in allowing it to dry more easily. This was because the chimney-free hearth in the central section gave off enough warmth to protect at least part of the grain stored above from damage. The *Hallenhaus* soon became the standard farmhouse in the north precisely because it provided sufficient space to fulfil numerous functions under a single roof. It combined the essential functions of peasant life and work: housing, the keeping of livestock, and the storing of produce and provisions. It was essentially these multiple functions which caused this genuine 'peasant invention'[19] to achieve considerable popularity in the lowlands of northern Germany, and it is hardly surprising to see that from the twelfth and thirteenth centuries peasant settlers from the north began to introduce it into the colonized eastern territories too.

As in northern Germany, but in contrast to the central parts of the country, there was also a marked trend to standard multi-purpose farmhouses in southern Germany.[20] In contrast to the situation in the north, however, it is still unclear when this trend began in the south, although most evidence suggests the high Middle Ages. The *Mittertennhaus* (see figure 9) could well be the oldest standard farmhouse in southern Germany – provided that its being one of the most successful southern types of farmhouse in the fourteenth, fifteenth and sixteenth centuries can be taken as a hint at possible predecessors in the high Middle Ages. The early rise in the number and size of urban communities, which affected the south of Germany too, and the growth of the market and the money economy in the regions near to towns, also suggest that the rural architecture of the south underwent considerable change in the high Middle Ages. The equally impressive farmhouse of the Black Forest, the *Schwarzwaldhaus*, probably evolved in its basic form in the thirteenth and fourteenth centuries and attained its 'optimal' form in the late fifteenth century.[21] This was yet another type of compact farmhouse which included stores, stables and peasant lodgings. Its design was perfect for meeting the specific needs of farming in the Black Forest, particularly the need for ample storage rooms for hay and straw to winter the animals at altitudes where spring would often come as late as May. Although the peasant family and its livestock lived under a common roof as in the *Hallenhaus*, lodgings and stables in the *Schwarzwaldhaus* were separated by a wall to prevent the damp air from the stables penetrating into the bedrooms and living areas.

In the land between the Danube and Lake Constance, another type of compact farmhouse known as the *Dreisässenhaus* developed out of the older Alemannic farm. These were of ridge-post constructions horizontally divided to include threshing floors, stables and bedrooms. Other compact farmhouses laid out in this manner – where living rooms, working quarters and stables also formed a row and each section was equally accessible through a door from the outside, as well from the inside – can be found all over southern Germany. The most common variant, the *Mittertennhaus*, predominated in Upper Bavaria, and Upper Swabia, in addition to such regions as the Vorarlberg in Austria, Mittelland in Switzerland, the Sundgau in southern Alsace, the Vosges mountain range west of the upper Rhine valley, and Lorraine. In its older form (see figure 9), the threshing floor divided the interior into living quarters, with a parlour and kitchen on one side, and stables on the other. In some parts of southern Germany this type of house acquired an upper storey which contained above the parlour bedrooms for the peasant's family and servants, and above the cattle stalls a storage room for grain and hay.

In many parts of southern Germany, however, the innovations of early medieval farms did not result in the development of compact farmhouses in the high Middle Ages, but in the formation of standard farms characterized by a complex of farm buildings. In the south-west for example, the carefully timbered *Schwarzwaldhaus* with its various functional compartments competed with a type of farm from the upper Rhine valley which was equally popular in the fourteenth century. It was here that farms gradually developed from a random assemblage of farm buildings into a regularly laid out type of farm. Living quarters, barns, stables and adjacent buildings were separate, but tended to form either a three- or four-sided farmyard. The division into separate functional buildings has been recorded in the land registers or *Urbare* of the upper Rhine valley, the most explicit descriptions of property of the time. The *Urbar* of the monastery at Tennenbach from the year 1341, for example, is a meticulous inventory of the furnishings of every single farm on its domain, and it often distinguishes clearly between farmhouse (*domus*) and barn (*horreum*), indicating that they are two separate buildings.[22]

The history of peasant housing in the central parts of Germany was similar to that in the upper Rhine valley. As a rule, regularly arranged farmyards were much more common than compact farmhouses. The need for more storage room in the wake of the increasing grain production in the high Middle Ages was partly met by extending the existing barns. According to land registers, other inventories and customals (*Weistümer*), barns were integral parts of farmhouses in the central areas of Germany. However, in other regions of central and western Europe the farmhouses were enlarged so as to include stables as well (*Wohnstallhäuser*) – the reason being that peasants in these regions had a great interest in protecting their precious livestock, especially cattle, against the cold winters and to have them always within easy reach for better care. Such farmhouses were very common in the British Isles, in northern France, central Germany, and also in many parts of eastern Europe. In a number of instances, rudimentary forms of this type of farmhouse continued to be used until well into the nineteenth and twentieth centuries.

The *Ernhaus* of central Germany, often called the 'Franconian farmhouse' in older works, was a specific variant of this integrated type of farmhouse (*Wohnstallhaus*). The farmhouses excavated at Hohenrode from the twelfth and thirteenth centuries, which were two-storey residential houses on stone foundations, are generally regarded as predecessors to the *Ernhaus*.[23] It seems that the farmhouses of that area were only later extended to provide sufficient room to include stables too. In Königshagen, however, which like Hohenrode was situated in the Harz Mountains in northern Germany, archaeologists discovered a farmhouse which must have been extended in the fourteenth century in order to add a stable.[24] Both settlements, in sum, introduced the basic concept of the peasant farm characteristic of central Germany, consisting of several separate farm buildings. But whereas the farms of Hohenrode had no regular form of layout to their buildings, in Königshagen, a clearance settlement of the later Middle Ages, we find rectangular farms, with buildings laid out in a regular order around a courtyard, sometimes even forming a closed quadrangle. The trend in central Germany during the later Middle Ages was towards a strict layout of individual buildings arranged around a central courtyard, a process which finally resulted in the 'Franconian farm', which was a quadrangular or rectangular yard enclosed by the various farm buildings on either three or four sides (see figure 9). There is reason to believe that such closed or U-shaped farmyards might also have existed in lower Bavaria by the thirteenth and fourteenth centuries.[25] The increased regularity in the arrangement of farm buildings has also been confirmed in the excavation of a fifteenth-century farm in Sindelfingen, Swabia.[26]

In the case of Swabian and Franconian villages with commons, the increase of farms with systematic ground-plans was caused, in particular, by the growth in population and in the number of local farms themselves. The increase in the number of farms had its origin in the growing popularity of partible inheritance, the tendency towards more specialized production, such as wine, and in the development of rural industries such as linen production. We can certainly not rule out a close correlation between farms with systematic ground plans and the growth of rural areas in which grain production or intensive viticulture predominated. The construction of new buildings occasioned by the boom of the later Middle Ages was restricted in many places to the confines of the village to avoid wasting precious arable land and to preserve the villages as a unified group of buildings. In a number of settlements in the south-west of Germany it was strictly prohibited to build on the fields outside the village fence (*Etter*), and lords as well as village authorities adhered to this principle rigorously.[27] The farm-buildings of small farm-towns (*Ackerbürgerstädte*) which were laid out in this manner, may have served as a model for the development of regular plans for village farm buildings because the pressure to save space was even more pronounced there than in the

Figure 10 The Prodigal Son. Copperplate engraving by Albrecht Dürer (1497). Dürer transposes the biblical parable of the prodigal son into a late medieval Franconian village

countryside. In any case, the much more compact farm of the late Middle Ages used far less space than the more extensive farm of the early Middle Ages.

The development of two-storey buildings and houses during the high Middle Ages arose from the same need to save space, as well as from the desire for greater display, above all in the farms of the upper strata of the peasantry. Here the towns, where multi-storey buildings had long since appeared as a result of lack of space, served as a model for rural architecture, while the development of a heated parlour or *Stube* led to the addition of an extra storey. As economic and cultural ties between towns and the country became closer with the high Middle Ages, wealthier peasants increasingly sought to gain greater social prestige by having two-storey buildings. The further development of half-timbering in the course of the late Middle Ages provided the basis for several-storey building and for a more efficient divison of the interior itself. These new buildings, however, tended to require the skill of professional carpenters since most peasants were simply unfamiliar with the more sophisticated construction methods of such buildings.

The social differentiation just touched upon was also reflected in the housing of the lower levels among the peasantry. It is safe to say that in the late Middle Ages the majority of peasants from the lower and middle strata continued to live in houses with one or two rooms, such as those excavated at Hohenrode and elsewhere. Their houses were generally much humbler than the homes of rich peasants.[28] An examination of language has confirmed this assumption. The names for members of the rural lower classes, such as *Seldner* in southern Germany, *Kobler* in Franconia and *Kötter* in Westphalia, were evidently derived from the type of houses they lived in, namely *Selden*, *Kobeln* and *Kotten*. All of these names refer essentially to cottagers. With the intensification of market relations and a money economy in the high Middle Ages, which brought about greater social differentiation of the peasantry itself, the peasant smallholders devised their own versions of the main farmhouse types. Generally speaking, their houses were comparatively small and had only a few adjacent buildings. The analysis of the older buildings in villages today has demonstrated that they were actually smaller versions of the farm buildings described above. In northern Germany, cottagers lived in smaller, compact farmhouses whereas the poorer peasants and day-labourers of southern Germany had to be content with relatively humble one-room houses. The farmhouses of the lower strata of peasants in central Germany had only one extension, which either stood at a right angle to the farmhouse or was simply added to it to form a type of elongated farm (*Streckhof*). And finally, the counterparts to these found in the south-west were either stud-frame constructions in the case of compact farmhouses, or various types of double-houses crowding two peasant households under a common roof.

Development in houses in other European regions

This section glances briefly at the peasant farms and houses in other European regions, keeping in mind the traditional elements of popular building, climatic conditions and the building materials available in the various regions. As a consequence of the warm climate near the Mediterranean, to provide one example, there was no particular need for sophisticated buildings to protect people and livestock from the cold, and owing to lack of timber most farmhouses were made of stone anyway. It should be noted that they had gently sloped roofs as early as the Middle Ages.[29] By contrast with the north, in the south of France stone farm buildings predominated at that time as well, and it appears that their construction may have been influenced by the architectural tradition of the *villae rusticae*, the Roman villa of late antiquity. Two-storey stone farmhouses with working areas at ground level, a type of building frequently used in the Mediterranean even today, might also have had their origin in the Middle Ages. In addition to the simple hearth-houses with open fires and smoke outlets, there were also one- or two-storey farmhouses with built-in chimneys in the prosperous north of Italy by the end of the Middle Ages.

The distribution of stone farmhouses north of the Alps in early modern times, particularly in such areas as Burgundy and Lorraine, was different from that in the Middle Ages. Since the late Middle Ages, stone buildings have gradually come to predominate among peasant building in northern France, Switzerland, the regions west of the Rhine and certain wine-growing areas in southern Germany.[30] The low prestige which timber had in Renaissance architecture, the predilection for stone castles and stone residences among the aristocracy, and particularly the prestigious stone buildings in the towns contributed to the high esteem of brick and stone houses in the rest of medieval Europe. These and other, more practical considerations, such as better protection from fire hazards, were responsible for the growing use of stone in regions with a long tradition of wood construction.

By far the most widespread use of timber construction was made in northern Europe to produce log-cabins. As in Scandinavia and the north of Russia, timber buildings were built in densely wooded mountainous areas such as the Alps and the Carpathians. Between the woodlands of Scandinavia and northern Russia in which timber houses predominated and the south of Europe where stone constructions prevailed, there was a zone including southern Sweden, England, northern France, the German Empire, and many parts of eastern Europe in which half-timbering was the most common building method.

In the course of Anglo-Saxon settlement in the fifth century, the rectangular, rather than the three-section farm buildings which had characterized the native lands of the Anglo-Saxons, came to be used in England.[31] These were either buildings at ground level or pit-houses. They served a variety of purposes and were often part of building complexes of different sizes. With the formation of the English farmhouse, the one-room houses of the early Middle Ages were gradually replaced by longhouses which were divided into several functional sections. Like some types of farmhouses on the Continent, these longhouses encompassed bedrooms, living-rooms, working rooms, as well as stables. Excellent archaeological work in England has demonstrated that until the twelfth-century English farmhouses were exclusively made of wood, peat and clay. It was only towards the end of the high Middle Ages that more durable building materials came into general use in the rural areas. Farmhouses until then were either frame constructions on stone foundations, or they were entirely made of stone. It is therefore hardly surprising that English farmhouses in the early Middle Ages were as short-lived as their counterparts on the Continent – and they were just as often shifted to be rebuilt after only one generation. Two types of farmhouse prevailed in England in the late Middle Ages. By far the commonest was the longhouse, which provided both living and working areas. A hall in the middle separated the rooms of the peasant family from the stables on the opposite side, and the hall was itself divided into a hearth-room with a fireplace and a bedroom. A regularly arranged type of farm has also been excavated whose living and working quarters formed a right angle around the yard. In addition to most medium-size and large farmhouses which were arranged in either of these ways, small one- or two-room farmhouses have been excavated which obviously served as the dwellings of the lower peasant strata.

In the north of France and many neighbouring areas farms without regular ground-plans were the rule in the early Middle Ages, while in the late Middle Ages half-timber constructions predominated in Normandy and the north-western plain of France. The latter were half-timber buildings identical to the ones used in England at that time; however, they often had a greater length – which was mainly due to the extension of additional living and working rooms. In other instances the basic longhouse appears to have been transformed into a farmyard with several functional sections and a regular ground-plan. Furthermore, some European areas witnessed the survival of an older type of the two-room compact farmhouse called the *maison bi-cellulaire*. All in all, there was no fundamental difference between the farmhouses of northern France and those in England or Germany. The stone constructions of southern France, on the other hand, were designed in the indigenous style of the Mediterranean.

As a consequence of the great variety of geographical conditions, there was a remarkable diversity among Alpine farmhouse types. The Alemannian *Dreisässenhaus*, a variant of the compact house (*Einhaus*) of southern Germany, was built particularly in the foothills of the Swiss Alps.[32] To the south, that is along the northern slopes of the main Alpine ridges, there followed randomly arranged farms which for the most part consisted of log-houses. Their working quarters were separate from the farmhouses. Finally along the southern slopes the Mediterranean influence produced stone farmhouses with multiple storeys.

In the early Middle Ages, the Slavic farmhouse of eastern Europe was usually a two-room wooden house in the log-cabin style, or a post construction with latticework walls surrounded by various additional buildings.[33] Brick or stone heating ovens were introduced early in eastern Europe because of its severe winters, and, as they were used for cooking as well as for heating, they soon formed the centre of the fully-fledged heated parlour. The recent excavation of the deserted village Pfaffenschlag in Moravia has added to what was known about peasant housing in eastern Europe in the high and late Middle Ages.[34] Pfaffenschlag, a forest village which was founded as a clearance settlement at the end of the thirteenth century, consisted of stone farmhouses with two or three functional sections. Architecturally speaking, they were probably a further development of the traditional one-room houses of eastern Europe. As the ground-plans of Pfaffenschlag's farmhouses reveal, the room in the centre served as a hall which led to the bedrooms and the *Stube* (a heated parlour free from smoke) on the sides of the house. And once again this parlour must have been the room for the gatherings of the family, for it was equipped with a heating oven or at least a fireplace bedded in mortar. Living and working quarters had a standard layout and a yard between them. V. Nekuda, who directed the excavation of Pfaffenschlag, made a remark which is of a particular interest for the study of the development of farm buildings in Moravia in saying that 'the nineteenth- and twentieth-century farmhouse types all had their origin in those from the fourteenth century'.[35]

The heated parlour:
new stoves and the gradual development of the interior

Moreover, peasant housing in the high Middle Ages underwent considerable improvement not only in its architectural forms, but also in its internal living space. It was in particular the invention of the heating oven and the introduction of the *Stube* which must be regarded as an extremely important advance in the refinement of peasant housing in the Middle Ages.[36] What this new type of parlour really meant for the everyday life of the peasant was illustrated in the literature of the time, for example in the poetry of the Bavarian minnesinger Neidhart von Reuental, who is considered to be 'the creator of village poetry in the courtly style of the thirteenth century'. The *Stube* was a recurrent topic in his winter poems and those of his imitators in later decades. To summarize, his lament about the hardship of the winter season was followed by praise of this type of heated, smoke-free parlour as a genuine refuge, as the best place to be during the cold months of the year. The need to escape from storms and the cold into the heated parlour was contrasted with the joys of the hustle and bustle which it saw in wintertime. According to Neidhart, dancing and entertainment in the heated parlour in winter are the equivalent of the summer idyll below the linden tree or by the side of the village pond. Here is a quote from one of his winter poems which roughly translates as: 'Megenwart's *Stube* is large enough. So let us have a dance there on Sunday. His daughter asks you all to spread the news and come. Engelmar is preparing the dancing around the table.'[37] And another passage provides further evidence for the social importance of the parlour: 'Clear out the chairs and stools! Let's get the tables away! Tonight we will dance until we drop. And open the doors so that we have some fresh air!'[38]

Neidhart von Reuental was the first poet of the high Middle Ages whose works give a detailed description of this new type of parlour.[39] To him, it was the most important place for the peasant to spend his time during the winter months. Neidhart was surprisingly realistic in his account of the peasantry, but he recorded mainly the life-style of the wealthier peasants. The *Stube* referred to in his poems varied in size and quality: some were praised because they were particularly spacious or comfortable, such as Engelmar's. This was because the heated parlour was not only a refuge from the cold in winter, but also the social centre of peasant life. Consequently the best, the most comfortable heated and smoke-free parlours were usually owned by the wealthy peasants. However, it was for the peasants alone that the heated parlour had such an eminent social function. Despite the fact that this kind of parlour with a stove was also recorded in the residences of the nobility during the high Middle Ages, they appear to have served there exclusively as a warming room in winter. In place of the heated parlour, the aristocracy used a hall with an open fireplace, which served alongside the great hall (*Palas*), or heated apartments (*Kemenate*) as settings for courtly festivities and social activities. Hence, as a room, the courtly parlour was more or less private, a refuge especially for women. For the peasantry and townspeople, however, the parlour was the uncontested room for social gatherings, feasts and other activities during the winter.

The term *Stube*, itself refers, as mentioned earlier, to a heated and yet smokeless room which was warm even on extremely cold days. This was not necessarily the case in halls heated by fireplaces. Today's nostalgic enjoyment of open fires should not distort the real living, and especially the heating conditions in traditional farmhouses with their open fireplaces. Reliable measurements taken in the halls of the longhouses in northern Germany have illustrated that, even with a blazing fire in the hearth, temperatures were only a few degrees higher inside the house than outside, and that they could be well below freezing on severe winter nights.[40] Prior to the invention of heating ovens, heating was provided either by hearths or cooking-stoves. Hearths were no doubt older and more common, but cooking-stoves also go back a long time. Cooking-stoves constructed of stone or brick were able to help prevent fires and retain heat while providing warmth for the room, in addition to their use for cooking. For this reason they were common in areas with wooden farm buildings and harsh winters. Hearths were used almost exclusively in western, central and southern Europe, whereas cooking-stoves prevailed in the north and the east of the Continent, including the mountainous areas of central Europe. Unfortunately both types of heating had the one serious disadvantage that the living-rooms in which they were installed were always full of smoke. A saying from the eleventh century reflected this problem in stating that among the worst things that the owner of a house can suffer are a leaking roof, a malicious wife and smoke in the house (*sunt tria dampna domus, imber, mala femina, fumus*).[41]

In the Mediterranean lands, the introduction of chimneys eliminated this terrible nuisance.[42] In addition in the mild climate of these countries fireplaces supplied enough heating even in winter. North of the Alps, however, it was only the installation of cooking-stoves or hearths into a separate, self-contained room, the *Stube*, which permitted smokeless heating. The new type of heating oven was stoked from the back, which was outside the parlour, so that it remained completely free from smoke. In fact, these stone or clay ovens were operated from a separate hearth-room, often the kitchen, whereas its vault pointed into the parlour itself. Owing to this construction, the parlour was the most comfortable place in the house of the peasant and thus the focal point of his work and social life in winter. Without doubt it was one of the most 'effective in-novations' of housing in the Middle Ages,[43] and markedly improved the living conditions of the majority of both rural and urban population.

The origin of the heating oven is still disputed, although some scholars refer to Slavic and Roman influences, as well as to early medieval ovens which might also have served as models. The heated parlour was probably an invention of twelfth-century southern Germany, from where the idea was disseminated into the neighbouring regions in the course of the thirteenth and fourteenth centuries. By the beginning of the thirteenth century, most farmhouses in upper Bavaria, for instance, were furnished with the new type of parlour – as was confirmed in the poems of Neidhart von Reuental. Two of the houses of Hohenrode, the village mentioned above which existed from the twelfth to the fourteenth centuries, had also been heated with ovens.[44] Before long the town-dwellers of northern Germany introduced the new heating oven, and were followed by the inhabitants of the neighbouring rural communities. The *Stube* was also a common phenomenon in this part of the country in the fifteenth and sixteenth centuries, but it was particularly in areas where the longhouse had been introduced in the high Middle Ages that the peasants refrained from substituting the traditional hearths with those stoked from the back. There is evidence that even in the eighteenth century peasants in Westphalia refused to adopt the new heating method, although apparently they were well aware of the inadequacy of the traditional hearths – at least according to a local saying which roughly translates: 'A burn from the front, and an icicle on your backside.' Peasants in some areas of southern Germany, however, also had reservations about this innovation, for in some parts of Austria and the rest of the Alps peasants retained their antiquated heating ovens for centuries. Indeed in the eastern Alps, some of the old ovens remained in use even as late as the first half of the twentieth century.

Unfortunately there is little evidence on the kind of furniture used in medieval farmhouses.[45] What is known to date so far is that even after the introduction of the heated parlour, the furnishings remained scanty and inexpensive. Depending on their financial means and social position, peasants attempted to furnish and decorate their homes with better-quality handcrafted goods. A rack for drying clothes which was attached to the ceiling of the parlour near the oven is depicted in fifteenth-century paintings. Simple shelves on the walls of bedrooms and the parlour provided storage room for various household items such as bowls and jars, while clothes and tools were hung on simple wooden pegs. In most cases, the furniture of the new heated parlours consisted of tables, stools, and benches. The trestle tables called *Schragen* were large enough for all family members to sit around them. The furnishing of the living-rooms of farmhouses without the smokeless parlour was essentially unsophisticated because smoke would have ruined any delicate painting on such items. Clothes, and particularly valuables, were generally stored in trunks or crude cupboards on the wall.

Peasants who did not have bedsteads used benches and primitive wooden racks padded with sacks of straw instead. Poorer peasants, who had even less furniture, slept on heaps of straw near the fireplace. From paintings and from written records there is some evidence on the arrangement of the interior of peasant living-rooms. It appears that tables and benches were usually placed in a corner opposite the fireplace, hearth or oven. And as befitted the patriarchial character of peasant families in the Middle Ages, the seats by the walls were reserved for the men while women were expected to sit by the oven to take care of the food and perform other domestic tasks.[46]

PART III

PEASANT CLOTHING, FOOD AND WORK, 1000–1400

6

CLOTHING AND FOOD

Clothes in the early Middle Ages

Within any particular culture, clothing serves not only to protect the wearer against the climate but to express an 'attitude, a way of life'.[1] During the Middle Ages this was true for the clothing of the nobility, the clergy, the urban population, as well as for the peasantry; indeed clothing should be considered in terms of its economic, social and cultural context. This is because, far more than food, clothing reflects the social and ideological position of an individual within society rather than being the result of purely vital needs. Moreover, the human urge for innovation produced considerable alterations in the form, quality and colour of clothes – although it seems that peasant garments changed less than the fashions at court or in the towns.[2] Above all, peasant clothing had to meet the practical requirements of everyday life, especially the various types of peasant work. Archaeological evidence, which has so often supplied excellent insights into many facets of peasant existence, is poor in this respect, since most medieval textiles have survived only under unusual conditions, such as in moors or other very damp soils. Consequently written sources, especially individual descriptions, clothing regulations and illustrations,[3] are the best sources for research into the forms and development of peasant clothing.

The most interesting aspects of the study of peasant clothing are those related to the transformation of men's as opposed to women's clothes, and to social, regional or economic variations, and generational differentiation. In addition it is interesting to observe the formal development of fashion and costume.[4] Until well into the nineteenth century, clothes were an unmistakable reflection of the social hierarchy of the villagers: as a rule, the wealthier peasants wore rich garments which were noticeably different from the clothes of day-labourers, small tenants and other members of the lower peasant classes. These differences were most prominent in Sunday clothes, as those of the upper classes were woven of precious and fine fabrics. The everyday and working garb of the peasants, however, was less differentiated. Hence the regional character of rural attire is found in the festive clothing which originated in the late Middle Ages.[5] In economic terms, raw materials and the production of clothes should be taken into account: is there any evidence, for instance, that linen, wool, and other fabrics were produced by the peasants themselves? Did peasants have access to imported textiles, and was the processing of these done by specialized trades?

There was no specific peasant attire in the early Middle Ages, and popular clothing at the time consisted basically of three items: a tunic, a covering for the lower body and a cloak.[6] As far as we can tell there were no major differences between the clothing of the Celtic, Germanic and Slavic branches of the European population. Men usually wore a tunic of wool or linen with long sleeves, trousers with a belt, and especially in winter a cloak of fur, animal skin or heavy wool. Pieces of leather wrapped around the feet and tied above the ankles served as shoes, and a hood, often attached to their cloaks, protected them from the wet and the cold. Peasant tunics were slit from the waist on both sides so that they would not impede work in the fields. Women wore them much longer: their coats covered the ankles and were held in place by decorated belts. Winter tunics always had long sleeves, and for further comfort finer linen shirts gradually came into use by both women and men.

Miniatures, fresco cycles and written sources from Carolingian times have been found helpful in sketching the history of medieval clothing, although these mainly give an impression of the costumes of the upper classes. One of the most informative written sources was Charlemagne's clothing decree of the year 808,[7] according to which neither women nor men were allowed to buy or sell finer coats for more than 20, and ordinary woollen ones for more than 10 shillings, while the use of marten, otter or other linings raised the price limit to 30 shillings. It is known from other contemporary accounts that Charlemagne strongly disapproved of excessive luxury in the clothing of his staff at court, in particular of silk, furs and foreign fashion. According to Einhard, his biographer, Charlemagne himself seems to have had a predilection for the garments of the common people.

The dress of the clergy and the laity became much more distinct in the course of the Middle Ages. In contrast to the relatively short tunics of the peasants, monks wore long habits without slashes on the sides under especially large hooded cloaks. Benedictine friars were known to wear dark woollen clothing whilst the Cistercians of the high Middle Ages preferred white or grey wool for their habits.[8] Long clothes covering the ankles came to be the characteristic dress of the monks and secular clergy, thus indicating that these groups did not have to engage in physical labour.

Changes in clothing during the high Middle Ages

The differentiation which with the high Middle Ages began to appear in the clothing of the chivalric and courtly upper classes and the rising bourgeoisie also had an impact on the clothing of the peasantry.[9] These changes appeared in many European regions during the twelfth and thirteenth centuries. It is clear that they had their origin in the close contact with Arabian and Byzantine fashions during the crusades, and in the changing attitude towards life in general and the human body in particular. From the eleventh century we see a growing preference for longer tunics among the wealthier members of society, until in the end they even reached the ankles. As a result of these changes men's clothes became increasingly similar to women's; in the illustrations to the Manesse collection of ballads, for example, we can see how little men and women at in the medieval courts differed in appearance from one other (see figure 11). Their tunics fit closely to the chest and the arms, but from the belt they dropped in deep folds so that they had to be gathered up. This was the favourite clothing for indoor life, whereas hunting and travelling parties, of course, preferred much shorter tunics, often turned up, to allow more freedom of movement. Peasants, however, and other groups of medieval society who had to work physically, continued to wear the old styles which barely covered the knee.

Another change in men's clothing deserves mention: the traditional long trousers which reached from the hips right down to the feet were in time replaced by two pieces of clothing. Close-fitting linen breeches covering hips and thighs, which were called *Bruch* in Germany, served as suspenders for the long stockings which were worn below them. This type of trousers predominated between the thirteenth and the sixteenth centuries. The bottom of these stockings was frequently supported by a leather sole, forming a kind of shoe. However, as a rule, the peasants wore either laced-up or wooden shoes, or simply crude pieces of leather wrapped around their feet. It was in particular the laced-up type of shoe, the *Bundschuh*, which was used in many regions until it even came to represent the peasant protest groups before the Great Peasants' War of 1525;[10] the reason for this was that it was the commonest type of shoe among the rural population of the time. These laced-up shoes were made of leather and held together by long thongs running through leather loops attached to the upper side of the shoe.

As opposed to court costumes which became increasingly colourful from the thirteenth century, the clothing of the peasants remained far less conspicuous as most clothing was either grey or another dark colour. Members of the upper strata of peasant society, who became wealthier under the favourable agrarian developments of the high Middle Ages, began in many regions to distinguish themselves from the bulk of the peasant population by wearing more colourful garments and emulating the fashions of court society.[11] This led to increasing concerns among the nobility about preserving the social hierarchy; they tried to maintain the marks of social difference between wealthier peasants and lesser knights by issuing a number of clothing regulations in the twelfth and thirteenth centuries. Their purpose was to reinforce the hierarchy among the orders by preserving outward distinctions in appearance. This trend was in many instances accompanied by a corresponding desire to prevent the use of luxuries and extravagant clothing which did not befit one's station. Indeed some of the regulations in the King's peace which affected peasants' clothing and the kind of arms they were allowed to carry must be seen as a result of the gradual social segregation of the nobility and the differentiation between them and the peasants.

Clothing regulations for peasants

One of the earliest documents reflecting the growing pressure on the peasantry to respect the arms and clothes regulations is the so-called imperial chronicle of the priest Konrad of the mid-twelfth century in which decrees allegedly issued by Charlemagne are quoted. According to this chronicle peasants should wear only black or grey clothes, using no more than seven ells of material for both shirt and trousers, and they should wear only leather shoes. Going to church on Sundays a peasant was free to take his rod (*gart* in Middle High German) with him, but not his sword:[12]

> Now I will tell you about the peasant,
> what he should wear when going to church:
> it is either black or grey, nothing else befits him.
> A rod he may carry by his side, as it fits his life;
> leather shoes,
> they will have to do;
> seven ells for shirt and for breeches
> of linen cloth.

As a source, the Bavarian Peace of 1244 is of particular interest because it links the arms prohibition for peasants with elaborate clothing regulations.[13] Peasants were not permitted to use expensive and colourful fabrics for making clothes, but only inexpensive and grey ones. Moreover, with the exception of those who had been committed to special tasks for their lords, all peasants were obliged to wear plain leather shoes. Improper clothes were to be confiscated and only returned to their owners on payment of a fine. Peasant women were also bound by these rules. They were not, for example, entitled to wear silk trimmings or expensive and colourful scarves. Another passage of the Peace even

Figure 11 Neidhart of Reuental, minnesinger and the creator of what is known as
courtly village poetry, surrounded by peasants.
Miniature from the Manesse collection of ballads (beginning of the fourteenth century)

restricted certain peasant hairstyles. Long hair, fashionable among the noblemen of the time, was prohibited for peasants. Their hair had to be short, that is no longer than ear level. As mentioned earlier, this regulation must be considered within the context of the hairstyles then fashionable in court society, the members of which, male and female alike, clearly cherished long hair. From the early Middle Ages onward, short hair was, in fact, the social mark of peasants and other dependent groups of the population, for whom it may also have been advantageous in the performance of heavy field labour.

The clothing regulations of the Peace of 1244 find their literary equivalent in a number of interesting comments by contemporary poets who, in dealing with the frequent tensions between peasants and nobility, also touch upon the clothing issue. In particular the poems of Neidhart von Reuental, a knight who wrote in the first decades of the thirteenth century, contain a number of attacks on peasant immodesty in clothing.[14] The wealthy peasants, whose boasting demeanour stood at the centre of Neidhart's critique of his time, were the first to spurn the traditional peasant costumes of plain grey clothes and unsophisticated hats and shoes. They had the means to buy colourful rather than grey clothes and soon embroidered them abundantly. Neidhart describes the fashionable overcoats of the wealthy peasants in much detail. They seem to have been studded with two rows of bright buttons below the neck and were held together by expensive belts. Peasant women were dressed very much like their men except for holidays and celebrations when they wore their hair loose and adorned themselves with valuable hair clasps. Wreaths of roses were popular for summer festivities, while other seasons saw wealthy countrywomen wear silken veils or tiny hoods with colourful ribbons. Their expensive linen dresses sometimes had long trains, or they fitted closely around the waist. They clearly sought to emulate court fashions with narrow belts decorated with pearls and small copper plates.

Although it must be assumed that some of Neidhart's descriptions are somewhat exaggerated, they still contain a number of relevant observations. What underlies his account of peasant clothing, customs and habits in upper Bavaria and Austria is an attempt to caricature and mock the pretentiousness of the newly rich peasants as they aped the outward appearance of the nobility – as if only to prove their foolish and boorish nature. Hence many of Neidhart's poems can be regarded as a reflection of the resentment engendered among the impoverished nobility by the emulation of courtly fashions and life-styles by newly rich peasants.

Another poet, Wernher der Gartenaere, also gives a picture of the luxurious outfits of wealthy peasants, and especially their sons, in his description of the clothes of one of his literary characters, the bailiff (*Meier*) Helmbrecht in a poem written around the middle of the thirteenth century.[15] On leaving his parents and his home he is depicted in what appears to be a truly proud array very much in the courtly style. His expensive clothes consist of a high-class woollen coat, a colourful shirt made of fine fabric and a costly hood embroidered with minute pictures. However, since in this account historical accuracy is only too often outweighed by poetic license, its description of peasant clothing should be accepted with considerable reservations. Seifried Helbing's poetry of the late thirteenth century proves, by contrast, to be much more reliable.[16] Like Neidhart, Seifried denounced the preposterous manner in which the wealthier peasants imitated the courtly clothing fashions and decried the narrowing of the social gap between peasants and nobles in Austria. He described the former more traditional peasant costume as follows:[17]

> At that time it was considered proper for the country
> to allow the wearing of grey, home-made breeches
> and blue ones for holidays
> of good, milled loden cloth.
> No better colour was permitted
> neither husband nor wife.

Seifried, however, further states that the costumes of his own time were radically different and that the nobility and the peasantry would often wear the same kinds of clothes because peasants had a propensity to imitate the courtly fashions in order to raise themselves beyond their estate.

Yet none of these admittedly detailed accounts about the clothing of the wealthier peasants should blind the reader to the fact that the majority of the peasant population was unobtrusively and plainly, if not poorly, dressed. At any rate, the low income of many small and medium-sized farms certainly did not permit their holders to spend much on sophisticated clothing or adornment. This was also because most peasant clothing was produced by the peasants themselves, with flax and wool being the predominant raw materials. The clothes produced domestically in this manner were without exception of coarse quality, and they were generally worn for a long time, hence becoming very shabby.

Extravagance in peasant clothing?

On the whole, the clothing regulations of the high and late Middle Ages, which were issued in France and Italy as well, cannot be taken as actual evidence for peasant prosperity and widespread luxury in peasant clothing.[18] Recent studies on such regulations, which were for the most part promulgated in towns, have rightly emphasized that these rules against immodest spending on clothing and adornment were clearly not the result of an attempt to combat wasteful expenditures. Hence what was intended with the issuing of such regulations was not the suppression of luxury in clothing, but the preservation of the social hierarchy; for clothing, especially in the 'society of orders' of the Middle Ages, had an important function as a status symbol for the privileged orders. This is why such regulations cannot be taken as a reliable source for the reconstruction of actual consumption or spending patterns in that period. Their significance lies in illustrating the privilege and prestige in clothing held by the nobility.

It follows that research on peasant clothing has to pay careful attention to the consumption patterns among the various levels of the peasantry. Many of them simply did not have the means for extravagance. Consequently if the term luxury applies at all to the clothing of the medieval peasantry, it existed exclusively among the upper strata of the peasantry. This also holds true for clothing regulations like the one included in the imperial decree of Lindau of 1497 which forbade 'the common peasant and the working populace both in towns and in the country to make clothes from fabrics which were worth more than half a guilder per ell, adorn them with gold, pearl, velvet, silk or patchwork, or allow their wives or children to wear such clothes'.[19]

The late Middle Ages saw a continuation of the tendency in clothes-making of the high Middle Ages to emphasize the natural proportions of the human physique.[20] As a result, the differences between men's and women's costumes were more than ever accentuated. Women's clothes fitted closely at the waist, falling in abundant pleats from the hips. Collars were now considerably wider, as a consequence of which the authorities saw good reason to issue regulations against excessively wide collars. Men's tunics became increasingly short until finally the breeches beneath them came into view. Furthermore, tunics were gradually replaced by jerkins which could be fitted snugly to the body by means of buttons and strings. These new clothes were first introduced by the nobility and the townspeople, but they were also soon to be adopted by the peasantry, who in the course of time developed a variety of regional styles. The exposure of the human body and the alleged immodesty accompanying it, as for example wide slits in women's tunics or skirts, or opulent cloaks and obtrusive breeches in the case of men's garments, aroused open disapproval among the clergymen and itinerant preachers of the time. The clergy was especially filled with indignation at men's fashion which barely covered the pubic region or which implied a spendthrift use of expensive fabrics. Geiler von Kaisersberg, for example, who was an Alsatian penitential preacher in the late fifteenth century, furiously attacked the luxury in clothing and other extravagances in his native Alsatian villages. He was particularly eager to condemn the indecencies of contemporary men's fashion, such as short vests, which were also worn by large numbers of peasants.[21]

The late medieval preachers who saw immodesty in peasant clothing also accused peasants of lacking restraint in eating and drinking.

Numerous chronicles, petitions and Shrovetide plays make complaints about peasant feasting and luxury, about boisterous banquets and excessive carousing in villages, as well as frequent drinking binges. In his work *The Ship of Fools* (1490) based on contemporary life in the upper Rhine Valley, Sebastian Brant castigated the immodesty and extravagant life-style of the indigenous peasants. He complained in particular that, as opposed to the past when peasants still lived a simple life, and justice had

Figure 12 Three peasants talking together.
Copperplate engraving by Albrecht Dürer (1471–1528)

made its home in their straw huts after it had been expelled from the towns, they were now the worst debtors because they refused to repay their loans on time – despite the fact that wine and grain had become rather expensive:

> Modesty has left the face of the earth;
> And peasants' pockets burst with money,
> For they hoard wine and wheat.[22]

Some years earlier Jakob Wimpfeling had similarly accused the peasants of his native Alsace:

> Wealth has corrupted the peasants of this and other lands in Germany. I have met peasant families who spend as much on the weddings of their sons and daughters, or christenings for that matter, as others on their homes, even with a plot and a vineyard. And it is the same wealth which makes them extremely spendthrift with food, clothing and expensive wines.[23]

However, we must ask whether these complaints represent the historical reality of the majority of the rural population in Europe. Are these indeed reliable sources for the actual living conditions of the peasantry in the late Middle Ages? Is it true that peasants had really become cocky as a result of the upturn in agriculture in the high Middle Ages, the indulgence and sumptuousness of their life-style making them ever more greedy?[24] What must be kept in mind, no matter how interesting the accounts of Shrovetide plays, sermons and decrees might be in reflecting the attitudes and motivations of their respective authors, is that they provide us with what is in fact only a very partial view of historical conditions. This is because Shrovetide plays, for example, present the reader with a highly stereotyped perception of the peasant, a character who amused the urban audience of the time with his rudeness, foolishness and his delight in brawling and feasting. However, the moralizing recommendations to live a life of asceticism and repentance, and the attack on human weaknesses and vices, which characterize the sermons, hardly appealed to either the common people or the nobility. Moreover, the luxury regulations decreed by the authorities were overtly designed to preserve the corporate order by maintaining in particular the obvious differences in rank between the clergy, the nobility, the burghers and the peasantry. The stereotypical view of sumptuous and indulgent feasts in peasant communities, and the idea that village celebrations are excessive, are impressed on the minds of many city-dwellers even today, so that such accounts from a distant past are only all too often accepted without due discrimination. Before considering the actual conditions of peasant nutrition in the late Middle Ages, brief mention must be made of the basic problems related to peasant diet and the changes which affected it from the early to the late Middle Ages.

Peasant diet

In contrast to clothes which were worn every day over a long period of time, food was one of the most short-lived products of the material culture of the Middle Ages and reacted extremely sensitively to fluctuations in the economy.[25] In addition to the dependence of peasant diet on the state of agriculture in a particular region at a given time, such as grain as opposed to cattle production, rising or falling grain prices and so forth, short-term crises such as bad harvests or epidemics among cattle also had an immediately disastrous effect on the quality of peasant diet. Times of hardship were therefore often accompanied by radical changes in the daily diet of the country populace. Nevertheless, what was hardly subject to change with the highs and lows of the economy was food consumption as a whole; this, unlike spending on clothing, adornment and housing, did not rise in proportion to larger incomes and social advancement. Generally speaking, peasant diet could vary in a number of ways despite the fact that it was strongly bound by tradition. This applies above all to the sequence of courses, especially on such occasions as weddings and funerals. Food preparation (cooking, roasting and baking), taste, and the daily and weekly menus were also aspects of peasant diet which could vary widely.

Two main forms, meat and vegetable foodstuffs, must be considered separately in dealing with peasant diet in the Middle Ages – the reason being not only that they formed the basis of any diet but also that the Middle Ages witnessed an astounding increase in the consumption of vegetable foodstuffs at the expense of meat. In marked contrast to the early Middle Ages when a comparatively small population could afford to use vast stretches of farmland as pasture, the population growth in the high Middle Ages led to a quantitatively much greater demand for foodstuffs in the first place – which meant in essence that productivity had to be intensified wherever possible. One of the most effective ways to arrive at greater yield ratios per acre was to turn pasture into cornfields, as a result of which grains and vegetables played a much greater role in peasant diet in the high Middle Ages than they had before.[26]

Among the country populace a gruel made from oats and millet was in fact the main food for centuries.[27] It was called *Mus* (mash) or *Brot* (bread) in some regions of the German Empire, and it appears to have been a highly valued dish, at least according to a number of fairy-tales which go back to that time. One of them, for instance, which is set in the 'land of milk and honey', imagines a situation in which people must eat their way through mountains of gruel; another is about sweet gruel pouring endlessly out of a cooking-pot. As opposed to bread, which was initially eaten almost exclusively by the clergy and the nobility and which only later became the daily food of the common people, gruel was at that time the main dish among the peasantry. It was made from ground grains, water or milk, and salt, which were boiled for a few minutes. Round flat dough-cakes of this mash were sometimes fried in a pan to make a primitive sort of round flat loaf. Actual bread, however, could only be produced with the help of a raising agent such as yeast or sour dough, which was added to the mash to make it much lighter and to turn the flat dough-cake into a risen round loaf of bread. Compared with gruel, bread was a major step forward in food-processing. In particular wheat bread came to be a highly esteemed gentlemen's dish which was prepared in a great variety of ways.

The cereals best suited for baking bread are wheat and rye; hence only wheat, rye and spelt are considered the primary bread-cereals. Most of the bread in France and England was made from wheat, whereas the south-west of Germany preferred spelt. The rest of central Europe used mainly rye. To serve good bread was regarded as a matter of good taste, and it was taken as a sign of stinginess if the head of a house provided his servants with coarse, bran-loaded bread.[28] Bread from oat-flour stood lowest in public opinion and it was commonly served to farm-labourers and poor peasants. Basically the same held true for bread from barley, which was also typical for peasant bread. In many parts of Germany, especially where spelt and rye were the prevailing cereals, bread was baked predominantly from these cereals although they were spurned by the nobility, who thought highly of their delicate wheaten bread.

Essential for successful bread production was the availability of optimum flour types and sufficient sifting methods to sort out the bran during the grinding process. Moreover, improved facilities were also necessary to increase output in bread production. Since the high Middle Ages it was common practice to build large communal ovens in manors and monasteries as well as in villages. They helped considerably to save time and fuel for heating. Professional baking in the towns led to the creation of the baking trade, which was soon in a position to offer its customers a surprising variety of bread types in addition to cakes and pastries. It should be noted that the development of the mill system was the cardinal precondition for the production of satisfactory flour qualities. Since flour, as opposed to grain, could not be stored for indefinite periods, peasants, insofar as they did not mill by hand, came to depend more and more on professional millers, and henceforth the trade played a key role in supplying the population with quality flour and bread. The lords, on the other hand, used their mills and their monopolies on them to further enlarge their incomes by compelling their tenants to grind exclusively in their mills.[29]

The following passage, often quoted in connection with peasant eating habits, was to apply for centuries: 'Peasant food is either poor-quality bread, gruel or boiled vegetables, and whey is what they usually drink' (*panis cibarius puls avenacea aut decoctum legumen cibus. aqua serumve potus*).[30] This statement by Johannes Boemus around the year 1520 was expressly designed to accentuate the contrast between the food of the peasantry and that of the other classes. Peasants usually did not eat the fine bread of the nobility and the burghers in the towns; they had to be content with gruel or vegetable stews which stood in marked contrast to the soups, meat dishes and additional side-dishes which were served in the homes of the wealthy. If Boemus is to be believed, water and whey were the main drinks in peasant households. Yet this does not exclude the possibility that there might have been others as well. There can be no doubt that peasants also drank beer, cider and wine, although mostly during holidays and local festivities. It is obvious that they also had some of the more refined dishes on holidays, and meat must have been served on some workdays too, which is even today held to be an indication of prosperity.

In fact, meat dishes were quite established in the peasant household during the Middle Ages, in spite of the fact that the proportion of meat consumption in the household as a whole varied according to the income of the particular family, its geographical location and the historical period in question. Peasants seem to have been particularly fond of fatty pork, which they even preferred to beef; this is also reflected in the price for pork in the Middle Ages: there is evidence that pork was one-third more expensive than lean beef in the late Middle Ages.[31] Horse-meat was eaten only in times of famine, while that of most of the smaller farmyard animals was eaten on a regular basis, including poultry. In order to increase both the flavour and the fattiness of meat new techniques of fattening were developed, although farmyard feeding continued to be the exception to the rule of pastoral agriculture. For many centuries, pig masting did not necessarily mean farmyard feeding, because the abundance of acorns in the nearby forests allowed peasants to keep them outdoors until late autumn. Farmyard feeding nevertheless grew constantly in importance for peasant agriculture in the Middle Ages, especially as with the land shortage of the high Middle Ages more and more woodland was developed for farming. This trend reduced the quantity of acorns available for pig masting, which soon derived more from leftovers from mills and bakeries.

The slaughtering of farmyard animals was part of domestic work which in the case of larger animals was done either by the peasant himself or by a farm-labourer. Virtually everything, even intestines, was used from the slaughtered animals.[32] Roasted joints were considered typical noblemen's dishes, as opposed to boiled meat which almost everyone could afford, while the intestines and sundry pieces of the animal such as feet, mouth, lungs, liver, kidneys or brain were the favourite dishes among the lower classes. They were especially fond of tripe, so specialized trades (*Kutter, Flecksieder*) for its processing and sale soon emerged. Of all the domestic animals pigs were the most productive, because in addition to their meat

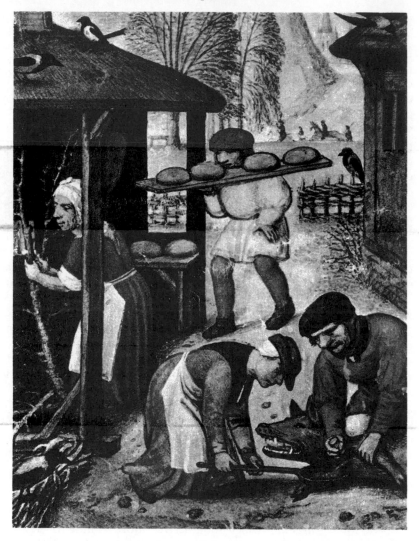

Figure 13 Bread-baking and pig-slaughtering, from a sixteenth-century
Flemish calendar

and offal their rind can be eaten as well as their blood, which is edible,
unlike that of other livestock. Similarly, pork provided most of the
sausage-meat. Generally speaking sausage was made from finely chopped,
spiced meat stuffed into edible entrails.

Apart from domestic animals, wild animals were also used to supply
the population with meat. Evidence from animal remains found in a
number of excavations of early medieval settlements reveals that wild

animals in fact contributed considerably to peasant diet.[33] From Carolingian times, however, the peasantry gradually lost their hunting rights with the development of the feudal system. Hunting rights were soon held exclusively by the nobility, who applied draconian measures to protect their privileges. This of course gradually reduced the proportion of game in the peasant diet. The same development applied to fishing rights,[34] and it had a lasting effect on the composition of the peasant diet because brooks, rivers and lakes were hardly polluted in the Middle Ages and thus contained both plentiful fish and crayfish.

Instead of bread and vegetable mash, families of herdsmen and peasants specializing in cattle-breeding tended to have milk and other dairy products as their principal foods.[35] Stock put out to pasture was milked either by the herdsmen themselves or under their supervision. They also made cheese and in other ways processed raw milk, but where stock was mainly kept indoors, or in wintertime, these tasks were taken over by the peasant's wife and her servants. On exceptionally large dairy-farms, however, as on the *Sennereien* or *Schwaighöfe* in the German-speaking Alps, for example, there was a great demand for male farmhands owing to the particular difficulties involved in this kind of farming and because of the much greater size of these farms. Before it became part of everyone's food in the high Middle Ages, butter was almost exclusively consumed by the nobility. Monastic life contributed substantially to the increase in butter production, because the monastic orders were inclined to give up meat in the attempt to lead an ascetic life and thus developed new vegetarian and dairy dishes. In the Middle Ages, butter consumption was highest in the northern regions of Europe, while the inhabitants of the Mediterranean countries preferred vegetable oil to butter. The large dairies and farms which specialized in stock production used most of their milk to make a variety of cheeses, which also served as rents and dues. All in all, cheese was an important part of the peasant diet, and it would be offered to guests and visitors along with bread if for some reason there was no hot meal.

In addition to bread, meat and dairy products, vegetables and fruit need mentioning as essential foodstuffs of the peasant household in the Middle Ages.[36] Fruit and vegetables, especially legumes, were grown in the garden by the farmhouse, and they were either cooked fresh, or dried and stored for winter supplies. The favourite vegetable crops were turnips and various cabbages; turnips were held in high esteem, particularly by the lower classes, and so acquired many peasant nicknames. Neidhart von Reuental, for example, teases his peasant sweetheart with her special liking for turnips. However, not merely turnips, cabbages and other vegetables found their way into the everyday cooking of the peasantry, but also wild plants such as dock and sorrel, lamb's lettuce and sundry herbs which were often collected and served as alternatives to the standard dishes. Apples, pears, plums, cherries and strawberries were the commonest fruits, and dried pears and apples supplemented the peasant menu in winter.

Among beverages, it was particularly mead and its beer derivatives,[37] in addition to water and milk, which were popular north of the Alps – with mead enjoying the longest tradition. It was made from a mixture of water and honey, was then boiled and left to ferment; but since it was highly perishable it had to be consumed quickly, as opposed to wine, which became the favourite alcoholic drink of the nobility during the course of the twelfth century. This change was also partly brought on by the influence of the courtly life-style, until eventually it was only among peasants and simple people that mead maintained its popularity. Yet even this changed with the development of a new and more difficult technique for brewing, in which hops were added to grains, such as oats and barley, thus creating beer. From then on the much tastier beer, which also kept much better, was on its way to replacing mead completely. The monasteries in particular were considerably involved in the improvement of brewing methods. Before long village breweries were built under the direction of the lords of the local manors; nevertheless, it was not until towns also began to use their know-how for brewing that the brewing trade came to full flower. Depending on their recipes and source materials, the various regions of Europe developed a wide range of beers, and in the north, where grapes were not grown, beer soon became the main alcoholic drink of the population.

From the late Middle Ages, the production as well as the consumption of wine were extremely popular in central Europe.[38] Even the north of Germany made its own wine, which was grown as far north as Münster and Brunswick on the western side, Lübeck and Stettin in the far north, and East Prussia in the north-east. Originally introduced into Germany by the Romans, vines were widely cultivated along the rivers Rhine and Moselle. The south and the west of Germany belonged to the regions with the best vines and therefore had a widespread popularity and tradition of wine consumption. Vineyards were not only planted along river-banks and close to the villages as in earlier centuries, but also at higher altitudes, and this without a loss of quality. Rhine, Moselle and Alsatian wines were exported to many foreign lands although they were equally popular in the areas where they were grown. In years of high productivity wine prices fell nearly to the level of beer prices, as a consequence of which wine consumption grew substantially among the peasants too. Yet regions with a preference for either wine or beer are often hard to distinguish – despite the fact that some areas in Germany, or France, rightly claim to be centres for either one of them. As far as wine is concerned, the main area of production in Germany has indeed always been the south-west, which has an extremely favourable climate for wine-growing, whereas most of the beer in that country originates from the centre and the north. Because of high transport costs in the Middle Ages which bore heavily on final prices, the areas of production were also those with the highest consumption of either beer or wine.

With the exception of the typical wine-growing areas just mentioned, the quality of most of the other wines was often poor, and it was only in warm and sunny years that other areas managed to produce comparable qualities. In order to make the dry wines from the north more drinkable, they were often spiced and sweetened with honey. Such practices, however, were also known in lands with more favourable climates. Here wine producers also spiced and sweetened according to demand, diluted their products with water, or drank them warm in cold weather which was how *Glühwein* (hot mulled wine) became popular. In the early Middle Ages, wine was almost exclusively consumed by the nobility and the clergy, and it was not before the late Middle Ages that it became a popular drink for the rest of society. In villages where wine was the main product it was also an everyday beverage for peasant families. Basically the same applies to such Mediterranean lands as Spain, southern France or Italy, where wine was not only produced but consumed in great quantities by inhabitants of both town and country.

The growing importance of cereal foodstuffs

A look at the development of diet from the early to the late Middle Ages helps to highlight a number of important changes in the food consumption of the peasantry. The predominant mode of agriculture being cattle-breeding, the early Middle Ages form a marked contrast to the high Middle Ages,[39] and in fact there is evidence from the folk laws of the seventh and eighth centuries that the keeping of stock was far more important than arable cultivation: theft of pigs, cattle, goats, sheep or bees was severely punished according to a highly detailed catalogue of fines. The classification concerning pigs is especially detailed, with fines depending on the age and the quality of the animals, as well as their purposes, such as fat piglets, young pigs and breeding sows.[40] It is clear enough that pig-breeding played an important role in the agriculture of the time, and there can be no doubt that their production guaranteed the meat supply of most communities. Recent studies of the development of land division and farming methods have given insight into the relation between farming and stock-breeding in the economy of the early Middle Ages. An analysis of the use of farmland in northern Germany during the early Middle Ages has shown that the average farms had 3 hectares. Estimates of the food consumption of each household prove, then, that only a third to two-thirds of each family's calorie supply was covered by its own grain production.[41] The considerable gap which remained in the daily diet had to be filled by means of hunting, fishing and gathering of wild plants and fruit – but most importantly stock production. Owing to easy masting with the acorns from the nearby forests the keeping of pigs was especially profitable.

The high Middle Ages, by comparison, mark a decisive change in the history of peasant diet because grain production came to predominate over stock-breeding. The steady rise in population throughout Europe brought about an ever increasing demand for grain, as well as the farmland necessary to produce it. Land clearance and the settlement of hitherto underdeveloped regions were, as demonstrated earlier, the principal ways to provide more land for food production. From the eleventh century onwards grain production became increasingly important, supplying the population with their daily bread and gruel.[42] Expanding grain production, which reached its peak in the twelfth and thirteenth centuries, eventually entailed the use of soils hardly good enough for grain production. Not only land at high altitudes and along rainy coasts came under the plough, but fallows and woodlands, which until then had been used as pasture. As a result the structure of the European landscape changed radically.

From now on, stock-breeding was unmistakbly secondary to vegetable and especially grain production, but served to supply the necessary fertilizer as well as draught-animals such as oxen for the ploughing of the land. Vegetable foodstuffs predominated in the peasant diet of the high Middle Ages, while the importance of meat decreased by comparison. Apart from meat and grain dishes, the peasant diet in the high Middle Ages also consisted of fruit and vegetables and the produce of various other types of agriculture. Generally speaking, however, the situation in terms of food deteriorated markedly towards the late Middle Ages, mainly as a result of the enormous growth in population. The living conditions of the poorer peasants with their smallholdings and limited provisions were extremely modest and particularly vulnerable to crises of any kind. The rather low level of productive techniques, low grain yields and heavy dues to the feudal lords pushed the living standard of most peasants down to a relatively low level, the only exception being the upper strata among the peasantry.

What, then, was peasant nutrition really like in the late Middle Ages? Can such accounts as the ones quoted earlier really be trusted, which depict peasant life in plenteous and extravagant colours? In order to answer such questions as objectively as possible it is necessary to distinguish diet among the various levels of peasant society. Despite such improvements as the extension of the arable and better wages, the living standard of the majority of peasants with their small and medium-sized holdings continued to be quite poor. It was only very rarely that round, flat dough-cakes or gruel had to compete with quality meat or bread on their dinner tables. In summer, carrots, turnips and wild plants such as sorrel and stinging nettles supplemented their daily menu, and in autumn women and children went into the neighbouring woodlands to collect berries, nuts and fruit, some of which were stored as winter provisions. It is obvious, then, that the food and drink of the average peasant family was meagre most of the time, and occasionally even dangerously scarce. The families sat in a given order around a large dinner-table, using either their fingers or wooden spoons to eat out of one big common bowl. With the exception of iron knives, most of the kitchenware, such as forks, spoons, bowls, plates and coopered jugs were made of wood, hence so perishable that few of them have survived until today. From the thirteenth century, however, pottery bowls and jugs, in addition to massive jars made from crude green glass, gradually became part of the kitchenware of the peasantry too.[43]

The meal regulations for peasants who were obliged to perform labour services, as well as for day-labourers and other servants, contain some interesting information on the nutrition level of the rural population of the late Middle Ages. In 1497 Berthold von Henneberg, the Archbishop

Figure 14 Peasant open-air banquet.
Copperplate engraving by Daniel Hopfer (*c*.1500)

of Mainz, decreed that 'every labourer, no matter whether he works in the fields or elsewhere, shall receive soup with bread in the morning, stew with meat and vegetables, and half a pint of table-wine for lunch, and a meat-dish with bread or stew with bread for supper.[44] A similarly rich menu was provided for his labourers by Erasmus von Erbach in the Odenwald mountain range in 1483:

> Every hired labourer, dependent peasant, as well as servants and maids shall have two meat dishes and half a jug of wine per day with the exception of the days of fasting when they shall have fish or other nourishing dishes. Also those who have laboured during the week shall be served generous portions of bread and meat, in addition to half a jar of wine on Sundays and other holidays.[45]

According to such meal regulations and a number of available estimates there was plenty of meat in the meals of the late Middle Ages. In many parts of central Europe, the amount of meat consumed each year per person was approximately 100 kilogrammes, or 220 pounds. This figure seems exceptionally high, especially when compared with current estimates of prosperous West Germany where annual meat consumption per person in the 1980s is about 90 kilogrammes, or 200 pounds.[46] However, it must be borne in mind that virtually everything, from the head to the intestines of the slaughtered animals, and not merely tender meat, found its way into the stomachs of the medieval peasantry. Apart from that there were some regional differences in the composition of peasant diet which should be noted. In the south of France, for example, the rural population consumed far less meat, and more bread, than in central Europe. Research conducted by L. Stouff on the diet of the order of the Hospitallers in southern France was particularly helpful in reconstructing the composition of the daily peasant menu.[47] According to the meal regulations, the daily rations were fixed depending on the estate and social position of its members, and as a rule those who were furthest down the social ladder had the greatest share of bread in their food, and the least meat, fish, eggs, cheese, oil, spices and so forth (the *companagium*). The proportion of bread rose from 25 per cent in the case of the preceptor to 45 or 50 per cent for friars, and to 55 or even 70 per cent in the food of common labourers, who in turn only received a mere 15 to 20 per cent of the *companagium*, as opposed to 30 or 40 per cent for friars, and a truly meaty 55 or even 60 per cent share in the case of the preceptor. In Provence, as in many parts of Germany, diet had improved in terms of both quantity and quality in the course of the late Middle Ages.

Bad harvests and famines

Accounts of extravagant peasant feasts usually refer to the wealthiest peasants who were apparently willing to spend considerable sums on food and drink. Fine examples for regions with a fair number of exceptionally well-off peasants are the marshes along the North Sea coasts where stock-keeping was the very basis of the local agriculture, as well as in some of the fertile grain and wine-growing areas in southern Germany. The upper peasant stratum in such regions was evidently in a position to afford a life-style which stood in marked contrast to that of the poor cottagers.[48] Yet the majority of peasant families had such a small income that they had difficulty in storing sufficient supplies for lean years. Hence throughout the Middle Ages bad harvests or widespread cattle epidemics almost automatically entailed devastating famines among peasant communities.

Many regions in Europe suffered, for instance, from the terrible famine of 1437–8, which in terms of its duration, intensity and effect surpassed most of the preceding catastrophes of its kind.[49] Lands affected by this exceptionally severe famine included England, Flanders, France, most of Germany, and considerable parts of Switzerland. It was the result of a series of bad harvests in the wake of exceedingly cold winters and rainy summers. The war of the Hussites as well as crop damage from mice and hamsters did their share to aggravate the situation in central Europe, which culminated in deaths en masse, particularly in the year 1438. The chronicle of Thuringia recorded:

> The year 1438 saw a huge rise in prices in Thuringia and elsewhere which led to a great famine, killing many people in their villages, hamlets or in the streets, and there was no one to bury them for a long time . . . moreover, because people lay dead for so long the air became polluted with a swiftly killing pestilence which caused the cruel death of even more than had died of hunger before. Many villages, but also some smaller towns, became extinct in these years, with virtually no one to inhabit them.[50]

This statement demonstrates that villagers suffered no less from hunger than townspeople, an observation which is confirmed by the chronicle of Klingenberg in the north-west of Switzerland: 'Even in the country it was harsh, and there were a considerable number of people who had not had bread for six months, so that they were forced to feed on boiled cabbage, turnips, and other such things.[51]

It appears that this series of famines, epidemics and deaths affected in particular those areas of central and southern Germany where there was a comparatively large proportion of cottagers. The scarce provisions which their small fields and gardens or their keeping of livestock supplied were soon consumed in times of hardship. Such disasters usually started with famines producing malnutrition which in turn gave rise to disease and epidemics. Research on nutrition in Third World countries has shown that it is often malnutrition which causes the often frightening inertia and lack of drive among the local farmers.[52] The same vicious circle of bad harvests, famines, epidemics and malnutrition which is known to torment such developing countries as India or Mauritania was also at work in many rural areas of medieval Europe.

AGRICULTURAL IMPLEMENTS, LAND UTILIZATION AND AGRARIAN DEVELOPMENT

An Agrarian Revolution in the high Middle Ages?

The mechanization of agriculture, which has made rapid progress particularly in post-war Europe, illustrates how new methods of farming, by greatly increasing production levels, have transformed traditional agricultural and rural society. By contrast with 1850, when 55 per cent of the German population still earned their living from agriculture, only 6 per cent did so in 1985. Owing to the enormous increase in productivity and the replacement of human labour by modern machinery, the supply of basic foodstuffs is no longer a critical problem. However, technological innovations affected agriculture in the high Middle Ages and later centuries as well as the nineteenth and twentieth centuries. Adequate nourishment of the ever rising population in Europe during the Middle Ages, especially in the newly founded towns, was only possible because of the agricultural advances of the high Middle Ages. In view of the astonishing achievements in agriculture at that time some historians, such as G. Duby and L. White, have even talked about the 'agrarian revolution of the Middle Ages'.[1] In addition to evaluating this assertion, the present chapter looks at the principal technical innovations at work in medieval agriculture, as well as at improvements in agricultural implements,[2] working techniques and farming methods, all of which shaped the everyday life of the peasantry. Special heed will have to be given to changes in methods of cultivation and to the development of the necessary tools, not least because the growing population could only be fed on the basis of a considerable increase in grain production.[3]

The plough was certainly the most important agricultural implement in the Middle Ages and its improvement played a crucial role in achieving agricultural progress. However, the development and regional distribution of the various types of plough is hard to assess, especially during the early Middle Ages, owing to the piecemeal nature of such evidence as archaeological finds and pictorial depictions. Recent studies, none the less, have confirmed that the wheeled plough with its coulter and soil-turning ploughshare facilitated the development of farmland, especially the tilling of heavy soils in marshes during the agricultural boom of the high Middle Ages. The peasants of the early Middle Ages, by contrast, were only acquainted with hook-ploughs, which merely scratched the soil – a rather inadequate way to prepare it for the sowing.

The introduction of new ploughs

In order to reach a better understanding of the development of medieval agriculture, a distinction must be made between the two principal types of plough, namely the hook- and the wheeled plough.[4] The traditional hook-plough was a symmetrical device which, although it did break up the soil and let it crumble to either side of the ploughshare, failed to turn the soil over because it had only a very small or no mould-boards at all. The hook-plough permitted adjacent furrows to be ploughed, with its plough-bar serving as a shaft which had a double yoke for the draught-animals attached to its tip. Wheeled ploughs, an important innovation in ploughing technique, were asymmetric implements with a mould-board on one side to turn the soil over and create deep ridged furrows. Apart from this and the ploughshare, the coulter and a primitive wheel were the usual characteristics of the wheeled plough (see figure 15). Since the mould-board turned the furrow ridges to only one side of the plough, furrows next to each other could not be ploughed one after another. Instead the wheeled plough, after reaching the opposite side of the field, had to be turned either right or left without actually being in operation and return to the other side of the field, where it had commenced its course, to resume ploughing. Since turning the plough created difficulties, wheeled ploughs were particularly suited to plough long, rectangular strips of land where less effort had to be expended turning the plough, or reaching the section of the field where the ploughing started from the other side. Fields rising evenly from their sides towards their centre (*Hochäcker, Wölbäcker*) are still discernible in the vicinity of the deserted settlements of the late Middle Ages, especially around forest villages. Their characteristic form is the result of precisely this method of ploughing whereby in the course of centuries considerable quantities of soil were gradually transported from the sides of the fields towards their centres.[5] In contrast to the long, rectangular strips of arable land produced by wheeled ploughs, areas cultivated predominantly with the hook-plough are marked by rather square-shaped fields owing to the crosswise ploughing course. What also needs mentioning is the fact that wheeled ploughs were far easier to operate, and that because their shares reached much deeper into the ground they were much more suited to heavier soils.

Although wheeled ploughs, which 'introduced a new era in the history of agriculture because of their method of soil-turning',[6] were known in some Roman provinces and along the North Sea coast as early as late antiquity,[7] they were not used on any large scale until after the tenth century. Instead most of the archaeological and iconographic evidence points towards the use of hook-ploughs employing various types of ploughshare. Neither sufficient depth nor breadth of the furrows could be attained with this primitive ploughing implement, primarily because of the small size of its ploughshare. Consequently ploughing with the wheelless ploughs of the early Middle Ages was hardly effective, despite the effort put into it by the peasants. Hence little can be said in favour of Lynn White's conclusion that there was a radical change in the ploughing technique of that period.[8]

It was not before the eleventh century that the wheeled plough came to replace the hook-plough in most parts of Europe.[9] The surprising progress in the arable cultivation of the high Middle Ages, and the tremendous increase in grain production, were achieved not least due to improvements in ploughs.[10] Especially in the regions north of the Alps and the Loire with their rich soils and rainy summers, ploughing with the heavy wheeled ploughs proved to be much more rewarding than with its antecedents. During the early Middle Ages, peasants in central Europe had mostly cultivated the better drained, and therefore lighter, soils on higher ground. These, although much easier to plough, yielded less. Wheeled ploughs, by comparison, reached so much deeper into the topsoil that subsequent cross-ploughing, a characteristic of the old method, was no longer necessary. This saved the peasants a great deal of precious time and labour, and increased the productivity of farming in general. The wheeled plough soon ranked among the most important agricultural implements, and was fully exploited by making use of animal power and technical sophistication rather than the physical power of the human body. Turning over the soil also helped to control weeds and to increase the formation of humus as well as improving ventilation.

Without the new plough, the cultivation of the rich soils in the plains north of the Alps and of the damp but highly fertile marshes alongside rivers and lakes would hardly have been as successful as it was in the high Middle Ages. This was because the proper working of such soils guaranteed the local peasants far greater yields than that of the higher sandy soils. Labour-saving, improved drainage and the use of the best soils were the principal advantages of wheeled ploughs for arable cultivation in central and northern Europe, which permitted the increase in yield ratios so crucial for the ever growing population. In southern Europe, on the other hand, the wheeled plough failed to gain general acceptance owing to the contrasting soil and climatic conditions in the Mediterranean,[11]

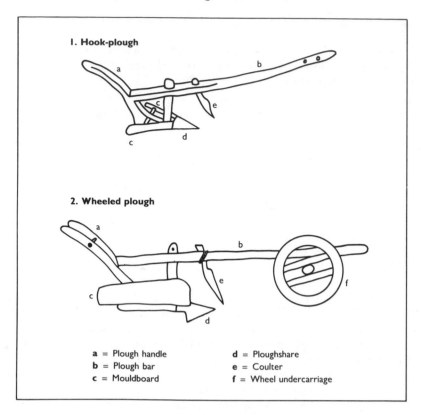

1. Hook-plough

2. Wheeled plough

a = Plough handle   d = Ploughshare
b = Plough bar   e = Coulter
c = Mouldboard   f = Wheel undercarriage

Figure 15 Hook-plough and wheeled plough

where the traditional hook-plough retained its importance. Since all that the wheelless plough did was to break up the topsoil rather than turn it over, over-extensive drying of the soil could be avoided. Hence the utilization of hook-ploughs in southern Europe both helped to reduce extensive evaporation of soil moisture and increased the fertility of the land by stimulating the capillary distribution of minerals from deep-level soil strata.

The long-held view that the German peasants of the newly settled eastern marches were agriculturally more advanced than the indigenous Slavs because of their iron-mounted, wheeled ploughs can no longer be maintained in the face of recent archaeological studies. They have in fact proved that wheeled ploughs were used by Slavic peoples even before the colonization movement of the high Middle Ages.[12] Yet hook-ploughs were used just as much in eastern Europe as in some peripheral regions in the Mediterranean. They retained their value in certain climates as well as on newly cleared woodlands, where ploughing was much easier with wheelless ploughs because the smaller ploughshare was far less impeded by the many roots and stones which had not yet been cleared out. Also, difficult mountainous soils such as in the Black Forest, the eastern parts of the Alps, and even in agriculturally well-developed regions like Mecklenburg, hook-ploughs remained in use beyond the Middle Ages.[13] In today's Third World Countries 75 per cent of the ploughing implements must also be considered wheelless, for most of their peasants still work with exceedingly primitive hook-ploughs, spades, digging-sticks, and other tools like those their ancestors had also used in struggling to produce the little that saved them from starvation.[14]

Horses and harnessings

One factor, namely improved tractive power, facilitated the development of wheeled ploughs during the high Middle Ages; basically the much greater weight of the new ploughs required greater strength to operate than the traditional wheelless ploughs, and hence required in addition new types of harnesses.[15] These problems were often tackled by using draught-oxen, but also by making better use of horses. This was because although naturally much more energetic than cattle, horses need especially sophisticated harnessing to perform at their best in ploughing and drawing. Despite the fact that oxen were the preferred draught-animals for ploughing in many European regions in the high and late Middle Ages, the twelfth and thirteenth centuries saw the emergence of the use of horses as draught-animals for wheeled ploughs, a trend which appears to have started in northern Europe. Progress in harnessing was made especially by the development of more efficient breast-pieces and horse-collars to replace the older inadequate harnessings. However, although they were recorded as early as Carolingian times, it was only in the high Middle Ages that the new-style harnesses came to be the prevailing types. The cardinal disadvantage of the older types had been that they constricted the animals far too much when they had arduous work to do. This is why in antiquity horses were only used to draw extremely light chariots, and almost never heavy carts.

It seems that the new harnesses, which appeared in central Europe from the early Middle Ages, were developed by Eurasian herdsmen and horsemen and came to Europe through the mediation of the Slavs. The new horse-collars were well cushioned and especially designed to fit better onto the horses' shoulders, thus enabling them to breathe normally and enjoy undisturbed blood circulation. The new harnesses were connected to the carts by means of either side-traces or side-poles, so that the horses could put all their weight into them, drawing even extremely heavy loads. According to recent tests, the nominal draught power of horses equals that of oxen, but the work performance of horses is about

50 per cent higher, mostly owning to the fact that they move much faster. Moreover, horses have much greater staying power, which enables them to work more hours per day. The much greater energy and labour of horses was particularly valuable in central and northern European climates, because in these areas satisfactory yield ratios depended largely on taking immediate advantage of favourable weather conditions during the cultivation and above all the harvesting of the crops.

Figure 16 Ox-harnessing for ploughing. The oxen are harnessed to a double yoke which is put around their necks; this wheeled plough has a convertible mouldboard and a device to adjust the coulter.
Herrad of Landsberg, *Hortus deliciarum* (twelfth century)

Notwithstanding the obvious merits of the new horse harnesses, the importance of horses for the agrarian economy of the high Middle Ages has all too often been overrated. Horse-lovers frequently have a biased view concerning the economic value of horses as draught-animals and the actual geographical distribution of the new harness types. Although considerably more horses were used for heavy agricultural labour in some regions, in general most draught-animals were still cattle.[16] In any case, it simply is not appropriate to claim, as in some more popular scholarly writings, that horses revolutionized the agrarian economy of the twelfth and thirteenth centuries as much as the tractor in the twentieth century. Horses indeed have a much better draught performance, and they are also much faster, yet oxen retained their value as animals for slaughter even after they became useless as draught-animals. Furthermore, oxen needed less food and also lower-quality food, and they were much easier to keep in good health than horses which are notoriously susceptible to illnesses.

The keeping of horses also required local access to grain production; hence there was a close connection between the two in many parts of Europe.

In southern Germany, by contrast, peasants continued to use cattle as draught-animals in ploughing even after the high Middle Ages. According to the manorial law of 1150, the bondsmen of the priory of Muri, now in the Swiss canton of Aargau, were compelled to use their ox-carts to drive all of the hay of the convent into the barns which belonged to it (*cum suis bobus*).[17] Dependants who received a holding from the monastic administration were also equipped with a plough (*aratrum*) as well as a cart with four oxen (*plaustrum cum quatuor bobus*).[18] Thus there is reason to believe that the average peasant holding in the twelfth century was likely to have four oxen in use to draw either the plough or carts as well as other heavy agricultural implements for fieldwork. In the twelfth and thirteenth centuries, the phrase *aratrum cum bobus* developed into a standard legal formula which referred to ploughing services by dependent peasants.[19] As a rule, two persons conducted the heavy labour of ploughing on the difficult arable terrains: the ploughman, who guided the plough, and the ploughboy, who led the team in front of the plough and drove the animals with a firm rod.

In many villages in the plains of northern Germany, however, horses had replaced cattle as the predominant draught-animals by the thirteenth century, and soon many other regions followed their example. Information on the kind of draught-animals used in the neighbouring areas is provided by the *Sachsenspiegel*, a Saxon legal code of the thirteenth century. It appears that both horses (the Middle High German term employed was *veltperde*) and oxen (*tochossen*) were used in southern Saxony.[20] It is evident, nevertheless, that in most regions particularly the poorer peasants continued to use oxen as draught-animals to keep expenses at a minimum. For the wealthier peasants, however, horse-raising was also extremely prestigious.

From the high Middle Ages, horses became increasingly important for transport and haulage with carts and wagons. Above all swiftness and low running costs for long-distance transport were the main advantages of horses as draught-animals after the introduction of such efficient equipment as the new breast-pieces for harnesses, the cushioned horse-collars and traces, as well as the new technique of horseshoeing. On the other hand, little is known about the development of the vehicles which were now drawn by the much better harnessed and shod horses.[21] Most of the wagons in Roman and early medieval times had only two wheels, and from the twelfth century these were increasingly supplemented by big four-wheel carts. One of the decisive characteristics of the peasant cart was the fact that it was a multi-purpose vehicle, serving to transport the harvest and manure as well as for general transport. Horse-carts facilitated peasant access to the markets in the nearby towns and to distant fields, a saving of time which was especially valuable during the hay and the grain harvest.

The use of horses for ploughing was preceded by their use in harrowing,[22] because the inadequate ploughing of the Middle Ages required further work to prepare the fields effectively for sowing. This, in return, was greatly improved by the use of the new harnesses. The soil had to be harrowed several times in order to break up the furrow ridges, even out the hollow spaces in the furrows and uproot weeds. The effect of harrowing was markedly greater when it was done faster, and this is why horses were much better than oxen at producing the various effects of thorough harrowing. Even in those areas where peasants continued to use cattle as draught-animals for ploughing, harrowing was done exclusively with the help of horses. In contrast to the plough, whose main components, the share and the coulter, were made of iron, the harrows of the high Middle Ages did not have any metal parts whatsoever. The wooden prongs of the contemporary framed harrows were inserted into beams which were in turn held by sheaths.

The improvement of agricultural implements

This detailed account of the development of ploughing implements and harnesses has served to illustrate the development of agricultural technology in the Middle Ages in its decisive aspects. The discussion of other agrarian implements will therefore be limited to the most important points. According to the depictions available, the sickle remained the only instrument for grain harvesting in the high Middle Ages – just as it had been in early medieval times.[23] Pictures and archaeological finds show that the blades of medieval sickles were usually saw-edged, so that the

Figure 17 Horse team harnessed to empty harvest cart without racks. Cart with swivel stool, long beam and stakes.
From the illuminated manuscript of the Saxon Code at Heidelberg (fourteenth century)

Figure 18 Grain-harvesting with a serrated, bow-
shaped sickle.
Herrad of Landsberg, *Hortus deliciarum* (twelfth century)

ripe ears received as little shaking as possible in the process of harvesting. This was important as it kept the loss of grain to a minimum. The fourteenth century, at the earliest, saw the transition to the much more effective harvesting with scythe in highly developed areas of grain production such as northern France, Flanders and the Rhineland. This transition was, of course, preceded by technical improvements which continued into early modern times, making the scythe the most efficient implement for grain-harvesting for centuries to come. It would seem that the development of the scythe into its modern form started in the twelfth and thirteenth centuries, when it was used for cutting hay. By that time it already had an edged back which held the connecting piece to the long wooden handle. This handle, which was as high as a man, allowed the mower to work in an upright position and to use all his physical strength to swing the scythe.

While the scythe was not widely used for grain-harvesting until the fourteenth century, it had long had a place in the development of pasture cultivation, as well as in haymaking by the high Middle Ages. Foliage had been used for centuries as winter fodder, but the actual cultivation of pasture and the production of quality hay only began with the regular mowing of the pastures by means of effective scythes.[24] This was because the regular working of pasture, which some villages started in the early

Middle Ages, required an implement which could mow at a very low height in order to prevent the regeneration of poisonous plants and to stimulate the growth of the nutritious ones. Different techniques of haymaking were employed in the various European regions which cannot be discussed in detail here. Farms stressing stock production, however, such as the Alpine dairies or smallholdings, profited from this improvement in haymaking, since the availability of hay facilitated the wintering of livestock and contributed to improving food supplies.

The threshing of grain was for the most part done indoors, in barns, halls, or other farm-buildings, and could last well into the winter months.[25] The much cheaper flail was adopted more rapidly by medieval peasants than the relatively dear scythe. The thirteenth century marked only the beginning of its enormous popularity in most regions of Europe. It consisted of two parts which were used to beat the corn ears powerfully, a technique which was extremely efficient. As mentioned above, another advantage of the flail was its price, because thanks to the fact that it was made of leather and not of any metal components, even the poorest tenant could afford it. It is believed to have originated in Frankish Gaul, yet flails were soon used all over central, northern and even parts of eastern Europe. In Italy, however, it was introduced only in the north, while the south, like most of the other Mediterranean countries, retained the traditional threshing method of either driving cattle, sheep or goats over the grain while it lay spread out on the outdoor threshing floors, or else a threshing sledge was used to separate out the grain from the ears.

Seen as a whole, the technical development of agricultural implements reached a much higher level at the beginning of the fourteenth century than during the early Middle Ages. Indeed it reached a standard 'which in many respects was so influential that it provided a model reaching beyond its own for generations to come'.[26] Hence the twelfth and thirteenth centuries were indeed a decisive period, because the extensive development of arable, which went hand in hand with the rise of the towns, was paralleled by important innovations in agricultural tools which paved the way for a higher level of progress in agriculture. Among the innovations which gained acceptance in the high Middle Ages and survived into later centuries were the wheeled plough, draught-horses with their improved harnesses and iron horseshoes, the modern scythe, cart, flail, water- and wind-mills, and not least the three-field system which will be discussed in the last section of this chapter. Technical development, however, was by no means even but depended on the region and its proximity to major trade routes. Some of the improvements were accepted rapidly, and others only very slowly. Even in the nineteenth and twentieth centuries ethnological researchers met with altogether astoundingly varied levels of technical development when they first attempted to produce a systematic inventory of peasant implements in different regions. Some regions retained traditional tools and methods with great stubborness even though neighbouring areas might have already reached the latest level of agricultural improvement.

What is more, the high Middle Ages were characterized by an increase in the number of iron parts used in peasant implements, as a result of which these implements lasted much longer and were also much more productive. This applies to ploughs and carts, as well as sickles, scythes and spades. The increase in iron production and the quality in the processing of metals facilitated this development considerably.[27] Although the urban trades participated in the production of agricultural implements, rural craft seems to have played a much greater role in it. Apart from wheelwrights, blacksmiths need particular mention in this context, chiefly because they had an essential function in the production of ploughshares and scythe-blades, as well as other iron parts.[28] As far as possible, peasants made wooden tools and components for agricultural implements themselves, especially handles for sickles, poles for scythes and spades, harrow frames, and wooden plough parts. In order to do so they went to the village commons to get the wood they needed. Home production of agricultural implements thus played a dominant role in the Middle Ages; however, this was increasingly supplemented by professional craft production. The growing dependence of the peasant economy on the market thus even started to affect the production of agricultural implements.

Changes in land utilization

A decisive factor in the development of agriculture in the high Middle Ages was the growing use of the three-field system.[29] It is true that the very beginnings of this cropping method go back to Carolingian times; however, its application then was usually limited to a handful of manors. The actual development of the three-field system as a rotation of three open fields did not start until the high Middle Ages, although its utilization progressed so rapidly in most of Europe that it had become the prevailing cropping method by the late Middle Ages. Many studies on the types and the first use of the three-field system should, none the less, be treated with great caution, largely because of their tendency to blur the distinctive phases of this development. As discussed earlier,[30] the three-field system existed when the arable of a village was divided into three main fields and peasants followed a compulsory system of rotation involving winter crops, summer crops and fallow. This system of common and compulsory uses did not find general acceptance before the twelfth and thirteenth centuries, although it was in itself a result of both the transition from predominantly livestock to predominantly grain production and the much more intensive farming of the village lands – two developments which had a tremendous effect on medieval agriculture.[31] In any case, there is no reason to believe that this method of land division is a legacy of early Germanic times, as nineteenth-century scholars suggested. It was rather the result of the general trend towards technological innovation which characterized the high Middle Ages. After all, the unification of the individual holdings into three open fields was not, to any great extent, recorded prior to the eleventh century and must be regarded as being closely connected with the rationalization of grain production. Notwithstanding the fact that there is little evidence on the dating of the introduction and initial spread of this method of cultivation in individual regions – which would be hard to supply anyway – it is widely accepted today that the three-field system developed first in the vast grain-belts of northern France, the Low Countries, and western Germany. Likewise, there seems to be no doubt that some of the neighbouring areas adopted the new method of cultivation more rapidly than others.

The best way to illustrate the advantages of the three-field system is to see it in contrast to the older methods of cultivation.[32] Most of the arable in the early Middle Ages was farmed extensively, that is alternating with fallow grassland; hence the production of grain was often interrupted. In itself however, this method was already an advance on even older methods of crop rotation which used the land for only a few years and then abandoned it to be overgrown and regenerated by wild plants (*Urwechselwirtschaft*). This regeneration period could last years or even decades until the land was eventually cleared again for new crops. Fallow grassland was only rarely ploughed for crops and essentially retained its character as pasture. This cultivation rhythm, mostly a two- or three–year cultivation of rye, spelt or oats, did not require fertilizer. During the times when fallow grassland served as pasture, other strips of land in the vicinity provided the soil for these short-term crops. This method was in particular used on the outskirts of the arable of the villages, as opposed to the fields closer to the centres of settlement, which were frequently manured and much more intensively farmed.

Another cropping method similar to this was the *Egartwirtschaft* adopted essentially in the Alps and in southern Germany.[33] The *Egärten* were fields used for many years as meadow or pasture before being used to raise grain or vegetables. And on other low fertility soils, on mountainous terrains or in the moors and sandy plains, grain crops alternated with woodland or heathland. Yet another extensive farming method consisted of burning the fields and then a few years of cultivation. This method had different names in the various regions of Europe.[34] After clearing the woodlands, heaths, or moor flora with fire, peasants used either ploughs or hoes to mingle the ashes with the soil as a method of fertilizing the land for up to two years of grain production, frequently followed by another year during which the same strip of land served as pasture before it was again left fallow. The same cycle was then started on the neighbouring strip of land and so so on, so that cultivation gradually travelled across a considerable part of the local heath or woodland. In the face of the notorious shortage of manure in medieval agriculture this was also a good method to provide the poor soils of low mountain ranges and heaths with the necessary nutrients.

Some areas which retained the older, primitive methods of crop rotation nevertheless developed more advanced forms which survived until the twentieth century. The *Hauberg* method of cultivation, which was used in the mountainous area along the River Sieg east of Bonn, scheduled about twenty portions of arable land for systematic use for periods of various lengths.[35] The bark of young trees, mostly oak trees, was peeled off the tree-trunks, dried and then used as tannin for leather-making. The wood itself was turned into charcoal or served the peasants as fuel. The land thus cleared was farmed with grain crops for one year, afterwards serving as pasture.

This brief survey of the older methods of crop rotation suggests that, despite the predominance of the three-field system, numerous other farming systems were stubbornly retained during the late Middle Ages, and even in modern times. In fact, their number is far greater than estimated in the scholarly works of the past. Among these other methods particular mention should be made of the two-field system, an annual alternation between tilling and fallow periods which is also called ley farming.[36] It met the needs particularly of wine-producing areas where peasants spent most of their time and energy on their vineyards rather than on their grain fields. Because of this, and the corresponding lack of manure for the cereal crops in such areas, grain yields were relatively meagre. These circumstances might help to account for the fact that relatively extensive cropping methods such as the two-field system survived in fertile regions in combination with special crops like wine, such as in the upper Rhine valley.

The spread of the three-field system

What were the advantages which stimulated the development of the three-field system ever since the high Middle Ages? What kind of influence did it have on the development of agriculture as a whole? There were three essential advantages in using the three-field as opposed to previous cropping methods, such as the two-field system.[37] First of all, the new methods, when carefully applied, raised the grain yields considerably; it has even been estimated that a 50 per cent increase was by no means an exception.[38] Secondly, the labour of ploughing, sowing and harvesting was spread much more evenly over the entire year, thus increasing the efficiency of peasant labour. The harvesting of winter and summer crops could now be done in one stretch from July to August; the spring months were reserved for the ploughing and the sowing of the summer crops; and while the preparations for the winter crops fell into the autumn period, there was plenty of time to plough the fallow land in early summer. Thirdly, the main field intended for the winter crops could now be farmed and manured much more intensively than before. This improved the nutrient balance of the soil and thus prevented its premature exhaustion. And the ploughing of the fallow also helped to control weeds which otherwise would have diminished the yields in grain farming, especially in the case of long-term production.

With the sowing and growth phases divided over the various seasons there was less danger of famine, as peasants now had a chance to compensate for a bad winter harvest with a good summer harvest. The overall increase in oat production also stimulated the introduction of horses as draught-animals into the peasant economy because oats were by and large the best horse fodder. The increasing use of horses in agriculture thus helped to raise the productivity of peasant labour. All in all, the three-field system combined with common practices guaranteed 'an extremely regular and thus comparatively productive succession of the most important summer and winter crops, and a regular one-year fallow which increased the fertility of the soil and provided additional fodder for livestock because it meant that more of the available land could be used as pasture'.[39]

The three-field system, which was used for almost a thousand years in some regions, was equally advantageous for the majority of peasants in Europe. Yet there can be no doubt that the common usages which accompanied it also constricted the economic freedom of the individual peasant. In later centuries, moreover, compulsory rotation frequently obstructed further advances in the three-field system, such as the cultivation of the fallow land. Some areas like the lower Rhine or Flanders saw the sowing of fodder crops, vegetables and legumes on fallow land as early as the end of the high Middle Ages. This was in fact the beginning of the further development of the three-field system, which was to continue into early modern times.[40] Extensive vegetable and fruit plantations developed in the vicinity of big towns, and the growing of wine prospered on favourable sites. Since the constrictions of the common field system did not apply to gardens, cultivation was much more flexible there and produced considerable yields of vegetables, hops, peas and plants for spinning fibres and dyeing from the high Middle Ages onwards.

The development of cropping methods within the context of the agricultural expansion in the high Middle Ages as a whole demonstrates the undoubted importance of the three-field system for agricultural progress. Along with the enormous extension of arable, the expansion of grain production, the improvement of agricultural implements and the intensification of farming in general, the three-field system provided the basis for the surprising boom in agriculture during the twelfth and thirteenth centuries. The increase of yields laid the foundation for the extraordinary rise in population, the growth of the economy in general and the prosperity of commerce and trades, and if is only against this background that the emergence of the urban economy and culture, feudal lordship and chivalry can be fully comprehended. Although the formula 'agricultural and technological "revolution" of the high Middle Ages', which has been used by some historians,[41] is somewhat exaggerated, it is clear that the conditions of agriculture improved markedly during this period.

PEASANT LABOUR AND ECONOMY

The specific characteristics of the peasant family economy

Owing to its aim of selling specialized produce at the highest possible profit on the market, a modern farming enterprise cannot be compared with a medieval peasant farm. The peasant economy was a unique system in which the household provided both the basic food requirements and everyday goods, all with the aim of managing its own household and work with as little interference from the outside as possible. Peasant labour was not primarily directed at gaining high profits. Its main goal was to secure the subsistence of the family. In order to understand this particular social and economic phenomenon, which has become alien to modern society and economy, we cannot but draw attention to the specific character of the peasant economy in pre-industrial Europe. To a degree unknown in today's agriculture, this encompassed both production and consumption in the household and the family.[1] Although bound within the framework of the manorial system, the peasant household economy was for centuries at the heart of medieval and early modern agrarian society in Europe. Moreover, the peasant economy is still central to those countries outside Europe dominated by an agrarian economy, particularly in the developing regions of Africa, Asia and Latin America.

According to W. H. Riehl and O. Brunner, the term 'household economy' refers to the house of the peasant in a larger sense, hence to 'the entire house'.[2] The peasant household or family economy actually includes the contributions of all family members in addition to the servants, and the entirety of their activities in both field and farmhouse. The medieval economy represents what is meant by the Greek word *oikos*, 'the entire house', that is peasant economy in the broadest possible sense.[3] In fact, what this 'theory of the house and its economy' deals with is the basic form of peasant economy and culture from the high Middle

Ages to the nineteenth century. The peasant economy was the foundation of the economic and social structure in pre-industrial Europe. It was little affected, in its core, by the numerous political changes in the social superstructure. Even in the wake of today's trade economy, and in contrast to other economic forms, it has managed to preserve the ability to survive without becoming too dependent on the market. This is why the peasant economy had comparatively little trouble in surviving the major economic crises which accompanied the formation of our highly developed market economy.

The peasant economy's tenacious power to survive originated from the fact that the peasant did not regard his farm as a means of production which could be disposed of when it was no longer profitable. For him, the farm was above all the basis of his existence. A pre-industrial farmer would continue to work even if his revenues dropped below the local average wages, thus maintaining his means of existence for the future even when the economy might change. Precisely because it was not paid labour but the effort of the family that lay at the heart of the peasant economy, it could remain self-sufficient even when conditions deteriorated. It follows that peasants secured their subsistence on the one hand by a decrease in consumption and, on the other, by an increase in the work done by the family – that is by means of sacrifices which were, economically speaking, unprofitable. This holds true particularly for the high Middle Ages, when the market integration of farms was relatively low and peasants were less affected by economic crises.

A number of valuable insights into the structure of the peasant family economy were advanced by the Russian agronomist A. Chayanov, whose empirical study of the peasant economy in Russia before 1914 led to a general theory of the peasant family economy in the pre-industrial period.[4] Chayanov emphasized that the autonomy of production and consumption in the peasant household economy manifests itself in the fact that peasant work does not aim primarily at the highest possible profit but at securing the family's subsistence. What is essential to the peasant family economy is, in fact, the gross amount, and not the net surplus of family labour. Whenever the returns of the peasant family economy drop, for example after an unprofitable fragmentation of the holding or in times of overpopulation, the peasant family reacts by increasing its work rate. This increase may well surpass what we usually find under the conditions of wage labour, and it is maintained until the subsistence of the family is secured and returns are sufficient again. It is not economic considerations nor an interest in the highest possible revenue for their labour input that determines how the peasant will react when the subsistence of the family is threatened but an interest in raising the common work effort. This is how the household's chances of survival are guaranteed even in difficult circumstances. In case of rising returns, however, it is no longer necessary to sustain the additional work effort;

consequently, the intensity of peasant labour slackens off and the surplus results in higher consumption.

Hence according to Chayanov there is an apparent balance between production and consumption, that is, between the size of returns and the degree of consumption. Although it is clear that the peasant economy does take advantage of its chances to make a surplus, it none the less pursues only limited economic aims. More important than producing profits is the satisfaction of the traditional, culturally sanctioned needs which belong to the life of the peasant. This reaction proves that 'the peasant family never exploits its full work capacity, and that it stops working as soon as needs are met and the economic balance has been re-established.'[5]

Contributions from cultural anthropology

R. H. Hilton has made some interesting comments on the specific structure and development of the peasant economy of the Middle Ages,[6] including critical remarks on pronouncements made by such anthropologists as T. Shanin, E. R. Wolf, and R. Redfield about the peasant economy.[7] In so doing he has stressed the unique character of its medieval form. Some recent anthropologists have distinguished the 'peasant economy' from the forms of production in primitive tribal communities or modern industrial societies. As a 'society within society', the peasantry comprises the majority of the population, as well as the basis of the political and economic system – especially in these agrarian societies with their functional unity of production, consumption and generative reproduction. Yields exceeding personal needs were either sold on the market or had to be delivered in substantial quantities to powerful outsiders.

Quite rightly, R. H. Hilton has stressed that the peasant economy should not be seen in isolation from its historical context. Feudal society and the stages of its development must, of course, be taken into account in studying the medieval peasant economy.[8] Despite the fact that it is possible to compare peasant societies and economies in various social systems, these comparisons still have to be handled with great care. The peasants of the Middle Ages did not live isolated from the rest of society. They were ruled by feudal lords to whom they were obliged to deliver the greater part of the commodities they produced and did not use personally. Throughout the medieval period there were fierce conflicts and struggles between feudal lords and peasants over the quantity of rents and services. In any case, the social and economic situation of the medieval peasant differed in a number of respects from the living conditions in other societies, and especially from those of today.

Characteristics of the peasant economy in the Middle Ages

What striking differences between the peasant of today and his medieval counterpart must be mentioned to facilitate an understanding of the socioeconomic position of the medieval peasant? As already noted, the decisive characteristic of the medieval peasant economy lies in its manorial dependence on feudal lords who siphoned off an essential portion of the peasant's return. The main obstacle to the independence of the peasant economy was the extensive labour which had to be done for the manorial household. In addition to feudal obligations it is the dependency on the village community and its characteristic three-field system which distinguishes the peasant economy of the Middle Ages from modern agriculture. The peasant had very little chance to farm according to his own initiative, particularly because he was obliged to farm under compulsory methods of cultivation. The communal forms of the use of meadows and woods also hampered the peasant's freedom of action at that time. What needs mentioning among the other distinguishing features is the low technical standards of agricultural implements in the Middle Ages – something which must be kept in mind in the face of today's mechanized agriculture. Owing to the low standard of agricultural technology, medieval farming was low in productivity too. As for the cultivation of cereals, yields only three or four times the quantity of the seed sown were normal. Considering yields as low as these, it is clear that bad harvests had a devastating impact on the nutrition of peasant families, causing severe famines and preparing the way for epidemics.

If we take into account such circumstances as modest technical standards, low yields, and the burden of manorial rents and dues, it is plain how difficult the work of the medieval peasant must have been. The laboriousness of peasant work can hardly be imagined by outsiders, yet it must be said that despite much improvement it has in many areas remained this way. At the beginning of the sixteenth century, Johannes Boemus wrote an unadorned report on the work of the contemporary peasant:

> The lowliest estate is that of those living in villages and homesteads in the countryside, cultivating the soil, whence they are called peasants and country-folk. Their situation is rather miserable and harsh. They live isolated from one other, in very poor conditions, with many of their relatives and their cattle. These people can never enjoy any leisure, they are ever at work and are unclean. To towns nearby they bring what they can sell, what can be gained from fields and stock, and here they buy what they need . . . They perform services for their lords many times a year; they farm their lord's land, sow their seed, harvest the fruits of their fields and store it in barns, saw wood, build houses, dig ditches. There is nothing this oppressed and miserable people does not seem to owe them, nothing they can without risk

decline to do when ordered, for the guilty will be severely punished. Yet what is most bitter for these people is the fact that the larger part of the holdings they possess is in fact owned by the lords and that they have to pay them a considerable portion of the annual harvest in order to keep their tenure.[9]

A basic measure of land allotment in the Middle Ages was the hide (German *Hufe*, Latin *mansus*). With the development and consolidation of the early medieval manorial system, the hide became the standard representing a peasant family in terms of land, means of production and legal rights to the common land within the context of the manor. Moreover, this unit of land served as a basis for the quantity of services in money and kind which the lords demanded from a self-sufficient, originally indivisible peasant holding. As we can see from W. Schlesingers's studies, the hide emerged under the influence of the Carolingian kings. The Frankish *Hufe* corresponded to that in the Anglo-Saxon kingdoms as well as to its equivalent in the Scandinavian regions, where it was called *bol*, and described a normal, fully endowed peasant holding.[10] At a certain stage in the process of the consolidation of royal authority in the early Middle Ages it was thought desirable to normalize the entire agrarian order so as to facilitate claims for certain services. In this context the hide was 'not just the unit for the manorial demands for dues and services, but at the same time a unit for taxation in general'.[11]

The individual hide differed in size according to soil quality, manorial affiliation and time of introduction. This is why we have trouble trying to determine a universally valid average size for a hide. For example, given that there are 30 yokes to a hide and that a yoke equals a third of a hectare, a fully endowed farm would have as much as 10 hectares. After the steep rise in population in the high Middle Ages, however, hides were increasingly split up into half- and even quarter-hides, especially in a number of densely populated areas. This formation of small farms further increased the disparity in size of peasant holdings. Nevertheless the majority of peasant households continued to be sufficiently endowed with land, implements and labour so as to provide for the adequate nourishment of the family. Only such whole, undivided hides, however, managed to fulfil their duties to the manor and thus kept the manorial regime alive.

The cultivation of cereals

The cultivation of cereals was the most important branch of the peasant economy in the high Middle Ages, the only one which could supply the growing population with basic foodstuffs.[12] Hence the cultivation and maintenance of grain fields stood at the centre of peasant work. The well-being and survival of entire regions depended on their grain crops. In most villages the production of cereals was conducted collectively on the basis of the three-field system, and the predominant crop rotation consisted of rye, oats and fallow. Rather than rye, some regions cultivated wheat or spelt, and barley instead of oats. With the intensification of grain production in the twelfth century, some regions specialized in the cultivation of certain cereals. In the south-west of Germany, for instance, common wheat or spelt predominated for centuries. Spelt was more popular than other cereals, its production can be traced from the valleys of the Alps up to the Moselle region, and from Alsace deep into Bavaria. It is no longer possible to assume a close connection between the growing of spelt and the territories of the Alemannian tribe.[13] This theory ignored the fact that spelt was after all produced far away from the Alemannian lands too, for example in France or in Thuringia. This was because unlike wheat, spelt was less dependent on particular climatic and soil conditions, as a result of which it could also be grown in regions with less favourable soils and climates.

Figure 19 Work in the fields: ploughing, harrowing, hoeing, scaring off the birds.
Wood engraving from Virgil, *Georgics*, Strasburg, 1502

Wheat, by contrast, was so demanding that it could hardly be grown in harsh climates such as in Scandinavia and the north of eastern Europe; but it was the predominant cereal in the large grain-belts of western Europe, where its cultivation was facilitated by favourable soil conditions.[14] In most of central Europe, however, and especially in north-eastern Germany, rye was by far the most important cereal for the production of bread. Owing to its outstanding hardiness and generous yields, rye was the ideal cereal for farmsteads with less fertile soils. Like rye, oats were also grown mainly north of the Alps because they grew quickly enough to be sown after long winters and were less affected by dampness. The cultivation of barley was widespread over all of Europe, being grown virtually everywhere from Scandinavia to the Mediterranean. Above all its adaptability to difficult climatic conditions accounted for its popularity: it could survive the long droughts of the Mediterranean just as well as it could grow after the long winters of the northern regions.

The increase in grain production required extra effort on the part of the peasants, both in terms of labour and the amount of time they had to spend in the fields. The three open fields had to be ploughed at least three times per year, and sowing and harvesting were equally labour-intensive. Hence peasants were generally concerned about having similar-sized portions of arable land in the three open fields to secure similar returns each season. This was extremely difficult to achieve in areas where forms of partible inheritance such as *Realteilung* prevailed, and the land was divided into equal portions among heirs – an inheritance custom similar to gavelkind in England.

More and more peasants used either manure or marl to fertilize their fields, but particularly the latter was not always available. There is evidence that in the fourteenth century Alsatian peasants rented marl pits in the vicinity of their fields in order to use them collectively.[15] Manure was scarce on many farms, because most of them had neither enough room in their stables nor enough fodder to winter all of their cattle. Hence peasants kept their cattle out at pasture as long as they possibly could, and after bringing them back home in autumn, slaughtered all those animals which could not be fed for the winter. The constant manure shortage was undoubtedly one of the main problems for grain production in the high Middle Ages, particularly since the little that was available was used preferably to fertilize vineyards and orchards. The importance of manure for the peasant economy is reflected in a fourteenth-century village law from the south-west of Germany in which the word manure-heap functioned as a synonym for the peasant farm as a whole. Peasants who were obliged to plough the manorial land were allowed to leave in the course of the afternoon so that they could 'reach their own manure-heap' by nightfall.[16]

An interesting regional peculiarity in the high Middle Ages is the so-called one-field system *(Einfeldwirtschaft)* of the north-west of Germany. This term refers to the constant cultivation of a single kind of crop year after year on the same field. In particular the north-west of Germany was known for its continous cultivation of rye in a special type of field, the *Eschboden*.[17] This method was still used in Westphalia and the area between the Rivers Weser and Ems even after the three-field system had been introduced in the neighbouring regions. The *Esch* was a closed system of long strips of arable land which were often protected by hedges against damage from grazing livestock or wild animals. The elevated ground in these fields resulted from the fact that they were regularly fertilized with sod cut from the heath in the village commons which, in addition, was enriched with manure. As a result of the permanent improvement of the topsoil with nutrients, the *Esch* could be sown continuously with grain. In the course of the centuries, this type of fertilization created layers of topsoil which in some instances were a metre high. A number of villages continued to use this method until the introduction of artificial fertilizers in the nineteenth century, and in the Middle Ages it was also applied in the Low Countries and in Denmark. Fertilization of this kind required large heaths nearby and led to the uprooting of most of the woodland in the vicinity and thus to a considerable change in the landscape as a whole. Sod fertilization was first introduced into the north-west of Germany in the tenth and eleventh centuries as a by-product of the intensified cultivation of rye which, as described above, also accounts for the fundamental change in the architecture of the peasant houses in those regions. For this was the time when the longhouse of northern Germany was developed, providing much more storage for grain under its massive roof space.[18]

In the peasant economy as a whole, it was the garden in addition to the farmhouse and the inner realm of the farmyard which was reserved for the private use of the peasant family.[19] The fenced-in garden near the peasant house was important for food supplies. Above all, plants which needed either intensive care or particular protection from grazing livestock or wild animals were kept here, such as vegetables, legumes and spices needed in everyday cooking. Peasant gardens were typical kitchen rather than ornamental gardens, a type of agriculturally productive land which produced everything needed for the peasant diet apart from bread. Millet, turnips, flax, hemp and peas also ranged among the typical garden plants in peasant kitchen gardens, and in some parts of Germany cabbage patches were actually called cabbage gardens. In particular the cultivation of legumes such as peas, beans and lentils goes back a long time in history, and this is why they are among the traditional vegetables in the everyday cooking of the peasantry, just as are turnips, herbs, leek and cabbage. The evolution of gardens in the today's sense was gradual and was paralleled by the development of fruit and herb cultivation as well as orchards. Ornamental gardens were primarily located in the vicinity of castle and monastic complexes, and were only rarely found on the average farm. The most important among the gardening implements was the spade, which helped to loosen the topsoil so as to prepare it for the sowing or planting of the more delicate garden plants.

In addition to the land which was collectively farmed within the open fields, there were often other parcels of farmland which were exempt from communal use. As well as the gardens which belonged to each

Figure 20 Work in the fields and gardens: ploughing, fence-making, clearing
trees.
Wood engraving from Virgil, *Georgics*, Strasburg, 1502

peasant farm there were some pieces of garden land in the commons
which were also farmed intensively. Their names varied from region to
region; in Germany they were frequently called *Gärten, Bündten,
Beunden or Bifänge*.[20] In legal terms, these gardens within the commons
were not part of the land which had to be farmed according to the three-
field system. They were subject to the garden laws which let their owners
have free use of their land. These gardens were fenced in as well, and
peasants used them especially to grow legumes such as peas and lentils,
vegetables such as turnips and cabbages, plants for textile-making such as
flax and hemp, or plants for dyeing such as madder and woad. These
specialized cultures, including vineyards, were increasingly developed in
the high Middle Ages as they grew in importance for the peasant
economy. They were farmed mostly by less wealthy peasants who put
considerable effort and care into their modest holdings. Among the plants
which supplied raw materials for commercial production, those for
textile-making were grown most frequently in this type of garden. Many
peasants used large parts of them to grow flax, the raw material used for
making various fabrics and clothes. Payment in flax or linen was for a
long time part of the peasant dues to feudal lords, and from the thirteenth
century on linen production was a widespread supplementary source of
income for peasant households.[21]

In the high Middle Ages, areas with more intensive farming and agricultural production were mainly located on the periphery of big towns and in heavily urbanized regions, such as Flanders or Lombardy. The farmland and gardens near towns were particularly well maintained and manured, and thus able to produce a large variety of vegetables and fruit to satisfy the tastes of an urban clientele. There were a number of intensively farmed areas, particularly along the Rivers Rhine, Moselle and Neckar, which were known for their specialized production to meet the growing demand from the towns for such plant products as madder and woad, as well as fruits and vegetables, and not least wine. A written source from the thirteenth century reads like a proud enumeration of the impressive variety of Alsatian farm produce, including wheat, rye, barley and oats; legumes, vetch and lentils; as well as a whole range of other crops (*crescit ibi frumentum, sigulum, hordeum et avena. Crescunt et legumina, faba, pisa, vicia, lentes; et ibidem multarum herbarum semina generantur*).[22]

One of the specialized cultures which has hardly been discussed so far is wine production, an important branch of the peasant economy in certain regions.[23] In the high and late Middle Ages, wine production prospered essentially in good climates and even reached its maximum geographical development in Germany. It became one of the most important sectors of the peasant economy along the Rivers Rhine, Moselle, Neckar and Main. In France, however, there were areas which depended even more on viniculture, particularly near big towns and along such important waterways as the Rhône and the Loire which facilitated the transport of wine.

Despite some remarkable improvements in the agricultural production of the high Middle Ages, the yields of grain production, on which the nourishment of the populace depended, were far from satisfactory.[24] There is no exact information available on yields per hectare before the middle of the twelfth century, and even for the thirteenth century consistent figures on the development of harvests and yield ratios are only available thanks to a number of excellent sources which allow some insight into this period of England's agricultural history. The returns of medieval agriculture, like any other, depended on soil quality, on climate, on the amount and quality of the fertilizers used, and on the tending of the crops. Moreover, annual weather conditions tended to affect the yields of medieval agriculture much more severely than they do nowadays. In 1156, the estates of the abbey of Cluny in Burgundy produced a seed–yield ratio of approximately 1:3 for wheat, 1:5 for rye, and 1:2.5 for barley.[25] Some evidence for the thirteenth century in England provides us with ratios of 2.4–3.9 for wheat, 3.8–4.2 for barley, and 1.9–2.7 for oats.[26] In some regions, however, there was evidence for much higher yield ratios during the thirteenth and fourteen centuries. Some of the manors of the abbey at St Denis, for instance, which were located in the basin of the River Seine, produced an average seed–yield ratio of 1:8 for wheat. On the land of a manor in the Artois this ratio even increased to 1:15 in 1335.[27]

Despite some reservations it seems likely that most peasants in the Middle Ages were satisfied when they produced harvests three or four times the seed sown. The comparatively low rate of productivity in the twelfth and thirteenth centuries is, nevertheless, notably higher than the rate of the ninth century, which is estimated to have only rarely exceeded a mere 1:2 seed–yield ratio.[28] An increase in the yield ratio to 1:3 thus meant real progress in terms of productivity, providing the peasants with returns twice as high as in the ninth century. This was because in order to continue grain production at about the same level in the following year the peasant had to save the same amount of seed which he had sown in the previous year, and this means that all yield figures given above must be reduced by one unit in order to arrive at the net returns. A peasant could use merely two-thirds of the average seed–yield ratio of 1:3 to pay his tributes and tithes, as well as to cover the requirements of his household as a whole. Since only two-thirds of the arable land could be used for grain production in the case of the three-field system, and only 50 per cent in that of the two-field system, peasants were forced to reserve a substantial part of their farmland to produce the grain for their daily bread.

Famines, a constant threat to the populace in the Middle Ages, were mainly triggered by bad harvests, yet the deeper cause lies in the low yields.[29] The lower the seed–yield ratios fell, the more threatening were the consequences of harsh winters, rainy summers, hail or drought upon the margins of peasant subsistence. This, and the fact that bad harvests could not be balanced by grain imports for lack of a developed grain trade, provided one of the main reasons for hunger in the Middle Ages. In addition, grain storage was limited, and when stored could suffer from rotting as well as be eaten by mice. This is why it was vital for the subsistence of the peasant family to have access to provisions other than grain products when harvests were threatened.

Stock production

Although important, the production of livestock played only a secondary role in the peasant economy of the high Middle Ages when compared with grain production and everything that went with it.[30] Yet the two were closely linked to each other, and this was because extensive grain production required not only draught-animals but considerable quantities of fertilizer in the form of manure. However, the keeping of cattle was restricted by the lack of pasture. This was because the extension of the village into nearby land and the increase in the number of peasant farms in the thirteenth century led to a noticeable reduction of that portion of the

Figure 21 Sheep-farming
Wood engraving from Virgil, *Georgics*, Strasburg, 1502

commons which had traditionally served as pasture. In response to the shortage of pasture lands, manorial and peasant regulations worked to limit the number of cattle in villages and on farmsteads according to the size of the individual holding and its capacity for wintering.

A more systematic use of meadows, beginning with the high Middle Ages, certainly helped to compensate for the limited availability of food for livestock.[31] Through drainage and irrigation the development of meadows progressed especially in low mountain ranges and in the Alps. Initially, most of the meadows were not grazed by cattle but mown by the peasants, who cut the grass and harvested the hay as winter fodder for their stock. Unlike crops, meadows were only fenced in for limited periods. Also, meadows were from time to time ploughed and otherwise prepared for temporary grain production. Meadows with dry and thin soils were regularly fertilized and watered with the help of nearby rivers and brooks in order to raise their yields. Average meadows, however, provided hay only once a year and were used as pasture thereafter. In addition to hay, straw and foliage were used as fodder for livestock in the winter.

In the course of the high and late Middle Ages, the keeping of cattle prevailed in grassland regions, such as the marsh along the coasts, as well as in lands at higher altitudes, such as low mountain ranges and the Alps. The marshes along the North Sea coast provided particularly fertile soils for meadows. As a result an important part of farming in those regions consisted of breeding cattle for export to both neighbouring and more distant areas, which in return financed the import of grain.[32] Above all, the Frisian marshes were famous for their cattle, which provided not only meat but also butter, milk, and cheese in considerable quantities. This specialization of Frisian agriculture was further stimulated by the increase in the export of cheese, butter and beef in the late Middle Ages, a factor which accounts for the wealth of the upper strata of peasant society in Frisia at that time.

In mountainous regions, the trend towards specialization in cattle production seems to have started somewhat later than in the marshes along the coasts. The twelfth and thirteenth centuries saw the foundation of a great number of such specialized peasant farms in southern Germany, Alsace, Switzerland, the Tyrol, and in Carinthia, where such livestock operations were called *Schwaigen* in the German land registers, or *vaccariae* in Latin documents.[33] These Alpine holdings were not farmed in summer only; rather, they were permanent peasant enterprises at fairly high altitudes specializing in pasture and cattle production. Some of them were located as high as 2,000 metres above sea level in the Tyrol and Carinthia during the fourteenth century. The bulk of their production consisted of butter and cheese. The farms in the Tyrol even had to pay their rents and dues in cheese. As a rule, the larger *Schwaigen* paid rents of 300 cheeses per year on the basis of an average stock of about twelve cows and two oxen. These are the figures recorded in an Austrian land register of the fourteenth century which reads as follows: '*swaiga dicitur, que habet 12 vaccas et 2 boves et solvuntur 300 casei.*'[34]

The quality of cattle breeds in the high Middle Ages appears to have been rather low.[35] Bone finds show that most of these animals were small, an observation which is confirmed by the analysis of the paintings and drawings of the time. The overall difficulties of stock-keeping left little room for systematic breeding. Since most of the village cattle were kept mixed on the commons from spring to autumn, procreation happened as nature wished it. Little effort was made to keep a balance between male and female animals, and separate bull-keeping was hardly practised. With the introduction of a tithe for breeding animals the keeping of such animals was often considered an equivalent for the payment of such tithes. Consequently parsons who often had the task of collecting the tithes were also obliged to keep such breeding animals. In many villages, none the less, it was the feudal lord or his representative who held this office, as the analysis of the *Weistümer* or village customals shows. On the leasehold farm of Gallenweiler, for example, which belonged to the monastery at St Blasien in the Black Forest, it was one of the duties of the bailiff to supply bulls and boars for breeding purposes.[36] In the parish of

Simmern in the upper Palatinate, by contrast, the feudal lord shared the duty of administering the breeding of local livestock. The feudal lord was in charge of bulls and boars whilst the parson had the task of keeping rams and ganders.[37] The keeping of the male breeding animals was, however, always regarded as an irksome duty; an attitude which did not help the development of systematic breeding.

In most parts of medieval Europe, the bulk of the meat consumed was pork.[38] Bone finds of pigs, which were unearthed in excavations of medieval settlements, indicate that the domestic pigs of that time very closely resembled their wild boar relatives, particularly in the extended shape of their skulls and their long legs. Medieval illustrations confirm the archaeological evidence, leaving no doubt that steps to breed pigs systematically had hardly been taken by the high Middle Ages. In peasant households, nevertheless, pigs were highly esteemed domestic animals for two reasons. First, because they grew fast to a stage where they were ready for slaughter, and secondly because they were omnivores, hence easy to feed. Central to the keeping of domestic pigs was their fattening in the woodlands near medieval settlements under the supervision of a swineherd, especially since beechnuts and acorns provided an excellent mast. The high esteem of pig-rearing in the Middle Ages is reflected in the fact that the size of forests was frequently estimated according to the number of pigs which could be fattened in them. With the increase of woodland clearance, however, the capability to feed and maintain pig herds decreased, so that extensive pig-raising became extremely difficult for the majority of the rural population. As a result of the shortage of pasture pig-raising was soon subject to strict regulation. In the case of the large Schwaderloch Forest near Lake Constance which had long been the rightful pig pasture of the neighbouring villages and manors, the threat of excessive grazing led in the year 1274 to limiting the number of pigs allowed in the forest and to the detailed regulation of its use as pasture.[39] A good example of the significance of pig-raising in the late Middle Ages is the pasture regulation for the Lusshardt Forest near Bruchsal in the south-west of Germany. In 1437, at least 43,000 pigs from the surrounding villages were fattened there every year against payment of a special fee (*Dehmen* or pannage).[40]

A considerable number of Alpine dairies kept sheep rather than cattle, or both of them in varying proportions. Alpine dairies specializing in sheep-raising had to pay their lords in sheep, lamb, wool or cloth.[41] The undemanding nature of these animals was one of the main reasons for their popularity, especially in less fertile areas or under unfavourable climatic conditions, such as heaths, woodlands, at higher altitudes or in rather barren grasslands. Sheep yielded not only milk which could be further processed to make cheese and other dairy products, but also more importantly wool, a raw material for textiles which was in constant demand. Sheep-rearing was not practised by the peasants alone. There is

Figure 22 A cattle deal, *c.*1500
Wood engraving by Hans L. Schäufelein

evidence that some shepherds migrated long distances and at various altitudes with their animals as early as the thirteenth and fourteenth centuries.[42] The range of their journeys was limited in such mountainous areas as the Alps or the Apennines. Seasonal migrations over long distances took place particularly in the Pyrenees, where in springtime herds of sheep were guided from their winter pastures below the snow-line to summer pastures at much higher altitudes. Peasant life and labour conditions in the Pyrenees village of Montaillou have been analysed splendidly by the French historian E. Le Roy Ladurie.[43] According to his study fierce conflicts broke out in many villages between the local peasants and migrating shepherds because the latter took the manorial flocks to the village commons for pasture without having obtained the permission of the peasants. Moreover, such practices often did lasting damage to the vegetation of the commons, for sheep do not merely graze on small plants but also on young trees and bushes.

The other branches of peasant livestock-raising cannot be discussed in detail within the limits of this study. General mention, however, must be made of the increasing importance of horse-breeding in the peasant economy and of the keeping of small domestic animals, such as goats, geese, chickens and ducks. Chickens and their eggs had an important place in peasant diet. Furthermore, many peasants kept them as a means to pay their taxes to their feudal lords. An important supplementary source of income for peasants in the woodlands and heaths of north-west Germany and eastern Europe was beekeeping,[44] since honey was a much sought-after sweetener and many wine makers used it to upgrade their products. Beehives were kept on many farmsteads, and every spring their owners brought them into the woodlands and heaths. Rules against the theft of beehives can be found in the folk-laws (*Volksrechte*) of the early Middle Ages, and in later centuries peasants were often obliged to pay dues in wax and honey to their lords.

Although many farmsteads, particularly in typical grassland zones such as the Alps, specialized in cattle and sheep-keeping, it is important to bear in mind that livestock production, on the whole, decreased in the course of the high Middle Ages in proportion to the production of grains. As a consequence of the increase in settlements as well as arable land, many meadows and woods came under the plough. The intensification of grain cultivation reduced the availability of grazing land for livestock in the cases of both open meadows and woodlands which had traditionally served the rural population as pasture for animals. This had a strong impact on cattle- and pig-raising. Cattle and swine stocks had to be reduced, as the main focus of the peasant economy shifted to working on the more fertile soils. By 1300, this aspect of medieval agriculture clearly dominated peasant labour. For it was owing only to the increase in grain production (to the detriment of meat production) that the basic food supply of the rapidly growing population could be secured.

Individual and collective methods of farming

After this analysis of the various branches of peasant production, it is equally necessary to discuss the close connection between the individual and the collective forms of agrarian production. In this context, K. S. Bader even went so far as to state that 'the real problem of land utilization in the medieval village' was the conflict between individual and collective land rights.[45] The integration of the individual household economy into a network of collective rights and duties was particularly developed in villages farming according to the three-field system, which in its fully-fledged form entailed compulsory forms of cultivation and the use of collectively held land. Owing to the fact that the three open fields of this type of village consisted literally of a mosaic of individual holdings, there was a strong communal pressure towards co-operation which tended to constrain even the most reluctant peasant. Transit rights had to be defined, new crops had to be protected, fences had to be built, and most individual jobs had to be co-ordinated. In hamlets, by contrast, where communal fields were only one aspect of local agriculture, the individual peasant was less constricted by the communal farming system, and compulsory rotation was less developed. In some regions there were also farms which were not interspersed with someone else's holdings; this was especially common among forest villages which were arranged in a straight line with strips of farmland extending behind each house (*Waldhufendörfer*). These holdings could be farmed by their holders as they thought best, for there was hardly any interference from other peasants' holdings. But even the communities of hamlets and settlements where the holding structure permitted individual farming methods, required a minimum of organization to regulate access to communal resources such as water, pasture or woodland.

The collective forms of land utilization particularly affected tilling methods, because farming was conducted according to compulsory crop rotation. Between sowing and harvesting, however, peasants were free to tend their holdings at their own discretion. When harvesting was over, the stubble-fields were again used collectively as village pasture. On the one hand, these constraints had positive effects, insofar as they forced sluggish individuals among the peasants to finish seasonal tasks in the fields, particularly harvest works, on time. On the other hand they could also mean a considerable burden to those peasants who wished to experiment with the traditional rotation of crops in order to make it more productive. Hence they could be a real obstacle to agricultural innovation.

In many regions, the tenants of smallholdings were often dependent on their neighbours, for instance if they did not have ploughs or draught-animals of their own. A plough team, no matter whether made up of oxen or horses, was an extremely expensive investment, and as a rule it was only the peasant with a medium or large-size holding who was able to afford one. An analysis of holdings in the English diocese of Winchester has shown that in the thirteenth century as much as 40 per cent of the dependent peasants did not have a team of their own; this observation is confirmed by French evidence from the same time which indicates that those with teams and ploughs, or *laboratores*, had a social and economic position radically different from those peasant groups who could not afford them and continued to farm their fields using the traditional manual implements.[46] Even as late as the early nineteenth century, it was only the larger farmsteads in many villages in southern Germany that actually had ploughs and teams of their own,[47] while cottagers (*Seldner*, *Schupposer* etc.) were forced to join with others to buy such expensive equipment, and hence did the ploughing together, or borrowed plough and draught-animals from the wealthier peasants in exchange for labour services on certain days of the year. Such forms of neighbourly help gave rise to a multi-faceted range of mutual dependencies within the community which undoubtedly left their imprint on daily life in the village.

The co-operative elements were most apparent in the communal pasture on the village commons. Peasants were obliged to give all their livestock into the safekeeping of the village herdsman. As far as the village commons were concerned, it was difficult to make a sharp distinction between the common pasture and the common woodlands. First, because the two often merged into each other without visible boundary, and secondly because the value of the common woodland consisted not only of the utilization of the wood itself but also in its use as pasture. By means of strict regulations, village communities sought to protect their common woodlands which, in addition to firewood and timber, supplied the rural population with foliage to feed their stock, game, herbs and various kinds of fruit. The commons, with their pastures and woodlands, were an irreplaceable asset for the medieval peasant economy which had to be protected effectively against misuse by unauthorized persons and overexploitation.[48] In short the collective aspect of the medieval peasant economy was most obvious in the use of the village commons.

The dues and payments of the medieval peasantry

What now also needs to be mentioned is the impact of the various modes of feudal dependence on the peasant economy of the Middle Ages. However, the scope of this chapter does not permit a thorough discussion of this complex area of conflict between the manor and the peasants as a whole. The remainder of this section will therefore focus on the question to what extent the peasant economy of the high Middle Ages was actually influenced in economic terms by the feudal system and how much in rents, dues and services peasants had to hand over to their lords. First of all, the gradual dissolution of the manorial, or *Fronhof* system – the most developed form of the manorial system in south-west Germany and France during the Carolingian period – and the decline of demesne farming[49] led to a marked reduction in labour services which, by the end of the thirteenth century, had lost most of their former harshness. Yet some dues continued to be demanded and could still be a considerable burden on the peasant economy and its seasonal work rhythm, especially when labour services were demanded in springtime, during harvesting in summer, or other peak times for agricultural work.

Most of the dues paid to the lords of the manor, personal lords and the judicial authorities of the thirteenth century were, however, payable in kind or in money. In the face of the unbelievable variety of feudal dues such as rents, personal dues, tithes, bailiff charges, merchets and heriots, fees for the use of such monopolies as mills, communal ovens and breweries, and taxes – all of which were recorded in an abundance of different terms and phrases – it is extremely difficult to arrive at exact figures on the actual burden on the peasants as a whole.[50] Nevertheless, it is possible to calculate the total burden on individual holdings if a principal burden is focused upon; then the remaining dues can at least be estimated in approximation. As far as the Rhineland and the Moselle region were concerned, K. Lamprecht reported that peasant dues in the high Middle Ages amounted to about a third of the gross proceeds from the grain produced by peasant tenants.[51] A good survey on the size and forms of peasant dues can also be gathered from subcontracts delineating in great detail the burdens and payments of tenants and lessors. In the thirteenth century, large grain farms were often let to peasants against the payment of a third or half of the gross proceeds of their grain output. In those cases where it was agreed that half the gross proceeds were to be paid, it was usually the manor which supplied the seed and supported its tenants with subsidies for harvesting and fertilizer. M. Postan has estimated that, as far as the English peasant economy was concerned, the dependent peasantry often had to hand over up to 50 per cent of their gross proceeds. This seems to indicate that in the high Middle Ages peasants in England had to cope with a higher burden of dues than in Germany, for example.[52]

The economic balance of the peasant economy

W. Abel's detailed calculations of costs, yields and sundry burdens on both grain and stock-producing farm types, as well as of the total budget of landholdings in the high Middle Ages, reveal the heavy burden of the feudal system on the peasant economy.[53] Dues of about a third of the grain harvest consumed almost all of the surplus produced by a medium-

Figure 23 Haymaking (Flanders)
Miniature by Simon Bening (1483–1561), seasonal picture for July

sized holding on top of what its occupiers needed themselves for sustenance. Conservative estimates on gross yields from agriculture, gardening and other branches of the peasant economy show clearly that many holdings retained close to nothing to store or save after deductions for the various rents and dues, as well as what was needed simply for subsistence. Most of the farms had to put up with considerable feudal rents, so that owing to the low productivity of agriculture, the majority of peasants had no chance to produce any profits, no matter how good harvests had been. Bad harvests, however, drove many peasants into precarious circumstances. If low yields coincided with more bad luck, such as cattle plagues, epidemics or warfare, large parts of the medieval peasantry were likely to suffer severely.

In dealing with the economic situation of the rural population, due attention must, none the less, be paid to the various strata among the peasantry of the high Middle Ages. Judgements on the precarious condition of the peasant refer primarily to the cottagers, who saw a frightening increase in their numbers in many regions, especially towards the end of the high Middle Ages. The peasants with larger holdings, by contrast, enjoyed better opportunities for trade on local markets, as a result of which they had better incomes than ever before. Furthermore, it is extremely difficult to produce precise calculations of the incomes and yields of these types of family economies, because their main interest lay in subsistence farming. The widely held view that 'most peasants had hardly enough to live on' proves under close scrutiny to be far too sweeping and does not help to draw an accurate picture of the peasantry in the feudal society of the high Middle Ages.

In retrospect, W. Abel was certainly right in stating that most peasant households were constricted by harsh burdens during the high Middle Ages and that the peasant economy as a whole teetered 'on the precipice'.[54] The slightest strain put its delicate balance at risk, and this is precisely what happened in the late Middle Ages as a consequence of the agrarian crisis.[55] The unfolding of a more complex trade economy helped open the hitherto almost autarkic peasant economy to new trends in commerce and trade as well as to the urban market. Increasing exchange in money meant that, in addition to the payment of taxes and other dues, peasant incomes also had to cover the ever increasing expenses for such essential agricultural implements as ploughs and scythes. Although it varied according to the region, the nature of production, and the size of the individual holdings, the growing dependence on the market made the peasant economy much more vulnerable to fluctuations of the economy as a whole. This development proved to be detrimental, particularly in the wake of the economic crisis in the late Middle Ages. However, the degree of peasant dependence on the market should not be exaggerated. The family economy was still basically self-sufficient, as far as the production of foodstuffs, raw materials and even utensils was concerned. The desire to produce for and profit from the market, however, was certainly not the principal economic goal of the peasant family, which was rather to produce enough for its own immediate needs and pay the dues demanded by its lord.

PART IV

SOCIAL PATTERNS, 1000–1400

9

NEIGHBOURHOOD AND VILLAGE COMMUNITY

The Markgenossenschaft: origin of the village community

Many regional studies associate the village and its everyday life with highly emotive values such as security and a communal spirit, and contrast these with the anonymity and isolation of modern urban life. The changes which affected the city in the course of the Industrial Revolution, and the miserable condition of the working class that came with it, revealed the full scope of the urban and social crisis in the nineteenth century – a development which was soon critically portrayed in innumerable monographs on the city as well as in studies on popular culture. The spectre of the city, chaotic and filled with a threatening proletariat, was contrasted with the allegedly unimpaired social ties within the village. Literature and social studies presented their readers with a nightmarish view of the city which was diametrically opposed to what seemed to be the idyllic and untainted historical development of the village.[1] W. H. Riehl, for example, who during the nineteenth century was one of the leading figures in the study of German popular culture, characterized modern city life as follows:

> The modern city, no matter what its actual size, annihilates the unique character of traditional urban life in Germany and can be regarded as the water on the brain of modern civilization. It is no secret that water on the brain is often accompanied by precocious and highly excitable emotions. Yet no one would want to infer from this observation that intelligence and the ability to survive increase with the amount of water on the brain.[2]

Riehl's view of the rural community was markedly different:

> The common people [*Volk*] can only know and conceive the state through the image of the village community [*die ländliche Gemeinde*]. For the majority of the peasantry, political sense is first of all communal sense . . .

The community is not merely a political, but primarily a social body. The mutuality of work, occupation and settlement lies at the heart of communal life, and it is only through the state that communal life receives a secondary political form.[3]

Is it true that the village was a place of unbroken tradition, solidarity and security? Does the idyllic picture of the village and its community, which specialists in popular culture (*Volkskunde*) and regional writers drew especially in nineteenth-century Germany, really conform to the historical reality of the traditional village? Or did this view of the native village represent rather an immediate reflection of the crisis which affected the village and the peasant world in face of radical economic and political changes? In spite of the opinion of such eminent men as Riehl and Ganghofer, since the mid-nineteenth century the village has in fact also been affected by the unaccustomed and by innovation which have altered its traditional structure completely.[4] The structural change within the village was accompanied by a wave of emotionally stereotyped village stories and regional novels. The contradictions and breaks with the past, which affected the village just as relentlessly as the city, were usually concealed, so that a superficial spectator was led to believe in what appeared to be the idyll of a golden past.

Yet even the medieval village was not a wholesome world exclusively characterized by communal sense and harmony. Detailed studies of the social, economic, cultural and political development of the medieval village suggest that the traditional village community was above all a social amalgamation of peasants in which all sought to solve everyday problems by forms of co-operation and on which the destiny of each individual depended. This functional interdependence of the peasants within the village lies at the heart of traditional village organization. The unique character of life in the medieval village was in particular formed by the varied needs of mutually dependent producers in the village. Important aspects of peasant life were administered by the co-operative to allow the optimum use of farmland and forest. 'The village community had absolutely nothing to do with emotions, and it had little to do with what we now call a community [*Gemeinschaft*]; it was much more a specifically structured form of exchange under certain economic conditions.'[5]

As demonstrated above,[6] even the traditional village and the rural community were not primordial forms of social organization. After all, the village community had been influenced by many factors in its development and took its characteristic shape between the eleventh and the fourteenth centuries. As opposed to the chapter on changes in the village which focused on settlement history and economic factors related to the formation of the European village, this section takes a close look at the legal, social and political aspects involved in its development. The rise and composition of the rural commune will be discussed along with issues related to the demarcation between the peasants as a community of neighbours (*Nachbarschaft*), a village co-operative (*Dorfgenossenschaft*) and a village community (*Dorfgemeinde*). Different forms of communities as well as their administration and office holders will also be considered. Regional differences and divergences in time will be taken into account as far as possible without blurring the common elements in the development of the rural community in Europe or the overall picture of the medieval village.

For the discussion of these issues it is important to know that in the nineteenth century legal historians argued that the late medieval village, characterized by its system of compulsory crop rotation and common lands, originated in the so-called Germanic mark association (*Markgenossenschaft*).[7] Eventually these arguments became obsolete as the concept of the 'Germanic mark community' was abandoned by most historians. It was criticized and discredited especially by specialists in settlement and economic history who emphasized the importance of local settlement and the agrarian origins of the medieval village.[8] According to the old theory, large co-operatives of free mark communities formed the beginnings of the village. This research simply did not consider the idea of a gradual development of the village community from small groups of families and neighbours who eventually formed larger co-operatives. However, today it is now known that the typical peasant settlements of the early Middle Ages were hamlets, groups of farmsteads and small villages. They were loosely joined in neighbourly co-operatives which assisted the common life of several peasant families living together in one settlement in performing the various tasks and needs which were much easier to cope with as a co-operative. These communal responsibilities included the laying out of paths and fences, the marking of village boundaries, negotiations on the setting up of farmsteads and fields, and the use of communal facilities such as wells and baking-ovens. The continual struggle with the local manorial lord possessing land in the village also contributed to the evolution of the village from village association to village commune. K. S. Bader was certainly right in pointing out that the formation of the village community was much stronger when the various rights of lordship were entangled and there was competition and conflict among different lords over rights, land tenure, servile tenants and the division of jurisdiction.[9]

Now we must ask how the relation between village associations and village communes as corporate bodies can be described, and how these two aspects of peasant organisation can be distinguished from each other.[10] The historical sources, which tend to use terms such as *genossame*, *gebursame*, or *universitas rusticorum* for the village association as opposed to *gemein*, *gemeinde* or *communitas villae* for the village commune, often confuse the two concepts, as a result of which it is not easy to keep the concepts separate in the study of the sources. Still one

Figure 24 Late medieval village enclosed by village boundary fence
From a Swiss chronicle by Johannes Stumpf

can detect a gradual change from peasants simply residing next to one another to peasants sharing a life and sharing economic activities as they deliberate together or represent themselves communally to the outside world. From their early undeveloped forms, the association and co-operation of neighbours eventually evolved into the village community as a body politic; this process lasted from the high to the late Middle Ages until the village community finally emerged as a distinct legal and administrative association. In the sources, however, this development is often only discernible underneath what was still expressed in the traditional neighbourly and manorial terminology. According to a strictly legal point of view, then, the term village association applies to neighbourly co-operation, especially in regard to use of the village commons. On the other hand one may only speak of a village commune when the villagers began to exercise their rights 'to justify and exert its authority in matters transcending co-operative issues'.[11]

Owing to the great variety of different types of settlement and political as well as social conditions, neither the origins nor the actual forms of rural communities in Europe can be subsumed under a single formula. This was also the reason why it is difficult to make universally valid statements about the form and development of the various types of rural communes. In any case, rural communes did not arise from a single root but were subject to conflicting influences over a long period of historical development.[12] Most European regions saw the formation of the village commune during the high and late Middle Ages, but there is evidence that in some places this process was completed only in early modern times. Obvious temporal differences in the development of rural communes, in addition to the differences in their respective functional structures, must account for the historical and regional variety of village formation in Europe during the Middle Ages.

Modern approaches to the development of the rural community

In particular the views of F. Steinbach,[13] A. Dopsch and K. S. Bader on the origins of the medieval village community have had a lasting impact on later studies of the legal history of village communities. F. Steinbach saw the origin of the village community in the decentralized jurisdictional districts of that time: 'The rural community developed as communal administration and self-government split from the existing jurisdictional districts, either within the confines of the same district or through the formation of a subdivision of the jurisdictional district'.[14] A. Dopsch, by contrast, regarded the *familia*, or early medieval band of dependents of the manor (*Hofgenossenschaft*) as the root of the village community and its legal and administrative organization.[15] According to his view, the *familia* was first of all an economic and legal co-operative, and this was why it served as a model for the formation of the village community. Within the village the members of the *familia* continued to exercise their traditional rights as they had under the manorial lord, something easily done since the village commune had many of the same functions.

Nevertheless, the study of the village in general and the study of the village as a legal and administrative community has been stimulated particularly by the legal historian K. S. Bader, who has concentrated on the development of the village in south-western Germany rather than producing yet another survey of the various forms of constitutional organization throughout the country.[16] He has rejected Dopsch's views by stressing that instances were rare in which the manorial *familia* in fact formed the original cell of village organization. By singling out villages with more than one feudal lord, Bader has made it clear that in his opinion the legal relations on the manor did not serve as a model for the development of the village community. To him, the origins of the village community as a legal and administrative body are much more complex and cannot be found solely in the manorial system.[17] Steinbach's conclusions were also rejected, mainly because his research was limited to the Rhineland, which Bader argued was not at all typical of the development of the village, and also because the connections with earlier jurisdictional districts were negligible among the village communes of south-western Germany studied by Bader. 'The formation of the village community in the region we investigated was not influenced by institutions such as the Frankish hundred. It was much more tied to later constitutional developments, primarily the jurisdiction of the advocate [*Vogtei*].'[18]

In cases where the jurisdiction of advocates was limited to the village itself, a type of village rule emerged which was based on *Zwing und Bann* (essentially lower jurisdictional rights), as well as law and order. This transformed advocacy evolved jurisdictional rights which were more powerful than those of the *familia* and more effective in creating a village commune. Bader further argued that the formation of the village as a legal and administrative body was subject to a number of forces and influences, such as neighbourly, manorial, and lordly jurisdictional elements which gradually brought together the villagers into a true village community.[19]

The diverging views on the development of the village community as illustrated by the three German researchers have shown that the medieval village had more than just one root. Considering the variety of forms and legal origins of the village, it seems appropriate to outline the principal issues involved in this process. Of particular importance, despite the conflicting theories on the formation of the village community, is the fact that the foundations for the emergence of the rural community were primarily laid during the settlement period. Hence it is necessary to make a clear distinction between the older settlements, newly developed territories, and regions in which single farms or villages predominated.[20] There can be no doubt that in older settlements the evolution of the village community was indeed closely related to that of the traditional manor. In many of the older villages, the compulsory field systems and the use of common lands were supervised by a bailiff (*Meier*), and the village court met on the main farm of the feudal lord. Such links between the manor and the *familia* cannot be found in the clearance settlements of the high Middle Ages; hence this factor did not come into play in the formation of the village community in these areas. By contrast with the villages in the older settled lands, the newly founded villages both east and the west of the Rivers Elbe and Saale were much less marked in their layout by the communal use of the land. There were even colonial settlements, such as forest villages with long strips of farmland extending behind each house (*Waldhufendörfer*), which did not have village commons. It should also be borne in mind that some of the older villages adopted the advanced three-field system only in the late Middle Ages, so that the village community which emerged in the high Middle Ages was not modelled on established peasant co-operation concerned with communal agricultural practices.

As opposed to the village in south-western Germany which saw the gradual emergence of jurisdiction under the advocates (*Vögte*), the colonial villages to the east of central Germany had the status of jurisdictional communities from the time of their establishment. It seems that the element of jurisdictional lordship was also much more important for the development of villages as legal and administrative bodies in such areas as Westphalia or the Rhineland than elsewhere. Another important stimulus for the emergence of village communities were the guilds, whose influence is still discernible today in folk customs.[21] This factor in the history of the village community must be duly considered, particularly for the widely spread settlements of north-western Germany where the communities consisted in the main of single farms. These communities in fact bore close resemblance to guilds.

The emergence of the village as a complex process

On the whole, the formation of the village community was a complex process influenced by the interaction of both lordship and community. It produced a specific structure of executive authority with manorial and co-operative traits. The origins of this legal and administrative entity go back as far as the early Middle Ages when the Frankish rulers reorganized the development of the country on a larger scale, in part by creating co-operative judical, military and parish institutions for the settled inhabitants. The hundreds and similar institutions from the times of Frankish rule (*Zentene, Huntare*) can be regarded as an early stage in the formation of the village community in its constitutional aspects, although as legal and administrative bodies villages were by no means fully developed in Germany before the twelfth century.[22] Fully-fledged rural communes, however, must be carefully distinguished from the various forms of neighbourhoods and communal co-operatives. In addition to the various economic, legal and political functions of village communities the maintenance of the public peace is especially noteworthy. The local observance of justice, the call for neighbourly help as well as the maintenance of territorial regulations, and more specifically apprehension of criminals and bringing them before the courts were in many regions the responsibilities of medieval village communities.[23] The degree of co-operative self-determination among the peasantry nevertheless depended on how much they actually took their affairs, such as self-protection, into their own hands.

The use of the term 'rural community' should imply a certain awareness of its specific character, because particularly in its German rendition as *Landgemeinde* it is primarily derived from modern legal jargon; it is not found in medieval sources. In any case, it is difficult to use a modern term like *Landgemeinde* to describe conditions in the Middle Ages, because it refers specifically to a historically unique type of rural body politic created by a radically different type of authority in the nineteenth century, which furnished the *Landgemeinde* with all those competences in lower communal administration provided by the new laws of that time.[24] The modern rural district, then, included many villages, which was not the case in the Middle Ages when the village was a legal district separate from the surrounding territory. Furthermore, not only medieval villages were characterized by their own legal competence, but so were neighbourhoods and various other types of peasant associations. In certain regions a number of villages would form a large jurisdictional community, as for example in the mountain valleys of southern Germany, where the local administration had been endowed with special rights and privileges by the territorial prince.

In order to get a fuller understanding of the process of the formation of the village community, changes in settlement patterns and other agrarian structures must be considered along with the various forms of land development, the innovations in the agrarian economy which were caused by the increase in grain production and cropping in general, as well as the transition from the traditional *Fronhof* system to a manorial system based on rent. Special heed in this context should be paid not merely to the changes in the agrarian economy, the consolidation of peasant property rights, or the levelling of differences in legal status among the various peasant groups, but also to the increasing territorialization of political rule and the emergence of various forms of local rule.[25] The formation of territories was a process which progressed continually throughout the twelfth and thirteenth centuries. It already bore the traits of what were to become the territorial principalities in the late Middle Ages. On the lower level of political rule, the high Middle Ages saw the emergence of small-scale territories which in many instances encompassed only a single village or a motley assemblage of settlements. Within these small territories, however, the lords did not hesitate to defend their privileges by force. The descriptive formula for these manorial rights and competences in south-western Germany, which were often entrusted to the village authorities in later centuries, was *Zwing und Bann*, meaning the right 'to command and prohibit' within the bounds of the village; this formula became the basic concept of village lordship.[26] The most important institution of local rule was the village court, and one of its main functions was to ensure that village laws were obeyed.

With the emergence of such small lordships, the territory of a village came to represent the smallest unit of local political power. In this context, the village was not only a communal but also a lordly entity. This double function is reflected in a number of institutions and offices in the village. In some villages in south-western Germany, the *Schultheiss* or village mayor was the representative of the lord and at the same time an agent of the village community. Lordship and co-operative self-administration often went hand in hand within the realm of rural communities, and in many instances they influenced each other.

Therefore the extent of peasant rights in the village was determined by both communal forces and the actual strength of the village lord.

The various types of village and rural communities

Owing to the various conditions in settlement and economy, the huge social and cultural differences and the considerable divergence in the types of lordship, the formation of the rural commune took many shapes in the various regions and produced distinct types of rural community.[27] The village community became particularly important during the high and late Middle Ages in Swabia and Franconia, where it often provided the basis for the formation of local principalities. In Bavaria and Austria, by contrast, rural communities were apparently far less important. Although village courts were a common phenomenon in Bavaria, they were often the achievement of later centuries. It was only in the fifteenth century that they were granted the status of *Hofmarken*, yet this did not do much to augment their influence since it gave them immunity solely against claims by the district judge. The village communities in the Tyrol, which do not appear in the sources earlier than the twelfth century, were distinguished by their close relation with the sovereign, who used them as a counterbalance against the ambitious nobility. There is evidence for free peasants under the special patronage of the count of the Tyrol, who had a far-reaching autonomy in their native villages. In the neighbouring territory of the archbishops of Salzburg the emergence of rural communities is particularly interesting. From the thirteenth century on the larger regional courts were also jurisdictional communities. The latter were subdivided into districts of various sizes with different names which were mainly concerned with the military organization of the district courts. The relative importance of the jurisdictional communities of Salzburg lay in the fact that they were responsible for local conscription, and this may well be the reason why they took part in the meetings of the *Landtag* or diet in the late Middle Ages. Another factor favouring the formation of regional communes in Salzburg was its geography; the extremely mountainous countryside was only sparsely populated and had many tiny settlements between wide stretches of uninhabited mountain slopes.

North-west Germany was characterized by a form of rural community called *Bauerschaft*. (In other areas it was called *Burschaft*; the modern German form is *Bauernschaft*). Again a distinction must be made between areas where actual villages prevailed and those which were characterized by single farmsteads. In the first case, village communities were, of course, much more economic co-operatives than in the second where there was little need for compulsory rotation systems and the use of collectively held land. It was here that the local peasantry formed the

Bauerschaft (peasant group) under the supervision of a peasant master
and a peasant judge. Its predecessor was a loose form of neighbourhood
co-operation. Their members had to be holders of full-size holdings and
usually farmed the oldest fields of the developed farmland in the area. The
peasant court (*Burgericht*), known since the twelfth century, heard only
cases concerning disputes between neighbours and not concerning
conveyances of land. Another communal institution in such areas was the
Mark whose members were usually the holders of full-size peasant farms.
Neither materially nor personally did the *mark* have anything to do with
the *Burschaft*. The owners of full-size peasant farmsteads consequently
belonged to the *Burschaft*, the *mark*, and certain lordships with their
respective courts.

In the area between the Rivers Weser and Elbe it was the parish which
served as a juridical unit. The *Bauerschaft* in these areas was mainly an
organization concerned with feuds and defence, and the lowest level unit in
military levies. The free peasants, who could be found living in great
numbers in the marshes along the North Sea coast and its rivers, had a legal
position similar to that of the inhabitants of clearance settlements in
woodlands, for both groups had been awarded considerable rights and
autonomy for their development of such hitherto unpopulated territories.
In Frisia it was the hundred, which was identical with the parish, which
provided the basis for the formation of the village community. As
everywhere along the North Sea coast, the struggle with the sea had a great
impact on this process. The land had to be drained for farming, and it had to
be secured with dikes against exceptionally high tides and other assaults
from the sea. Political powers like the counts of Flanders helped
considerably to promote peasant land reclamation in a systematic manner,
and they used their influence to extend their territories by means of
embankments and institutional regulations.[28] The Dutch, who were well
acquainted with the most advanced techniques of dike-building as well as
the drainage of low-level farmland, were soon much consulted experts for
similar measures along the German and the Danish North Sea coast as well
as on the banks of the lower Weser and Elbe rivers.[29] The law of the Dutch
settlements in these areas served for centuries as a model for the
establishment of a great number of free village communities in the north of
Germany which were essentially marked by a large degree of self-
administration and a far-reaching autonomy.

In the colonial territories in the east of Germany,[30] the formation of
village communities as political bodies was largely influenced by legal
conditions imported from their native countries, particularly the Low
Countries and Flanders. Fully developed village communities are known
in these regions from the twelfth century; as co-operatives and legally
responsible associations, they organized the daily life of all their members
and helped to maintain peace by enforcing law and order on everyone
living within the boundaries of the village. In this context it is interesting

Figure 25 The foundation of a clearance village. The lord of the manor
presents a charter granting heritable rental terms to the peasant master
From the illuminated manuscript of the Saxon Code at Heidelberg (fourteenth
century)

to note that the office of *Schulze* or village mayor, which was
characteristic of many clearance settlements, seems to have been of Dutch
origin. Towards the end of the Middle Ages and in early modern times,
however, the position of the village mayor and of the rural community in
general deteriorated even in the lands east of the Elbe and Saale where
during the high Middle Ages the local communities had been especially
successful in self administration. The decline of their power and
independence was a repercussion of the development of a special form of
manorial system with extensive demesne farming (*Gutsherrschaft*) in late
medieval and early modern times.

The development of rural communes with their own legal and
administrative authority followed to some degree the same pattern in the
rest of Europe. In the Mediterranean, the legacy of the Roman Empire
was reflected in a number of typically Roman-influenced constitutional
forms and public institutions. Italy became increasingly divided between
the Lombard influences in the northern and central parts of the country
and the Byzantine, and later Norman, influences in the south.[31] In the
north of the country, rural communities were often under pressure from
the expanding urban communes which acted systematically in an attempt
to create regional territories of their own and forced the neighbouring
rural communities into dependency upon them. The city-states for the
most part respected the wishes of the local communities to preserve their
self-administration, but with three exceptions. Rural communities were
obliged to supply active military aid against any enemy of the city, to
reserve their products and their personnel for economic exchanges with

the city, and to accept the jurisdictional superiority of the city court. This explains why villages had statutes of their own which served as guidelines for the independent administration of their social and political life. Country statutes of this kind were known all over Italy during the thirteenth century and reflected the economic, social and legal peculiarities of everyday life in these rural communities.

The extent to which Roman influences affected the regions of France varied in part according to their political history. The Saracens brought considerable destruction to the south while the Franconians left their imprint on the rural constitution of the north with institutions and social conventions of Germanic origin. In central France, by contrast, which had been least affected by the post-Roman changes, many dependent peasants achieved a greater degree of independence from their lords. This did not, however, result in the formation of autonomous village communities, for there was a substantial preservation of lordly authority. We first hear of the rights of a peasant settlement in 1182 with the *loi de Beaumont*, which guaranteed communal self-administration including the election of the holders of judicial and administrative offices; thus here we see the genuine development of the village as a body politic.[32] The origin of the *loi de Beaumont* lies in the privilege which was given to the newly founded village of Beaumont south of Verdun by the archbishop of Reims in the year 1182, whereby Beaumont became a 'liberated' village. Thereafter more than 500 villages in the border regions between France and Germany were granted the rights of Beaumont, fifty of which were in German-speaking areas. At the same time more than 200 villages in the regions between the Rivers Rhine and Meuse were granted the privileged status of a *Freiheit* or a *Tal*, or they were allowed village laws modelled after the city laws of Frankfurt.[33] According to the laws of Beaumont, these liberated villages had the right to elect the village head and the jurors at their own discretion; in contrast, under the city laws of Frankfurt both the village court and administration were presided over by a *Schultheiss* or village mayor chosen by the village lord.

This movement towards the franchise of villages started in the north-east of France and combined urban and rural elements. It was an attempt to clarify the legal position of rural communities which had often been the victims of conflicting legal norms. This had led to a great deal of legal insecurity and long-term litigation. The liberation of villages was part of the overall liberation of communities in towns as well as smaller rural settlements during the high Middle Ages,[34] all of which gave peasants much better chances to improve their social, legal and economic positions. At a time when many peasants sought a less restricted life in clearance settlements or found better living and working conditions in the towns, many lords found themselves under pressure to grant the villages more rights if they did not want to lose their tenants. Enfranchised villages (those with a far-reaching degree of self-administration) could be found particularly in the diocese of Verdun, the county of Luxemburg, the Moselle region, and most of all in the Rhineland and some of its neighbouring areas.

The emergence of 'liberated' villages was part of a development characterized by a partial assimilation of the town and the country during the high Middle Ages which has even left its traces on the outward appearance of many villages. Like towns and castles, villages at that time were fortified with walls, especially those villages which lay in strategically important areas or in border regions; for additional defences increased the military strength of the nearby territorial powers and also served to counterbalance the growing power of the towns.[35] The residential area of many villages, particularly in southern Germany, was protected by a wattle-fence or hedge called an *Etter* which surrounded the nucleus of the village and was only interrupted by gates and thoroughfares. Within the villages themselves, fortified churches and churchyards often provided the inhabitants of rural settlements with some protection against raids of various kinds. In times of feuds or warfare peasants used to drive their livestock into the houses or stables adjacent to the churchyard walls, which were the best sites available for defence against hostile forces. The square in the vicinity of the church was the favourite place for festivities and markets, especially for commercial fairs and the annual parish fair. The part of the village inside the village fence was particularly safe, and this is why it was often to become a specially protected legal and military area.[36] It was mainly in southern Germany that the centre of the village had a legally protected status, which sometimes manifested itself in the fact that it became the seat of certain village courts (*Ettergerichte*).

The oral tradition of the law and village laws

Before analysing the legal and administrative structure of rural communities and their competences, it is necessary to comment briefly on village customals or *Weistümer*, which are the main sources for the study of the legal constitution of the medieval village. Diverging views have been held concerning both the nature and the origin of these sources. The principal difficulty lies in the question of what particular circumstances gave rise to such village customals. Some, like Jacob Grimm and his followers, argued that the customals were a late echo of the traditional common laws of the peasantry. A different stand was taken by researchers who thought that the lords had ordered the customals to be drawn up. Consequently it was particularly manorial interests which stood behind the village customals of the Middle Ages.[37] The *Weistümer*, however, can by no means be regarded as testimonies which allow a genuine insight into the legal norms of early Germanic times. Although some of them are phrased in an admittedly archaic legal jargon, they cannot be taken as either echoes of an autonomous communal life of the peasantry, or as the sole product of manorial initiative. The reason for this is that although the lords of the manor or the village tried to influence the regulations which were recorded in the customals, it was essentially the legally informed villagers, that is the peasants of the particular village or a larger jurisdictional district, who determined their contents. Hence in a sense the village customals came out of the womb of the village community or the neighbourhood. Yet even if they 'spoke the laws' the villagers could not alone determine their contents. In fact the manorial lord and the village community shared in their composition. The two parties virtually met on the level of the village in order to 'find' the village customs. Moreover, it was in accord with venerable practices that peasants were the possessors of oral tradition including village customs, although the manorial lord often took the first step towards their actual recording.

Weistümer and other village laws appeared under very different names in various regions of Europe. They were called *Dinghofrodeln* in the upper Rhine valley, *Öffnungen* in Switzerland, *Ehaftrechte* in Bavaria, and *Taidinge* or *Banntaidinge* in Austria. The term *Weistum* itself was mainly used in the Rhine and Moselle area, as well as the extreme south-west of Germany, in Austria and in Switzerland. In the north and east of Germany, by contrast, *Weistümer* are comparatively infrequent or in many places not found at all. The reasons for this uneven occurrence are not clear, although there is an interesting congruity between their appearance and that of areas with well developed village communities. Areas in which great numbers of *Weistümer* are formed, such as the south-west of Germany, were also marked by a high village density and highly developed communal life during the late Middle Ages. Moreover, the German south-west was also the main arena of the Great Peasants' War of 1525 – a coincidence which can hardly be purely accidental. Nevertheless, only a small proportion of the surviving customals date back to the twelfth and thirteenth centuries during the most important phase of the formation of rural communities. Most of them were drawn up in the late Middle Ages.[38]

The neighbourhood as a peasant community

A good starting-point for a discussion of the basic social structure of the medieval village community is a brief analysis of life and society in the rural neighbourhood. This is because the neighbourhood was the very basis for the development of communal life among the peasantry, and even in the fully developed village community of the late Middle Ages continued to be one of the cardinal pillars of peasant life.[39] Varying between areas with a high density of villages or a predominance of single settlements, and according to the extent to which social contacts had already developed, the peasant neighbourhood emerged from informal coexistence into regulated modes of co-operative labour and neighbourly assistance. Even the English word 'neighbour', or its German equivalent *Nachbar*, ultimately stems from the root *bur* signifying 'house', which means that the term 'neighbour' originally referred to a 'fellow lodger', and only later to what we mean by neighbour and fellow citizen.[40] The relation to the farmhouse was thus essential for the 'neighbour' who was a fully entitled proprietor of a house and hearth. 'House' meant more than a mere dwelling and a roof – it meant family in a larger sense. In the early days of rural settlement when peasants lived in groups of farmsteads or hamlets, the co-operative elements worked to keep individualistic attitudes among families to a minimum. The coexisting families and various members of large households were forced to adopt a communal life-style in order to secure the optimum use of the farmland for the benefit of the community as a whole. The basic human need for help and protection lay at the heart of the continous development of neighbourly ties and relationships which, as far as peasant communities were concerned, flourished particularly in the high and late Middle Ages. At first, the term 'neighbourhood' referred exclusively to a group of people at a given place. In time, however, it developed a new connotation which characterized the relationships and the attitudes among neighbours, which is why people still talk of 'good' as opposed to 'bad' neighbours.

An interesting source for the study of neighbourly relationships in the village of the high Middle Ages is the *Sachsenspiegel* of the first half of the thirteenth century, which describes the farmyard and garden of the peasant as being enclosed by a fence. In any case, peasants who lived in villages were advised to fence in their gardens for their own good as well as that of their neighbours.[41] Baking-ovens, privies and pigsties should be 3 feet from the fence, and branches of trees not allowed to reach over the fence into the neighbour's property if this caused damage to the neighbour (*Sinir bowmezelgen sollen obir den zun nicht gen sime nackebure zu schaden*)[42] – cf. figure 26. If hops sent forth their tendrils over the fence, the owner of the plant was obliged to pull the tendrils back on to his side, and what he managed to pull over was his, and what was left torn off on the other side was the lawful property of the neighbour.[43] In the villages of eastern Saxony, which the author of the *Sachsenspiegel* had in mind, the farms lay close to one another, and because of this there was often cause for quarrel. Apart from ovens and pigsties having to be built at a certain distance from fences, peasants were also advised to keep an eye on their oven and other fires to prevent embers from flying into the neighbouring plot. In addition, everyone was obliged to prevent damage to the neighbour from negligence. Whoever shot or threw something at birds, for instance, had to make sure that in doing so he or she would not hurt either humans or livestock.[44]

In some village laws and regulations mention was made of certain

Figure 26 Setting the territorial boundary between neighbours. Pigsties, privy
and baking-oven had to be at least 3 feet away from the fence; cutting branches
jutting over from the neighbour's land was permitted
From the illuminated manuscript of the Saxon Code at Heidelberg (fourteenth century)

neighbourly duties, such as the obligation to help in emergencies and on
such occasions as weddings, births and deaths.[45] Among the prime
neighbourly duties which were related to the household itself was the
obligation to help in house-building. It was common practice almost
everywhere that neighbours assisted one another as much as they possibly
could with the construction of new houses, which at that time were
mostly built by peasants themselves. In agricultural matters, by contrast,
the commitment to neighbourly help was subject to great variation
between different neighbourhoods. In many villages it was normal

practice to lend out draught-animals and agricultural implements, although at harvest-time assistance was asked for only in real need or when someone fell sick. Fire-fighting was also one of the most important neighbourly duties, and indeed everyone was obliged to help with putting out fires. Peasant families who came to be homeless after a fire were put up by their neighbours, and stock was distributed between their stables and fed as long as possible.

Births, christenings, weddings and deaths were the principal occasions in the Middle Ages when peasants required the help of their neighbours. Childbirth was supervised by midwives with the assistance of female neighbours who also helped in the household during the first days after the actual birth and during the preparations for the baptismal festivities.[46] The neighbourly obligation both to give practical help and to share in celebrations came together especially at weddings. In many regions, these were genuine celebrations of neighbourliness because of the local customs and habits that went with them. Many village laws and rules of the late Middle Ages included regulations for peasant weddings and the 'excesses' which they produced. It seems that most peasant weddings were attended by the entire neighbourhood, which also participated in the extensive celebrations and banquets. These could last for days, as shown in the wedding feast in Heinrich Wittenweiler's *Der Ring*.[47] Strict regulations apparently applied to deaths and funerals from very early times. Funeral cortèges and obsequies became central aspects of neighbourly relations in some regions, and neighbourly duties like the preparation of the corpse, the bearing of the coffin and the holding of the funeral banquet followed strict rules.

In many regions, the term 'neighbourhood' was subject to one substantial restriction in the course of the high and late Middle Ages, such as in Holstein where only the holders of a full-size farm or entire holding were considered true neighbours. There a neighbourhood consisted exclusively of such fully entitled 'hidemen' (*Hufner*), while the other inhabitants of the village were not considered neighbours.[48] Towards the end of the late Middle Ages, neighbours were often merely those peasants in a village who had inherited their holding.[49] Consequently the term 'neighbour' was reserved for the occupier of a farm with full rights, which meant that the size and the quality of his holding entitled him to unlimited use of the common pasture land and the common woodlands. Since neighbourhoods tended to set themselves apart, strangers could become members only when they married into the neighbourhood or bought a fully entitled holding. Newcomers gave a house-warming party with beer or wine. In some areas they even had to pay a neighbourhood initiation fee.

The development from the various forms of neighbourly social groupings to village co-operatives and village communes was, as mentioned in earlier chapters, primarily caused by the ever increasing density in settlement and by the economic changes of the time.[50] As far as form and intensity were concerned, the growth of groups of farms and hamlets into villages and the emergence of rural communities depended on regional conditions. In some instances, especially in the south-west of Germany, villages attained a remarkable compactness in the course of the high and late Middle Ages. In places where villages flourished, inhabitants had to move closer together – no matter whether they were individuals or entire families. 'The rise in population density was accompanied by an even greater variety of social and legal relations, associations and tensions.'[51] Everyday life in the village required a high degree of consideration on everybody's part, even the sacrifice of interests that were too individualistic to conform to those of the community.

Administration and office-holders in the medieval village

The development of the neighbourhood into the village association in the wake of social aggregation had immediate influence on the village economy and culture. The transition to the three-field system in the high Middle Ages produced a network of social conventions which reached far beyond the limits of neighbourly goodwill into the realm of legal constraint. The advanced three-field system, with its compulsory crop rotation and scattered land parcels, was an important reason for forming a village co-operative – a development which was largely independent of the manor. 'The village co-operative thus became an . . . economic union.'[52] As a result, most of the regulations in village customals and other law codes refer to the economic controversies in peasant everyday life, such as the use of pasture and commons by individual villagers and the maintenance of rules pertaining to the proper use of arable, pasture and woodlands. In addition to these economic phenomena in the village, some of the less obvious cultural, ecclesiastical and political aspects of co-operative life also had their origins in the growing settlement density at that time. These issues are touched upon whenever mention is made of the extension of the village church, the maintenance of the parson,[53] or charity matters such as the responsibility for the sick or poor. Two of the more important police tasks were the maintenance of peace inside and outside the community, as well as the eviction of both beggars and vagrants from other parts of the country. What continued to remain exclusively within the context of the neighbourhood and village co-operative 'was everything pertaining to village customs and rituals during the seasons and on holidays, some of which became institutionalized in forms similar to these in guilds and corporations'.[54] As far as the fully-fledged village community of the high and late Middle Ages was concerned, the village council of all fully entitled members of the village community was the most important organ of peasant administration in the village or parish.[55] It met at least once a year on certain set days. The favourite gathering-point in early times was under the linden tree, in the churchyard or in the village green at the centre of the village; in later times assemblies preferred the village parlour (*Gemeindestube*) or the house of the mayor. Attendence was mandatory for the male members of the community, and wives or children were not allowed to represent them. The main task of the village council consisted in the control of the village budget, the regulation of crop rotation within the framework of the three-field system, the promulgation of the village laws and the election of the village officials.

As a rule, village administration was led by an office-holder who was clearly superior to all others; his title varied from region to region. The commonest titles in the north and the east of Germany were *Schulze* (in medieval Latin *scultetus*) or *Bauermeister* (in medieval German *burmester*); in the south of the country the title was *Schultheiss*, *Ammann*, or *Vogt*. The Thuringian version *Heimbürge* had its origin in the middle Rhine area and in the south-west of Germany. This head of the village council was often appointed by the lord or had at least to be confirmed by him despite the fact that he was chosen by the local peasantry. It is obvious that he had a double function, because he was the 'confidant' of the lord as well as the spokesman of the village community. This explains why the village or territorial lord had a great interest in having a say in his appointment. The duties of the village head included leading the village council, presiding in the village court and acting as chief administrative officer of the village community.

First among the administrative institutions and office-holders appointed by the village council was an assembly, which was named after the number of its members. This appears in the sources, for example as the board of four, five, twelve etc. Since its members had to take an oath to the village council and the lord, they were often called jurors (*iurati* – sworn men). On the whole these were experienced men who took on various tasks within the village, such as the maintenance of village and farmland boundaries, the surveillance of fire regulations, and the control of weights and measures. In addition to these regulatory, police-like functions they were in many cases also members of the jury in the village court.

Depending on the size and location of the villages, there were sometimes a number of lower-level offices with varying names, such as the field-constable (German names included *Bannwart*, *Flurschütz* and *Flurhai*), who had to monitor the keeping of farmland as well as regulations of the commons; the forester (*Forstwart*, *Förster*, *Waldschütz*) for the same task within the woodlands of the community; the surveyor (*Untergänger*), who surveyed boundaries and reported on boundary violations; and the beadle (*Büttel*) who had to go on errands on behalf of the village council, the village bailiff, or the board of four etc. Another office which is noteworthy is that of the village herdsman. This position grew in importance as a consequence of the development of the village and its livestock, which in turn caused the introduction of special day or night herdsmen, cowherds, shepherds and swineherds. In some places, however, village communities only appointed one chief herdsman who was himself responsible to the community for the activities of the men he chose to employ.

It is extremely difficult to produce universally valid descriptions of the competence of the village court in the Middle Ages because jurisdictional matters were subject to much variation at that time. The members of the village court – judge, jurors and sentencers – were in some villages elected by the community, while in others they were appointed through a complicated system of co-operation between the manor and the village community. In areas where courts of jurors were used, the local court consisted mostly of a board of twelve jurors presided over by the village mayor as the head of the court. Village courts were entitled to deal with minor civil and criminal suits which fell under the jurisdiction of the local village authorities, such as disturbing the peace, physical injuries, or the violation of property rights by ploughing or mowing someone else's land. Among the administrative functions of the village court were the division of landholdings and the co-operation of its staff in the compilation of manorial land registers and rentals (*Urbare* and *Zinsbücher*).

Village courts naturally varied greatly in the authority they enjoyed to perform certain tasks and in their degree of self-government. Hence it is difficult to define clearly both the historical and the geographical development of the fully-fledged village commune throughout central Europe as a whole. Therefore, to conclude this discussion of the village commune, it seems worthwhile to take a close and more comprehensive look at the structure of a single village type, taking as an example the villages in south-eastern Saxony in the middle of the thirteenth century. The reliable *Sachsenspiegel*, supported by additional evidence, makes it in fact possible to describe the Eastphalian village commune with remarkable accuracy.[56]

The area between the Harz, a low mountain range towards the north of Germany, and the Rivers Elbe and Saale on the eastern fringes of central Germany was traditionally under the sway of early Saxon constitutional principles. From the high Middle Ages, a type of rural commune developed under the direction of a *Bauermeister* which combined the functions of both a jurisdictional community and a neighbourhood association. At the same time it also fulfilled the various tasks of a parish. Its authority was not limited to the actual village but also included the fields. It administered the commons as well as roads and paths, baking and communal houses, village inns and in some places mills too. The head of this type of rural community was assisted by a village council called *burding* or *burmal*. The *Sachsenspiegel* stated explicitly that the *Bauer-*

meister (peasant master) made decisions in accordance with the majority of the local peasants, and that these decisions could not be overturned by the minority.[57] It follows that the medieval village was a legal entity which could make its own laws. This is shown by many legal actions in which the *Bauermeister* acted on behalf of the commune and was backed by witnesses from among the locals, sometimes even the entire village.

Detailed information on the responsibilities of the *Bauermeister* to both the manor and the village community is also provided by the *Sachsenspiegel*. His function was to be the prime representative of the village in important legal and administrative affairs and in its relations with the outside world. He had to pass the sentences in the three annual sessions of the manorial court, and during the absence of the *Vogt* or bailiff it was his duty to preside over the lower village court. This was the body which judged such cases as minor theft up to 3 shillings in value, the illegal use of weights and measures, slander, bodily injury, debts and inheritance cases, the purchase and exchange of land as well as violations against village and farmland laws. Certain police-like functions were also closely connected with this judicial authority. The *Bauermeister* represented the village whenever someone accused of committing a breach of the peace had taken refuge within its bounds and his pursuers demanded that he be handed over. In manorial court sessions as well as in those of the advocate the *Bauermeister* was obliged to censure various misdeeds and offences which were committed within the boundaries of his village. He or his servant collected part of the manorial dues on behalf of the lord, and he also took care of other matters pertaining to village lordship. Moreover, in later times he was also in charge of the village treasury and the financial accounts of the rural commune.

Apart from the *Bauermeister*, the common herdsman was another important person in the Eastphalian village. His office was different from that of the 'private herdsman', who could only be employed by peasants who owned more than 3 hides of farmland. The unbroken development of village communities in eastern parts of Saxony can be gathered particularly from the fact that these villages had their own meeting and court places, and from the thirteenth century even special assembly halls and courthouses.[58] The German term *Tie*, which was used for such communal meeting places, suggests that this juridical institution had in fact a long tradition in the village. In sum, the Eastphalian village commune of the thirteenth century can safely be regarded as a co-operative which was firmly rooted in the overall structure of the village and its arable land.

It is obvious that economic interests gave it its particular character, but other interests of its inhabitants were almost equally important, such as the administration of justice, or the maintenance of peace. The village commune had considerable authority over its inhabitants as well as over strangers in the village. This power had not been granted from above, but rather had its historical origin from below, and this is why it was so original. Without having been designed by the king or other superiors . . . the village community fulfilled essentially the same tasks in its area as the municipality in the city-commune or the king with his hierarchically structured feudal power in other, higher realms.[59]

PEASANT FAMILY AND KINSHIP

The peasant family: a special type of family?

It is generally assumed that the family is a timeless institution which has always provided society with a stable foundation. Many people see the family primarily as a 'natural' form of social life, an unchanging element in human life. There were times when so much emphasis was placed on the biological aspects of the family that it was almost only biologists who concerned themselves with the family. By contrast, social scientists and historians of the family have recently been at great pains to point out that although the family is indeed strongly influenced by biological factors and therefore a stable element in human society, it has nevertheless changed considerably in the course of history. In fact, it has presented itself in such a great variety of forms that it is certainly wrong to speak of it as an unchanging element of human life.[1] On the contrary, the family is a social phenomenon which in the course of historical development has changed just as much as has its social context. This, of course, also applies to the peasant family which has in particular been regarded as a timeless constant. In response to changes in the state, economy and society in the Middle Ages as well as in later centuries, the structure of peasant families has been transformed just as much as the family structures of other groups in society, such as craftsmen, merchants or the nobility. A process of reciprocal influence can be observed between changes in the family and those in wider social groups.

How much, then, does the structure of the peasant family really differ from that of other social groups and occupations? Are there any features at all which belong exclusively to the peasant family? Sociological research on modern farm families in West Germany after 1950 has shown that even today the constitution of the farm family has retained a number of its traditional peculiarities, including the composition and size of the household, generational structures, and the sheer number and role of its children.[2] As opposed to the modern family which, as a rule, consists of the standard nuclear family, the traditional peasant family was characterized by at least two, but in most cases three generations. In fact, the peasant family was often much larger than other families because it included the unmarried brothers and sisters of the peasant proprietor and distant relatives who also lived on the farm, as well as servants. One of the structural peculiarities of the peasant family is the fact that it is not merely a community of consumers but a basic organizational unit of production. The peasant family is an association for the ownership of property whose agrarian foundation lies at the heart of its existence. This circumstance is responsible for the marked immobility of the peasant family. The needs of farming force the heir to the farm to stay on his father's property and to share it with his wife – who has to give up her residence to live with him. While other families are usually relatively independent in the choice of their residence, young peasant families are what has been termed patrilocal, that is they are virtually attached to the soil of their forefathers. However, as far as patrilocality is concerned, the young couple, but in particular the peasant wife, is at a serious disadvantage in developing her own personality as well as a family style of her own. 'Patrilocality is indeed the most important source of peasant traditionalism and encourages . . . patriarchal authority.'[3] Another characteristic of the peasant family is the social security of the individual within the community of the family. This is because the peasant family is obliged to support those family members who are either too old or unfit for work. This often entails serious conflicts within the family, especially in regard to succession to the holding, which is also the reason why the older generation often delays the transfer of property as long as it possibly can.

The peasant family as the social form of 'the whole house'

Within the German academic community opinions on the characteristics and development of the peasant family have for a long time been decisively influenced by the views of W. H. Riehl, one of the pioneers of family sociology.[4] Riehl came to the following conclusion on the social form of 'the whole house' which he still found functioning in the peasant world of the mid-nineteenth century:

'The whole family' is closely related to 'the whole house'. Unfortunately modern times are merely familiar with 'the whole family' and no longer with 'the whole house'. As friendly and 'cosy' as it is, the term 'the whole house' includes not only the natural family members, but similarly all those voluntary companions and fellow workers in the family who are commonly called domestic servants. In 'the whole house', the blessing of the family also reaches the entire groups of people who are otherwise without a family. As in an adoption, these people are drawn into the family's moral relationships of authority and piety.[5]

Elsewhere, Riehl described the coexistence of three generations in a single domestic community as particularly characteristic of the peasant family: 'The idea of "the whole house" also means that parents and grandparents live in the house of their children after they have retired. Hence people in the country often reserve a room for their parents.'[6]

Does this harmonious, even idyllic picture of the traditional peasant family correspond with the actual conditions in earlier centuries? The basis for Riehl's attention to the family forms of the past was his critical attitude towards the development of German society in the nineteenth century. The changes and crises within the family, society and state in the wake of the Industrial Revolution were in his opinion to be overcome by a revival of the traditional forms of the family and traditional values in general. Riehl believed that a healthier society would result from the restoration of traditional family structures, paternal authority and the traditional norms that he saw in decline in his day. Wishful thinking concerning the reorganization of society from elements of the old order of society blended with his empirical analysis of the historical manifestations of the family.[7] The egoism and individualism of the modern family were contrasted with the alleged unselfishness of the traditional family and its active help for needy family members, the impersonal social relations of the present with the close ties within the family of the past, and the waning of authority with the patriarchical hierarchy of the traditional family. This idealization of the old forms of the family and the modes of dependence that accompanied it, the emphasis on the authority of the father and the dependent status of his wife, served Riehl and other conservatives to underpin their critique of contemporary society. These distorting viewpoints must therefore be disregarded when dealing with the peasant family in the Middle Ages and trying to analyse peasant social forms as unbiasedly as possible.

Terms like 'domestic community' and 'household family' seem to be particularly helpful in characterizing the peasant family in the high Middle Ages. They indicate that the peasant family at that time was primarily a community of producers and consumers – the social form of 'the whole house' which has been examined in its economic aspects in the chapter on the peasant economy of the high Middle Ages.[8] The peasant and his wife presided over the domestic community in their functions as father and mother of the family, by organizing the maintenance of the peasant household and by stipulating the rules of conduct for the everyday life of all of its members. In essence, the peasant household family was less marked by blood relationships than by communal living and labour, and this was why servants had an active part in that family.

As a 'domestic science', medieval economics was in particular concerned with the optimum structure of the large household family and the best way to organize the domestic economy.[9] It dealt with the wide range of human relations and activities in the house, including the relationships between father and mother, parents and children, householder and servants. In addition, the domestic economics of the Middle Ages also described the organization of the household and agricultural tasks. A work on domestic economics by Konrad von Megenberg which was written in the years 1348–52 pondered in its first volume the questions and problems that could arise between father and mother, parents and children, master and servants, and the goods required in domestic production.[10] The medieval writings on domestic housekeeping in this sense, which were succeeded in early modern times by numerous works on the head of the household, thus contained basic advice on the structuring of everyday life in household and family, on home rules and children's education, and on the supervision of servants, as well as general guidance on household management and agriculture.

There can be no doubt that the social form of 'the whole house' was most prominent in the realm of the peasant economy with its unity of production, consumption and generative reproduction in household and family. The head of the house, who directed the medieval peasant household, presided not only over an economic unit in the modern sense but also over his servants and family. He managed the people in the house, its means of production as well as its goods for consumption, and gave directives concerning labour arrangements, cultivation and consumption. The peasant economy, which was in essence based on the unpaid labour of all family members, was thus a social form which encompassed human as well as economic relations. This was because the medieval 'house' was more than a dwelling; it was a place which granted its occupiers legal protection and security, and this is why it was a basic element in the social order of the Middle Ages. The house was a sphere characterized by a unique kind of peace, and in German law this is still reflected by specific regulations against disturbances of the domestic peace (*Hausfriedensbruch*). In a society in which self-help was frequently practised the peasant householder had considerable power over the members of his household. He even held considerable rights to impose corporal punishment. In addition the peasant was privileged in the village community in his function as a householder since the ownership of a house was the fundamental prerequisite for the exertion of the full rights in the neighbourhood as well as the village.

Owing to insufficient evidence it is hardly possible to come to reliable conclusions about the structure of the peasant family in the early days of the Middle Ages. It is extremely difficult to determine to what extent the Germanic tribes at the time of the Teutonic invasions actually consisted of large, complex family types – as has been held for a long time in research. Still, the extensive stock production of the early Middle Ages can be considered an indication for the predominance of extended family structures. Anthropological studies have shown that stock-producing societies and pastoral tribes are in fact distinguished by larger families than societies where arable cultivation prevails.[11] Livestock can easily be multiplied, and extended families facilitate its keeping, especially when the available pastures can only be used collectively.

Influence and significance of kinship

It seems worthwhile to comment briefly on the relationship between family and kinship. As opposed to other social forms in the Middle Ages, such as the house and the family, the size and competences of kindreds are much harder to define. The term 'kinship' is generally used to describe the types of social associations which are based on blood relationship and which are larger than families in the modern sense.[12] For the Germanic tribes, kinship relations were almost as important as the family or the household community. Researchers use the term 'agnatic kinship' for a group of people whose blood relationship is founded on descent in the male line, and hence it is identical with male lineage. In contrast to this clearly defined social formation, cognatic kinship refers to the entirety of blood relationship ties of an individual, including his female relatives. Nineteenth-century historians, who thought that the clan played a dominating role in the life of medieval society, assumed that kindreds were associations under the guidance of a kinship council and a kinship leader. They thought that this was why kindreds held the guardianship over dependent children and widows and even had a criminal law of their own. As far as outside relations were concerned, it was believed that kindreds, which were meant to provide mutual help, functioned mainly in the case of feuds and vendettas, the collection of wergeld, and the swearing of oaths. Moreover, it was assumed that kinships had formed settlement associations under the direction of their elders in the times of the Germanic invasions and that these in later centuries developed into mark co-operatives. Recent studies, however, have completely revised these exaggerated views on the influence and historical significance of kinships. They have also demonstrated that cognatic kinships did not have the legal authority nineteenth-century historians had presumed them to have and that, owing to their highly unstable social composition, it is extremely difficult to regard them as social institutions at all.[13] Hence kinships were associations whose composition was extremely fluid and in which, as opposed to the hierarchy in the family, house descent was not clearly defined in terms of rank or relations.

Kinships or clans, which were exclusively based on male lineage, manifested themselves particularly in times of feuds or vendettas. In addition to feuds among knights, which have always caught the interest of historians because of their violent excesses in the late Middle Ages,[14] there is also evidence of feuding among peasants in many regions until well into early modern times. Especially in a number of free peasant communities along the North Sea coast and in the Alps, feuds and vendettas are known to have continued without any apparent interruption from the early to the late Middle Ages.[15] While peasants in other regions lost the right to carry on feuds and vendettas following new regulations concerning arms-bearing and the introduction of public peaces in the high Middle Ages, regions such as Frisia and the marshes north of the lower Elbe retained their primitive form of armed self-defence and peasant law for a long time.

The vendetta and peasant feuds

In the sources, the term feud refers to the state of hostility between a lawbreaker and a victim. The main form of peasant feud was the blood feud or vendetta which was the redress for manslaughter or murder,[16] but there were many other reasons to carry on a feud. As a rule, the kindred of the victim fought against the clan of the suspected culprit, yet the circle of relatives involved in his punishment varied between regions.

This form of justice among families and kindreds did in fact survive in Frisia until the end of the late Middle Ages, despite the fact that the use of such violence had been substantially reduced as early as Frankish times by the compulsory introduction of a system based on fines for compensation and punishment, and despite later attempts to reduce feuds and vendettas by means of court decrees and regulations for the keeping of the peace.[17] As late as 1539, the provincial law of Dithmarschen still acknowledged the legitimacy of vendettas. It was said that the victim's friends who had slain the culprit were obliged 'to lay the corpse of the murderer next to his victim'.[18] Even in 1507 Peter Swyn, in his day one of the most influential men in the province of Dithmarschen, restored the honour of his family by personally setting fire in a barn to both a young kinswoman, who had had an affair, and her illegitimate child. The feud which ensued involved the entire parish and was fought with extraordinary violence.[19] A fourteenth-century chronicler from the Hanseatic town of Lübeck testified to peasant feuds in the neighbouring county of Holstein by stating that the local peasants were frequently engaged in the evil custom of fighting and killing one another in extensive feuds. He wrote that when the father, brother or cousin of a peasant was slain, and the murderer had a father, brother or cousin himself, either one of them would inexorably be killed as soon as the victim's kin got hold of him – even if he regretted the murder, knew nothing about it or had been away at the time of the crime.[20]

Feuds were also recorded in East Frisia until well into the late Middle

Ages, although the province had obviously been under the influence of the peace movement of the eleventh and twelfth centuries.[21] The reason why the Frisian clans refused to accept the introduction of criminal law lay in the fact that it meant embarrassment for the peace-breaker, as a consequence of which they defended the feud as an act which could only be atoned for by a substantial payment in money. The demand for an appeal to a court in the case of a lawful vendetta, as can be found in the records of the neighbouring areas at that time, does not appear in the Frisian sources. With 'the law of self-defence' and peasant blood feuds continuing unabated in many communities peasant kindreds remained powerful institutions which retained some of their primitive constitution and their traditional attitudes against the introduction of public peaces. Thomas of Chantimpré, a Brabant clergyman of the thirteenth century, has left us with a vivid description of the feud in Frisia. Apparently feuding was still practised in Frisia in his day, and to the Frisians the killing of a relative was only fully atoned with the death of at least one of the culprit's kin. To be constantly reminded of their bloody duty the bereaved kindred kept the corpse of their dead kinsman in one of their houses until revenge was achieved, and it was only then that the corpse was buried in the customary way.[22]

Around the year 1200 the Cistercian Caesarius of Heisterbach recorded that peasant feuds and vendettas were also still widespread in the lower Rhine area. His reports are lively descriptions of how violent the hostilities between peasant kinships could be, and that they often culminated in manslaughter and arson. For example Caesarius depicted an especially bloody quarrel between two enemy houses from the peasantry (*duae generationes rusticorum inimicitias mortales exercebant*) for which there was no atonement for a long time because the extremely aggressive disposition of their chiefs constantly provoked new clashes between the hostile families.[23]

As far as central Europe is concerned, in a number of Swiss cantons peasant feuds continued for a surprisingly long time. Even the Gersau chronicle of 1605 stated that it was lawful to take revenge upon the foreign assassin who fled into Gersau if he had been declared 'disreputable' in that region. As late as the seventeenth century it was customary in the County of Kiburg to deliver the corpse of the assassin to the relatives of the victim.[24] The reason why feuds survived for such a long time in the Swiss Confederation can be found in the extremely close solidarity among the peasant houses, their unbroken family tradition, and not least in the fact that the rural communities of Switzerland long retained traditional customary law.[25] It is widely known, of course, that in some other European regions, such as Corsica, Albania and Montenegro, blood feuds continued to be pursued even until well into the twentieth century. The reluctance to abandon them was due mainly to the unimpaired importance of family and kinship ties in certain regions. In the Middle

Ages, kinship solidarity manifested itself principally in court sessions where kinsmen covered up for each other in the swearing of oaths. In addition they sought to settle internal disputes as quickly as possible. The individual kinsman or kinswoman was obliged to assist his or her family and kin both in general emergencies and particularly in cases of manslaughter, where the clan supported a culprit with as much money as they possibly could. The aim was to come to an agreement with the victim's family, and thus enable the fugitive to return home without getting killed. The country law of Dithmarschen even listed atonement fees explicitly under the most important legal duties ensuing from kinship.[26]

The structure of the peasant family in the Middle Ages

Land registers, manorial laws and other seigniorial sources allow some insight into the social composition and development of peasant families and households between the ninth and the eleventh centuries. On the great domains the demesne farm of the manor was usually run by a steward or bailiff and his family, assisted by a number of dependent domestics who were also members of his household community. Moreover, there were married servants of both sexes on the larger farms who worked exclusively for the demesne farm and other fields of the lord. Hence it is justifiable to regard the associations of people who lived on such main farms as large household communities which were in fact composed of several families. Bonded peasant labourers (*servi, mancipia*), perhaps better considered domestic slaves, also played a considerable role on the farms of free peasants.

Detailed studies on the condition of peasant families on a number of ecclesiastical estates in the Frankish Empire have helped considerably to shed light on the relationship between the house and the family during the ninth century.[27] These studies have shown that two forms of dependent peasant households must be distinguished. On the one hand there were peasant households with a single family nucleus which employed various other family members to farm their holding, such as the father's unmarried brothers and sisters, as well as other servants who were not related by blood. On the other hand there is evidence for peasant households which consisted of several family nuclei who shared the property and inheritance. This was often the case when married brothers, each with a wife and children of his own, shared a single hide; however, such holdings were always at risk of being divided into separate households each surviving on half or even quarter hides.

The two household types were by no means mutually exclusive; both types could develop from, or into, the other. Large household communities could shrink into single families, whereas a small household could turn into a community of heirs composed of the families of the sons of the deceased peasant holder. The division of holdings depended not just on the influence of the local manor, but also on their size and how many people they could support. The feudal lords often had an interest in preserving the holdings as units thus prohibiting their division, in order to ensure the maximum productivity of the holdings. A younger son was faced with a choice: a life as an unmarried labourer on the farm of the eldest who possessed the holding, or to gain a holding for himself in one of the clearance settlements. Within the peasant family itself men clearly had precedence over women, and married over unmarried individuals. As mentioned above, another important characteristic of the traditional peasant family was patrilocality, which meant that after the wedding most peasant women moved into the homes of their husbands. On the whole, the nuclear family consisting of parents and children prevailed among the dependent peasantry of the ninth century, whereas families which included three generations under one roof were comparatively rare. Many peasant households, however, included both male and female servants.[28]

The trend towards nuclear families as the predominant form of peasant family increased with the rise in population, the extension of the cultivated area and the corresponding decline in livestock farming. The overall intensification of agricultural production and the considerable increase in the number of cottagers as well as settlement density contributed to the tendency to limit the number of households in each village. This was because the family holdings, which were increasingly split into parcels scattered throughout the arable land of the village, could only support a limited number of people, particularly in densely populated areas. The narrow margin of subsistence made it extremely difficult to preserve the larger family structures characteristic of traditional stock-rearing societies. In most regions of central and western Europe, therefore, the radical change in agriculture in the wake of the widespread development of arable farmland in the high Middle Ages was accompanied by a growing trend towards the nuclear family as the predominant form of peasant family.[29] Where more complex family forms existed they included families with two or three nuclei of married brothers and their families who lived in a common household. Some regions of France, for instance, saw the emergence of *frérèches* towards the end of the Middle Ages – a common type of extended family consisting of the families of several brothers.[30] The reason for the development of this complex type of peasant family lay in the tax system, in which levies were assessed according to households, so that it was much cheaper for people to live in extended household communities. Larger family groupings are also known in south-eastern Europe – such as the South-Slavic *Zadrugas*,[31] which were mainly found in areas where stock production was predominant.

The development of marriage laws

The structure and changes in marital relations among peasants can only be fully understood in their interrelation with the development of family types. In areas which had been influenced by Germanic law, marriage had in the early Middle Ages been primarily a legal contract between two peasant kinships or families which gave the wife a certain degree of legal protection and social security. Corresponding to the legal character of these marriages, the wedding act was still essentially a legal transaction even at the beginning of the high Middle Ages as the bride and her dowry (*dos*) were transferred to the groom and his kindred.[32] In the early phase of the courtship the two parties generally agreed on such conditions as the size of the dowry and the wedding-day. This marriage contract and the engagement were followed by the actual legal act on the wedding-day when bride and groom met in the company of their families and blood relatives. The order of events was ritualized; first the two families formed a circle around bride and groom who were then, according to a traditional formula, asked by the father of the bride or a legally experienced man of either family about their desire to marry. *Meier Helmbrecht*, a famous thirteenth-century poem in Middle High German, includes a good example of such a wedding formula:[33]

Figure 27 Wedding scene in front of a church
From a wood engraving by Hans Sebald Beham (1535)

Now we must give young Gotelind
As wife to youthful Lämmerslint,
And we must give young Lämmerslint
As man, in turn, to Gotelind.
A grey-haired man now did arise
Who in the use of words was wise;
Well versed he was in marrying.
He stood both parties in a ring.
Then first he spoke to Lämmerslint:
'And will you take this Gotelind
To be your wife? If so, say "aye".'
'Gladly', the young man did reply.
And when he asked the same once more,
He answered 'Gladly' as before.
And then he asked a third time still:
'And do you this of your own free will?'
He answered: 'By my soul and life,
I gladly take her as my wife.'
The man then spoke to Gotelind:
'And do you, too, take Lämmerslint
Willingly, your man to be?'
'I do, sir, if God grants him me.'
Again he asked the same of her,
Again she said: 'I'm willing, sir!'
And then upon his third demand:
'I'm willing, sir, here is my hand!'
They gave away thus Gotelind
To be the wife of Lämmerslint,
And thus they gave young Lämmerslint
To be the man of Gotelind.
And now they sang, the questions put,
And Lämmerslint trod her on the foot.

The custom mentioned in the last line, according to which the groom has to step on the foot of the bride at the end of the ceremony, is an unmistakable hint at the legal character of this wedding because it imitates similar customs in business deals and literally refers to the seizure of an article of property.[34] Consequently this custom cannot be interpreted, as by some authors, as a symbolic ritual for male supremacy in marriage.

Furthermore, it is evident that peasant marriages in the Middle Ages were by no means love matches, or the wedding ritual an emotional ceremony, but rather a sober legal contract between two clans. In many respects the bride was merely a legal object in the hands of the male relatives, and not a legally responsible individual. In most cases it was the father of the bride, or her next of kin acting as her family guardian, who conducted the engagement as well as the marriage itself. In the course of centuries the two steps of marriage – the engagement as the agreement to a legal contract and the marriage itself as the execution of that contract –

moved closer together. The wedding was usually followed by a wedding banquet and by a symbolic wedding in the presence of all wedding guests, particularly the representatives of both kindreds. It was only then that the marriage was legally effective.

It was only with effort that the church managed to place greater emphasis on religious consecration at the expense of the secular marriage procedures and shifted the site of marriage from the house of the family to the church-porch where the legal transaction was now conducted in the presence of the priest.[35] He would bless the young couple at the end of the worldly or legally binding part of the marriage ceremony, and proceeded to say a mass for the wedding party. From the thirteenth century, the wedding ceremony itself was conducted by a priest, and the church started to prohibit marriages by laymen. This development had its repercussions on the site of the ceremony in all of its phases, for from then on the entire wedding procedure had to be conducted within the church itself. The Council of Trent (1545–63) eventually ruled that a church wedding was the only legitimate form of marriage, thereby endowing the priest with an effective means of controlling any possible obstacles to marriages. Instead of equality in rank and wealth and the priority of the welfare of the kinship as a whole, which were the main goals of the traditional forms of marriage, the church, from the high Middle Ages, continually emphasized the importance of the religious bond and faithfulness in wedlock. In addition, the church expected the willing consent of both bride and groom and insisted on the duty of the husband to support and protect his wife and children.

In the Middle Ages maintaining material equality in marriage was a deeply rooted practice particularly among the peasantry and continued to be of great relevance for them. Such criteria as status and wealth played a decisive role in the choice of a suitable match for son or daughter which, in any case, was mainly made by the parents. The negotiations between the two families on the size of the dowry and the material support of the bride were the most important steps in arranging the actual marriage. It must be assumed that the majority of marriages among the poorer peasant classes were conducted on a much more private scale, for the simple reason that the courtship did not involve intricate financial arrangements. Furthermore, it seems very likely that many of the less wealthy peasant couples in the high Middle Ages were not even formally married.

Among serfs, their manorial and personal lords strongly influenced their marriage and family circumstances.[36] In any case, a free choice of partners was out of the question on most manors. From the viewpoint of the lords the marriage of their personal dependants was inseparable from economic considerations, especially property rights, and peasant land tenure. Lords were not only entitled to prohibit peasant marriages, especially to outsiders; some manorial laws even permitted lords to force their dependants into marriages. Although in most regions this right did

Figure 28 Peasant wedding
Wood engraving by Nicolas Solis, *c.*1550

not survive, or was at least rarely applied during the high Middle Ages, it was none the less persistently applied in a few areas. In Weitenau, a monastic estate in the southern Black Forest, for example, as late as 1344 the manor claimed the right to force every Christian householder from the age of eighteen or twenty, and every girl from the age of fourteen, into a marriage of the lord's choice.[37] Even widows and widowers who held land from the monastery were not exempt from this regulation.

Originally it was only within the narrow confines of the lord's *familia* that marriage was relatively unrestricted, and it was not until the late Middle Ages that these regulations allowed marriage among all dependent peasants of a manor, including those outside the lord's *familia*. A general right for the lord to prohibit the marriage of bondsmen and bondswomen is found primarily on the older manors, where marriage between peasants of unequal status, such as between free and bonded peasants, as well as between dependants of different lordships, was prohibited. Although the church demanded the indissolubility of even these marriages, it took a

long time to put this into effect; it was decreed as late as 1035 – when the
German Emperor Konrad II laid down the rights of the Limburg
monastery – that the abbot was in fact entitled to abrogate the marriage
between his peasants and women from other manors.[38] The prohibition
of marriage between dependants of different lordships (the German term
is *Ungenossame*) was widespread, as is attested by numerous collections
of manorial rights and customary law codes. Offences against such
prohibitions were heavily fined, and sometimes the peasants had to face
serious losses of property or certain rights of inheritance. Occasionally
they were even driven from their holdings.[39] The children produced by
marriages between the dependants of different lordships were often
divided equally between the respective lords or at least the rights over
them were divided.

In some regions of western and central Europe dependants were
obliged to pay merchet – a marriage due – when they intended to marry, a
fee which seems to have been the charge for the lord's consent to the
marriage.[40] In France, where such marriage dues were very common, it
was called *maritagium* when the two marriage partners belonged to the
same manor, and *forismaritagium* (formariage) when one married
'outside' the manor. In north-west Germany such marriage dues were
called *Bedemund*.[41] A certain proportion had to be paid to the lord of the
bridegroom, another to the lord of the bride if she belonged to another
lord. It appears that there was no legal connection between the obligation
to pay merchet and the often quoted *ius primae noctis*.[42] This is important
to emphasize because the alleged privilege of the feudal lord to have
sexual intercourse with the bride prior to her bridegroom on the
wedding-night has stirred the imagination of some historians, leading
them to conclusions having nothing to do with actual conditions in the
high Middle Ages. There can be no doubt, however, that in some regions
feudal lords had a considerable influence even on the personal life of their
peasants, including their families, and that sexual relationships between
feudal lords and female serfs were not exceptional.

For most of the medieval peasantry the main purpose of marriage lay in
the procreation of children. When marrying, a medieval peasant did not
primarily hope to establish a partnership or a love relationship for life.
The prime goal of wedlock was children and the reproduction of the
family. This attitude was also reflected in village customals (*Weistümer*),
the most important source on peasant life and peasant mentality in the
Middle Ages. For a long time the Christian ideal of lifelong monogamy,
the obligation of faithfulness and protection for wife and children, as well
as the idea of equality between the sexes, did not enter the mind of the
peasantry.[43] Yet it was in accordance with the peasant notion of marriage
that both partners could expect the fulfilment of marital duties. If the
husband failed to do so, various village laws in lower Saxony allowed the
wife to have sexual intercourse outside marriage and advised the husband

to send the unfortunate woman to a neighbour who 'could lavish on her enough care and attention to satisfy her'.[44] A Westphalian customal (*Weistum*) contains a humorously formulated passage on the same issue which sends the wife to the annual fair in case the neighbour was unable or unwilling to satisfy her. The peasant husband was advised 'to send his wife to the next annual fair in the vicinity, and to see that she would be cleanly dressed and had adorned herself. She should also be given a purse with plenty of money so that she could treat herself to something; yet if she returned home without being cured it was only for the devil to help her.'[45]

Legal position and tasks of peasant women

Many customals granted pregnant peasant women a number of privileges, all of which prove that pregnant women enjoyed a high reputation in the eyes of the medieval population.[46] Pregnant peasant women enjoyed the right to pick fruit and grapes wherever they wanted. Nor did the strict hunting and fishing regulations apply to them, and even in places where fishing was otherwise severely punished, such as by gouging out the eyes of the offender, pregnant women were free to fish with the permission of the local fisherman or under the supervision of witnesses. After childbirth, peasant women enjoyed additional privileges, such as the relaxation of dues and feudal labour obligations, as well as larger firewood rations. In the *Weistümer* frequent mention was made of exemptions from payment of the chicken dues, which were very common, and when the bailiff or *Vogt* came to collect them he was only allowed to take their heads so as to leave the remainder to the family of the pregnant woman.

The inferior legal position of peasant women as opposed to their husbands was mirrored particularly in what was called *Munt* in Old Germany, which was the legal expression of the relationship between husband and wife in respect of protection and authority in wedlock. For as long as she lived, the countrywoman stood under the guardianship of her husband and was subject to his 'rule'.[47] The laconic phrasing of a customal from the year 1424 reads: 'A woman must do what a man wishes.'[48] The husband was regarded as the master in the house and as the person who was in charge of all the family's possessions, including the property of his wife. Although he was obliged to obtain the consent of his wife if he intended to sell any of these goods he was still entitled to exert all his domestic rights in spite of such restrictions. It appears from the statements of peasant women in the Pyrenees village of Montaillou that fear of their husbands accompanied many of them in their daily lives.[49] As a result of his guardianship, and his wife's duty to obey him which was entailed by it, a husband also had the right to inflict corporal punishment on his wife. Husbands had the right to punish wives, for instance, if they wronged outsiders and insulted them in the course of the ensuing argument. In some areas the right to corporal punishment even became a duty, and the husband who did not punish his wife was liable to a fine.[50] In most parts of France in the high Middle Ages it was also considered a customary right of the husband to punish his wife. A thirteenth-century legal clause from the Beauvaisis stated that: 'A husband ought to beat his wife, although without injuring or killing her, if she has lied to him. '[51] In the Bergerac region the husband had the right to flog his wife until she bled if this was done with the honourable intention to make her mend her ways. On the other hand, the village population treated those husbands with toughness and contempt who were incapable of asserting themselves. In the Senlis, for instance, it was common practice in the fourteenth century to force those husbands who let their wives beat them to ride on a donkey through the village.[52]

The harshness and roughness of rural life in the Middle Ages considerably affected the daily life of peasant women. Owing to early marriages and lack of consideration on the part of their husbands, birth-rates were extremely high. Insufficient hygiene, illnesses, the filthiness and cramped space of peasant housing were the main reasons for high infant mortality, as a result of which only about three to five children in each family survived out of a far greater number of childbirths.[53] What should not be forgotten is that many women died during childbirth, which is why their life was particularly at risk between the ages of twenty and forty. Frequent childbirth and excessive labour in the household and in the fields also weakened the health of the peasant woman and made her even more prone to illnesses. It is obvious, therefore, that women's position improved from the time they were physically incapable of conceiving, and women between forty and sixty had a much better chance to survive longer than men. It is no secret that life-expectancy was low not only among the peasants but throughout the medieval population. Detailed studies on the average age of the deceased in a number of villages in the diocese of Winchester around the year 1300 have shown that individuals who had reached the age of twenty could only expect to live another twenty years.[54]

In addition to human needs, above all economic considerations compelled the peasants to find a new partner soon after the death of their spouse. Hence second and third marriages were by no means exceptional in the Middle Ages. Peasant women often suffered more under the burden of daily labour than men, especially among the lower peasant classes. The church, which generally proclaimed the intellectual and sexual inferiority of women and called for their subordination, did little to alleviate the situation of women.[55] As far as the position of women in the divine order of this world was concerned, the message was obedience, humble submission and patient endurance even of corporal punishment

Figure 29 Men and women harvesting grain, using sickles
Wood engraving of the sixteenth century

from their husbands. From the twelfth and thirteenth centuries, however, the position as well as the esteem of women improved substantially among both the nobility and the peasantry. The chivalrous concept of love, the Christian ideal of marriage and the development of the cults of Mary attributed a new ethic of dignity to the public image of the woman and mother. These new ideals and the higher esteem of women gradually permeated the world of the peasant as well, and increased the reputation of the woman in the family as well as in society in general.

The tasks of the peasant woman encompassed many household and farm duties, including work in the fields.[56] Evidence from the high and late Middle Ages does not confirm the view that women were exclusively responsible for housework and other light work, and that the Middle Ages were characterized by the same form of the division of labour as nowadays. Contemporary illustrations of the various seasonal operations in peasant work, such as in calendars, drawings and book illustrations, indicate that women usually performed the same functions as men (see figure 29). This applies to all branches of agricultural labour and even heavy jobs which in later centuries were generally performed only by men. At harvest-time, for instance, women participated not only in sheaf-binding, but also in reaping with sickles. Scything eventually became the typical labour for men – first in hay-making, and from the fourteenth century onwards in grain harvesting too.[57] This happened only after the scythe had developed into the most important cropping implement, which in many regions is not documented before the end of the Middle Ages. The well-known image of the male reaper and the female binder, therefore, does not stem from the medieval period.

Illustrations present the spectator with various agricultural tasks which were performed by women,[58] such as reaping and hay-making in addition to housework, gardening and threshing, or work related to livestock production, such as the processing of milk into butter and cheese or the slaughtering of domestic animals. Women had to perform labour services on manors, and in their functions as housewives they supervised the essential tasks within the household, or they worked as servants and wage-labourers in the households of feudal lords and wealthy peasants. The common duties of women in the household included the maintenance of the hearth-fire, the preparation of meals, the storing of provisions, as well as the supervision of female servants and the education of children. The processing of flax and hemp, in addition to spinning and weaving, were also considered typical women's tasks. In areas specialized in sheep production women were in particular responsible for the preparation of wool and the production of woollen sheets and clothes.

It is plain that the peasant housewife stood at the heart of the peasant household and was irreplaceable in the peasant economy as a whole. It was virtually impossible to maintain a peasant household without her. Her daily life was determined by hard work and full of privation from dawn to dusk, and by constant care for the family, the household and production in general, all of which left her with very little time for relaxation. Although men and women had equal shares in supporting the

Figure 30 Peasant woman slaughtering a chicken
Etching by Marcus Geeraerts (1555–1635)

peasant family, and despite the fact that sex was not the decisive criterion for the division of labour in the Middle Ages, there were already obvious disparities in the payment of the sexes for identical labour. Female servants were always paid less than their male counterparts, and women performing heavy work received only as much as servants who did the most menial jobs. There is an example from England of a female servant on an estate of the bishop of Worcester, who received 7 shillings for skilled dairy work as opposed to the lowliest among the male servants who was paid 8 for unskilled labour.[59]

In terms of human labour children were an important asset to the peasant household, partly because they provided for their parents after their retirement.[60] Young children began by performing small jobs and were thus ushered step by step into the adult world. This gradual introduction into the requirements of peasant labour also acquainted them from an early age with the basics of peasant life in an everyday context, such as the use of agricultural tools, treatment and care for domestic animals, and the codes of social behaviour in the village and in rural society in general. In villages ruled by feudal lords, even young children could be found working on manors, or they worked as farmhands for wealthy peasants. Although peasant children entered the working world at a very early age, it is likely that there was one respect in which they were privileged in comparison to other children of that age: they spent their childhood with their parents and were not sent into monasteries or other households as were children of the nobility. According to a thirteenth-century preacher young noblemen were often treated much more roughly and flogged much harder than peasant children. He stated that peasant children were swamped with love from their parents, and that they were only put behind the plough when they had grown up.[61]

The influence of peasant inheritance customs on the structure of rural families

To conclude this analysis of the basic aspects of the peasant family in the Middle Ages, mention must be made of the relationship between the structure of the peasant family and the inheritance customs of the medieval peasantry. In essence, the composition and size of peasant families depended on both inheritance laws and regional inheritance customs.[62] In areas in which partible inheritance was the predominant form of inheritance and holdings were divided according to the number of heirs, small farms and thus small families prevailed, whereas areas in which the holding was in fact inherited by the first-born tended to have much larger households. The genesis of these regionally divergent inheritance traditions has long been subject to speculation, and although many of the theories contain a grain of truth, none of them can claim ultimate validity for all regional variations.[63] There can be no doubt that the development of such peasant inheritance customs lies in a complex interaction of several influences and conditions, the impact of which varied from epoch to epoch. However, the attempt to impose the regional distribution of inheritance customs found during the late nineteenth century indiscriminately on the high Middle Ages must be rejected. This is because the regional distribution of the various inheritance customs became consolidated in the centuries after the Middle Ages, and there is even evidence for fundamental alterations in several areas (see figure 31).[64]

In any case, attempts to ascribe peasant inheritance laws to the legacy of early Germanic folk laws (*Volksrechte*) can no longer be maintained. Such attempts were very popular in Nazi Germany as part of the ideological support for the 1933 *Reichserbhofgesetz* which regulated the inheritance of peasant farms. B. Huppertz, for example, thought that having 'single heirs was a characteristic of the Nordic–Germanic world and its folklore' and claimed that the origin of this inheritance custom lies in the 'physical and geographical peculiarity and the overall racial, national and cultural development' of central and northern Europe.[65] Such statements are invalidated by the fact that the division of holdings is documented throughout the Germanic-speaking lands, and that this practice was common even before the eighteenth century in Scandinavia – that region of Europe which Huppertz had always cited as the main support for his assumptions.

Three aspects must be considered in the analysis of peasant inheritance rules in the Middle Ages: the influence of the manor, local conditions such as soil, climate and economic development, and the attitude of the peasantry towards the inheritance rules. In most cases landlords urged their peasants to leave their holding to a single heir to safeguard their profitability by keeping farms sufficiently large. This mattered more to them than the question whether the oldest, the youngest, or any other son actually inherited the farm. The changes in agrarian conditions, the alleviation of manorial dependence and the growth in population in the high Middle Ages gave rise to increased fragmentation of hides and landholdings in many regions in central and western Europe, particularly in the north of France and in the south-west of Germany. Other regions, such as Bavaria and the north-west of Germany, showed by contrast a marked tendency towards impartible inheritance (*Anerbenrecht*). Landlords often had difficulty in imposing their will upon the peasantry, largely because in many regions circumstances were favourable to an increasing fragmentation of the holdings. Among the most important ones were the rise in population, good soil conditions and large-scale urbanization, as well as the intensification and specialization of agrarian production. This applied in particular to regions where peasants held propitious property rights.

In areas where the manors shaped the structure of agriculture as well as inheritance rules, manorial lords usually demanded the indivisibility of the holdings. As long as the property of dependent holdings was not freely heritable, the manor usually allowed only one successor to the holding. Often enough the successor was appointed while the former holder was still alive, and he would retire to a cottage or a separate part of the farmhouse after a maintenance contract had been made.[66] Some regions retained the principle of the indivisibility of peasant holdings even after the easing of manorial pressures, which gave the peasants much more freedom to dispose of their lands as they wished. This was partly due to the influence of nearby regions which had impartible inheritance systems. In some areas a mixed form developed which was called *Trägerei* – which meant that the holder of the largest share collected dues from the others and paid them to the lord for the holding as a whole.[67] With the help of this system manorial lords tried to preserve the original size of the holding at least in regard to the collection of rents and dues, and it also served to prevent an even further division of the land. In some villages the heirs to a farm continued to live and farm as a single household community without actually dividing the holding; this occurred in the *Gemeinderschaften* in Switzerland and in the southern Black Forest in the late Middle Ages.[68]

The effects of local inheritance customs on the structure of both the family and the household were considerable. In areas dominated by equal division of inheritances many small farms and households emerged which were usually composed of a nuclear family of parents and children. In these areas, often the longest-settled regions characterized by numerous villages, neighbourhood associations and village communes prevailed. In areas whose laws favoured impartible inheritance, large holdings were preserved as well as large households which thus included the siblings who were not entitled to inherit land. The continuity which was guaranteed by the principle of impartibility and the corresponding inheritance regulations gave rise to a relatively homogeneous and wealthy upper stratum possessing large and medium-size holdings. Below them were numerous peasants possessing little land or none at all. These families were marked by a division between the future heir to the farm and the remaining sons: only the successor to the holding inherited both the land and the prestige of being a 'full peasant' (*Vollbauer*) while the others had to be content with being day-labourers, cottagers or craftsmen, often having only small incomes. The heirs to the holdings often took the side of the wealthier peasants in village politics, especially in issues related to the use of the commons, whereas the younger brothers naturally identified with the cause of the poorer peasants and cottagers.

Family ties were thus often eclipsed by interests which reflected the social position of the individual family members within the neighbourhood and the village community. Hence, regions marked by impartible inheritance were also known for less developed ties among siblings – in contrast to regions of partible inheritance where families developed complex and less tightly knit contacts.[69]

THE SOCIAL STRATIFICATION
OF THE PEASANT POPULATION

Factors of social differentiation within rural populations

The medieval village community, often regarded as a stronghold of
equality, harmony and peaceful social life, was not, in reality, a
monolithic society of equals who valued the aims and goals of the
community above their personal interests. The social composition of the
peasantry in general and the village community in particular were highly
diversified and consisted of a variety of different layers and levels. While
it is true that the social form of the village suggests a degree of
egalitarianism, and to a certain extent could indeed serve to harmonize
social and political differences, it would be wrong to ignore the various
degrees of social, economic and legal inequality among its inhabitants.
Basic elements of this social inequality were already rooted in the
constitution of the Germanic tribes at the time of the invasions and the
settlement period which followed; for, in fact, no evidence has been
found for a primitive peasant democracy in the early Germanic period,
which some have argued was organized in free mark associations.
Moreover, the differences in peasant status increased with the development of feudal society and the consolidation of the manorial regime – a
tendency which gained additional momentum during the large-scale land
development in the high Middle Ages and the boom in agriculture which
accompanied it. This, on top of demographic change, economic innovation
and rising production for the market, contributed to widening the gap
between individual peasant families and thus stimulated social differentiation within the village community as a whole.

The present chapter will focus on the stratification of peasant society in
the high and late Middle Ages. Hence such general issues as the social
stratification of the feudal society of the Middle Ages, or the theoretical
shortcomings of what is known as stratification analysis, cannot be
discussed within the scope of this chapter. We can also only handle

briefly the interesting question whether such historiographical labels as estate, order or class can be usefully applied to the medieval peasantry.[1] Furthermore, this analysis of the social stratification of select communities and regions will not be concerned with the form and extent of peasant dependence and bondage to personal lords within the manorial regime, which are treated in the following chapter. In general this analysis of social stratification will be guided by a greater emphasis on such objective aspects as the size of landed holdings, income, and the financial situation of peasant groups than by subjective judgements.[2] The great variety of terms which, depending on region and period, serve to describe peasant groups and associations often makes it difficult to locate them unambiguously on the social scale. However, although the terminology in the records is indeed very important and must be considered in the analysis of the various peasant strata, it should not blind us to the essential structural aspects and criteria which are involved in the study of the development of medieval society.

Interest in the social stratifiction of the peasantry has essentially been aroused by the universal phenomenon of social inequality.[3] But what, then, were the specific causes for the social inequalities occurring in peasant communities? Which factors in particular led to social differentiation in peasant society, and which long-term changes accounted for it? Five principal factors are especially important in this context because they, more than others, accelerated social differentiation among rural populations. Firstly, the various peasant groups had long been distinguished by the size of their holdings, with a spectrum ranging from large farms to medium-sized holdings and cottages. The size of the holdings depended to a large extent on regional demographic development, since a rise in population could cause further changes in the extent of peasant holdings. Owing to the fact that the extension of arable and the growth in the number of farms per village had natural limits, population growth must be regarded as one of the decisive factors for the increase in the number of cottagers and poorer peasants in the village. Secondly, social differentiation was further stimulated by the dynamism of the feudal system itself, the circumstances of manorial dependence, and differences in legal status, especially between freedom and bondage. Peasants who had to pay comparatively low feudal dues and perform fewer services, and those who were in advantageous legal positions, had a better opportunity to accumulate supplies and to acquire more land and livestock.

Thirdly, the varying degree of peasant participation in production for the market was an important factor in creating social differentiation among the rural population. Those who owned sufficiently large farms found it much easier to produce a surplus, the proceeds of which could either be reinvested in their farms or used as lucrative credits in financial arrangements with the proprietors of neighbouring holdings. Peasant social structures were especially diverse in the fertile wine- and grain-producing areas where both urbanization and the development of the market progressed rapidly as from the high Middle Ages. Fourthly, new opportunities to earn money outside agriculture, such as in linen manufacture in some areas, also had a part in improving the situation of some sections of the country populace by creating supplementary incomes – a factor which applied particularly to the lower peasant classes in the medieval village. The fifth factor which contributed considerably to the social differentiation of the peasantry was the various inheritance customs. Their influence on the structure of the peasant family was examined in the previous chapter. Villages in which only one heir was entitled to inherit the land of his parents were characterized by a pronounced contrast between a relatively homogeneous upper stratum of proprietors of large and medium-size farms and a lower peasant group of cottagers. The latter depended on additional sources of income from agrarian wage labour or artisan production. The continuous land fragmentation in areas in which holdings were divided according to the number of children, a practice which was similar to gavelkind in England, gave rise to a marked increase in population, in the numbers of farms in the villages and in the number of cottagers. This was why these areas produced large scattered villages whose arable land was divided into many small portions, and where landed property was generally subject to great mobility among tenants. In addition to these five factors, of course, further influences on the social stratification of the peasantry should be taken into account, such as the degree of technological and economic development in a given region, as well as the chances of the local peasants to emigrate to towns – a decision which often helped to alleviate the economic and legal position of those left behind. In brief, it was the interaction of these various forces which brought about the growing social differentiation of the peasantry found throughout the high and late Middle Ages.

The social stratification of the manorial servants and dependants

It is useful to precede the analysis of this process in a number of select villages and regions with a look at the social stratification of the rural population within the framework of the manorial regime between the ninth and the twelfth centuries. The people who farmed the land of lay and ecclesiastical lords in the early Middle Ages formed an association of peasants known as the *familia*. The *familia* consisted of all the dependants of the lord of the manor. In geographical, legal and economic terms, the *familia* had its centre in the demesne farms, the manors and other forms of feudal lordship. K. Bosl was certainly right to consider the *familia* as 'one of the most comprehensive and complex foundations' of early feudal

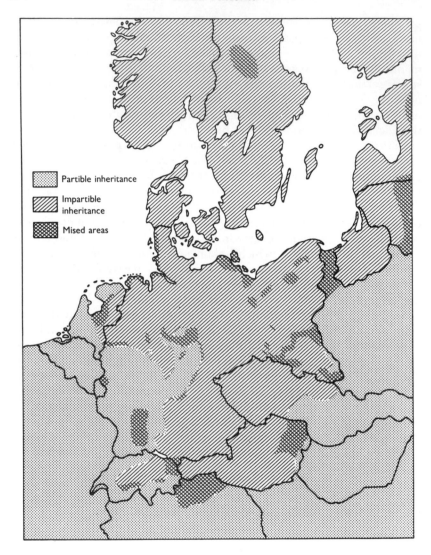

Figure 31 Peasant inheritance customs in central and northern Europe
(after B. Huppertz)

society – for the *familia* included the bulk of the rural population at the
zenith of the early medieval seigniorial system, out of which developed
the various social strata and estates in the early days of the high Middle
Ages.[4]

Dependants settled on hides (*servi casati, manentes*) clearly formed the
majority of the dependent peasant population. The second main group

consisted of day-labourers, artisans and servile domestics (*servi cottidiani, mancipia*) who lived and worked on landed estates.[5] But an accurate description of the legal and social position of these groups is difficult because they appear in the sources under the rather sweeping term *servi*. Both groups were members of the *familia*, and because they were all *servi*, they formed a uniform group whose legal status was markedly different from that of freemen (*liberi*). They were the heritable property of their masters and subject to his jurisdiction. With the exception of presents from their lords, domestic servants did not have property of their own. There can be no question that the male and female servants (*mancipia intra domum* or *prebendarii*) were serfs; they received their daily food rations on the manors, and had the lowest status of all bondsmen. They were not paid for their work, and their services in the lord's household, in his workshops and in his fields were unlimited and arbitrary.

The records of ecclesiastical estates are the principal source for the study of the development and differentiation within the band of lordly dependants. This also applies to manorial laws which regulated the legal position of the various groups within the *familia*. Most of these regulations too have survived only in ecclesiastical sources. These bands of dependants were, nevertheless, equally important on the landed estates of kings, lay princes and numerous other noble lords. Not only the bishops and the abbots of the Holy Roman Empire but also counts and freemen of noble birth controlled their own bands of male and female dependants, which could differ widely both in size and internal organization. The external differences between the *familiae*, which were mainly determined by the status of their lords, corresponded to their internal social and legal differentiation. The numerous dependent peasants living on the manors of the early Middle Ages were by no means uniform. Their composition was very complex, and subgroups and individuals differed considerably from each other in terms of their rights, duties and functions. The growing social differentiation within the *familia*, and the fact that access to skilled jobs was easier in the eleventh century, resulted from the overall acceleration in economic and social development and in the impressive expansion of trade and commerce. This trend was partly reflected in the emergence of privileges for certain subgroups among the dependants of the manor. An upper layer of tenants, those who according to special legal privileges such as the *Zensualenrecht* were only liable to annual rent payments, gradually distinguished themselves from the rest of the dependent peasants.[6] The lowest subgroup, which bore the worst legal status of all dependent peasants, consisted of serfs (*mancipia*) who were obliged to perform unlimited services.

The manorial laws of the eleventh and twelfth centuries, which were often decreed and recorded with the explicit consent of the particular *familia*, allow detailed studies of the rights and duties of the various groups and officials among the dependent men and women of a manor. The manorial laws for the Limburg monastery, which was founded by the house of the Salian rulers of the Holy Roman Empire, were ordered to be put into writing by the German Emperor Konrad II in 1035 and can be read as an explicit listing of the rights, tasks and duties of the dependants of the manor towards their ecclesiastical lords. They were subject to a great number of dues and services. Some of them had to serve their lord on a daily basis, others only once a week. All of them were obliged to pay heriot, a form of inheritance tax levied at the death of a tenant, as well as merchet, a marriage tax.[7] The chronicle of the Alsatian monastery of Ebersheim recorded in 1163 that on the estates of the bishopric of Strasburg, which were scattered around Alsace, the *familia* consisted of three main groups.[8] The leading position among them was taken by a group of military estate officials (*familia ministerialis*) who were of servile origin but who clearly aimed at climbing into the knighthood and gradually distinguished themselves in status from other dependants. Below the *ministeriales* stood the group forming the upper layer among the peasant dependants, a group which enjoyed an advantageous legal position (in Latin, *familia censualis et oboediens permagnifica et sui iuris contenta*). The third group consisted of the bulk of the dependent peasants (*familia servilis et censualis*).

Ample evidence in the form of documents and informative descriptions by chroniclers have permitted a thorough analysis of the social structure of the *familia* of the Benedictine monastery of Zwiefalten in Swabia at the beginning of the twelfth century.[9] The peasant dependants of this monastery included various subgroups whose position was clearly distinguished according to the size of their holdings, their legal status and the status of their office. In legal terms the dependants of the monastery fell into two distinct groups. On the one hand there was a privileged group of tenants (*tributarii*) who had to pay their rents in money or wax. They were much better off than the large group of peasant serfs (*servi*) who were liable to services on top of the payment of the usual feudal dues. The greater part of the dependants lived on holdings of various sizes, while the remainder worked as field-labourers and servants on the demesne farms. Considering their principal occupations, the manorial dependants of this monastery not only consisted of peasants or field-labourers, but of artisans and traders.

This demonstrates that the peasant groups and associations, which formed subgroups of dependants in the early high Middle Ages, cannot be regarded as homogeneous associations of equals. There is evidence from the *Urbare* and other land registers of the ninth century for a marked social differentiation within the peasant population. The villages and settlements owned by the wealthy monastery of St Germain-des-Prés in the vicinity of Paris were characterized by substantial differences in the holdings of the peasants during the ninth century.[10] Some of the dependants of this monastery possessed standard hide-sized holdings, while others held only a few acres of farmland. It seems that cottagers farmed their modest plots with hoes and spades, whereas dependants who held arable land of a sufficient size owned teams and ploughs. In some of the more densely populated villages of a number of specially fertile regions peasant holdings were sometimes occupied by two or even three families, so that several large households had to live off the produce of a single farm.

Substantial differences in the size of holdings and their production are also known to have existed in the ninth century on the ecclesiastical estate of Prüm in the Eifel, a low mountain range south of Cologne.[11] In addition to the large majority of full hides there were also half- and quarter-hides, although the actual size of these holdings varied considerably from region to region. The size of the holdings and their complement of stock and agricultural implements had a great influence on the social differentiation of the peasantry as a whole. In addition to economic differences there were differences in estate and legal status, as a result of which distinctions were made between free, half-free and dependent hides, with corresponding types of feudal dues, duties and service obligations. Although most of the dependants of Prüm were 'full peasants' (*Vollbauern*) possessing full hides, there was also a large number of landless farm labourers and servants who worked on the lord's demesne. Between these two groups were day-labourers and formerly free peasants who had sought the protection of the ecclesiastical lord. This third group lived on modest holdings and paid comparatively low rents.

The emergence of the peasantry as an order

The various groups and social strata of manorial dependants in the early days of feudalism gradually amalgamated in the high Middle Ages into a relatively uniform peasant estate, but one nevertheless clearly differentiated within itself. By the thirteenth century at the latest, the peasantry formed a social entity distinct from other estates, especially the lower knighthood and the burghers of the towns. Yet how did the country populace develop from its highly amorphous social, legal and economic composition during the early Middle Ages into the much more uniform peasant estate of later centuries? Which forces were at work to bridge the huge differences between free and dependent peasants, or between the relatively well-off peasants who paid rents and the almost rightless personal serfs? Why did eleventh- and twelfth-centuries sources begin to distinguish between such occupational estates as knights (*miles*) and peasants (*rustici*), whereas the traditional distinction between the hereditary estates of freemen (*liberi*) and serfs (*servi*) increasingly lost importance? Many questions in the difficult field of social change at the beginning of the high Middle Ages have not yet been fully answered but it is possible to outline some of the important aspects of the social differentiation of the peasantry at that time.

Semantic studies on the word *gebure*, the Middle High German term for peasant, have shown that it was originally reserved for members of villages and neighbourhoods. It was only in the eleventh century that *gebure* came to mean peasant in the modern sense.[12] This shift in meaning seems to have accompanied the formation of new social groups and estates with specific characteristics, such as the *ministeriales*, who were estate officials of servile origin, the knighthood, and the bourgeoisie in the towns and cities. In the wake of this development the rural population was also increasingly identified with its occupation, with the work performed in the fields. In contrast to the knights in their well-fortified castles and the burghers who also dwelt safely within town walls, the peasantry, who formed the great majority of the medieval population, lived unprotected in the countryside until the introduction of the public peaces of the eleventh and twelfth centuries.

The social and corporative differentiation of society in the high Middle Ages and the emergence of a peasant estate were closely connected with fundamental changes in settlement structure, economy, warfare and political rule – all of which occurred between the eleventh and thirteenth centuries. The gradual dissolution of the traditional structure of the manor and its economy, together with the transition from services to rent payments, relaxed the ties between serfs and their manorial lords.[13] In the villages this development manifested itself in the emergence of village communities with new social and economic forms out of what had been distinct groups of manorial dependants with distinct rights under various lords.[14] The transformation of the traditional seigniorial system and the improvement of peasant property rights was paralleled by an alleviation of the legal differences among the various peasant groups, a relaxation of dependence on the manor, and an assimilation of the corporative positions of those for whom the village had become their social centre. The traditional social stratification based on differences of birth took a new shape. The old differences between the free and dependants, between merely rent-paying peasants such as the *Zensualen*, the semi-free and serfs increasingly lost importance under the altered social and economic conditions in the village of the high Middle Ages. Besides, there were new groups of free peasants in the newly settled areas who held an intermediate position between the bulk of the dependent peasants and what was left of the old peasant freemen from the early Middle Ages.[15] Such colonizers were granted favourable rights for their efforts in clearing woodlands and marshes, and this also had liberalizing repercussions on the condition of the peasantry in the older areas of settlement.

The traditional manor and the corresponding categories of dependants had gradually been transformed by the social amalgamation of the various peasant groups of the old *familia* – a process which united particularly serfs who had been granted a holding of their own with the former peasant freemen who had commended themselves to the powerful for protection. Their legal assimilation lasted until the twelfth and thirteenth centuries and produced a peasantry with a fairly uniform legal position. The original legal position of the peasant subgroups ceased to matter in comparison with their economic position. In brief, economic differences gained in importance to the detriment of the old legal distinctions. Moreover, the reorientation of the peasant economy towards the flourishing markets and urban centres stimulated the process of economic differentiation among the peasantry and created a many-sided hierarchy within peasant society

With his seminal study on the development of rural society in Bavaria from the ninth to the thirteenth centuries Philippe Dollinger has provided a detailed regional study of these social changes.[16] He has shown that the profound transformation in the social structure of the peasantry must be seen in close connection with the dissolution of the traditional manor and the overall economic, social and political advances during the high Middle Ages. By the middle of the thirteenth century, the status of free as opposed to bonded peasants had become so similar that it was hard to determine the actual differences between the two groups.[17] All manorial dependants were liable to the same basic dues and payments such as merchet and heriot, and subject to restrictions on marriages to outsiders and the free disposal of their holdings. The social stratification of the peasantry was thus increasingly determined by social and professional, rather than legal criteria. The proprietors of peasant holdings now formed the greater part of the peasantry, and their status depended on the size of their holdings and the rules governing their tenure.

In comparison with the social development in Bavaria there was even less variety among peasant subgroups and their respective status in the north of France.[18] This region was marked by an earlier levelling of the social differences among the peasant groups in the high Middle Ages which put an end to what was originally a similarly complex social stratification of the dependent population. As early as the beginning of the high Middle Ages all peasant dependants amalgamated into a single group. In addition to the majority of dependent peasants who fell under marriage restrictions and the obligation to pay merchet and heriot, there were still various groups of free peasants in this part of France who were exempt from such regulations. Their numbers increased for brief periods in the thirteenth century because of large-scale manumissions.

The social composition of the village at the beginning of the fourteenth century

The study of the social stratification of the peasantry towards the end of the thirteenth century is particularly rewarding in those areas in which sufficient evidence allows insight into the composition of the rural population. Research on the social stratification in a number of villages near the town of Freiburg in the Black Forest is comparatively advanced owing to the ample evidence from records and land registers of a number of important estates such as St Blasien and Tennenbach. These sources contain detailed information on the social structure in the villages ruled by these monasteries.[19] The social and economic differentiation of the local villagers was in particular stimulated by their inclusion into the expanding money and market relations in the upper Rhine region.

Figure 32 Open-air peasant dance
Copperplate engraving by Daniel Hopfer, c.1500

Peasant households who participated to a relatively great extent in the market were in a good position to increase their income and add to their property. Differentiation in terms of property was thus increasing among the local peasants – a process which widened the gap between rich and poor peasants.

Many villages in the Breisgau area saw a substantial rise in population as a result of the general increase in population density in the upper Rhine region. Large villages with impressive landed properties emerged, particularly in areas where intensive grain and wine production was accompanied by partible inheritance as the prevailing inheritance system, which in the course of time produced a considerable degree of farmland fragmentation. The division of holdings was especially marked in the long-settled nuclear villages which possessed large commons. By the end of the thirteenth century some villages already had a majority of cottagers as a consequence of the continuous fragmentation of hides and other farms in the high Middle Ages. The members of the upper peasant groups consisted mainly of those who held large properties, in particular the former demesnes of the manor or other big leasehold farms which served as collecting points for peasant dues or as the seat of the local court. Such farms were not only exceptional because of their size or status, but also because they had prestigious farmhouses and large farm buildings, including barns and stables. The wealthy proprietors of these farms often held responsible posts and offices in the administration of the manor, as a result of which they appear as tax collectors, bailiffs and mayors in the records. Members of this group were also appointed heads of the village and members of the village court. In the course of the thirteenth century this privileged group of the village population, which stood out in terms of property size, reputation and access to influential posts in the service of the feudal lords, were called *meliores* or *honestiores villani* in the records. In later centuries they consolidated their position. It is also plain from the records that this group was comparatively small, and that in the social hierarchy it was followed by the middling peasants who held either full or half-hides. Finally the majority were poor peasants and cottagers. Their proportion increased to an alarming extent, particularly in fertile regions and on the peripheries of towns. The lower strata in the village were generally not able to live off their modest holdings, and most of them depended on supplementary sources of income from agricultural wage labour and commercial production.

In quite a few respects the social structure in several villages near Brunswick was similar to those in the Freiburg region; in others it was not. A number of land acquisitions by the Cistercian monastery Riddagshausen near a village by the name of Wobeck, made in the late thirteenth and early fourteenth centuries, allow a detailed study of the social structure of the local communities and the social position of a number of influential families.[20] The Robbe family, for one example, had quite substantial holdings which they leased from several lords. Around 1320 Hennecke Robbe was a registered citizen of the neighbouring town of Schöningen which, because of its salt deposits, had risen to become a leading market town. Thus one member of the wealthy Robbes family crowned its success by moving into the town. Another family from the upper peasant class in Wobeck was that of a man called Konrad Advocati. His landed property was far more extensive than what must be considered the average holding of a peasant at that time. This is also suggested by the fact that either he himself or one of his ancestors had been appointed to supervise the clearing of new lands for cultivation, in return for which they were possibly awarded with a fairly large piece of land which he must then have added to his farm. In addition to the nucleus of the Advocati property there were also portions of land which the family rented on a variety of terms and conditions, and the head of the Advocatis also fulfilled a number of functions in the name of the local manor. His daughter Gertrud evidently managed to rise above the peasant estate by marrying into a knightly family. Around 1300, then, Wobeck had an upper peasant stratum, which held key positions in the village because of the size of their holdings and also because they were influential office-holders on behalf of the village community. At the same time family connections to the bourgeoisie and the lower nobility existed which underlined the prestigious positions of these families within the village hierarchy.

A number of interesting comments in the land register issued in 1375 by Emperor Charles IV for the Mark Brandenburg have greatly helped to cast more light on the social stratification of the villages in that region.[21] The size of the holdings in the Altmark varied not only from farm to farm but also from village to village. The average peasant holding consisted of two hides, although there was also much variation among the individual levels of the peasantry. Calculated on the basis of 7.5 hectares per hide we can arrive at the following figures: 6 per cent of the peasants held small farms of between 0.5 and 5 hectares, 70 per cent possessed between 5 and 20 hectares, whereas 24 per cent of the peasantry in that region possessed holdings of between 20 and 40 hectares.[22] It is obvious that the latter formed the upper stratum of the peasantry. These figures illustrate that the region was characterized by a large group of medium and large holdings and that cottagers were a small and rather unimportant group. In contrast to the villages near Freiburg, which in 1300 had a much larger group of cottagers, the Altmark villages in Brandenburg were clearly dominated by medium and large holders.

Moreover, in the Brandenburg villages east of the River Elbe peasants had been granted advantageous rental terms according to which they held indivisible but freely heritable farms.[23] Here the top layers of peasant society were surpassed only by the mayor or head of the village. Holders of this office were furnished with holdings as large as two to four, and in some instances even up to eight rent-free hides. Obviously the social gap between the numerous wealthier peasants and the cottagers (*Kossäten*) was rather wide in the Brandenburg villages of the fourteenth century, especially in terms of their standing and the property division in the villages. According to the original meaning of the word, *Kossäten* or *Kotsassen* were the occupiers of a cottage or a small house with garden who possessed neither a substantial portion of farmland nor draught-animals. This is why they were often forced to work as farmhands to feed their families.[24] It would seem that this group often helped to farm the property of the local nobility of the village mayors and parsons. The members of this underprivileged group were the younger brothers of the successors to their parents' holding. Another large group among the lower strata in the village consisted of servants who earned their living on the farms of the wealthy peasants or in the manor-houses of the nobility where they also found their lodging.[25] Day-labourers and rural workers, by contrast, usually lived in separate houses erected on the property of the lord or wealthy peasants. The village records of the time also mentioned herdsmen and shepherds, blacksmiths and wheelwrights, but only a few other village craftsmen. The innkeeper had a special social position in the village. In many cases he owned a small portion of land, brewed and sold the local beer, kept some cattle and pigs, but farmed only rarely.

The proportion of the peasantry in lower strata

Unlike the conditions in the Brandenburg villages, the agricultural development in many regions in western Europe during the high Middle Ages resulted in a much higher settlement density and in the emergence of a much larger group of cottagers. The Belgian Low Countries, for instance, saw a much more pronounced fragmentation of arable land and the appearance of far more cottagers as a consequence of the enormous rise in population, as well as the large-scale urbanization and the growth of the markets in that region. By the end of the thirteenth century the development of agriculture in Flanders, Hainault and Namur had resulted in an average size of only 3 hectares per peasant holding.[26] The studies of L. Genicot on the social stratification of the peasantry in the county of Namur have illustrated that in the year 1289 38, 54 and 72 per cent of peasants in three select villages held less than 4 hectares of farmland.[27] Considering the relatively low productivity of the soil at the time it is doubtful whether such cottagers were at all capable of producing enough for the subsistence of their families, despite the fact that farming at that time progressed remarkably in terms of the intensification and specialization of production. In any case, a large proportion of the lower classes in the country relied on supplementary sources of income, such as from wage

labour on the large farms in the vicinity, or from artisan production. By
the second half of the thirteenth century the rural wool and linen trade in
the most densely populated areas of Flanders and Hainault experienced a
tremendous boom. This commercialization of agriculture, which occurred
especially in the peripheries of larger towns, accelerated the social
differentiation of the country population.

The increase in population, the shortage of farmland and the
continuous fragmentation of holdings were also responsible for the social
differentiation of the neighbouring agricultural regions in the north of
France, where they produced a substantial growth among the lower
peasant strata.[28] Towards the close of the thirteenth century the French
peasantry was divided into two distinct groups. On the one hand there
were the *laboureurs* who owned teams and ploughs, and on the other the
manouvriers who had to farm their land by hand.[29] Such draught-animals
as oxen or horses were so dear that only wealthy peasants could afford to
own them. Many cottagers had no access at all to such efficient means of
farming; hence they had no choice but to work their land with their own
hands. Only the owners of larger holdings were in a position to produce a
surplus which could then be sold profitably on the market. Technical
innovations in agriculture, such as wheeled ploughs, harrows and so
forth, increased the competitiveness of the owners of teams and ploughs
even further, which is why they had much better chances to raise their
yields and acquire even more land. Moreover, the shortage of available
farmland aggravated the economic position of the cottagers and other
almost landless groups in France. They were increasingly forced to find
supplementary sources of income, mostly in agricultural wage labour.
Differences in respect of the legal critera of freedom and bondage were
clearly supplanted around 1300 by economic differences.

Detailed studies on the rural population in England in the high Middle
Ages have not produced a radically different picture.[30] As early as 1300,
the number of cottagers in several south-eastern parts of the country had
risen to more than half of the entire peasant population. According to the
Hundred Rolls, a series of documents from 1279 registering detailed
information about 20,000 farms, only 6 per cent of the peasants owned
very large holdings; 21 per cent owned little more than twenty-two acres;
30 per cent had hardly enough land to feed their families; and 43 per cent
held even less.[31] M. M. Postan's calculations on the social composition of
the peasantry on representative manors have shown that 22 per cent of the
peasant population must be considered among the upper layer; 33 per
cent who held about 11 acres were in the middle layer; and 45 per cent
were in the lower layers.[32] It seems the growth of the English population
was also accompanied by a rapid reduction in the number of medium-size
peasant holdings, and at the same time the feudal dues per holding had
been raised. In any case, a large group of cottagers dominated the English
village by the end of the thirteenth century.

This survey of the social development of the peasant population in various lands and regions has demonstrated that as a result of the agricultural expansion in the high Middle Ages the extent of social differentiation increased in almost all of Europe. The proportion of cottagers and lower strata within the peasantry as a whole varied considerably from region to region, but it seems to have been extraordinarily high in areas where fertile soils, partible inheritance, urbanization and the growth of the market stimulated the emergence of cottagers. In Germany, the proportion of cottages rose particularly along the upper Rhine, in the Neckar area, in lower Franconia, and in the Rhineland, where partible inheritance, specialized agriculture and the growth of towns and markets facilitated this development. Large and medium-size farms, by contrast, were more predominant in Westphalia, Lower Saxony, Bavaria and especially in the newly settled areas in the north-east of the country where pioneer settlers had been granted larger holdings. Furthermore, some areas stood out because of a marked twofold division of rural society. On the one hand there was a group of full peasants who were equipped with sufficient farmland, livestock and agricultural implements, and on the other day-labourers and almost landless cottagers. This was in some regions even reflected in a linguistic distinction between peasants in contrast to smallholders, or cottagers: Swabian sources differentiate between *Hofbauer* and *Seldner*, Swiss between *Bauer* and *Tanner*,[33] Westphalian between *Hufebauer* and *Kotsasse*, and obviously the French distinction between *laboureurs* and *manouvriers* mirrored the same distinction.

The upper levels of the peasantry

The analysis of the social stratification of the peasantry in the regions mentioned has also shown that most villages were dominated by a handful of families from among the top layers of village society who held important offices.[34] Members of these families, who appear as *meliores* or *preudhommes* in the records, controlled the leading posts in village administration. They fulfilled important functions in the service of manors and judicial lords, and they owned particularly large holdings. Membership of this 'upper crust' among the peasantry, which in some areas actually developed into a 'village patriciate',[35] was based above all on wealth, reputation and the performance of important administrative functions. The old peasant householder of *Meier Helmbrecht* is a lively portrait of a member of this class of wealthy peasants in Bavaria and Austria, as found in the thirteenth century. Meier Helmbrecht (a reeve or bailiff) is the owner of a considerable amount of livestock and controls many servants, but his ambitious son falls victim to pride by violating the accepted social barriers and embarks on a disastrous career as a robber-baron.[36] Moreover, wealthy peasants frequently claimed a larger portion of the commons than peasants with average or even smaller holdings because they had to put far more livestock out to pasture. Their close contacts to the manors were the reason why they were often granted favourable terms for their holdings, which the lords often bestowed upon them as a heritable holding. There is evidence that they tried to increase the size of their farms by systematically selling surplus farm produce on the urban markets. The profits were often reinvested in their households or given as lucrative credits to less successful neighbours, as a result of which the latter often became their debtors and lost their influence in the village community to the wealthy farmers on whose goodwill they depended. Furthermore, many rich peasants obviously knew how to preserve the integrity of their holdings by clever inheritance arrangements which allowed them to secure the continuity of their families for many centuries.

Members of the 'middling peasantry', that is those just below the wealthiest peasants, had modest properties and income which sufficed for the basic subsistence of their families. Around 1300, this group comprised approximately 25 to 30 per cent of the entire peasant population, and in some areas even more than 50 per cent.[37] In areas where the land was not divided but inherited by a principal heir (*Anerbe*), the middling and upper layers of village society amalgamated to form a new class of 'full' peasants which were known as *Erben, Meier* and *Hufner*. Prime examples of such areas are Westphalia, lower Saxony and Brandenburg, where 'full' peasants were clearly prevalent. The majority of the members of the lower peasant ranks, which in some regions formed more than half of the rural population by 1300, came from a wide spectrum of small peasants, cottagers, day-labourers and servants.[38] They appear under a number of names in the various European regions, such as *Kötter, Seldner, Gärtner, manouvriers* or cotters. These people simply could not afford ploughs and draught-animals, and many of them lived on the periphery of the village, on a separate part of the manor or else were cramped into close rows of houses. Their arable plots and gardens were so small that they rarely yielded enough to feed their families, and thus such people depended on supplementary sources of income either from paid labour for lords and rich peasants or from artisanal production.

In eastern Swabia, for example, where the holding was inherited by a principal heir only, a much larger layer of cottagers emerged who were soon called *Seldner*.[39] They were originally landless day-labourers and artisans who could only afford small houses (*Selden*) with a small strip of garden. Most of their owners were the younger brothers of the peasant son who had inherited the family farm. They gradually managed to acquire landed property and rights to the commons, although in many areas they met with the fierce resistance of the full peasants. Many cottagers found their income in rural textile production. In the southern parts of the upper Rhine the lower classes in the village were called *Schupposer* or *Tagewerker*.[40] Lower peasant ranks whose situation was similar to those in the south-west of Germany can also be found in other densely populated regions of central and western Europe, such as in Hainault, Picardy and the south-east of England, where they formed very large parts of the rural populace.[41] It is evident that the propitious agricultural development in the high Middle Ages was largely responsible for this trend. This observation is confirmed not least by the fact that the crisis of agriculture in the late Middle Ages reduced the number of cottagers drastically, whereas the number of peasants with medium-sized holdings became considerably higher.[42]

PART V

MANORIAL RELATIONS
AND LAW, 1000–1400

MANORIAL DEPENDENCE

Aspects of lordship in the Middle Ages

There can be no doubt that bondage stands out as one of the main characteristics of the peasantry in the Middle Ages. With the exception of a varying number of free peasants who will be discussed in the next chapter, the majority of the medieval peasantry were subject to a variety of forms of lordship including landlordship, servile lordship and judical lordship (*Grundherrschaft, Leibherrschaft* and *Gerichtsherrschaft*). According to Max Weber the origin of peasant bondage lay in both the seigniorial possession of land and the seigniorial possession of the people who lived on the land – two factors which were often accompanied by the exercise of judicial authority by the same lords.[1] In contrast to the status of slaves in antiquity, medieval serfdom (*servitus*) falls into two distinct forms, namely the seigniorial possession of land and the seigniorial possession of serfs, although these two forms of lordship were often closely connected and therefore cannot be seen in isolation from one another. Personal dependence, however, which predates the manorial system, evolved over time and was not a static condition during the Middle Ages; hence the *servi* of late antiquity and the *mancipia* of the Carolingian period should not be confused with the personal serfs and other bondsmen of the later Middle Ages. Furthermore, lordship over serfs and manors provided its holders with not only economic but also social and political authority. The possession of judicial authority was of exceptional importance because it enabled the lord to discipline and hence rule more effectively over his bondsmen; in addition it often allowed manorial lords to create districts where land possession was coupled with jurisdictional authority.

The majority of the medieval peasantry were encompassed by the manor (*Grundherrschaft*), which can be characterized as 'lordship and domination over land and its occupiers' (F. Lütge). The manor was a specific form of lordship in which both lords and peasants were connected by economic and legal, as well as social and political, ties.[2] It is for this reason that the manorial regime should not be confused with the ownership of landed property: it included control over people. This can be seen from the abolition of peasant bondage to the soil and other traditional restrictions to their personal freedom in Germany in the nineteenth century, in a process which turned manorial lords into mere landowners. Some historians have been at pains to emphasize that the lords of the manors and their peasants existed in a relationship of mutual dependence in which loyalty was the price for protection and vice versa. They argued that it was not plain subjection which tied the peasants to their lords, but a 'moral relationship of reciprocity' moulded by bonds of loyalty.[3] The dependent landholders were allegedly obliged 'to serve and assist' their lords, while the lords had to offer their peasants 'protection'.[4] It is also claimed that a service relationship with a lord was the origin of freedom and honour, especially if the lord was high in rank. Moreover, since kindreds could no longer provide security after the dissolution of the traditional forms of social life, it had become vital to win the protection of powerful lords. A passage in the *Sachsenspiegel*, the most important legal document in southern Germany in the thirteenth century, is one of the most quoted sources in this context: 'We shall serve our lords so that they must protect us. If they do not protect us we are not bound by the law to serve them.'[5]

The manorial system

The realization that the exercise of manorial lordship included certain forms of protection towards the dependent peasantry should not beguile the reader into an all too idealistic interpretation of the relationship between the manor and its peasants or of this protective aspect. For it must be objected that manorial lordship was above all a relationship grounded on power and by no means the result of a voluntary labour agreement. According to K. Borchardt the manorial regime was a 'specific form for appropriating shares of agricultural surpluses by the powerful'.[6] This illustrates that the manor was much more a means of appropriation by the powerful than an expression of peasant protection. Owing to their rights of disposal over the land, feudal lords were in a position to grant their dependent peasants land use on unequal and forced terms. The numerous conflicts between feudal lords and peasants concerning dues and services, and especially the extremely violent peasant revolts of the high and late Middle Ages, are irrefutable arguments against an unrealistic evaluation of the relationship between lords and peasants. Such issues as the amount of peasant dues, the use of woodlands and pastures, and the difficult question of delimiting manorial from peasant rights were among the vital interests which affected the daily life of the peasant population.

Economically speaking the manorial system was characterized by the fact that most lords did not farm their landed property themselves but rented it out in exchange for dues and services. The early medieval form of the manor, however, often involved demesne farming by the lord himself. To this end the lord of the manor would use the labour of his serfs, peasants obliged to perform socage labour, or wage labourers. In legal respects, the manorial regime required the development of leasehold terms for peasant tenures and land use which did not affect the actual property rights of the manor. The laws of the Germanic tribes did not provide for such a clear-cut conception of property as found in Roman law. In Germanic law the right to the land was divided between the direct ownership of the lord and the rights of usage of the peasant. In addition to economic and legal aspects, particularly the social side of the manor must be considered in the analysis of the manorial system as a whole, because it was in essence a complex relationship between manorial lords and dependent peasants. These principal aspects of manorial lordship were accompanied by other types of lordship including protective, servile and jurisdictional forms.

What must be emphasized with respect to the historical significance of the manorial system is the fact that it provided the basis for the entire social, economic and cultural life of the Middle Ages. It was the economic foundation for the secular as well as the ecclesiastical elites, administrative bodies, the church and the representatives of cultural life. In a society which was for the most part based upon agricultural production and subsistence farming the manorial system was the economic basis for all those social groups which held superior functions in state and society. Therefore it cannot be ignored in any serious study of the medieval peasantry, particularly because it included the majority of the rural population and shaped their entire life. The social position of the peasant within the manorial system depended very largely on the size of the demesne in relation to the size of his holdings. It was also determined by the nature of his obligations, especially whether these were labour services, or dues payable in cash or kind. It was especially the impact of the increase in population, the spread of trade and market relations, in addition to long-term developments in agriculture, which gave rise to a number of structural changes on the medieval manor. The 'classic' manor of the early Middle Ages, in which the farming of the demesne formed the bulk of manorial production, gradually evolved into the manorial economy of the late Middle Ages, characterized by rent payments to the manorial lords.

Following both Roman forms of leaseholding and the Germanic form of lordship, the manorial system was adopted in most parts of the west, thereby affecting the very nature of medieval agrarian society. As mentioned in an earlier chapter, the integration of various elements into the fully-fledged manor and the development of the great domains took place chiefly during the Merovingian and Carolingian periods.[7] The expansion and consolidation of the manorial system between the ninth and the twelfth centuries was the culmination of developments which had their origin in the heart of the Frankish Empire. This 'classic' manorial system, which survived until the transformation of rural life in the twelfth and thirteenth centuries, incorporated seigniorial control over the land and its occupiers as well as judicial authority into an extremely compact type of rule. By a great variety of means it tied dependants to the manor and compelled them to pay or perform a wide spectrum of dues and services. The exercise of 'socage' rights (*Bannrechte, banalités*), which characterized feudal immunities, and the corresponding strengthening of jurisdictional authority reinforced the authoritarian character of the manorial regime, until it reached its historical peak in the high Middle Ages. There was, however, considerable variation in the size of manors from the great number of small manors, which commanded only a few dependants, to the great domains of the king and other lay or ecclesiastical lords of high rank who controlled thousands of peasant holdings.

Peasant dependence within the *Fronhof* system

The best understanding of the position of the dependent peasantry can be gained from sources concerning the *Fronhöfe*, the most developed form of the manorial system in Carolingian and post-Carolingian times.[8] Here the 'classic' manor, with its characteristic division between the lord's demesne and dependent peasant tenures, was regulated in great detail down to the rights and duties of all members of the manorial estate. The services and dues of the bondsmen depended on their legal and economic status as well as on the size of their holdings. In addition to the great number of peasant dependants who lived on the hides (*mansuarii*) there were also many bondsmen and bondswomen who earned their living as servants on the lord's home farm or in the manor-house itself. They were called *servi* or *mancipia* and had the lowest social status on the estate. They were obliged to be at their lord's service at any time of the day and were fully integrated into the lord's household. Other groups of dependent labourers lived somewhat less constricted in their own cottages (*servi casati*). They were for the most part cottagers and the holders of modest gardens. In terms of their social, economic, and legal position they were already similar to the peasants settled on holdings who had to perform all those tasks on the demesne which exceeded the work capacity of the labourers and the domestic serfs.

Much of the work on the great domains, which survived until the twelfth century, was conducted in close co-operation between the landed peasants and the domestic servants who worked on the demesne farm or in the manor-house itself. The tenants of the holdings had to bring their own teams and ploughs to till the demesne; moreover, they were also responsible for the grain and hay harvests, for the fencing of the fields of the manor, for the grazing of its livestock and for the masting of the pigs in the woodlands. Mainly those servants who lived on the lord's home farm were in charge of the processing of raw materials for everyday necessities, yet they were on many occasions assisted by the tenants of the holdings and their families. The obligations of the latter also included repair work on the demesne with its various outbuildings, threshing, the manufacture and repair of agricultural implements, brewing and bread-baking. Other obligations which took much of their time were errands and deliveries on behalf of the feudal lord, as well as the duty to lodge him and his guests, and, for peasant women, a wide range of domestic work, such as spinning and weaving. This heavy burden of peasant duties on the lord's home farm was partially alleviated by the fact that many lords granted them fixed shares of the production and food provisions for the time when they and their families worked on the demesne, but this was by no means an adequate compensation.

The extent of demesne services, which was one of the principal characteristics of the early medieval manorial regime, varied according to the legal status of the peasant, the size of his holding, the terms of the leasehold agreement with his lord, and the conditions under which he or his ancestors had entered the manor.[9] As far as the so-called free hide-tenants were concerned, the annual work-load consisted of only a few days, but the other groups of manorial dependants were usually compelled to serve for several weeks spread over spring, summer and autumn. In many regions of the Carolingian empire, however, tenants of dependent holdings owed three days of service each week, which meant that they served their lords for half of the working week. Unfortunately it is not possible to arrive at a systematic and universally valid estimate of the individual service obligations of the various peasant groups because of the great differences between regions, estates and even among individual manors. One must distinguish between two main groups of peasant holdings, the so-called free hides (*mansi ingenuiles*) and the 'unfree' or bonded hides (*mansi serviles*). The tenants of the former were indeed less burdened with dues than the holders of the latter. Such legal differences, however, gradually eroded, so that eventually no essential distinctions remained between the two groups of holdings in terms of the kind and size of their obligations. Moreover, 'free' hides were often farmed by bondsmen and the hides of the latter by the so-called free peasants, as a result of which there ceased to be a correspondence between the legal position of the peasant and the status of his holding.

Variations among the types of peasant dues were even greater than variations among labour services.[10] These dues included grain, wine, chickens and eggs, livestock and its products, such as pigs, sheep and

Figure 33 Peasants paying dues
Wood engraving, Augsburg, 1479

cheese, but also garden produce, honey, wax, as well as flax, linen, wool
and finished textiles. In areas where peasants had access to markets the
tributes in kind could be partially replaced by cash payments. Although
this wide range of peasant dues in money and kind was only rarely
demanded in full, it nevertheless gives a good impression of the potential
variety and burden of peasant dues.

Three interlocking legal justifications can be distinguished for peasant
dues in the days when the 'classic' manor still prevailed. First of all there
was the actual rent for the holding, which was demanded for the fact that
the lord permitted the peasant to use his land and the farm buildings
located on it. Secondly there were personal dues which originated in the
old property rights over the person of the peasant and in the charges for
his protection. In some instances these taxes were paid in addition to the
dues in kind, but as a rule they were only demanded of bondsmen and
their families who did not have a holding of their own. Thirdly lords
would also collect certain public dues, such as military taxes and church
tithes. A number of other dues were demanded of the peasants of a manor
on top of these principal ones, such as tributes for special rights and
privileges. These included charges for the use of the forests of the manor,
or for the lord's honour on special occasions. In the course of the high
Middle Ages many charges were increased, especially for the immunities
and other dues paid to jurisdictional and territorial authorities; above all
the demands of the advocate and various taxes were subject to substantial

rises. Owing to the difficulties which are involved in calculating the exact value of labour services, and because of the lack of a reliable gauge for the value of the various tributes in kind, it is virtually impossible to assess the full burden of peasant dues within the demesne system, a problem aggravated by regional variations. Free leaseholdings were usually charged half, a third, or a quarter of their agricultural yields, whereas the dues of customary holdings were fixed and thus not linked to the success of their harvests. Some peasant groups were comparatively well-off because they were merely charged a symbolic fee in recognition of seigniorial property rights.

In addition to regular dues a number of taxes and services were due on special occasions. There can be no question that the *mortuarium* or heriot, which was payable to the lord on the death of a tenant, weighed very heavily on the peasantry.[11] In some places lords were even entitled to all personal effects of a deceased bondsman, but this was rarely put into practice as it would have left the holding and thus the successor without the necessary means of production. What was claimed in most cases was a certain portion of the inheritance or an animal of the peasant's stock. At the death of the dependant's wife on the other hand the customary charge consisted of her best dress. Another extraordinary payment was due when a bondsman or bondswoman obtained permission to marry. On such occasions presents had to be given to the feudal lord which in later centuries were replaced by fixed marriage fees (*maritagium, Bedemund*).[12]

An early tenth-century land register from the imperial monastery of Werden for the manor of Friersheim on the lower Rhine helps to illustrate the position of the dependent peasantry.[13] The scattered holdings of Werden in the vicinity of the Friersheim manor formed a network of holdings farmed by dependent peasants. In all, this manor had almost 400 hectares of demesne supported by 121.5 holdings owing services, which means that the ratio between the size of the lord's home farm and the holdings of his tenants was roughly one to three. The rural population which belonged to this manor can be divided into three main groups: serfs without holdings of their own, tenants of holdings liable to socage services, and peasants who only paid rents. The first group was obliged to perform services at the will of the lord, and its members were either servants who worked in the manor-house or cottagers who lived in its vicinity. They formed about 25 per cent of the dependants of the lordship. The third group consisted of rent-payers liable to fixed payments in either money or kind. They were exempt from labour services, and the weight of their burdens was far smaller than that of the tenants on holdings.

The duties of the other, and by far the largest group on the Friersheim manor involved primarily labour sevices for the lord's home farm. They were obliged to perform two weeks of sowing work each spring and autumn, which meant that they had to plough about 3.6 acres and prepare them for the actual sowing of the seed. An additional two weeks of service was due in June, and they were also obliged to help with the hay and grain harvests, to undertake various tasks in the lord's garden and to aid in the masting of the manorial pigs. On top of that all bondsmen of that lordship had to perform their share when communal bread was baked, beer brewed, the flax harvest prepared for further processing, and in sundry other tasks. All in all, the service of these tenants amounted to ten weeks, hence a fifth of the year. In addition to this considerable work-load they had to pay 56 pfennigs, 3 chickens, 10 eggs and 12 bushels of grain.

It is obvious that the dependants of Friersheim struggled hard to cope with the work obligations towards their lords, so that it must remain doubtful whether they always had enough time for farming their own holdings adequately. This priority of labour dues demonstrates that it was the scarcity of human labour in comparison to the availability of arable land in the early Middle Ages which characterized the manorial regime, and the economy of the great domains. In other areas, however, where the Werden monastery possessed many separate holdings, as in Westphalia and Frisia, the demesne lands were not farmed as intensively as in Friersheim. In such areas the manor served above all as collecting-point for dues in money and kind.[14] It follows that in the period from the tenth to the twelfth centuries the great domain of the Werden monastery was represented not only by manors of the Friersheim type but also by tenancy arrangements based on rent payments, which were to become the predominant type of manorial organization in the late Middle Ages.

The structural transformation of the traditional manor in the high Middle Ages

The social position of the dependent peasantry changed in particular as a consequence of the transformation of the manorial system in the high Middle Ages, especially the dissolution of the great domains which reached its peak in the twelfth and thirteenth centuries. From the eleventh and twelfth centuries, lay and ecclesiastical lords started to lease their demesnes, particularly in areas where they had been dominant in the previous centuries, so that the old type of manor soon lost its former social and economic importance.[15] The essence of this change was the reduction of the demesne. The dissolution of the great domains followed a simple pattern: the demesne was divided into a varying number of holdings which were all rented to the dependent peasantry. As labour services lost their value in the course of this process, they were increasingly replaced by monetary obligations. Another important effect of this development was the economic separation of the lords' home farms from the farming of the tenants which worked to increase the independence of the peasant economy.

The complex changes which marked the overall expansion of market and monetary relations and the rise of the towns in the high Middle Ages were accompanied by a radical transformation of conditions both in agriculture and in rural society. The geographical mobility of the peasants grew following the introduction of advantageous landholding terms in the clearance areas, and the prospering towns also attracted people, especially from nearby areas. In particular the clearance settlements offered the newcomers a high degree of personal freedom, more direct responsibility in economic matters and much lower rents in comparison to the traditional manors. On top of that they relieved the peasants from the extreme pressure from the traditional obligations. Moreover, the expansion of commercial and monetary relations permitted the lords to buy better-quality goods at lower prices on the urban markets, and in order to do so they were in need of cash rather than service obligations. It was this tendency too which stimulated their willingness to turn their holdings into rent-producing tenures.

The interaction of all these forces eventually brought about the collapse of the 'classic' manor and opened what would become a new era which made room for a freer and economically more independent peasantry within the framework of a new form of manorial organization. Feudal lords were now confronted with the real danger of a rural exodus – a challenge which obviously left them at a loss for some time. The best way, however, to prevent their tenants from leaving was to offer more favourable conditions. The most unpopular dues, such as heriot and merchet, were lowered or totally abolished. The detested labour obligations were also substantially reduced. In many places they were limited to only a few days per year. Whereas in the past peasants had been compelled to work mainly in the fields and behind the plough, they were now primarily obliged to undertake much lighter transport tasks, especially at harvest-time. This, incidentally was almost the only time when they had to labour directly for their lords at all. Owing to the rising revenues from the sale of produce on the markets, peasants were now also increasingly able to commute the most onerous dues and obligations, either by the payment of annual fees or by the payment of a lump sum.

The compass of this study does not leave enough room for a detailed account of the changes which affected the manorial system in the high Middle Ages, particularly because they followed different regional patterns, and also because this study focuses primarily on the effects these changes had on the condition of the peasantry. The dissolution of the great domains, the fragmentation of the demesne into separate holdings and the overall transformation of the traditional form of rural economy commenced at different times in different regions; yet it is safe to say that they reached their climax in the twelfth and thirteenth centuries. In some

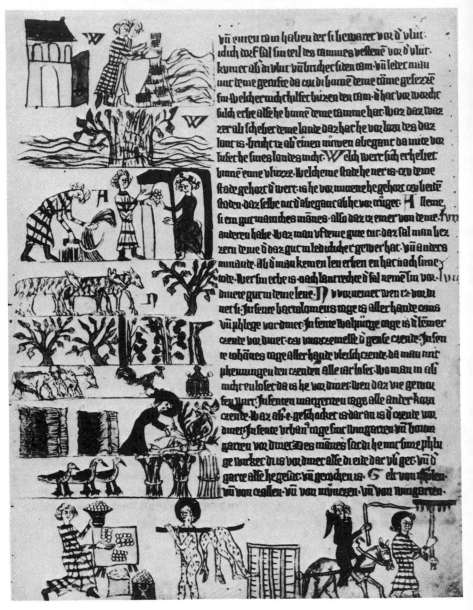

Figure 34 Schedule of dates for payment of peasant dues. A peasant calendar illustrates
the individual deadlines: the centre picture of the three lambs, for instance, is a reminder
of the lamb tithe due on Valpurgis (1 May)
From the illuminated manuscript of the Saxon Code at Heidelberg (fourteenth century)

parts of northern France this process started even as early as the eleventh century,[16] whereas Austria changed comparatively late. The transition to freer rent arrangements on the estates of Friersheim occurred mainly in the twelfth century.[17] However, research on the exact course of this transformation in different lands and manors is impeded by the lack of adequate regional studies, since the duration and the intensity of this development as well as its consequences for the peasant population can only be determined on the basis of detailed regional studies. What can be said, however, is that this was one of the most important changes in the history of agriculture in the high Middle Ages. Philippe Dollinger, who has produced a number of excellent contributions to research on the dissolution of the medieval manor in Bavaria, has called this process an 'economic revolution'.[18]

In addition to the change in the *Fronhof* system, other important changes affected the manorial system. The rise of the *ministeriales* and the formation of a distinct order of knighthood resulted in the emergence of numerous small lordships and a progressive fragmentation of feudal rights.[19] Now, owing to the increasing number of knights, *ministeriales* and small vassals, the peasants found not only the number of authorities much enlarged, but their dues increased as well. Various territorial and jurisdictional rights, based on castles, advocacies (*Vogteien*), local courts and administrative positions, were exploited to increase the taxes levied on the peasantry. Furthermore the old manorial rights of lordship over land, bondsmen and legal subjects, which were formerly held by a single lord, were increasingly split among several lords. The seignorial authority of the lord over land was no longer always combined with authority over servile peasants, and immunity rights were no longer always combined with local jurisdictional authority. In addition, the rights of the advocates, which had become extremely lucrative sources of income, were also defined in much narrower terms. They were frequently sold or mortgaged, and thus often changed ownership. Manorial rights became increasingly depersonalized, and the rights of lordship changed hands so often that it stimulated the development of various forms of legal contracts, such as short-term leases.

'Peasant liberation' in the high Middle Ages?

Generally speaking the structural transformation of the manorial system had one principal effect: it led to a marked loosening of the ties between lords and peasants. Some historians have interpreted this as a 'peasant liberation', or as the end of the 'first serfdom'.[20] There can be no doubt that the old forms of bondage lost in importance, and that rent obligations came to play a much more prominent role than the former legal position of the peasant. Now solely the size and the kind of dues and services can be taken as a rough indication of the original legal status of certain groups of peasants. Former bondsmen who had advanced to become independent peasants, and the remainder of the free peasants who from the early Middle Ages had commended themselves to the protection of a lord amalgamated into a relatively homogeneous peasantry, even if still to some degree dependent on lordship. In the eleventh and twelfth centuries, however, they merged into a fully-fledged peasant estate distinct from the other estates, such as the knights, the clergy and the early burghers. The more the obligations of formerly bonded peasants were reduced to purely economic obligations, the less relevance was attributed to the traditional distinction between the old types of freemen and bondsmen. All in all the peasants gained much more personal freedom, a much more secure and safer legal position and better property rights. The transformation of labour obligations into rent payments was what enhanced their independence and made their labour much more lucrative, especially where peasants were able to trade in urban markets.

By the end of the thirteenth century the social and legal position of the peasantry had improved considerably in most regions. Reservations to this should, however, be kept in mind because some sections of the peasantry continued to struggle and crises in agrarian society continued to erupt.[21] The rise in population had caused a notable increase in the division of peasant holdings, particularly in densely populated areas, as a result of which a large group of cottagers emerged who found it more and more difficult to support their families from agriculture alone. They depended on supplementary sources of income from wage labour and artisan production. The beginning of the fourteenth century finally saw the first signs of stagnation and crisis, such as an obvious decrease in clearing activities and a growth in the number of serious famines.

Manorial structures in the later Middle Ages

Despite its transformation and the partial easing of social relations which accompanied the dissolution of the *Fronhöfe*, the manor continued to be an institution which had an immediate effect on the daily life of the peasantry. By comparison with previous centuries there existed a far greater number of types of manorial organization in the Late Middle Ages, and some regions developed their own specific variants.[22] In addition to the manorial lords, territorial lords also increased their efforts to influence the condition of rural society as well as the legal relations among its members. They sought to standardize the manorial laws for their territories, to delimit the manorial privileges more clearly from each other and in many instances to protect the peasants from excessive demands from manorial lords; yet in doing so they also pursued their own fiscal interests. After all it was not least the balance of power between the sovereigns, the manorial lords and the dependent peasantry which determined the regional density and the influence of each individual local lordship. Four types of authority who left their imprint on the manor of the late Middle Ages can be distinguished: the territorial princes, the local nobility, the church and the urban elite. In Germany the estates of the princes corresponded to the royal domains in other lands, since they were also characterized by the combination of manorial and high jurisdictional authority.

The economic and social aspects of the crisis in the fourteenth and fifteenth centuries, which resulted in a drastic loss in population, the desertion of settlements and a depression in agriculture, did of course also leave their mark on agrarian conditions and legal relations, the organization of the manor and the social condition of the peasantry. Although this development will be discussed in depth in the last chapter of this study,[23] it is interesting to note in this context that it led to increased peasant dependence and to the gradual evolution of a new type of manorial regime in the lands east of the River Elbe; Marxists have called this a 'second serfdom'.[24] Most parts of western Germany, by contrast, were spared this aggravation of the condition of the peasantry, but the effects of the crisis made themselves felt there too. In the south-west, for example, feudal lordship over dependants became more important.[25] The western provinces of Germany and western Europe as a whole, however, witnessed a reduction of demesne farming and a restructuring of the manor towards fixed peasant dues. Peasant property rights improved in many regions and the forms of tenure limited in time were gradually replaced by customary rights of inheritance or even by freehold. In the northern Rhineland, and especially in Italy, peasant rights to use land became governed by leases which were distinguished by a proportional division of the agricultural yield.[26] In general in most regions of Europe, however, one finds a more independent and market-orientated peasant economy.

13

PEASANT FREEDOM AND INDEPENDENT PEASANT COMMUNITIES

The problem of the term 'freedom'

Although the great majority of the medieval peasantry were the dependants of feudal lords, there were also many free peasants and independent peasant communities in various parts of Europe.[1] These were generally the immediate subjects of a king or one of the German princes, which meant that they paid him taxes, fought his wars, but did not have to serve any of the smaller manorial lords. It is astounding to see in the sources of the high and late Middle Ages how many peasants were in fact free, particularly since one would have expected the number of free peasants to be greatly reduced at that point because of the extent of feudalization in the early Middle Ages and the consolidation of the manorial system in later centuries. What kind of freemen, then, were the free peasants of the high Middle Ages? In which countries, settlement zones and types of principalities were they most prominent, and what was their legal status?

In order to arrive at a fuller understanding of peasant freedom it is necessary to comment briefly on the medieval conception of freedom. Concepts such as 'free' and 'freedom' were subject to considerable shifts in meaning from the early to the late Middle Ages, so that the old Teutonic freemen, for example, held a position which was markedly different from that of the Carolingian freemen, or from that of the free peasants of the high Middle Ages. The modern notion of freedom, which is firmly established in Western constitutions, refers to the wide scope of human and basic rights which were obviously only developed much later and finally found their way into modern national constitutions between the eighteenth and the twentieth centuries.[2] A critical look at the political reality today reveals not merely striking differences in civil rights and liberties in various countries, but also in the concept of freedom held by individual groups within each society. Freedom is a relative concept, often ambiguous in its meaning, and given quite different meanings within differing contexts and situations. Typically enough, the term 'freedom' is employed by almost all political movements to justify their demands; nevertheless, they all have their own understanding of freedom, so that there really is a wide gulf between the freedom of the old imperial nobility of the Holy Roman Empire and the conception of freedom as it was cherished during the French Revolution.

Historians doing research on the various types of freedom in the Middle Ages[3] have often found it helpful to ask the following basic questions: freedom from what? What obligations and bonds did a certain group of freemen manage to escape? This initial step of questioning is closely related to a second one: free to do what? What actions and initiatives were open to the group of freemen in question? These two paths of enquiry are guided by the realization that freedom to do something does not necessarily exclude some other form of dependence, and that some services could also confer certain liberties.

The study of peasant freedom in the Middle Ages has traditionally been approached from two different standpoints. The view inherited from the nineteenth century was that peasant freedom is an absolute factor; consequently it was not regarded as something granted by governments, but as an older pre-existing status which itself created and moulded state and society.[4] According to the alternative view peasant freedom was not a clear-cut and invariable quantity. It should rather be approached as a relative phenomenon determined by medieval political, social and economic conditions.[5] Recent studies in constitutional history usually follow this view, as a result of which a distinction is made between two groups of free peasants: the descendants of the early medieval freemen, and those who were granted their liberty at some later point.

The theory of the royal freemen

Before discussing the kind of free status which characterized clearance settlements, a brief comment is necessary on the theory of the so-called 'royal freemen' (*Königsfreie*). This is necessary because the controversy on the status of freemen in Merovingian and Carolingian times continues despite the abandonment of the old conception that the tribal society of the Teutonic peoples had been based on a community of free warriors and peasants who allegedly held equal rights. This assumption gave way to the realization that Germanic society, even in the days of Tacitus, had been divided into bondsmen, the free and the nobility. T. Mayer and H. Dannenbauer, among others, argued that there did exist a class of free peasants – the royal freemen – who had been granted their free status by the crown. These authors often doubted whether the freemen of the Frankish period had any historical links at all with the common freemen described by Tacitus.[6] They answered the crucial problem of the historical origin of the royal freemen by arguing that their privileged status was the product of the development of the Frankish state; this development had led to the formation of a new class of independent peasants who were direct subjects to the king, hence the name 'royal men'. Members of this group were not born into the estate of freemen, but earned their privileged status by performing important functions for the crown. Moreover, the class of freemen which had formerly been described as common freemen (*Gemeinfreie*) were in fact royal freemen who were liable to military and other services as well as tax payments to the crown, in return for which they had received their holdings. According to T. Mayer this class of royal soldiers had formed the core of the Carolingian army and functioned as military guards throughout the Empire.

> They were obliged to do military and public service, to maintain the bridges and roads in the Empire, and to pay certain tributes to the crown. In exchange for these services they were provided with holdings which, however, they were not allowed to leave or sell without permission; besides this, they were not entitled to place themselves under the overlordship of the church to evade military service. The king, on the other hand, had the right to give them to someone else.[7]

Older research primarily asked why the common freemen of early medieval times had become dependent in Carolingian times in such large numbers; subsequent research turned to discussion on a new class of freemen. The emergence of this discussion can, however, only be understood in the context of a new trend in legal and constitutional history in Germany during the 1930s which won widespread support for some time. It emphasized particularly the role of the nobility in the history of the early Middle Ages and regarded the autogenous rule of this class as one of the principal foundations of the medieval constitution from very early times.[8] It was further argued that the authority of the nobility was grounded upon original rights and included legal competences which had not been delegated by the king.

Critics of this view have rightly warned not to overestimate the importance of groups who were taxed only by the Carolingian crown (*Königsfreie* or *Königszinser*). They demanded careful studies on the relationship between the royal freemen and other groups of freemen.[9] Some of them rejected the view that the tribal society of the early Middle Ages consisted in essence of noblemen, bondsmen and bondswomen and claimed that the majority of the early medieval population had been freemen who retained their privileged status for some centuries. In addition some historians claimed that a substantial number of the early medieval common freemen survived even until Carolingian times. H. K. Schulze, on the other hand, completely rejected the idea of a class of royal freemen who had allegedly won their freedom through such services as clearances. He summarized his criticism by stating that

> there is no evidence in the sources that certain groups were granted privileged legal positions in exchange for either clearance, settlement, military or other services to the crown. Owing to the fact that the orders of early medieval society were primarily determined by birth it is unlikely that such privileges ever existed . . . The admittedly large number of freemen during the reign of the Carolingians was essentially composed of the remainder of the freemen from early medieval times in addition to freed men.[10]

Following the development of the manorial regime and the progressing feudalization of state and society after the ninth century the majority of free peasants fell into dependence on secular and ecclesiastical lords of the manor. These freemen, however, rarely lost all the attributes of their former status immediately. They usually retained certain privileges and peculiar titles for many generations, although in many cases it is not clear in which respects their status really differed from the rest of the dependent peasantry. In any case, only very small groups of freemen from the early Middle Ages managed to maintain their status until the beginning of the high Middle Ages, and they lived in a handful of remote areas. A new class of free peasants emerged in the high Middle Ages as a result of the massive land development and the rapid increase in clearance settlements.[11] What, then, were the characteristics of free peasants in the clearance areas of the high Middle Ages? Furthermore, to what extent is it legitimate to speak of 'freedom through clearance' (*Rodungsfreiheit*)?

'Freedom through clearance' in the high Middle Ages

Although there is good reason to believe that some of the settlements of free peasants go back as far as the eleventh or even earlier centuries, reliable sources are only available beginning with the twelfth century. When in 1106 the archbishop of Bremen granted some of his marshland on the lower Weser to Dutch settlers, he issued an interesting document which has already been mentioned in a previous chapter.[12] From this time until the middle of the fourteenth century there is ample evidence on the foundation of settlements of free peasants throughout central Europe – a process which must be regarded as a unique development in the constitutional history of rural areas at that time. In northern Germany numerous clearance settlements were made by peasants from the Low Countries or Flanders. They settled in particular in the fluvial marshes of the Elbe and Weser, as well as further to the east, for example in the Harz, a low mountain range south of Brunswick, or in the Fläming, a hilly area to the south-west of Berlin.[13] Moreover, the peasant settlements along the upper Weser and Leine rivers were privileged through special laws (*Hagenrecht*) which were exported from here into such remote regions as Mecklenburg and Pomerania.[14] The newly colonized areas in the east of Germany supply by far the richest documentation of pioneer settlements in the high Middle Ages, including the establishment of free peasant communities. Southern Germany also had an impressive number of settlements of free peasants, but evidence for the earliest of these is scanty, and can only be reconstructed with the help of records from later centuries.

Settlement privileges have given valuable insight into the various forms of settlement and the specific rights of the colonists.[15] It appears that there were many cases in which settlement was based on systematic ground-plans, as a result of which settlers received equal holdings with standard dues and service obligations. Heritable property rights without manorial dependence of the old type were among the particular 'privileges' which were granted to the occupiers of pioneer settlements. This meant that peasants held landed property which was freely heritable, that they had much more personal freedom than in the old regions of settlement, and that they were exempt from the payment of heriot to either the village lords or the local prince. As far as the constitutional status of the villages was concerned, most of the newly founded colonist settlements were also furnished with special communal and jurisdictional rights. They were often granted a far-reaching communal autonomy, free election of village judges, and independence from existing courts. This body of privileges formed the essence of what peasants could attain in the high Middle Ages. Compared to older settlements where freemen had to attend the courts of the advocate and counts, while the dependent populace attended the manorial courts, the colonists were not only much freer but there was even more equality, since they were all subject to the same court.

After this glance at a few of the privileges of settlement in the high Middle Ages the more central issue will have to be pondered: is it historically accurate to use the formula 'peasant freedom through clearance'? Although the assumption of an independent class of royal freemen is highly questionable, many recent assessments on the privileged status of peasants in clearances must also be rejected because they are based on a very rigid conception of freedom. Their arguments are not convincing because they ignore the subtle gradation of privileges as well as the changes in the legal and political conditions of the high Middle Ages.[16] While it is true that the term 'freedom through clearance' does not appear in the sources, it is useful in describing the privileged legal status of settlers in most clearance areas. There is such an obvious connection between clearance and peasant freedom in the high Middle Ages that it would be unwise to neglect this important aspect of the social history of the peasantry.

The concept of freedom through clearance, then, is useful after all because it draws our attention to the advantageous position of the settlers in newly colonized areas, particularly in terms of their liberties and property rights, including the right to inherit land at stable rents. Yet the phrase can only be correctly applied to communities whose members were really granted more personal freedom and better property rights. The basis for this reservation lies in the fact that many clearances stood under the direction of manorial lords who were not interested in releasing the settlers from manorial dependency or furnishing them with substantial rights and privileges. Freedom through clearance applied above all to the twelfth and thirteenth centuries and particularly the large-scale colonization of the areas east of the Rivers Elbe and Saale.[17] Privileged settlements, nevertheless, were not limited to the high Middle Ages. Indeed special privileges accompanied efforts at developing regions in eastern Europe until well into the eighteenth century, as in Russia and Galicia. There is in fact written evidence from the high Middle Ages, that efforts at clearing were rewarded with certain privileges, for example in the marsh colonies in the north-west of Germany. Although the peasants who helped to open these areas were not officially released from bondage, the colonists gradually formed a community of freemen and dependants who held equal rights – a trend which eventually produced a new class of relatively independent peasants responsible only to the territorial prince.[18]

The privileges which peasant communities were granted in the clearance areas of the high Middle Ages corresponded to the rights and liberties of townspeople.[19] The urban regulations included unrestricted inheritance rights for registered citizens, the free election of judges, a special constitution for the courts and far-reaching rights of self-government, all of which closely resembled the rights and liberties of clearance settlements. In short, there were numerous parallels between the great number of urban foundations and the colonization of the countryside;[20] most notably, the freedom which dependants were granted after a year and a day when they settled in a town or city corresponded to the privileged status granted to the colonists in cleared lands. In an age marked by the intensive development of land resources, to offer improved legal conditions, even if it limited the authority of the urban or territorial ruler, was an effective means of encouraging the venturesome to advance both urban and rural development. 'Freedom through settlement' was a phenomenon of the age which the townspeople on the one hand and the colonists on the other had in common. It gave considerable momentum to the dissolution of the traditional manor and made large parts of the population the immediate subjects of urban or territorial rulers.

Free peasants' privileges in clearance areas

In northern Germany free peasants existed in great numbers; in addition, this part of the Holy Roman Empire was also characterized by a surprising variety of subgroups of independent peasants.[21] One of them was a group of descendants of early medieval freemen who were solely responsible to the court of the local counts (*Grafschaftsfreie*). In terms of tenure they were freeholders, that is only liable to the payment of tolls to either the king or the counts. Another group of free peasants were the 'imperial freemen' (*Reichsfreie*), who lived on the large imperial domains. A third group were the *Häger*, peasant communities which had been granted a relatively free status as a compensation for their efforts at clearing the land between the south of the Teutoburg Forest and the eastern fringes of the River Leine. From the beginning of the twelfth century the bishops of Hildesheim and other magnates had promoted settlement either on virgin soil, near existing villages, or in newly created hamlets and individual farmsteads. Advocates had jurisdiction over this group of free peasants and supervised the sale of their holdings. In some instances, these *Häger* settlements retained their unique legal position until well into the nineteenth century.

Special privileges for peasants were prominent among the Dutch and Flemish clearance settlements between the lower Weser and Elbe rivers. As mentioned in an earlier chapter, the Flemish and Dutch settlers introduced their native property and civil regulations (*Hollerrecht*) into these clearance areas and won recognition for them through the rulers in these territories.[22] These rulers granted such privileges because the settlers were great experts in draining swamps and marshes, technical know-how for which they were allowed a considerable degree of communal autonomy and even their own courts. These were presided over by *locatores*, bailiffs who had supervised the clearance and settlement of the land. The property rights of these peasants entitled them to heritable tenure for which they merely paid a recognition fee. The formation of peasant autonomy and self-administration in the marshes of the Elbe was decisively influenced by the Dutch settlers whose communities and parishes in clearance areas consisted exclusively of free tenants.[23] Thanks to their advantageous property and personal rights the descendants of the Dutch settlers in the marshes managed for centuries to secure their privileges against the old-established occupiers of the higher dry lands in the vicinity. The development in the Dutch settlements on the banks of the lower Weser, by contrast, was radically different. Owing to the disastrous outcome of the *Stedinger* wars the peasant communities of this area had lost many of their privileges as early as the thirteenth century.[24]

As in the northern parts of the country, so in southern Germany the extension of cultivated lands gave rise to the emergence of free peasant communities.[25] They could be found in the clearance settlements of low mountain ranges as well as in the Alpine countries, but it has proved to be difficult to determine the proportion of one-time freemen amongst them. In the south-west, clearance settlements appeared particularly in areas where influential houses of the nobility like the Zähringer or Staufer sought to extend their territories by granting peasant settlers a privileged status as an incentive. In the wake of the political and economic development of their principalities and the attempt to create consolidated territories out of their scattered holdings they often used various forms of settlement to establish privileged peasants as their immediate subjects in order to exclude interference from their vassals.[26] The privileges granted encompassed more personal freedom and better property rights, but not necessarily a complete exemption from taxes and services. In comparison to northern Germany, peasants in the south-west generally seem to have attained less freedom and fewer privileges.

The considerable degree of personal independence which characterized the status of peasants in the Tyrol had its origin in particular in the fact that they had a privileged relationship with their ruler.[27] Early on, the counts of the Tyrol had taken steps to the benefit of their peasants by enforcing laws which freed the rural population from many personal and economic obligations towards the manorial lords and made them their immediate subjects. Furthermore, this enabled the political bodies representing the local peasantry, that is the local judicial and village communities, to attend the provincial parliament as an estate of its own like the nobility, the clergy and the towns. Extensive military and tax obligations, on the other hand, were also characteristic of peasant conditions in the Tyrol at that time.

It is beyond doubt that the colonists in eastern Germany enjoyed what was the greatest degree of peasant freedom anywhere in the high Middle Ages.[28] Large-scale settlement in the twelfth century radically changed the character of the lands east of the Rivers Elbe and Saale, and many of the farms, hamlets and villages which were built in these territories were endowed with remarkable privileges and thus soon had a relatively independent peasant population. The settlement of the peasant colonists was conducted in various ways, and only the general pattern of this process can be described in this study. In woodland clearings, for example, peasants often received hereditary rights to their land and owed a quit-rent (*Erbzinsleihe*) which was comparatively small. Special mention must be made of the settlement methods of Archbishop Wichmann in Magdeburg, under whom peasant freedom reached its first fruition in the second half of the twelfth century.[29] The colonists settled under the supervision of a locator and were allowed a substantial degree of personal freedom. Characteristic of these colonial settlements were the propitious terms for peasant holdings, which in some places even became the peasants' own property, but at the least were hereditary, as well as the

Figure 35 Peasants under the linden tree at the village centre
From the illustrated chronicle by Diepold Schilling at Lucerne (1513)

formation of well-developed rural communities, with associative self-administration within villages or rural districts and a privileged juridical position.

The granting of considerable rights and liberties for the clearance efforts of the peasant settlers was just as much a common feature throughout Europe as was the development of new landed resources. Vast stretches of coastland were reclaimed under the direction of the counts of Flanders in the twelfth century, as a result of which conditions improved not only for the participating settlers but for the Flemish peasantry as a whole.[30] The manorial dependence of the peasants was considerably loosened if not completely abolished, and their social and legal position was considerably ameliorated. As a result, we find reflected in the sources that the peasants in the Flemish clearance areas enjoyed a privileged status by the twelfth century. In the twelfth and thirteenth centuries new settlements were also established in the south-west of France, and such expressions as *castelnaux*, *sauvetés* and *bastides* suggest that their occupiers held a comparatively independent legal status.[31] The settlement pattern of south-western France was also completely reshaped by large-scale clearings, massive colonization and the founding of many villages and farmsteads between the eleventh and the thirteenth centuries. The various forms of systematic settlement in this region also led to the alleviation of manorial dependence. The occupiers of the *sauvetés* were free, although in some cases they were charged a head tax in kind. The peasants of the *bastides* were also legally free: all they had to pay were very modest tributes in money or kind. The especially privileged position of many villages in the north of France, where in the twelfth and thirteenth centuries many villages were liberated after the model of Beaumont, has been examined in a previous chapter.[32]

Free peasant communities

During the high and late Middle Ages in areas where they formed a large part of the population, free peasants were particularly active in the formation of the village communities and regional administrative bodies. Here it was on the level of local jurisdiction that they made their first steps toward an active participation in communal life. They met in village and district courts and made use of their right of self-administration in all matters pertaining to the community. In certain areas, particularly in Frisia, Dithmarschen and Switzerland, they further developed their legal and political position, and it was here that they gained political competences on a much higher level, so that their peasant associations and alliances of independent communities began to design their own associative forms of political and territorial rule.[33] With the exception of the Swiss Confederation, however, political rule by peasant communities, or their alliances, did not survive for long.

The thirteenth and fourteenth centuries, which were marked by a decisive consolidation of the political influence of territorial rulers – and in many respects the dawn of the early modern state – also witnessed the considerable development of free peasant communities.[34] Under the influence of the great upswing of urban centres the communal movement also found new followers in rural areas and produced peasant co-operatives with territorial possessions of their own in Switzerland as well as on the North Sea coast. In other areas of the German Empire, by contrast, such as the Tyrol and Vorarlberg, the development of peasant communities came to a halt at the level of self-administered communities and freemens' associations.[35] Federal initiatives, which had more than a purely regional significance, were usually restricted to areas where free peasants were particularly numerous, and where they had maintained a

Figure 36 Dance under the linden tree at the village centre. Shrovetide
diversion in the Swiss canton of Schwyz
From the illustrated chronicle by Diepold Schilling at Lucerne (1513)

warlike attitude and hence could defend independent rural communities. In coastal areas the fighting of floods, the raising of dikes and embankments, and the communal organization of land reclamations definitely promoted the formation of free peasant associations,[36] whereas the difficult access and geographical isolation along with the martial attitude of a society of herdsmen contributed to the emergence of peasant autonomy in remote parts of the Alps.

The Swiss Confederation

The valley associations (*Talgenossenschaften*) in the interior of Switzerland gained their political basis through the grant of privileges for the imperial peace which made the peasant communities immediate subjects of the Holy Roman Empire.[37] As early as 1231 and 1240 Emperor Frederick II granted the populations of Uri and Schwyz the immediate protection of the Empire, a privilege which involved considerable independence and made them active associates of the Empire in the protection of the Alpine passes. The development of federal ideas in urban communities during the thirteenth century was soon adopted by the Swiss, who incorporated the new institutions and remodelled them for their own purposes. The valley associations which resulted from this process soon found themselves under threat of the territorial ambitions of the Habsburgs, whom they defied in the year 1291 by founding the famous league of the three forest cantons. The growth and renewal of the original alliance was guaranteed through the agreement of several cities to join them, and from now on the confederation had a much more permanent character, although it continued to spend most of its energy in putting up an effective resistance against the territorial ambitions of the Habsburgs. The Swiss Confederation of towns and provinces defended its independent position and rights of autonomy in a series of violent battles in which its peasant armies defeated the splendid knights of the Habsburgs. Nevertheless it took the Swiss Confederation a long time to tackle larger political tasks, and it was only in 1499 that it finally left the Empire.

Dithmarschen

The peasant communities of Dithmarschen,[38] which will be examined briefly as a supplement to the Swiss model of the formation of peasant sovereignty, had no urban allies in developing their political organization. The geographical position of Dithmarschen was politically speaking peripheral, and this facilitated the efforts of the rural communities towards greater independence. Dithmarschen is situated between the lower Elbe and the coast of North Frisia, and although it formally belonged to the archbishopric of Bremen and Hamburg, the archbishops had very early on left the peasant communities considerable autonomy. The political basis of the province was formed when peasant 'clans' (*Geschlechter*) associated in co-operatives to settle the marshes along the North Sea coast and to reclaim additional land with the help of dikes and embankments. These 'clans' were sworn communities (*Schwurgemein-schaften*) who helped their members in court trials as well as on other occasions, which meant in practice that they fulfilled the various tasks involved in the maintenance of law and the territorial peace on a local level. The peasant 'clans' and the parishes gradually merged into the province of Dithmarschen, and the solidarity of its members grew during the fourteenth and fifteenth centuries with the need to defend their independence against hostile forces. In a series of wars, in which the population of Dithmarschen resisted annexation by the counts of Holstein, the experienced army of the peasant communes of Dithmarschen stood the test and defended their independence. In 1447 a new constitution was proclaimed under which forty-eight men from the 'clans' were elected to be the judges and political leaders of the province. At the same time were compiled the territorial laws of Dithmarschen which are one of the foremost sources for reconstructing the peasant law of Frisia. Between 1447 and 1559 Dithmarschen was at the height of its independence, and in 1500 the province even managed to crush the superior army of the attacking Danes in the memorable battle of Hemmingstedt – a success which preserved the independence of the 'peasant republic' for another sixty years.[39]

14

PEASANT REVOLTS AND RESISTANCE, 1000–1400

The causes of peasant rebellions

In his well-known work on French rural history Marc Bloch examined the problem of peasant revolts in the society of the Old Regime. He arrived at the conclusion that peasant revolts, in a feudal society, play the same role as strikes in modern industrial society. For him it was clear that from a historian's viewpoint peasant revolts were as inseparable from the manorial regime as strikes from large capitalist enterprises.[1] It is not necessarily a reversion to rigid class-war truisms to acknowledge that peasant revolts and peasant resistance occurred throughout the Middle Ages, although they were more frequent in some centuries than in others. Owing to their special features and intensity, however, most historical studies so far have concentrated on the peasant insurrections of the late Middle Ages.[2] Consequently the fact has only all too often been neglected that peasant revolts occurred in the high Middle Ages too, although it is true that peasant resistance at that time was generally less spectacular and took on different forms than in the late Middle Ages.

In the final analysis, peasant revolts resulted from the obvious opposition between manorial lords and dependent peasants, particularly from the clash of interests between the two groups, which must be regarded as the decisive cause for the countless tensions, conflicts and struggles between the two groups. The alleged mutuality of rights and duties, and the overaccentuation of the protection-for-loyalty element in the relationship between lords and peasants do not correspond with the actual circumstances of peasant life in medieval society. Similarly unconvincing is Otto Brunner's assertion that 'the mutual dependence' of peasants and lords, and the protection-for-assistance agreement, would in spite of everything overcome the innumerable conflicts which occurred on the manor.[3] Peasant revolts and peasant wars illustrate that the transformation of the manor as well as the continuous effort of the nobility to extend peasant service obligations, dues and taxes entailed conflicts which simply could not be settled on the basis of friendly agreements. Yet the gulf between the attitude of the nobility and the world of their peasant dependants, who were at times extremely dissatisfied with their position, produced not only violent riots but also less conspicuous forms of peasant resistance.

According to medieval authors, who saw lords and their dependants in a relationship of mutual obligation, peasant resistance was lawful provided that the lords violated their duties in a gross manner. In this context reference must be made to the famous passage from the Swabian Code of the thirteenth century which stated that the duty of the peasant dependants to serve their lord ceased with the failure of the latter to protect them.[4] Whenever lords were unable to provide adequate protection peasants often no longer felt obliged to serve them and, given that this did not entail too great a risk, sought the patronage of more powerful lords. The military protection provided by powerful manorial lords and the introduction of the public peace made peasant life tolerably secure; indeed they were the essential prerequisites for the rural population to farm their fields and pursue their work at home and in the village. The lords of the manor were obliged to protect their serfs in court and in times of feud and other warfare, and they also had the duty to defend their and their peasants' rights in all matters heard by higher courts.[5] The peasants demanded this protection especially when feuds and warfare threatened them directly. Moreover, it was also plainly in the lord's own interest to protect his peasants from the economic and personal damage caused by the feuds of knights and other lords in the Middle Ages because they tried to weaken their enemies essentially by plundering their peasants and by setting fire to their homes and crops.

Basic patterns of peasant resistance

Peasant resistance to such assaults or to gross violations of the lords' duties could take a great variety of forms, ranging all the way from refusing to serve or pay dues, to deserting or fleeing the manor, or to violent protests of numerous kinds. Over the last decades an increasing number of studies on peasant resistance in the Middle Ages and in early modern times have treated both the concept and the forms of peasant conflict with feudal authorities in great detail.[6] Aspects analysed include for example the circumstances and criteria which may justify the use of the phrase 'peasant resistance', the distinction between open resistance and everyday behaviour of rural dependants, as well as the forms of peasant resistance. The study of peasant resistance has been strongly influenced by the Russian historian B. F. Porchnev,[7] who discussed three basic forms of resistance, namely partial resistance, flight and revolt; and

Figure 37 The three orders and their functions:
clergy (prayer); nobility and knights (the granting
of protection); peasants (labour)
Wood engraving by Jacob Meydenbach from
Lichtenberger's 'Prognosticatio', Mainz, 1492

he also stimulated research on peasant resistance with his differentiation
between 'primary' and 'secondary' forms of resistance. The notion of
partial resistance encompasses the individual and the collective rejection
of certain regulations and demands, the violation of prohibitions, as well
as legal disputes between peasants and lords concerning their respective
rights and duties. Peasant flight from the manor was defined as an
escalation of peasant resistance which meant not only that peasants
disagreed with certain demands of the lord but also that they intended to
break with him completely and were prepared to seek better terms
elsewhere. Peasant revolts finally were conceived as the open declaration
of war on the part of the peasants in order to change the existing
conditions to their benefit.

Critics of Porchnev's approach, while applauding the typology he
proposed as well as his subtle subdivision of the various forms of peasant

resistance, rejected his proposal to include the peasants' efforts to increase their agricultural production in the general question of peasant struggle.[8] In order to replace the problematic differentiation between 'primary' and 'secondary' forms of resistance a distinction between 'manifest' and 'latent' forms has been suggested,[9] because this terminological refinement corresponds much better to the various stages and levels of conflict. The relevance of a stage of 'latent' forms of resistance lies mainly in the fact that it draws attention to the element of time, that is to the growth of peasant dissatisfaction until reaching the crucial 'threshold' where latent resistance would turn into open aggression. Beyond this crucial point the forms of active resistance depended mainly on the economic and legal status of the peasantry, the organization of the manor and the political aims of their protest movements.

The distinction between non-violent and violent forms of resistance, which many analyses attempt to determine, proves to be more difficult than it seems at first glance because there is no clear-cut difference between peasant revolts and other forms of conflict.[10] This is because the historical interpretation of peasant revolts cannot be separated from the overall political context and other, less militant forms of resistance. Peasant revolts were usually the result of long-term developments in the course of which the peaceful forms of everyday protest gradually turned into militant action. However, it is extremely difficult to determine the crucial point that pushed limited resistance into full-scale revolts, that is the 'threshold' where peaceful protest became militant action. Is the collective refusal to pay feudal dues or to perform labour services already an act of violence, or must this term be reserved for open attacks on institutions and officials in the service of the lord of the manor? In asking such questions it should always be remembered that rigid limitations and classifications can detract from a realistic and sensitive understanding of the course of peasant revolts as a whole.

The analysis of peasant revolts should never be isolated from the conditions and circumstances which led to the formation of such movements. In legal and economic terms particular heed must be given to the correlation between local agrarian structures and conditions and the forms of protest. The various types of manorial regime, the extent of demesne farming, the composition of dues and services, the degree of independence of the peasant economy, and property rights – all of these factors had a decisive influence on the form and intensity of peasant resistance against the demands of the lords of the manor. On the traditional manor with its time-consuming labour obligations,[11] the economic and legal position of the peasant was radically different from his position on the manor of the late Middle Ages where payments determined not only the relationship between lord and peasant, but also his social status within the village as well as the forms of his protest. Furthermore the property rights of peasant holdings were subject to great

Figure 38 Peasant beating bailiff
Wood engraving by the Master of the Petrarca, Augsburg, 1532

changes in the course of the Middle Ages, so that a large variety of such rights developed which ranged from the disadvantageous *Freistift* lease, which had to be renewed annually, to the more favourable hereditary leases. Peasant resistance against excessive demands from manorial, jurisdictional or territorial lords was most successful in those areas where independent family enterprises were the predominant form of husbandry and where the peasants were organized in neighbourhood groups and village communities.

Research on peasant revolts in the Middle Ages, which has increased considerably over the last decades, has usually concentrated on the fourteenth and fifteenth centuries, especially in Germany.[12] This trend is not purely accidental, nor is it only the result of the actual increase in peasant revolts during the crisis of the late Middle Ages. It has rather been the Great Peasants' War of 1525 which has stimulated interest in the revolts of the preceding centuries. However, this highly simplified perspective has induced G. Franz for one to regard each and every peasant revolt of the fourteenth and fifteenth centuries as a 'precursor' of the Peasants' War of 1525.[13] Even Peter Blickle, the author of the most recent comprehensive study of this event, has endorsed this view with his apodictic statement that 'in the late Middle Ages Europe saw itself confronted with a phenomenon which had been unknown in the previous history of the west – the peasant rebellion.'[14] Yet is it really true that both the early and the high Middle Ages, the period when feudal society came to full fruition, were without peasant revolts and acts of peasant resistance? What future research should take into account, besides considering that little effort has been made so far to describe the peasant revolts of the high Middle Ages, is the fact that peasant protest took less spectacular forms in that period and occurred at other levels of political activity than in the following centuries.

The first known acts of peasant resistance in the early Middle Ages were a response to the progressive feudalization and the extension of manorial dependence.[15] The year 579 saw a major peasant insurrection which was directed against the rule of the Merovingian king Chilperich, in the course of which many peasants in the vicinity of Limoges left their holdings to escape excessive tax burdens. Tax collectors were threatened with death by the infuriated mob, so that in the end military force was used to stop the rebellion.[16] During the reign of the Carolingian kings peasant resistance was apparently limited to non-violent actions and other such protests against the consolidation of the manorial system. A number of refusals to perform services and to pay dues were recorded as well as other forms of protest against the growing demands of the lords of the manor. In many cases unfree peasants tried to escape from their lords – a form of resistance which entailed more severe punishment for runaway dependants.

The biggest peasant rebellion in Carolingian times occurred in 841 when the peasants of Stellinga in Saxony protested against the Frankish type of feudal rule.[17] In Saxony, which had only recently been subjugated by the Frankish rulers, the process of feudalization was much slower than in the other provinces of the Frankish Empire. Hence the traditional social structure of nobles, freemen (*Frilinge*) and half-free (*Liten*) survived longer in Saxony than elsewhere in the Empire. The position of freemen and half-free, who had fought most persistently against the Frankish conquerors, had deteriorated markedly with the invasion of the Franks and the introduction of their rule. Encouraged by open dissent among the sons of King Louis 'the Pious', the Saxon freemen and half-free arose in a big rebellious movement between 841 and 843. This Stellinga movement encompassed both dependent and free peasant groups and was primarily directed against lay and ecclesiastical manorial lords whose position had improved since the Frankish conquest to the detriment of the peasantry. It took King Louis and the Saxon nobility several extremely violent campaigns to suppress the insurrection, which had spread over large parts of Saxony.

Peasant resistance in the high Middle Ages

In the high Middle Ages, that is between the eleventh and the thirteenth centuries, peasant resistance against the feudal regime assumed a surprising variety of forms, especially in the wake of the consolidation of the manorial system during the Carolingian era – when many peasants became dependants.[18] Forms ranged from everyday passive resistance, such as the refusal of services and the striving for better property rights, or emigration and flight from the manors, to more developed forms such as peasant revolts and peasant wars. Since most peasants were now incorporated into the manorial system and subject to its obligations such as labour services, peasant resistance until the end of the twelfth century was mainly limited to activities on the domains and the individual manors themselves. At the same time, and not least because of the resistance of the peasants, the traditional form of manorial regime began to crumble and to change into a new type based on more favourable forms of tenure and other manorial duties.

In the twelfth and thirteenth centuries more and more peasants refused to pay dues and to perform their labour services, or they protested by neglecting their duties. Lay and ecclesiastical lords answered by threatening them with heavy punishments and advised them to pay their tributes in full and on time. In 1145, for example, the dependants of the monastery of St Georgenberg near Goslar were presented with a written stipulation of their obligations, and were emphatically admonished not to violate the regulations of the manor out of negligence.[19] Those who failed to pay on the day agreed or who did not submit their grain dues in time were fined 12 shillings by the administration of the monastery. This was a comparatively heavy fine, but by no means exceptional at that time. A considerable number of comparable warnings concerning punctual payment of taxes and tithes suggest that medieval peasants often refused to submit their dues as agreed.

Labour obligations were obviously the main target of the resistance of the peasants because they were a key factor for the functioning of the traditional manor. Everywhere the manorial lords complained that labour services were performed only reluctantly and with poor results, and that the peasants showed little willingness to produce the agreed quality standards. When in 1117 the abbot of the Alsatian monastery at Maursmünster converted the traditional labour service of three days per week into a cash payment, he justified the abandonment of the labour services by referring explicitly to the fact that the peasants had performed their services only with extreme sluggishness and negligence, even grudgingly, as a result of which they had caused the monastery more harm than good.[20] About the year 1150 the land register of the monastery at Helmstedt in the east of Saxony also referred to the reluctance of the peasants in proper performance of their labour duties. Dependants who failed to do their service, or performed it without due care, were punished with severe flogging or paid a fine as a subsitute for thirty strokes with the rod.[21] It was not exceptional for peasants to miss their services on purpose or to perform them with carelessness. Thus it was not least the resistance of the peasants against labour dues, in addition to other factors discussed earlier in this study,[22] which caused the lords of the twelfth and thirteenth centuries to abandon the traditional organization of the manor. By leasing the demesne farm to the dependants of the manor the traditional labour obligations became superfluous and could be converted into money payments.

Peasant resistance against the heavy demands of the manorial lords grew in the high Middle Ages with the rise of urban centres and the intensive development of landed resources which offered alternative livelihoods and often brought the peasants more personal freedom. In many regions the growing tensions and conflicts between lords and peasants provoked the latter either to move or, if necessary, to flee into clearance settlements or towns. Since both lay and ecclesiastical lords depended on a sufficient number of settlers for the colonization of their territories, they could not but offer them lucrative terms in addition to substantial economic, legal and political privileges. At the same time the many prospering towns could also provide a great number of people with employment, career opportunities and enticing personal privileges of all kinds. Thus it was not surprising to see that many peasants escaped from their lords into the towns, where they could apply for the status of free citizens after a year and a day.[23] As early as the middle of the twelfth century interesting information was recorded on the population drain in the lower Rhine area. A document of a Cologne monastery by the name of St Pantaleon from the year 1141 stated that the dependants of two manors had been oppressed to the point where they had left their homes and holdings to seek better conditions elsewhere.[24] Moreover, in 1158 the archbishop of Cologne confirmed a regulation whereby the feudal dues of the dependants of the monastery were reduced. This was because excessive dues and labour obligations had prompted an alarming emigration among serfs and other dependants of that convent.[25]

During the thirteenth century population drain and the problems accompanying it increased parallel to the growth in the number of new towns, which were founded everywhere. Ecclesiastical and lay lords reacted by introducing strict regulations which prohibited their peasants from moving into the towns; yet they met not only with resistance from their dependants but also with the opposition of many town patrons, who had a great interest in further growth and thus the unrestricted flow of countryfolk into the urban foundations within their territories. Imperial prohibition decreed by Emperor Frederick II (1212–50), which were designed to stop the influx of the dependants of their counts into the free towns, turned out to have very little effect at all.[26] Moreover, the sheer number of peasants emigrating to towns and clearance areas forced manorial lords to make considerable concessions to the serfs who stayed behind. Consequently the position of the peasants in the earliest settled regions also improved at that time. In many places they were granted a reduction of labour services, greater mobility and fixed dues.

The formation and consolidation of the village community and the increasing amalgamation of the various peasant groups into the village of the high Middle Ages also contributed to the solidarity of the peasantry as an estate and fostered a greater willingness to resist the excessive demands of their lords. The growing self-confidence of the peasant communities resulted in more frequent disputes with their lords concerning rights to woodlands and pastures In 1210 a conflict was finally settled concerning the use of the woodlands between the monastery of Salem and the peasants of Oberzell, a village to the north of Lake Constance, which had lasted for several years. It had escalated particularly in 1198 when the inhabitants of Oberzell devastated a farm of the monastery at Adelsreute, an action for which they were sentenced to heavy ecclesiastical punishment.[27] A stubborn conflict which was also related to the use of the commons was recorded between the abbey of Himmerode and a number of its villages. It was above all the peasants of Dudeldorf, Pickliessem and Gindorf who felt defrauded of their traditional right to use a large stretch of woodland, as a result of which they attacked a farm belonging to the monastery, seized its cattle and threw stones at the lay servants of the monastery.[28] It was only after the inhabitants of the villages concerned were faced with the possibility of being excommunicated that in 1228 a compromise between the conflicting parties was eventually reached which put an end to the aggression on both sides. Similar struggles between assertive peasant communities and manorial lords who tried to restrict their rights to the commons were also recorded in many other regions during the thirteenth century. The number of conflicts grew as arable land became scarce with the intensified development of land resources – a trend which incited many feudal lords to try and raise their revenues by limiting peasant rights to the commons.

It must be recognized that peasants did have some success in fighting excessive demands by their refusal to pay dues, by emigrating to towns or clearance areas, or by other forms of resistance; yet they were in a particularly unfortunate position in their struggle with the most powerful of the feudal lords, who tried to consolidate their scattered holdings with the help of castles, judicial monopolies and the appointment of knights as administrative officials. In the thirteenth and fourteenth centuries peasant communities clashed with ambitious rulers, especially in the Alpine provinces and along the coastlines of the North Sea where the rural population had fought hard to obtain a relatively independent social position and far-reaching autonomy in communal matters.[29] Yet as some of the more influential lords tried to expand their influence into areas occupied by relatively independent peasant communities with developed co-operative structures, they encountered the determined resistance of these rural peasant communities. In the thirteenth century, for example, peasant insurrections and even long peasant wars shook particularly such regions as Drente, West and East Frisia, the Stedingerland and Dithmarschen.[30]

There can be no doubt that the insurrection of the Stedingers was one of the most impressive peasant revolts of the high Middle Ages. The Stedinger communities in the lower Weser area waged a major war against the archbishops of Bremen and the counts of Oldenburg in an effort to preserve their independence. Yet although they fought for years, they were not as successful as the Frisians and eventually lost against the combined forces of their enemies.[31] It has been mentioned earlier that as early as the twelfth century the archbishops of Bremen had promoted peasant settlement as a means to turn the swamps and marshes along the lower Weser river into profitable farmland.[32] As an incentive for the arduous clearing work the archbishops granted the settlers considerable economic and legal privileges, including favourable dues, heritable holdings and a certain degree of autonomy in the lower jurisdictional courts. The agreements also allowed the settlers to administer their own affairs under the formal supervision of the archbishop. The dikes and channels which were soon built to drain the land and protect it from the periodic inundations by the North Sea required the joint effort of the entire population and greatly increased their sense of solidarity. Co-operation continued to be the means to survive even after the initial clearing and drainage measures, which manifested itself in the strictly organized dike-cooperatives of the Stedingers. These safeguarded their existence in the marshes and also provided a firm institutional basis for the recruitment of armed peasant units which soon fought highly successful battles in the struggle for their independence.

After the turn of the twelfth to the thirteenth century tensions increased as the archbishops of Bremen and the counts of Oldenburg sought to gain more control over the Stedinger territory with the erection of castles and the deployment of their vassals. At the same time the Stedingers continued to develop their village administrations and other co-operative institutions, adopted the name *Communitas terre Stedingorum* as a formula for the commonwealth of all Stedingers and even introduced their own seal as a symbol of their independence. The counter-offensive of the peasant communities against the attacks of the advancing feudal forces consisted in the destruction of castles and the expulsion of knightly *ministeriales*. In addition they fortified their villages and farmland with walls and moats and thus further improved their naturally advantageous defence position in the marshes. After an initial attack by the episcopal troops in 1207, which was designed to force payment of larger dues from the communities, their marshlands were again invaded by an army of knights sent in 1229 on behalf of the archbishop. As it happened they did not achieve very much, and the news of the military successes of the peasant defenders spread fast into the neighbouring provinces and carried the Stedingers considerable respect among the rural population in the other north-western provinces of the German Empire. The feudal authorities, on the other hand, were extremely alarmed. A chronicler of the Stade monastery wrote that 'a vast number of peasants near and far supported the Stedingers in words and showed a willingness to join them in their resistance as the opportunity arose.'[33]

After the Stedingers were accused of heresy by the Bremen synod of 1231 and Pope Gregory IX even proclaimed a crusade against them, a large army of crusaders gathered in Bremen and left for the Stedinger territory. The Stedingers, however, managed against all expectations to beat them heroically near Hemmelskamp. At this point all feudal lords and even princes in the north-west of the Empire feared for the foundation of their rule and summoned an even larger army of crusaders in 1234 which was composed of the knights and troops of the duke of Brabant and the counts of Holland and Cleves, as well as those of the archbishop of Bremen and the counts of Oldenburg. The concentrated forces of these crusaders were too powerful an enemy for the peasant army of the Stedingers, and despite their admirable defence their 3,000 peasants were crushed on 27 May 1234 in an extremely violent battle near Altenesch. It put an end to the remarkable degree of independence which the Stedingers had preserved for so long, and from now on their territory was under the full control of the archbishops of Bremen and the counts of Oldenburg. The peasants had to accept a marked deterioration of their status as dues and taxes were raised, and their heritable holdings were converted into much less favourable property rights. A substantial proportion of their land was confiscated for the knights who were now in charge of the local administration.

Considering peasant resistance in the high Middle Ages as a whole, it must be reiterated that it included many forms of peasant protest, ranging from such everyday actions as the refusal to pay dues or disputes concerning the use of the commons, to peasant flight and militant rebellions, and even full-scale warfare. As the Stedinger insurrection has illustrated, only those peasant communities were in the position to resist feudal interference in the long run which could rely on developed co-operative insitutions, such as dike and court associations, as well as on the solidarity of their members. In contrast to the Stedingers, the peasant communities of Dithmarschen, who were also formally the subjects of the archbishops of Bremen, managed not only to maintain but also to extend their impressive autonomy, as well as to resist the assaults of territorial rulers and to establish an independent peasant commonwealth which survived until the late sixteenth century.[34] The Swiss Confederation, which had emerged under the different circumstances and conditions of the Alpine provinces, was another example of the successful resistance of the peasantry.

Peasant revolts in France, England and Flanders

Three major peasant revolts outside Germany are particularly important when considering peasant resistance in the late Middle Ages: the revolt in Flanders between 1323 and 1328, the Jacquerie in northern France in 1358 – and not least the English peasant revolt of 1381.[35] The Jacquerie of 1358, which was essentially a revolt caused by peasant destitution, was unique because of its surprising geographical spread over a very small time-span.[36] Heavy tax demands, the vast devastation of the country as a result of the Hundred Years War and innumerable lootings by impoverished mercenaries had driven the defenceless peasantry to despair. Faced with the wretchedness and insecurity of their condition the peasants were allowed to form their own defence units to repulse the assaults of vagrant mercenary gangs. In the last days of May 1358 an open insurrection started in the Beauvais region which soon spread into Picardy and other neighbouring areas. In many places the rebellious peasant troops, which for the most part operated independent of each other, forced procrastinating individuals to join them. Great bitterness was felt towards a nobility which only pursued its own interests and often participated in pillaging

Figure 39 Knight surrounded by rebellious peasants carrying the flag of the Bundschuh movement
Wood engraving by the Master of the Petrarca, Augsburg, 1532

the countryside rather than protecting the peasants and their villages. Hence the peasants answered with the destruction of many castles and mansions, often driving away the owners. Most towns, however, were undecided, and only a few of them were active supporters of the revolt. It was soon plain that the insurrection was highly spontaneous in character and lacked a political perspective, for it collapsed after a few months despite its vast geographical extent.

By comparison with the Jacquerie, the English peasant revolt of the year 1381 was well organized and its leaders were far more determined.[37] The revolt started at the end of May 1381 in the south-western counties and was essentially crushed under the counter-offensives of the king and the nobility by the end of June of the same year. Although the revolt had broken out very suddenly, the leaders, who were supported by large parts of the urban population, followed a carefully thought-out political strategy. One of the principal demands of the rebellious peasants was the abolition of serfdom. The high tax burden and considerable feudal obligations affected the entire peasantry, so that not merely the poorer peasant groups but also many rich peasants joined the rebels. In particular the rich peasants were well organized and thus often took the lead on the local level. The programme of ideas of this rebellion was the product of such lesser clergymen as John Ball, who sympathized with the ideas of John Wyclif and the Lollards. All in all, despite the defeat of the rebels, the English peasant revolt of 1381 had positive effects on the position of the English peasantry because it accelerated the dissolution of serfdom and of the manorial dependence of the peasants.

As opposed to the peasant risings in England and France, the Flemish revolt lasted for several years, from 1323 to 1328.[38] The principal targets of this insurrection were lay manorial lords and administrative abuses by tax collectors and administrative officials. The centres of the rebellion were the coastal areas of Flanders where the peasants had won considerable independence in the high Middle Ages. It started in the vicinity of Bruges during the winter of 1323 and was at first directed against the excesses of the judicial authorities, who charged taxes and court fees in an arbitrary manner. The struggle against these individual abuses soon developed into a universal protest of assertive peasant communities who held much more far-reaching goals. In their rage the rebels launched their assaults mainly on the castles of the nobility, which were often pillaged and destroyed in the course of the rebellion. Without meeting any serious opposition the revolt soon affected the entire province and found the support of all towns except Ghent. The office-holders of the counts were replaced by representatives from the peasant estate, who maintained the normal administration for years. The decisive blow against the rebels eventually came from an army sent by the king of France at the request of the count of Flanders. After a big battle near Cassel in 1328 the Flemish peasant army was forced to surrender to the

French knights, and this defeat marked the final collapse of the insurrection.

Peasant uprisings in the German Empire during the later Middle Ages

In common with the German peasant revolts of the late Middle Ages, these three peasant revolts had a number of causes and crisis-points which also reflect the crisis of the late Middle Ages, which forms the subject of the final chapter.[39] Particular emphasis should be given to the agrarian crisis with all its adverse consequences for peasants and feudal lords alike, as well as to the crisis in feudalism in general and the attempts of the lords to balance their losses of income by greater pressure on the dependent peasantry. In addition, pressure was put on the peasantry by princes and sovereigns in their efforts to strengthen their territories by consolidating their scattered holdings into much larger, compact territories which were now governed with the help of a central administration. However, in doing so they were soon confronted with the resistance of the peasants, who were afraid to lose their traditional privileges and rights in local self-administration. Also among the causes of peasant movements in the late Middle Ages were the changing intellectual, religious and ecclesiastical currents, which were so powerful that they also left their traces on the movements among the peasantry.

The German peasant revolts in the late Middle Ages, which can only be mentioned in passing in this chapter, became much more frequent in the late fourteenth and the fifteenth centuries and had a much greater political impetus than their forerunners.[40] In the fourteenth century only four major peasant revolts were recorded while this number increased to fifteen in the first half and then to twenty-five in the second half of the fifteenth century.[41] The causes, aims and developments of these revolts, which mainly occurred in the south of Germany, were actually rather diverse. Some cannot be isolated from the contemporaneous pogroms against the Jews, such as the *Armleder* movement of 1336–9,[42] others were permeated by religious and 'nationalist' motives, such as the Hussite revolution in the first half of the fifteenth century.[43] Sometimes the peasant rebels developed new political schemes such as the adherents of the *Bund ob dem See* revolt in Appenzell, Switzerland.[44] Many of them, however, consisted of spontaneous actions devoid of any conscious political ambition. Although the Holy Roman Empire was not affected by revolts as widespread as the major peasant revolts in France and England, the German insurrections nevertheless had by no means a purely local character. They were unique because the peasants formed very large alliances which often went beyond the borders of a single territory and also because they were directed against several princes simultaneously. There can be no doubt, however, that the most far-reaching, radical and influential peasant uprising in Germany was the Great Peasants' War of 1525, which cannot be discussed in this study because it took place at the beginning of the early modern period.

PART VI

THE UPHEAVALS OF THE LATE MIDDLE AGES

THE PEASANTS AND
THE AGRARIAN CRISIS

Causes for settlement desertions in the later Middle Ages

Deserted settlements characterized many regions in Europe during the late Middle Ages. Even today a considerable number of areas bear witness to older abandoned fields and settlements that have long since disappeared. The only reminders of them are a few remains in forests and on pastures, or by old place-names. Keen observers may suddenly find dilapidated walls in the middle of thick woodland, or they may discover the overgrown terraces of former fields or heaps of stone which were once cleared from them. Even the ground-plans of old churches can sometimes be made out, and like the ruins of castles the remains of medieval settlements have always stirred the imagination of the common people, who have often spun all kinds of stories and folk tales to explain their desertion. Neighbours, when consulted about the time of the desertion of such a settlement, tend to say that it was destroyed in the Thirty Years War. Nevertheless the studies which have been published on this subject over the last decades have demonstrated that only a very small proportion of these deserted settlements were really abandoned after the devastations of the Thirty Years War, and that most of them were never occupied again after the late Middle Ages.[1] A much smaller proportion of them were deserted in either earlier or later centuries, such as in the high Middle Ages when settlements were abandoned which were situated in the vicinity of newly founded towns, or during the desertions which were recorded in eastern Germany during early modern times, when entire villages were absorbed by the new landed estates.

It is generally accepted that around the year 1300 approximately 170,000 settlements existed in the territory of Germany in its 1937 borders. By the end of the fifteenth century this number had decreased to about 130,000.[2] The proportion of deserted settlements, however, varied considerably from region to region and was by no means uniform

throughout Germany as a whole. It was particularly high in the north of
the Mark Brandenburg, in the Thuringian basin, east of the River Weser
and south of the Elbe, and in regions of higher altitude in Swabia, where in
some cases more than 40 per cent of the total number of settlements were
abandoned. On the other hand, deserted settlements were comparatively
rare in the thinly populated north-west of Germany and in the Rhine
area.[3] A careful distinction must be made between settlements which
were deserted while their fields continued to be farmed by the
neighbouring villages, and the complete desertion of arable land. The
term 'partial desertion' as opposed to 'total desertion' is often used to
describe the abandonment of certain parts of a village, hamlet or group of
farmsteads. This meant in most cases that the remaining parts of the
settlement continued to be occupied and farmed. The effects can still be
detected in the settlement pattern of central Europe today. What, then,
caused such an astounding number of settlements to be deserted? What
were the essential demographic, economic and social changes in the late
Middle Ages which led to the desertion of almost 25 per cent of the
settlements in Germany, for example?

Study of the causes for the desertion of settlements has produced a
great number of interesting hypotheses and explanations, but most of
them have been far too speculative. There was, for example, the war or
'security' theory, which was based on the assumption that wars were
responsible for the great number of deserted settlements. It was claimed
that the rest of the population moved into larger settlements which were
much easier to defend against the attacks of robber-barons and roaming
gangs of mercenaries. The theory of 'mistaken settlement' suggested that
many villages were deserted because of the poor quality of the farmland,
which eventually forced the peasants to abandon the unprofitable soils. In
addition there were the adherents of the 'intensification' theory who
argued that the intensified use of the fields close to the settlement centres
led to a reduction of the total land under the plough and thus in turn to
the partial desertion of the fields of the affected villages. Other causes
given included earthquakes, floods, fires, the expropriation of village land
by monasteries as well as the rise of the towns – all of which touched
upon certain aspects of historical developments as a whole. Yet none of
them came close to the real problem underlying this matter, and so a
convincing explanation of the overall development was for a long time
lacking. Moreover, many of these theories were developed at a time when
the extent of the late medieval population drop and its effect on
agriculture were still unknown.

The agrarian crisis of the later Middle Ages

There can be no doubt that the best explanation is the theory of an overall
agrarian crisis of the late Middle Ages which was first presented by

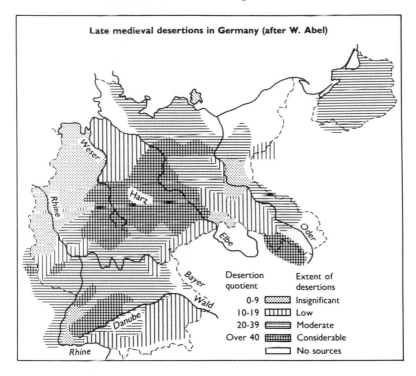

Figure 40 Late medieval desertions in Germany
(after W. Abel)

W. Abel and others.[4] Despite a number of objections and corrections which have been made, it is still by far the most convincing explanation of the great number of deserted settlements in the late Middle Ages. It focused on such factors as the decline in population, the development of prices for agrarian produce and commercial goods, and the level of wages; and it worked out the correlations between them. The change in the relation between prices for agrarian produce and prices for commercial goods, for instance, resulted in a marked drop in agricultural wages and thus caused a further decrease in rural population. According to Abel's theory it was precisely this decrease in population which was the main cause for the large-scale desertion of settlements. It began with the widespread famines of the first half of the fourteenth century and continued on an even more devastating scale with the onslaught of the plague.

It took only the first of them, the famous 'Black Death' of 1347–51, to wipe out about a quarter of the population in most countries of Europe.[5]

Additional outbreaks of the epidemic were recorded in 1360–1 and in 1380–3; they further diminished the population until by around 1460 the entire European population had been reduced to two-thirds of its former size. The immediate effect of the plagues was a kind of existential shock which made itself felt in every sphere of contemporary life as well as in the forms of human behaviour, causing reactions ranging from a fervent religiosity to a large variety of secular excesses. In the opinion of F. Lütge the serious drop in the population of the late Middle Ages was one of the turning-points in the history of Europe. He argued that it is literally impossible to understand historical developments in the following centuries without taking an event into account which had such serious consequences as the plagues. For this was more than death on a massive scale, this was something deeply distressing and incomprehensible, for which the men of the Middle Ages could find no solace. The Black Death was an apocalyptic event, incomparable to all previously known tragedy from famine to war.[6]

In analysing the causes for the desertion of rural settlements another factor must be mentioned in addition to the general decline in population, namely migration into urban centres. The peasants who moved away either made their living in the neighbouring towns which had often lost a great number of their inhabitants in the plagues, or they settled in villages where they found better economic conditions. This is what can be deduced from the fact that deserted settlements were much more frequent in areas with poor-quality soils. It is obvious in the case of the wooded areas in Thuringia and the lower Harz mountain range, for example, that those villages were first deserted which had been established under the difficult circumstances of the last phase of land development in the high Middle Ages.[7] The older settlements and villages, on the other hand, were least affected by the desertions since these desertions occurred mainly in other areas, such as on mountain slopes, poor soils and similar terrain which had been settled comparatively late. It must therefore be concluded that the peasants of the late Middle Ages abandoned the poorer soils and difficult agricultural terrain on mountain slopes, instead concentrating their efforts on better soils and profiting from the more developed transport in the valleys.

The decrease both in population and in the demand for grain corresponded with a long, steep fall in grain prices from the second half of the fourteenth century.[8] Since cereals counted among the basic foodstuffs, and were thus not subject to large fluctuations in consumption, and because their supply did not drop as fast as the demand, peasants produced a substantial grain surplus, causing a widespread and steady fall in grain prices which lasted for generations. In the case of France, where excellent data have been collected, the level of grain prices dropped from an assumed 100 per cent level between 1351 and 1375 to a mere 40 per cent a century later. It was only in the early sixteenth century that prices gradually reached their previous level.[9] As a consequence of the mass death caused by the plagues there was a marked reduction in the supply of labour, so that real wages rose considerably during the late Middle Ages. Owing to the fact that commercial goods retained their price level in contrast to farm produce, a disastrous discrepancy emerged between the prices for agrarian products as opposed to those for commercial goods. Agriculture, on the whole, saw itself confronted with rising costs in comparison to falling profits, at least on those manors where the lords depended on wage-labourers or where agricultural production required the purchase of a significant portion of commercial goods from the market. The drop in grain prices in the fourteenth century was unprecedented because earlier centuries, especially during the agricultural boom in the high Middle Ages, had for the most part seen a continuous rise in the prices for farm produce. This development had been to the benefit of both the lords and the peasants. The upward trend reached its peak in the late Middle Ages, and the agrarian crisis which followed hit feudal lords and peasants alike and had serious social consequences.

The decrease in the demand for basic foodstuffs and the fall in grain prices during the late Middle Ages gave rise to an important change in the use of land.[10] Poor soils were abandoned, cultivation continuing only on the richer ones, so that on the whole there was an increase in productivity. The reduction of the amount of farmland used for crops was thus accompanied by a corresponding extension of pasture which in turn provided the basis for an increase in livestock production. In many regions livestock production grew at the expense of crops and thereby supplied the population with a greater variety of meat products. This accounts for the undoubtedly higher per capita meat consumption in the late Middle Ages. The keeping of cattle continued to be the most important branch of livestock production because cattle were much easier to winter on meagre hay and straw provisions than pigs. Clearly the meat supply of the towns had never been better than in the late Middle Ages, and the fall in grain prices permitted the average consumer to spend a much greater share of income on meat products. At the same time the reduction of grain production was a stimulus for, and in turn caused by, the increased production of various other crops, like vegetables, for instance, or plants which were used for production of commercial goods. The cultivation of flax and other plants, such as madder and woad which were used for dye-making, supplied the expanding textile industries with the raw materials they needed, whereas other produce, such as wine, hops, fruit and vegetables, were also very welcome because they enriched the daily diet of the rural population. In Germany viniculture reached its maximum geographical development at a time when the production of grain hit rock bottom, and vines were even planted in areas where the conditions were far from adequate for satisfactory quality.[11]

How far the falling profits from agricultural labour and other aspects

**The Development of grain prices in Central Europe,
1351-1550 (after W. Abel)**

Figure 41 The development of grain prices in
central Europe, 1351–1550
(after W. Abel)

of the crisis influenced the daily life of the peasantry depended not least
on how the feudal lords responded to this transformation in agriculture.
In many regions the growing pressure from the manorial, servile and
jurisdictional lords on the rural population must be added to the highly
disadvantageous effects of the agrarian depression on peasant incomes.
Yet the lords of the manors and others who profited from incomes
derived from agriculture were hit even harder by the agrarian crisis than
the peasants themselves, because they had to cope with losses in income
which were even higher by comparison.[12] The incomes of the manorial
lords dropped essentially because of five factors which varied in degree
and intensity from region to region:

1 Many holdings could not be rented as a consequence of the decrease in
population, resulting in a substantial loss of dues in money and kind for
lords, particularly in areas with a high percentage of deserted holdings
and settlements. This inflicted disastrous loss of income on the church,
the monasteries and the lay nobility.

2 In order to find new tenants for such deserted holdings the lords had to
make considerable concessions, such as lower rents and dues, and offer
subsidies and investments for the resumption of farming of deserted

holdings. Faced with the shortage of human labour, feudal lords were sometimes forced to vie with each other for tenants, and the peasants were often lured with lucrative terms to take over vacant farms. In upper Bavaria, for example, a new type of law emerged in the wake of the attempt to fill deserted holdings which is known by the term *Ödrecht*. It stipulated that peasants who agreed to farm deserted holdings were for a certain number of years exempt from the payment of taxes as well as dues to the advocate. In 1385 twenty-seven of the holdings owned by the monastery of Tegernsee in the administrative district of Gevild in the plains south of Munich were deserted, and thirteen were rented on the favourable terms provided by the *Ödrecht*. Peasant dues in this district dropped from 60 pounds in 1350 to 26 in 1385, when the monastery at Tegernsee suffered the climax of its income losses in this district and recorded its greatest proportion of deserted holdings.[13]

3 The negative trend in manorial incomes increased with the drop in grain prices in the late Middle Ages. This affected in particular the manorial lords who received a considerable proportion of their feudal rents in kind, because they were forced, in the attempt to sell such farm produce, to accept the fluctuating conditions of sale on the markets. The bulk of the dues in kind, however, consisted of grain, and this was why the lords of the manors also suffered from losses due to falling grain prices. The recipients of tithes felt these losses more than other feudal lords because tithes were traditionally paid in kind.

4 In addition to the agrarian produce which they received as part of their feudal rents, manorial lords also had to sell the surplus from their own farming, provided that they still farmed to a significant extent. This, however, often required the labour of paid farmhands and day-labourers. Hence the wage increases of the fourteenth and fifteenth centuries came into play, since they had an additional negative effect on the production costs on manors, hence further reducing the net revenues of the demesne farms. On a great number of manors recommended wage rates and maximum wages were introduced to stop the increase of wages which followed the shortage of labour, but not even the strictest regulations had much effect on the long-term development of such wages. Abandonment or reduction of the farming of the demesne, or the transition to labour-extensive forms of cultivation were the only means by which the feudal lords could preserve the profitability of their manors.

5 Another factor which contributed to the reduction of manorial incomes was the decreasing purchasing power of the money rents, which were nominally fixed. They had not been raised for a long time; however, their loss in value increased as the purchasing power of money dropped owing to debasement of currency, inflationary tendencies and the changes in the overall price structure. Many lords were thus faced with a serious lack of money in the course of the economic crisis of the fourteenth-century, and some of them sold their rights to dues and taxes for a lump-

sum payment. Although this meant relief for the time being, it was nevertheless detrimental to a more permanent stabilization of their financial situation.

The difficulties of the lords of the manor

These five principal factors, in addition to others, contributed in their own way to the dramatic deterioration of the economic position of many lords in the fourteenth and fifteenth centuries. In analysing the reactions of the lay nobility to this crisis a careful distinction must be made between the various groups of the nobility. The less wealthy knights (*Ritter*) who had little land of their own were, of course, in a radically different situation from the feudal princes who ruled large territories. The latter had other sources of income besides the rents for landed property, such as their extremely lucrative tax revenues. Owing to reduced incomes from their own farming and the decrease in rents, the financial situation of the majority of the lower nobility deteriorated on a drastic scale during the fourteenth century. Many knightly families were impoverished or lost their economic basis completely, especially when they were unable to find additional sources of income, such as employment in the administration of the territorial princes and other rulers, or in their mercenary forces.

Detailed studies on the incomes of the nobility in various regions have shown that the financial difficulties of large proportions of the lay nobility began as early as 1300.[14] This seems to confirm observations made earlier in this study about the conditions of the peasantry, who at that time had to cope with similar problems created by the agrarian crisis.[15] It is obvious that the economic development of peasants on the one hand and feudal lords on the other can only be studied in tandem and that they reflect the social and economic problems which accumulated in trade, society and politics towards the turn of the thirteenth to the fourteenth century. The economic difficulties of the nobility, and the deterioration of their incomes, depended in various ways on the arrangements between lords and peasants, the development of the feudal system and the protection of their entitlement to rent. In any case, the first decades of the fourteenth century made it clear that feudal revenues were stagnating or even in decline, and that particularly the lesser nobility was affected by substantial losses in income and property. In the course of the fourteenth century the demographic and economic changes mentioned above turned the 'crisis of feudalism' into a much wider 'agrarian crisis' which was the actual reason for the crisis of aristocratic rule. The growing pressure of feudal lords on the peasants, the increase in dues and the development of peasant dependence contributed to the aggravation of the crisis in the late Middle Ages and laid the foundation for peasant revolts and insurrections. The following section will take a look at a few examples in order to arrive at a fuller understanding of this development.

Research on the economic situation of the nobility in the Ortenau, an area on the upper Rhine, has shown that the deterioration of the coinage in the late fourteenth century and the falling prices for agricultural products together reduced incomes of the knightly gentry to half of what they had been a century before.[16] In addition to the continuous diminution of their revenues, dues and rents were lost as a result of peasant migration as well as the decrease in population, so that the local manors might well be faced with a 60 to 70 per cent loss of their former incomes. Nevertheless, the analysis of the circumstances of sixteen knightly families in the Ortenau has also made it clear that their financial difficulties had already begun in the first half of the fourteenth century. The financial crisis of the nobility and the decrease of their rents culminated in the course of the fourteenth century in an agrarian crisis which was then characterized by even further economic difficulties. The Ortenau nobility was, for example, confronted with substantial losses in their income and in rents which affected particularly those families that depended entirely on agricultural income. A similar development of the economic position of the nobility and its income is known for many other regions and principalities. From the beginning of the fourteenth to the middle of the fifteenth centuries almost the entire nobility struggled with similar economic difficulties; this general impression cannot be invalidated by the counter-examples which undoubtedly exist. The first signs of financial recovery appear only at the end of the fifteenth century.

On the basis of a critical study of sources, G. Bois has produced an excellent regional study of the overall economic situation in the late Middle Ages, focusing particularly on the social relations between lords and peasants during the late medieval crisis in economy and society.[17]

In his study the author looks closely at the eastern areas of Normandy, where he examines in particular two aspects of the social transformations from the mid-thirteenth to the mid-sixteenth centuries, namely the symptoms of the agrarian crisis and the problems specific to feudal lordship often known as the 'crisis of feudalism'. Bois has placed the transformation of the economic and social position of feudal lords and peasants within the framework of the overall structural changes of the late Middle Ages, while also correlating these with their political, social and economic components.

Towards the close of the thirteenth century eastern Normandy was beginning to struggle with a growing imbalance between the rise in population and the scarcity of the available land resources. As a result of the enormous demographic upswing in the previous centuries, the country had now reached its limits in the development of arable. Feudal revenues were stagnating or had already started to drop, and problems in the agrarian economy and in political control increased, which led to conflicts over the division of wealth. The deterioration of the coinage, rising taxes and various military campaigns also contributed to put a further strain on the relations between lords and peasants. Desperate for supplementary sources of income, the nobility engaged in raids and local warfare which further undermined the social and economic situation. Such devastations gravely hampered agricultural production, while royal tax demands, designed to finance war, created additional burdens for the peasant population. This was how the crisis of the nobility paved the way for a universal crisis of society. The increasing pressure of the lords on the peasantry aggravated a situation which had already been considerably worsened by the enormous population losses during the plagues as well as by the effects of the crisis in agriculture which had destabilized the price structure. From the early fourteenth to the middle of the fifteenth centuries, the population of eastern Normandy decreased by 50 per cent, whereas wages tripled and grain prices fell considerably.

All the difficulties arising out of this crisis conspired to further weaken the economic position of the peasants in eastern Normandy, who had anyway long ceased to be able to render all their dues and taxes. The nobility began losing its moral authority as well as its social function, and warfare and general instability were unmistakable signs that they did not fulfil their duty to protect the peasants. The failure of the nobility to maintain legal security and public safety during this crisis turned the political scales in northern France in favour of the king and the rulers of the local principalities. Moreover, the inability of the nobility to protect the rural population and to preserve law and order also strengthened the political position of the villages in their function as peasant security organizations.

Although this study on Normandy contains a number of regional characteristics which simply cannot be applied to other areas, such as the extraordinary impact of the wars which affected northern France in the fourteenth century, it nevertheless represents a model study of social change in the late Middle Ages. However, it is still a matter of interpretation whether either G. Bois's term 'crisis of feudalism', or W. Abel's formula 'agrarian crisis' are really appropriate; therefore the question will be left open here.[18]

Feuds and robber-barons

The increasing number of feuds, and the aggressive activities of robber-barons known in many regions of Germany during the late Middle Ages, were undoubtedly also symptoms of the agrarian depression and the new crisis of the manorial system.[19] The rapid decrease in income and feudal rents, which in addition threatened a considerable loss of social prestige, encouraged many knights and noblemen to engage in military campaigns against wealthy merchants or to begin feuding with other local lords. To live the life of a robber-baron was simply a desperate attempt of some of the feudal nobility to escape economic ruin; however, it also aggravated the crisis even further because it hit the peasant economy at its core. For it was primarily the peasants who had to bear the brunt of this mode of acquisition, and their economic situation deteriorated in the late Middle Ages as feuding knights and robber-barons devastated the land with their raids and arson. The nature of the problem can be elucidated with the help of a few examples from the north-west of Germany. In the years 1364–5 the seneschal of Meppen reported on a raid by Otto, count of Tecklenburg,[20] who was said to have stolen 24 cows and a total of 1,005 sheep from the village of Dahlem, on top of 92 cows and 80 horses from Haselünne, and 111 cows, 50 pigs, 15 horses and other goods of considerable value from the village of Holte, where he even slew two peasants in the course of the pillage. Yet feuds and raids of that kind are known not only among such powerful lords as the count of Tecklenburg, but even more so among the members of the lower nobility. In 1395 robber-barons visited a farm in Garen which belonged to the monastery at Gertrudenberg, and despite the severe punishment which was inflicted upon them they appeared a second time and stole several pigs, horses and oxen.[21] Many alliances were formed to keep the peace and to put an end to the feuds which often harmed innocent people, but few of them were much of a success. In 1371, Charles IV renewed the King's Peace in Westphalia which, in the following year, was sworn to by the most important rulers of that country. They agreed to protect 'all churches, cemeteries, and the lives and property of all tenants, the ploughing of their fields including the draught-animals and the two people who were required in the ploughing operation, as well as wild horses, merchants, pilgrims and other travelling clergymen'.[22]

The intensification of serfdom

The ways in which the feudal lords responded to the economic difficulties in the wake of the agrarian crisis varied considerably from region to region. They depended very largely on regional political structures, types of lordship and on the means of power lords exercised over their peasants. Some manorial lords were bold enough to attempt to balance their tax and rent losses by demanding higher dues from their peasants. The feudal lords generally used a great number of methods to burden their dependents with higher, as well as additional, dues, or they tried to compensate tax losses from peasant migration by raising the dues for the peasants who stayed. Plenty of occasions and reasons were cited to justify tax rises, such as demands on the grounds of either manorial or personal dependence, and then there were the lucrative taxes which could be

Figure 42 Plunder of a village in the fifteenth century.
From what is known as the medieval house-chronicle of Count Waldburg-Wolfegg
(1460–1480)

charged by advocates and territorial rulers. These attempts were, however, limited by the economic means of the peasants and their willingness to pay. Excessive demands on the part of the feudal lords were often met with a more or less successful resistance, most importantly an increase in peasant migration, or even flight, into the towns. In some instances peasants moved into neighbouring areas whose rulers promised them better legal and economic conditions. Feudal lords who did not have the means to prevent peasant migration, for instance by decreeing effective limitations on their personal freedom, were often forced to grant them reductions on their dues and services as well as offer better property rights in order to ensure that they stayed.

In Styria Duke Rudolf of Austria and the bishop of Seckau decided in 1360 to grant tax and rent reductions for holdings which had been deserted in the course of severe plagues.[23] According to this agreement it was illegal to levy advocacy taxes on peasant holdings which were not occupied and which, therefore, could not pay rent to the Seckau cathedral chapter. The duke as advocate could only levy taxes when these holdings were occupied again, while tax reductions were granted on other holdings corresponding with any reductions in rent made by the chapter. Cases are known when several lords, sometimes of an entire territory, agreed upon concerted action to the benefit of the dependent peasantry. In 1433 Duke Henry of Brunswick negotiated with the prelates and knights of his territory to limit servile dues throughout Brunswick.[24] It was explicitly stated that the measure was necessary to improve the situation in a region which had been seriously affected by large-scale peasant emigration, the desertion of the settlements and other problems related to the population drain. The peasants had been burdened with dues such as heriot and merchet which were clearly too high, as a result of which an alarming number of them had escaped into neighbouring territories.

Nevertheless many feudal lords who had the means did not hesitate to use violence to prevent peasant migration and keep their revenues from tenant holdings. Such means ranged from forced promises of loyalty, migration taxes and regulations to limit the personal freedom of the peasants to measures which actually attached the peasants to their holdings. A number of monasteries in upper Bavaria demanded that their personal serfs swear oaths of allegiance and guarantee that they would never attempt to leave their personal lords by moving to towns or into territories of other lords, but stay within the territory of the monastery.[25] Some lords introduced drastic emigration fines to make it particularly difficult for peasants to move away. In other places peasants willing to move had to find a substitute, a rule which was probably a reflection of the idea that it was ultimately the entire peasant community which was liable for vacant holdings. In the Prussian territory of the Teutonic knights, which barely escaped financial ruin in the course of the economic crisis in the late Middle Ages, regulations from 1390 onwards prohibited peasants leaving their holdings unless they paid all arrears of rents and found substitutes for their holdings.[26] Gradually these rules were further stiffened, so that the peasants of east Prussia were becoming strictly attached to the soil, and they also had to provide the increasing number of manors with the human labour they required. Even in areas which had been famous for the relatively free status of their peasants, the disastrous consequences of the plagues gave rise to substantial losses of peasant freedom. A Tyrolean law of 1352, for instance, also tied peasants to their holdings and prohibited emigration without the consent of the lord. Peasants who moved into another lord's territory without permission could be prosecuted and legally forced to return. Peasants who refused to return to their rightful manor were fined the exceptionally high sum of 50 pounds and faced prosecution.[27]

In south-west Germany the grave consequences of the agrarian crisis induced many lords to strengthen the ties of personal lordship over their peasants so as to prevent them from moving elsewhere as well as to compensate for losses in income by charging higher dues.[28] Moreover, the rights over their serfs enabled them to force peasants to fill holdings which had been deserted during the agrarian crisis. The monastery of St Blasien in the southern Black Forest, for example, having suffered considerable financial losses during the agrarian crisis, began in the second half of the fourteenth century to make the personal dependence of its peasant bondsmen more onerous, and raised the associated dues such as heriot.[29] Around the year 1370 a serious conflict developed between the monastery at Hauenstein and its peasants concerning the terms of serfdom which finally culminated in an insurrection. The peasants had sought to escape from the monastery by moving into towns and refusing to pay the dues connected with their status as bondsmen. After years of conflict a legal agreement was reached in 1383 which permitted the peasants to move into those towns which acknowledged that it was legitimate for the monastery to demand the payment of heriot. In cases where a bondsman failed to obey this rule the monastery was entitled to confiscate both his moveable and unmoveable property.

A similar process took place on a number of manors in the south-west of Germany, no matter whether they were ruled by lay or eccclesiastical lords. There is evidence, for example, that the counts of Lupfen extended the terms of peasant dependence on their Hewen manor in the Hegau, an area to the north-west of Lake Constance. They also raised the amount of feudal labour obligations and increased the feudal burden by introducing additional dues.[30] But even lords who ruled much larger territories, such as the counts of Württemberg, lost considerable sums in the course of the agrarian crisis. The population drop caused by the plagues and the alarming extent of peasant migration to the towns in Württemberg provoked the counts to harden drastically the terms of bondage in 1383. In order to halt peasant migration they demanded penalties as well as declarations of the dependent status of their peasants.[31] Generally the conditions of personal bondage in the south-west of Germany were made harsher above all during the fourteenth century. The fifteenth century, by contrast, saw a notable alleviation of these conditions, until they finally lost their former importance towards the beginning of the sixteenth century. As the economic difficulties of the late Middle Ages were gradually surmounted, there was increasingly more room for reductions in feudal dues and for more personal freedom.

A look at the overall development of the legal and social position of peasants throughout western Europe demonstrates that most feudal lords did not succeed in raising the economic burden or worsening the legal position of the peasantry during the fourteenth and fifteenth centuries. Despite some initial successes, lords were generally unable in the long run to compensate for their financial losses at the expense of the peasantry. The influence of the towns, which never ceased to have a strong impact on the rural population, and other factors eventually gave rise to a liberalization of peasant conditions. In fact in many regions the property rights of the peasantry improved. Short-term leases were often replaced by heritable tenures or other agreements which practically allowed the peasants to own their holdings permanently. Despite the fierce resistance of lords, hereditary tenure became increasingly popular in upper Bavaria, where the territorial princes promoted the trend towards hereditary tenure to strengthen the peasant economy and to counterpoise migration into towns or other areas.[32] In Franconia heritable tenures even became the predominant form of tenure, and towards the close of the Middle Ages remnants of serfdom survived only in a few remote areas. Notwithstanding the fact that their legal position had improved considerably, the peasants in Franconia were still burdened with large manorial dues on top of the taxes to their ruler.[33]

During the fourteenth and fifteenth centuries the majority of the rural population in northern and western France, but especially in Flanders, Brabant and Hainault, were gradually granted a much higher degree of personal freedom and liberty.[34] The situation in these areas stood in marked contrast to the legal position of the peasantry in central and eastern France, where serfdom was still an important aspect of the peasant condition. Even though the English peasantry had suffered a great defeat in the great peasant revolt of 1381, this did not put an end to the trend towards the decline of serfdom which had begun much earlier.[35] The reduction of labour services made considerable progress in the fifteenth century and led to the abandonment of serfdom in the few areas which had retained it. In the course of this process servile tenures were replaced by the more advantageous terms of copyhold tenure. This improvement of property rights meant that rented holdings could hardly be distinguished from free landholdings. Feudal rents in England were relatively low, and since the feudal lords were more or less incapable of controlling or even constraining the personal freedom of the peasants, most feudal restrictions disappeared by the late fifteenth century.

The beginnings of a distinct type of manor in Eastern Germany

History took a completely different course in eastern Germany and eastern Europe as a whole: the gulf widened between agrarian conditions in the eastern as opposed to the western parts of Germany and thus created an agrarian dualism between eastern and western Europe.[36] In the course of the late Middle Ages the feudal lords east of the Elbe managed to develop arbitrary rights over the rural population, and by acquiring jurisdictional rights they were in a much better position to burden the peasants with further service obligations; these steps sufficed to consolidate their position permanently at the expense of the peasantry. The agrarian crisis of the fourteenth and fifteenth centuries, therefore, paved the way for the early modern type of manorial regime in eastern Germany. At a time when many holdings were vacant and the nobility exploited the weakness of the territorial rulers to obtain profitable jurisdictional rights, the peasants, on the other hand, lost most of their personal freedom and were increasingly forced to perform labour services. In the initial stages this development aggravated peasant dependence only in terms of their social and legal position; in the long run, however, it also gave rise to greater economic pressure as the feudal lords expanded production on their demesne farms. The territorial consolidation of the manors was mirrored in the intensification of personal obligations. The lord of the manor fulfilled several functions at the same time, as he was not merely the lord of an estate, but also personal and jurisdictional lord, and in many cases also the lowest representative of the ruler in the administration. This accumulation of rights and competences in the hands of a single lord increased peasant dependence, particularly in areas which had been famous for their legal and social liberty in the colonization period during the high Middle Ages. In the seventeenth and eighteenth centuries, in its most fully developed form, the manorial system (*Gutsherrschaft*) of eastern Germany was clearly the result of a long historical development which had its origin as far back as in the agrarian crisis of the late Middle Ages. The demesne farm of the Brandenburg nobility was still comparatively small in the fifteenth century; it was, however, the starting-point for the extension of manorial rights over the peasantry, the reduction of their personal freedom, the increase in their labour obligations and the conversion of hereditary tenures into much less advantageous ones.[37] By the sixteenth century a landowning aristocracy had emerged in Brandenburg whose influence rested on functions as both manorial and judicial lords, and whose members knew how to use this influence to make the peasants farm their estates.

The social position of the peasants in the later Middle Ages

After this survey of agrarian conditions and the legal position of the peasantry the following section returns to the central issue, the social and economic situation of the rural population in the fourteenth and fifteenth centuries – an issue which has led to extremely different viewpoints among historians. Some have argued that the condition of the peasantry worsened, others have claimed that it clearly improved and cited a number of sources to prove that peasants were relatively wealthy at that time. According to K. Lamprecht, the condition of the peasant in the late Middle Ages became 'increasingly desperate with each decade. In the second half of the thirteenth century a bright future was still smiling on the peasant, whereas now he rarely ever had enough to eat.'[38] Georg von Below, by contrast, held a completely different opinion: 'The land sufficed in every way to feed the rural populace, and an impoverished proletariat is nowhere to be found. In most areas it was the peasants rather than the manorial lords who profited from agricultural production.'[39] To these opposing interpretations many others could be added, but as they represent the two divergent trends in research they suffice to illustrate the range of opinions concerning the condition of the peasantry in the late Middle Ages.

In view of the variety of economic trends and peasant living conditions in different regions, it is virtually impossible to arrive at a balanced assessment of the situation of the peasantry in the fourteenth and fifteenth centuries.[40] Not only the feudal lords but also the peasants suffered from the consequences of the agrarian crisis. Yet in addition to the unfavourable development of incomes and costs in agriculture, the quantity of feudal dues determined the economic position of the individual peasant holding. However, it would be an oversimplification to claim that the position of the peasant generally declined during the agrarian crisis, since many peasants were now in a much better position to extend their holdings and cultivate more land than previously. In fact many of them increased the size of their holdings in the course of the second half of the fourteenth century; this was the more apparent as overpopulation and an unprofitable fragmentation of holdings had threatened the peasant economy in previous centuries. It has been mentioned above that the new expansion was accompanied by a widespread relaxation of manorial obligations which, at least as far as western and central Europe were concerned, had a strong impact on the conditions of the rural population. In any case, the prices for agricultural products should not be taken as the ultimate gauge of the peasant economy, particularly because the peasants sold only a small fraction of their farm produce on the markets and used a wide range of their products to meet their daily needs. Yet reductions of rents and services and improvements in property rights were not the only characteristics of the development in agriculture during the late Middle Ages. Many other areas saw a substantial rise in feudal obligations and taxes which were a heavy burden for the peasant economy. At the same time, and particularly in eastern Germany and in eastern Europe, the lords further limited the rights and independence of the peasantry.

The study of peasant conditions in the late Middle Ages should also be guided by a careful distinction between the various social strata and groups among the rural population. The agrarian crisis did most damage to large farms whose owners depended on the labour of paid farmhands and on conditions in the markets in order to produce and sell grain surpluses.[41] Tenants of large holdings were thus the hardest hit by the fluctuations in prices and costs, particularly since low grain prices were accompanied by rising wages as well as higher costs for materials. The position of the numerous peasants with medium-sized holdings was somewhat better because they employed few servants and relied essentially on the work of family members. For them the size of feudal dues in money and kind and the rises in taxes for the princes or kings were the decisive factors in their budget. When their dues amounted to a quarter, a third, or a half of their yields, such peasants had even in normal years great difficulty in fulfilling their obligations towards the manor. If, however, dues and taxes were raised, or production dropped because of warfare or bad harvests, emigration was often the only way to escape an unbearable future. It appears that the economic situation was best for the cottagers. After the high Middle Ages had seen a threatening growth of their proportion within the rural population as a whole, they were now increasingly able to improve their economic situation as well as to acquire more farmland. This was because farmland was cheap, or available on favourable terms, since many holdings and farms had been deserted during the first half of the fourteenth century. In particular the lower levels among the rural population, the day-labourers and the owners of extremely small holdings, profited from the agrarian crisis because their labour was in demand on other holdings and in artisan workshops.

Despite great differences on individual manors and among different regions or social groups, the overall condition of the peasantry in the late Middle Ages was far from enviable. Their yields and incomes were low, their feudal burdens were heavy, and the deductions for the various dues to the church, the manor and the state left them and their families with only very little for their own consumption. Many peasant families continued to live in extremely humble conditions; if, however, bad harvests, cattle diseases, warfare or raids occurred, the life of the average peasant could easily turn into a living nightmare. Notwithstanding the fact that they still bore the main burden of the economy in the late Middle Ages, the peasants never ceased to be regarded as the most despicable part of medieval society.[42] In addition they continued to be a regular target of ridicule from the higher orders. We find this in contemporary sayings like: 'The peasant is an ox, only one without horns.' Therefore W. Abel was certainly right to conclude that peasant labour was clearly 'undervalued' in the eyes of late medieval society. The peasants were well aware of this when they compared their lot with the flourishing urban economy and the advantageous living conditions in the towns. There can be no doubt that they realized that the legal position of townspeople was much freer, that to work there was much more lucrative and that the daily life there was much safer than in the country. 'This was the reason why so many of them emigrated, and when in addition to their everyday exigencies an epidemic afflicted their area, the half-emptied villages became completely deserted.'[43]

Symptoms of the crisis in the later Middle Ages

The other transformations and factors which affected peasant conditions will only be mentioned in passing. In the lands outside Germany, the growth in authority of the monarchies affected the constitutional status of rural communities as well as the general circumstances of peasant life in the fourteenth and fifteenth centuries.[44] Kings and other powerful feudal princes began to organize more modern jurisdictional and administrative systems and developed the institutions of the territorial state of the late Middle Ages as well as the sources for their fiscal revenues. Their aim was to tax all subjects in the same way, and the various state taxes which were added to the traditional feudal dues constricted the financial situation of the peasant population even further. What is more, the territorial rulers had almost no interest whatsoever in the old differences in estate. Their sole interest was to tax their subjects whenever they possibly could, or at least according to the financial means of each social group. The levelling of the differences in estate between the various social strata within the peasantry was a consequence of such ambitions which the new type of rulers willingly accepted, because it enabled them to tax all peasant subjects equally and irrespective of their legal position. The development of the territorial state thus led to a strengthening of the authority of the rulers at the expense of both the feudal middlemen and the autonomy of peasant communities. Encroachments on the independent administration of the village, as well as on the legal capacity of the community, and restrictions on the use of commons did, of course, also diminish the traditional rights of the village communities, but these moves were increasingly met by peasant resistance towards the close of the Middle Ages.

The growing influence of the territorial state automatically changed the traditional relation between lords and peasants, as well as the foundations on which the authority of ecclesiastical and lay lords rested. While kings and the most powerful of the feudal princes extended their authority, the options available to local magnates were increasingly limited, which in turn encouraged them to exert even more pressure on the peasants. The new types of political and military organization which emerged in the late Middle Ages deprived at least the local nobility of their ability to guarantee their dependents security in times of feuds and warfare. This meant that they were no longer able to fulfil their part of the agreement to protect the peasants. The increasing tensions and conflicts between lords and peasants which arose in many regions during the late Middle Ages were thus ultimately the symptoms of a changing relationship between lords and the rural population. The growing pressure which the nobility exerted on the peasants, the increasing demands of the territorial state, the conflicts over the distribution of wealth during the agrarian crisis, and the growing self-confidence of the peasantry in the late Middle Ages – these were the principal causes for the large number of peasant revolts and insurrections towards the close of the Middle Ages.[45]

A marked 'restlessness' among large parts of the population in the late Middle Ages can certainly be regarded as the expression of the crisis-filled nature of that period. The unmistakable signs of this crisis were responsible for the great interest which twentieth-century historians have shown for this period because they were themselves exposed to the crisis of modern society and civilization. The frequency and intensity of the various conflicts, revolts and upheavals in the cities, towns and villages of the fourteenth and fifteenth centuries must be taken as manifestations of the crisis in the late Middle Ages. In the opinion of F. Graus they give a good impression of the 'peculiar sensitivity' of that period. 'What must also be considered is the universal malaise which contemporaries articulated in literature and painting, which expressed itself again and again in the call for a change, a reformation.'[46] To the economic, political and social factors, various intellectual and religious tensions must be added. These manifested themselves in the Hussite movement, in the demand for a reform of the church, and finally in the Reformation at the beginning of the sixteenth century. The late Middle Ages and its 'crisis', therefore, can be regarded as the beginning of a new epoch in European history which lies beyond the compass of this study.

Despite the great variety and diversity of living conditions among the peasantry there is good reason to believe that, on the whole, their standard of living improved, rather than worsened, during the late Middle Ages. Owing to the fact that the population of the mid-fifteenth century was considerably smaller than a hundred years earlier, and also owing to the obvious loosening of manorial dependence, most peasants probably suffered less than their ancestors. In any case, they held more land than before, and they had larger pastures for their cattle and sheep than at the beginning of the fourteenth century when land was in much shorter supply. Moreover, beginning with the second half of the fifteenth century there were faint glimpses of a recovery in agriculture. These were signals of the beginning of a new expansion of the agrarian economy which came to full fruition in the sixteenth century.[47] The population grew again, new steps were taken towards the extension of arable, and deserted holdings were occupied by new tenants. In most lands however, the new growth was incomparable to both the extent of agrarian production and the density of settlement during the thirteenth century, when the unique intensity of peasant agriculture had provided the basis for the cultural ascendency of the high Middle Ages.

NOTES

INTRODUCTION

1 J. Seymour, *The Complete Book of Self-Sufficiency*, 1976.
2 For general information on the ecological movement see F. Klötzli, *Einführung in die Ökologie*, 1983; Klötzli, *Natur und Umweltschutz in der Bundesrepublik Deutschland*, 1977.

3 See F. -W. Henning, *Landwirtschaft und ländliche Gesellschaft in Deutschland*, vol. 2, Paderborn, 1978, p. 32.

4 See W. Landzettel (ed.), *Deutsche Dörfer*, 1982, pp. 27ff.

5 Ibid., p. 9. (Translator's note: Kempowski refers to the consolidation of the administration of villages and rural communities into larger administrative units (*Gebietsreform, Verwaltungsreform*) which has been carried out in the Federal Republic of Germany since the 1960s. This reform reduced the number of villages and rural administrations from 24,447 in 1964 to 10,390 in 1978 (see 'Verwaltungsreform' in *Deutscher Taschenbuch Verlag Brockhaus Lexikon*, Mannheim/Munich, 1986) and produced new compound place-names which in their abbreviated administrative form reduced long-familiar village names beyond recognition to capital letters, e.g. NBI.)

6 W. H. Riehl, *Die Naturgeschichte des deutschen Volkes*, ed. G. Ipsen, Leipzig, 1935. (The life and writings of W. H. Riehl are discussed in G. Ipsen and I. Weber-Kellermann, *Die Familie*, 1976, pp. vii, 69ff.

7 Riehl, *Naturgeschichte*, p. 221.

8 Ibid., p. 231.

9 Ibid., p. 232.

10 Ibid., p. 244.

11 See F. Sengle, 'Wunschbild Land und Schreckbild Stadt', in *Studium Generale*, xvi, 10 (1963), pp. 619–30; K. Bergmann, *Agrarromantik und Grosstadtfeindschaft*, 1970.

12 See esp. R. W. Darré, *Das Bauerntum als Lebensquell der Nordischen Rasse*, 2nd edn 1933; H. F. K. Günther, *Das Bauerntum als Lebens- und Gemeinschaftsform*, 2nd edn, 1941.

13 U. Jeggle, 'Alltag', in H. Bausinger et al. (eds), *Grundzüge der Volkskunde*, 1978, pp. 109f.

14 See A. Ilien and U. Jeggle, *Leben auf dem Dorf*, Opladen, 1978, p. 36; J. Kuczynski, *Geschichte des Alltags des deutschen Volkes*, vol. 1, 1980, pp. 124ff.

15 K. Lamprecht, *Deutsches Wirtschaftsleben im Mittelalter*, 3 vols, Leipzig, 1885/6; A. Dopsch, *Herrschaft und Bauer in der deutschen Kaiserzeit*, Jena, 1939; A. Dopsch, *Die ältere Wirtschafts- und Sozialgeschichte der Bauern in den Alpenländern Österreichs*, Oslo, 1930; R. Kötzschke, *Studien zur Verwaltungsgeschichte der Grossgrundherrschaft Werden an der Ruhr*, Leipzig, 1901; R. Kötzschke, *Ländliche Siedlung und Agrarwesen in Sachsen*, 1953.

16 See G. Franz (ed), *Deutsches Bauerntum im Mittelalter*, Darmstadt, 1976; T. Mayer (ed.), *Die Anfänge der Landgemeinde und ihr Wesen*, Konstanz, 1964.

17 W. Abel, *Geschichte der deutschen Landwirtschaft*, 3rd edn, Stuttgart, 1976; Abel, *Strukturen und Krisen der spätmittelalterlichen Wirtschaft*, Stuttgart 1980. (Translator's note: For an English translation of the work of W. Abel see W. Abel, *Agricultural Fluctuations in Europe from the Thirteenth to the Twentieth Centuries*, London/New York, 1980).

18 See David Warren Sabean, 'The Social Background to the Peasants' War of 1525 in Southern Upper Swabia', Ph.D. thesis, University of Wisconsin, 1969; Microfilm 69–12, 408 (German translation: D. W. Sabean, *Landbesitz und Gesellschaft am Vorabend des Bauernkriegs*, Stuttgart, 1972); Peter Blickle, 'Bäuerliche Erhebungen im spätmittelalterlichen deutschen Reich', *ZAA* 27 (1979), pp. 208–31; Peter Blickle, *The Revolution of 1525, The German Peasants' War from a New Perspective*, Baltimore, 1981; Peter Blickle (ed.), *Aufruhr und Empörung? Studien zum bäuerlichen Widerstand im Alten Reich*, Munich, 1980; W. Schulze, *Bäuerlicher Widerstand und feudale Herrschaft in*

der frühen Neuzeit, Stuttgart, 1980; W. Schulze (ed.), *Aufstände, Revolten, Prozesse. Beiträge zu bäuerlichen Widerstandsbewegungen im frühneuzeitlichen Europa*, 1983.

19 H. Dannenbauer, 'Adel, Burg und Herrschaft bei den Germanen' (1941), in H. Kämpf (ed.), *Herrschaft und Staat im Mittelalter*, 1956, pp. 66f.

20 Leopold von Ranke, *Deutsche Geschichte im Zeitalter der Reformation*, vol. 2, 6th edn, 1881, p. 147.

21 K. Bosl, 'Staat, Gesellschaft, Wirtschaft im deutschen Mittelalter', in Gebhardt (ed.), *Handbuch der deutschen Geschichte*, 9th edn, 1970, p. 706.

22 M. Bloch, *Les caractères originaux de l'histoire rurale française*, 3rd edn, Paris, 1960 (in English: *French Rural History: An Essay on its Basic Characteristics*, London, 1966); G. Duby, *L'économie rurale et la vie des campagnes dans l'Occident médiéval*, 2 vols, Paris, 1962 (in English: *Rural Economy and Country Life*, Columbia, SC, 1968); G. Fourquin, *Le paysan d'Occident au moyen âge*, Paris 1972; E. Le Roy Ladurie, *The Peasants of Languedoc*, Urbana, Ill., 1974; London, 1978; E. Le Roy Ladurie, *Montaillou: Cathars and Catholics in a French Village, 1294–1324*, London, 1978; R. Fossier, *La terre et les hommes en Picardie jusqu'à la fin du XIIIᵉ siècle*, 2 vols, Paris 1968. (See also the recent 4-volume study on French agrarian history by G. Duby and A. Wallon (eds), *Histoire de la France rurale*, 1975/6).

23 R. H. Hilton, *A Medieval Society: The West Midlands at the End of the Thirteenth Century*, London, 1966; Hilton, *Bond Men Made Free: Medieval Peasant Movements and the English Rising*, 1973; Hilton, *The English Peasantry in the Later Middle Ages*, Oxford, 1975; A. J. Raftis, *The Estates of Ramsey Abbey: A Study in Economic Growth and Organisation*, Toronto, 1956; Raftis, *Tenure and Mobility: Studies in the Social History of the Medieval English Village*, Toronto, 1964; Raftis (ed.), *Pathways to Medieval Peasants*, Toronto, 1981. See also Z. Razi, *Life, Marriage and Death in a Medieval Parish: Economy, Society and Demography in Halesowen 1270–1400*, Cambridge, 1980; J. Hatcher and E. Miller, *Medieval England: Rural Society and Economic Change 1086–1348*, London, 1978.

24 W. Lepenies, 'Probleme einer Historischen Anthropologie', in R. Rürup (ed.), *Historische Sozialwissenschaft*, 1977, pp. 126–59; E. R. Wolf, *Peasants*, Englewood Cliffs, NJ, 1966; E. R. Wolf and J. W. Cole, *The Hidden Frontier: Ecology and Ethnicity in an Alpine Valley*, New York, 1974; T. Shanin, (ed.), Oxford, 1987; *Peasants and Peasant Societies*, Harmondsworth, 1971; 2nd rev. edn, R. Redfield, *Peasant Society and Culture*, Chicago, 1969; G. Dalton, *Economic Anthropology and Development: Essays on Tribal and Peasant Economies*, New York, 1971; J. W. Cole, 'Gemeindestudien der Cultural Anthropology in Europa', in G. Wiegelmann (ed.), *Gemeinde im Wandel*, 1979, pp. 15–31. See also R. M. Berdahl et al., *Klassen und Kultur: Sozialanthropologische Perspektiven der Geschichtsschreibung*, 1982.

25 Wolf, *Peasants*.

26 See D. Nohlen and F. Nuscheler (eds), *Handbuch der Dritten Welt*, 4 vols, 1974–8; H. Elsenhans (ed.), *Agrarreformen in der Dritten Welt*, 1979.

27 See H. Jankuhn, *Einführung in die Siedlungsarchaeologie*, 1977; W. Janssen and H. Steuer (eds), *Zeitschrift für Archäeologie des Mittelalters*, 1 (1973) et seq.

28 U. Bentzien, *Bauernarbeit im Feudalismus*, Berlin, 1980; K.-S. Kramer, *Die Nachbarschaft als bäuerliche Gemeinschaft*, Munich, 1954; Kramer, *Grundriss einer rechtlichen Volkskunde*, 1975; G. Wiegelmann, *Alltags- und Festspeisen*, 1967; Wiegelmann (ed.), *Geschichte der Alltagskultur*, Münster, 1980.

29 H. Appelt, 'Mittelalterliche Realienkunde Österreichs als Forschungsaufgabe',

in *Europäische Sachkultur des Mittelalters*, Veröffentlichung des Instituts für mittelalterliche Realienkunde Österreichs 4, 1980, pp. 7–12; H. Kühnel, 'Realienkunde des Mittelalters und der frühen Neuzeit', *Jb. für Landeskunde von Niederösterreich*, NS 37 (1965–7), pp. 338ff.; *Bäuerliche Sachkultur des Spätmittelalters*, Veröffentlichung des Instituts für mittelalterliche Realienkunde Österreichs 7, 1984.

CHAPTER 1 THE FOUNDATIONS OF MEDIEVAL PEASANTRY

1 O. Spengler, *The Decline of the West*, 2 vols, tr. C. F. Atkinson, New York, 1926/8.
2 Ibid., p. 96.
3 The theory of the 'society of orders' has been analysed by W. Schwer, *Stand und Ständeordnung im Weltbild des Mittelalters*, 2nd edn, Paderborn, 1952; G. Duby, *The Three Orders: Feudal Society Imagined*, Chicago, 1980; O. G. Oexle, 'Tria genera hominum, Zur Geschichte eines Deutungsschemas der sozialen Wirklichkeit in Antike und Mittelalter', in *Festschrift J. Fleckenstein*, 1984, pp. 483–500.
4 G. Franz (ed.), *Quellen zur Geschichte des deutschen Bauernstands im Mittelalter*, 2nd edn, Darmstadt, 1974, p. 124, no. 49.
5 O. G. Oexle, 'Die funktionale Dreiteilung der "Gesellschaft" bei Adalbero von Laon', *Frühmittelalterliche Studien*, 12 (1978), pp. 1ff.
6 See R. Wenskus et al. (eds), *Wort und Begriff 'Bauer'*, Göttingen, 1975, pp. 11–28; Franz, *Bauernstand*, pp. 35ff.
7 G. Köbler, 'Bauer (agricola, colonus, rusticus) im Frühmittelalter', in Wenskus et al. (eds), *Bauer*, pp. 230ff.
8 See R. Schmidt-Wiegand, 'Der "Bauer" in der Lex Salica', in Wenskus (ed.), *Bauer*, pp. 128ff.
9 See J. Fleckenstein, 'Zur Frage der Abgrenzung von Bauer und Ritter', in Wenskus et al. (eds), *Bauer*, pp. 246ff; G. Köbler, 'Bäuerliche Rechtsstellung', in *Lexikon des Mittelalters*, vol. 1 (1980), cols 1571ff; W. Rösener, 'Bauer und Ritter im Hochmittelalter', in *Festschrift J. Fleckenstein*, Sigmaringen, 1984, pp. 665–92.
10 See J. Fleckenstein, 'Adel und Kriegertum und ihre Wandlung im Karolingerreich', in *Nascita dell'Europa ed Europa Carolingia: Un'equazione da verificare*, Settimani di studio del Centro italiano di studi sull'alto medioevo 27, Spoleto, 1981, pp. 67–94.
11 See H. Fehr, 'Das Waffenrecht der Bauern im Mittelalter', *ZRG GA* 35 (1914), pp. 111f; J. Gernhuber, *Die Landfriedensbewegung in Deutschland bis zum Mainzer Reichslandfrieden von 1235*, 1952, pp. 41ff.
12 M. Weber, 'Der Streit um den Charakter der altgermanischen Sozialverfassung in der Literatur des letzten Jahrzehnts', in *Gesammelte Aufsätze zur Wirtschafts- und Sozialgeschichte*, 1924, p. 538.
13 O. Brunner, 'Europäisches Bauerntum', in *Neue Wege der Verfassungs- und Sozialgeschichte*, 2nd edn, Göttingen, 1968, p. 203.
14 See Wenskus et al. (eds), *Bauer*, p. 27.
15 See the works by T. Shanin, E. R. Wolf and R. Redfield cited in Intro. n. 24, as well as E. Schlesier, 'Ethnologische Aspekte zum Begriff Bauer', in Wenskus et al. (eds), *Bauer*, pp. 46–57.
16 For general information on the development of agriculture see W. Abel, *Geschichte der deutschen Landwirtschaft*, Stuttgart, 1976, pp. 151; G. Duby,

The Early Growth of the European Economy: Warriors and Peasants from the Seventh to the Twelfth Century, Ithaca, NY, 1974, pp. 13ff; Pierre Riché, *Daily Life in the World of Charlemagne*, tr. A. McNamara, Liverpool, 1978, pp. 133f; W. Metz, 'Die Agrarwirtschaft im karolingischen Reiche', in *Karl der Grosse. Lebenswerk und Nachleben*, vol. 1, Düsseldorf, 1965, pp. 489ff.

17 On clearance and settlement in the early Middle Ages see M. Born, *Die Entwicklung der deutschen Agrarlandschaft*, Darmstadt, 1974, pp. 38ff; C. Higounet, 'Les forêts de l'Europe occidentale, du Vᶜ au XIᶜ siècle', in *Paysages et villages neufs du Moyen Age*, Bordeaux, 1975, pp. 37–63. See also the notes to ch. 3 below for further references.

18 For general information on the manorial system in the Middle Ages see H. K. Schulze, 'Grundherrschaft', in *HRG*, 1, (1971), cols 1834ff; W. Rösener, 'Die Erforschung der Grundherrschaft', *Mittelalterforschung: Forschung und Information*, 29 (1981), pp. 57–65; F. Lütge, 'Grundherrschaft und Gutsherrschaft', in *Handwörterbuch der Sozialwissenschaften*, vol. 4, 1965, pp. 682ff. On the manorial system in the early Middle Ages see T. Schieffer, 'Die wirtschaftlich-soziale Grundstruktur des frühen Europa', in T. Schieder (ed.), *Handbuch der europäischen Geschichte*, vol. 1, 1976, pp. 130ff; F. L. Ganshof, 'Das Fränkische Reich', in H. Kellenbenz (ed.), *Handbuch der europäischen Wirtschafts- und Sozialgeschichte*, vol. 2, Stuttgart, 1980, pp. 151ff.

19 O. Brunner, *Land und Herrschaft. Grundfragen der territorialen Verfassungsgeschichte Österreichs im Mittelalter*, 5th edn, Vienna, 1965, p. 242.

20 See O. Brunner, 'Feudalismus. Ein Beitrag zur Begriffsgeschichte', in *Neue Wege*, pp. 128ff; H. Wunder (ed.), *Feudalismus: Zehn Aufsätze*, Munich, 1974; L. Kuchenbuch and B. Michael (eds), *Feudalismus. Materialien zur Theorie und Geschichte*, Frankfurt a.M., 1977.

21 M. Bloch, *La société féodale*, 2 vols, 1939/40. (For an English translation, see M. Bloch, *Feudal Society*, tr. L. A. Manyon, 2 vols, London, 1961/2.)

22 The development of the manorial system in the early Middle Ages has been discussed by F. Lütge, *Die Agrarverfassung des frühen Mittelalters im mitteldeutschen Raum vornehmlich in der Karolingerzeit*, Stuttgart, 1967; M. Gockel, *Karolingische Königshofe am Mittelrhein*, 1970; A. I. Njeussychin, *Die Entstehung der abhängigen Bauernschaft als Klasse der frühfeudalen Gesellschaft in Westeuropa vom 6. bis 8.* Jahrhundert, Berlin, 1961; L. Kuchenbuch, *Bäuerliche Gesellschaft und Klosterherrschaft im 9. Jahrhundert: Studien zur Sozialstruktur der Familia der Abtei Prüm*, Wiesbaden, 1978; W. Rösener, 'Strukturformen der älteren Agrarverfassung im sächsischen Raum', *Niedersächsisches Jahrbuch für Landesgeschichte*, 52 (1980), pp. 107–43; A. Verhulst, 'La genèse du régime domanial classique' en France au haut moyen âge', in *Agricoltura e mondo rurale in Occidente nell'alto medioevo*, Spoleto, 1966, p. 135.

23 (Translator's note: for more information on the manorial system see ch. 12 n. 13.) On holdings (*Hufen*) see D. Herlihy, 'The Carolingian Mansus', *Economic Historical Review*, 13 (1960/1), pp. 79ff; W. Goffart, 'From Roman taxation to medieval seigneurie: three notes', *Speculum*, 47 (1972), pp. 165ff; W. Schlesinger, 'Die Hufe im Frankenreich', in H. Beck et al. (eds), *Untersuchungen zur eisenzeitlichen und frühmittelalterlichen Flur in Mitteleuropa und ihrer Nutzung*, vol. 1, Göttingen, 1979, pp. 41ff.

24 Verhulst, 'Genèse du régime domanial' p. 159.

25 *MGH*, ch. 1 pp. 83ff., no. 32.

26 A. Longnon (ed.), *Polyptyque de l'abbaye de Saint-Germain-des-Prés, redigé au temps de l'abbé Irminion*, 2 vols, 1886/96.

27 See Duby, *Early Growth of the European Economy*, p. 172.

28 For more information on the nobility and manorial rule see G. Tellenbach, 'Zur Erforschung des mittelalterlichen Adels (9.–12. Jahrhundert)', in *XIIe Congrès international des sciences historiques*, 1965, pp. 318–37; W. Störmer, *Früher Adel*, 1973; K. F. Werner, 'Adel', in *Lexikon des Mittelalters*, vol. 1, 1980, cols 118–29; Timothy Reuter (ed. and tr.), *The Medieval Nobility: Studies on the Ruling Class of France and Germany from the Sixth to the Twelfth Centuries*, Amsterdam, 1978.

29 H. Dannenbauer and T. Mayer were the first to put forward the 'Königsfreien' hypothesis: H. Dannenbauer, 'Die Freien im karolingischen Heer', in *Festschrift T. Mayer*, vol. 1 (1954), pp 49–64; T. Mayer, 'Die Königsfreien'und der Staat des frühen Mittelalters', in *Das Problem der Freiheit*, Sigmaringen, 1955, pp. 7ff. See also ch. 13 above, incl. notes.

30 P. Jones, 'Medieval Agrarian Society in its Prime: Italy', in M. M. Postan (ed.), *The Cambridge Economic History of Europe*, vol. 1, 2nd edn, 1966, pp. 395ff.

31 For general information on the military in the Middle Ages see W. Erben, *Kriegsgeschichte des Mittelalters*, 1929; F. Lot, *L'art militaire et les armées au moyen âge en Europe et dans le Proche-Orient*, 2 vols, 1946; J. F. Verbruggen, *The Art of Warfare in Western Europe during the Middle Ages*, Amsterdam 1977.

32 *MGH*, ch. 1, pp. 134ff, no. 807; pp. 137ff, no. 808.

33 See J. Fleckenstein, 'Adel und Kriegertum und ihre Wandlung im Karolingerreich', (n. 10 above), p. 93.

34 For more information on the levelling of social distinctions among the peasant groups on medieval manors see Kuchenbuch, *Bäuerliche Gesellschaft*, pp. 378ff. (particularly the author's discussion of the *familia* on the estates of the abbey at Prüm). K. H. Ganahl, *Studien zur Verfassungsgeschichte der Klosterherrschaft St. Gallen*, 1931, pp. 90ff.

CHAPTER 2 TRANSFORMATIONS IN THE HIGH MIDDLE AGES

1 M. Bloch, *Feudal Society*, (ch. 1, n. 21), p. 60.

2 Ibid., p. 69.

3 W. Abel, *Geschichte der deutschen Landwirtschaft*, Stuttgart, 1976, p. 55.

4 For general information on the transformation in the high Middle Ages see G. Duby, *The Early Growth of the European Economy*, Ithaca, NY, 1974, pp. 158ff; K. Bosl, *Europa im Aufbruch*, 1980; R. Fossier, *Enfance de l'Europe. Aspects économiques et sociaux*, 2 vols, Paris, 1982; J. Le Goff, *Das Hochmittelalter*, Frankfurt a.M., 1965; H. Fuhrmann, *Deutsche Geschichte im hohen Mittelalter*, 2nd edn, 1983.

5 See W. Abel, *Agrarkrisen und Agrarkonjunktur*, 3rd edn, Hamburg, 1978, pp. 27ff. (cf. W. Abel, *Agricultural Fluctuations in Europe from the Thirteenth to the Twentieth Centuries*, London/New York, 1980).

6 The demography of the Middle Ages is discussed by J. C. Russell, 'Population in Europe 500–1500', in C. M. Cipolla (ed.), *The Fontana Economic History of Europe*, vol. 1: *The Middle Ages*, Brighton, 1976, pp. 25ff; Abel, *Geschichte der deutschen Landwirtschaft*, pp. 28ff.

7 See M. Born, *Die Entwicklung der deutschen Agrarlandschaft*, Darmstadt, 1974, pp. 44ff; W. Schlesinger (ed.), *Die deutsche Ostsiedlung des Mittelalters als Problem der europäischen Geschichte*, Sigmaringen, 1975.

8 One of the first to study the interaction between the rise in population and the economic expansion was H. Aubin. One of his more recent articles is entitled

'Stufen und Triebkräfte der abendländischen Wirtschaftsentwicklung im frühen Mittelalter', *VSWG* 42 (1955), p. 21. H. Aubin contended that the rise in population was the decisive force behind the economic expansion. See also his article 'The lands east of the Elbe and German colonization eastwards', in M. M. Postan (ed.), *The Cambridge Economic History of Europe*, vol. 1: *The Agrarian Life of the Middle Ages*, Cambridge, 1971.

9 See Abel, *Agrarkrisen*, pp. 33, 118ff.

10 See ch. 7.

11 See Le Goff, *Hochmittelalter*, p. 45.

12 Consult the following works for more information on the rise of the towns in medieval Europe: E. Ennen, *The Medieval Town*, Natalie Fryde, Amsterdam, 1979, pp. 63ff (see the extensive bibliography for further references); C. Haase (ed.), *Die Stadt des Mittelalters*, 3 vols, WdF 243–5, 1973–6. On the development of commerce and trade see R. Sprangel, in H. Aubin and W. Zorn (eds), *Handbuch der deutschen Wirtschafts- und Sozialgeschichte*, vol. 1, 1971, pp. 202ff.

13 See H. Strahm, 'Stadtluft macht frei', in *Das Problem der Freiheit*, VF 2, Sigmaringen, 1955, pp. 103–21; T. Mayer, 'Bemerkungen und Nachträge zum Problem der freien Bauern', *ZWLG* 13 (1954), pp. 46ff; K. A. Kroeschell, 'Rodungssiedlung und Stadtgründung. Ländliches und städtisches Hagenrecht', *Blätter für deutsche Landesgeschichte*, 91 (1954), pp. 53ff.

14 H. Pirenne, *Sozial- und Wirtschaftsgeschichte Europas im Mittelalter*, 3rd edn, Munich, 1974, p. 19.

15 Cf. Paul M. Sweezy (ed.), *The Transition from Feudalism to Capitalism*, London, 1976.

16 Aubin, 'Stufen und Triebkräfte' (n. 8 above) p. 21.

17 R. Hilton, 'Ein Kommentar', in Sweezy, *Transition*, pp. 147ff; M. Dobb, 'Eine Erwiderung', in Sweezy *Transition*, pp. 74ff; H. Mottek, *Wirtschaftsgeschichte Deutschlands*, vol. 1, 5th edn, 1976, pp. 117ff.

18 See Duby, *Early Growth* (n. 4 above).

19 Ibid., p. 181.

20 For a general discussion of the dissolution of the manorial system see F. Lütge, *Die Agrarverfassung der frühen Mittelalters*, Stuttgart, 1967, pp. 83ff; F. L. Ganshof and A. Verhulst, 'Medieval agrarian society in its prime: France, The Low Countries and western Germany', in M. M. Postan (ed.), *The Cambridge Economic History of Europe*, 2nd edn, vol. 1, Cambridge, 1966, pp. 305ff; A. Dopsch, *Herrschaft und Bauer in der deutschen Kaiserzeit*, Jena, 1939, pp. 129ff; W. Wittich, *Die Grundherrschaft in Nordwestdeutschland*, Leipzig, 1896, pp. 301ff; P. Dollinger, *L'évolution des classes rurales en Bavière depuis la fin de l'époque carolingienne jusqu'au milieu du XIIIe siècle*, Paris, 1949.

21 Translator's note: For more information on the manorial or *Fronhof* system, see ch. 12 n. 13.) See also C.-E. Perrin, *Recherches sur la seigneurie rurale en Lorraine d'après les plus anciens censiers (IXe–XIIe siècle)*, Paris, 1935, pp. 626ff.

22 See Duby, *Early Growth* (n. 4 above), pp. 172ff; M. Mitterauer, 'Formen adliger Herrschaftsbildung im hochmittelalterlichen Österreich', *MIÖG* 80 (1972), pp. 121ff.

23 The development of territorial states has been discussed by O. Brunner, *Sozialgeschichte Europas im Mittelalter*, 1978, pp. 69ff; H. K. Schulze, *Adelsherrschaft und Landesherrschaft*, 1963.

24 See Genicot, *Le XIIIe siècle européen*, Paris, 1968, pp. 323 ff; S. D. Skazkin, *Der Bauer in Westeuropa während der Epoche des Feudalismus*, Berlin, 1976, pp. 191ff.

25 See ch. 4.
26 See J. Fleckenstein, 'Rittertum und höfische Kultur', in *Max-Planck-Gesellschaft Jahrbuch*, 1976, pp. 40–52.
27 For more information on peasant culture in the high Middle Ages see K. Ranke, 'Agrarische und dörfliche Denk- und Verhaltensweisen', in R. Wenskus et al. (eds), *Wort und Begriff 'Bauer'*, Göttingen, 1975, pp. 207ff; U. Bentzien, *Bauernarbeit im Feudalismus*, Berlin, 1980, pp. 57ff; W. Lammers, *Gottschalks Wanderung ins Jenseits. Zur Volksfrömmigkeit im 12. Jahrhundert nördlich der Elbe*, 1982.
28 Dopsch, *Herrschaft und Bauer*, pp. 218ff.
29 Ibid., p. 242.
30 F. Lütge, *Die bayrische Grundherrschaft*, 1949, p. 74.
31 Abel, *Geschichte der deutschen Landwirtschaft*, p. 109.

CHAPTER 3 NATURE AND ENVIRONMENT,
CLEARANCE AND SETTLEMENT

1 For general information on ecology and environmental protection see F. Klötzli, *Einführung in die Ökologie*, 1983; W. Zorn, 'Ansätze und Erscheinungsformen des Umweltschutzes aus sozial- und wirtschaftshistorischer Sicht', in *Festschrift H. Kellenbenz*, vol. 4 (1978), pp. 707ff; H. Stern, *Rettet den Wald*, 1979; W. Ritter, 'Waldverwüstung und Wiederbewaldung', in H. Kellenbenz (ed.), *Wirtschaftsentwicklung und Umweltbeeinflussung 14.–20. Jahrhundert*, Stuttgart, 1982, pp. 89–104.
2 See the essays in Kellenbenz (ed.), *Wirtschaftsentwicklung* (n. 1 above).
3 The ecological exigencies of Third World countries are discussed at length in Vereinigung deutscher Wissenschaftler (ed.), *Welternährungskrise oder: Ist eine Hungerkatastrophe unausweichlich?*, Reinbek, 1968; Independent Commission on Development Issues (ed.), *The Brandt Commission Papers: Selected Background Papers Prepared for the Independent Commission on International Development Issues, 1978/9*, 1981; P. von Blanckenburg and H. D. Cremer, *Handbuch der Landwirtschaft und Ernährung in den Entwicklungsländern*, 2 vols, 1967/8.
4 Mainly British studies have dealt with the crisis around 1300: M. M. Postan, 'The economic foundations of medieval economy', in Postan (ed.), *Essays on Medieval Agriculture and General Problems of the Medieval Economy*, Cambridge, 1973, pp. 9–27; J. Hatcher and E. Miller, *Medieval England*, London, 1978, pp. 240ff.
5 The demographic development has been analysed by W. Abel, *Handbuch der deutschen Sozial- und Wirtschaftsgeschichte*, vol. 1, 1971, p. 198; J. C. Russell, 'Population in Europe 500–1500', in C. M. Cipolla (ed.), *Fontana Economic History of Europe*, vol. 1, Brighton, 1976, pp. 25ff.
6 G. Duby, 'Medieval Agriculture 900–1500', in Cipolla (ed.), *Fontana Economic History of Europe*, vol. 1, p. 199.
7 See M. Born, *Die Entwicklung der deutschen Agrarlandschaft*, Darmstadt, 1974, pp. 38ff; K. H. Schröder and G. Schwarz, *Die ländlichen Siedlungsformen in Mitteleuropa*, 2nd edn, Bad Godesberg, 1978, pp. 12ff (see this work esp. for further references); W. Abel, 'Landwirtschaft', in H. Aubin and W. Zorn (eds), *Handbuch der deutschen Wirtschafts-und Sozialgeschichte*, vol. 1, Stuttgart, 1971, pp. 91ff.

8 For general information on the settlement and colonization of Europe in the high Middle Ages see Born, *Agrarlandschaft*, pp. 44–67 (cf. also the bibliography for reference works); Abel, 'Landwirtschaft', pp. 202ff; R. Koebner, 'The settlement and colonization of Europe', in M. M. Postan (ed.), *The Cambridge Economic History of Europe*, vol. 1, 2nd edn, Cambridge, 1966, pp. 1–91; J. A. van Houte, in H. Kellenbenz (ed.), *Handbuch der europäischen Wirtschafts- und Sozialgeschichte*, vol. 2, Stuttgart, 1980, pp. 24ff.

9 See F. Petri, 'Entstehung und Verbreitung der niederländischen Marsch-kolonisation in Europa', in W. Schlesinger (ed.), *Die deutsche Ostsiedlung des Mittelalters*, Sigmaringen, 1975, pp. 695ff; A. Verhulst, 'Die Binnenkolonisation und die Anfänge der Landgemeinde in Seeflandern', in T. Mayer (ed.), *Die Anfänge der Landgemeinde*, Konstanz, 1964, vol. 1, pp. 447ff.

10 See Born, *Agrarlandschaft*, pp. 49ff; Schröder and Schwarz, *Siedlungsformen*, pp. 19ff., pp 42ff; J. C. Tesdorpf, *Die Entstehung der Kulturlandschaft am westlichen Bodensee*, 1972, pp. 220ff; H.-J. Nitz (ed.), *Historisch-genetische Siedlungsforschung*, Darmstadt, 1974.

11 G. Franz (ed.), *Quellen zur Geschichte des deutschen Bauernstandes im Mittelalter*, 2nd edn, Darmstadt, 1974, pp. 168ff. See also L. Deike, *Die Entstehung der Grundherrschaft in den Hollerkolonien an der Niederweser*, 1959; H. Abel, 'Die Besiedlung von Geest und Marsch am rechten Weserufer bei Bremen', *Deutsche Geographische Blätter* 41 (1933), pp. 1–110.

12 R. Blohm, *Die Hagenhufendörfer in Schaumburg-Lippe*, 1943; Asch, 'Grund-herrschaft und Freiheit', pp. 107ff. 1943; J. Asch, 'Grundherrschaft und Freiheit. Entstehung und Entwicklung der Hägergerichte in Südniedersachsen', *Niedersächs. Jb. für Landesgeschichte*, 50 (1978), pp. 107ff.

13 K. Fehn, *Siedlungsgeschichtliche Grundlagen der Herrschafts- und Gesellschafts entwicklung in Mittelschwaben. Aufgezeichnet am Beispiel der spätmittel-alterlichen Rodungssiedlungen*, Augsburg, 1966.

14 For more information about German colonization in the lands east of the Elbe and Saale see Schlesinger (ed.), *Ostsiedlung* (n. 9 above); R. Kötzschke and W. Ebert, *Geschichte der ostdeutschen Kolonisation*, 1937; W. Ebert, *Ländliche Siedelformen im deutschen Osten*, 1936.

15 See W. Schlesinger, 'Zur Problematik der Erforschung der deutschen Ostsiedlung', in Schlesinger (ed.), *Ostsiedlung*, pp. 11ff.

16 The aspects of colonization in the east of central Europe are discussed by Kuhn, Zientara, Trawkowski, Fügedi, Helbig and Kubinyi in Schlesinger (ed.), *Ostsiedlung*.

17 See M. M. Postan, 'England', in Postan (ed.), *The Cambridge Economic History of Europe*, vol. 1, 2nd edn, Cambridge, 1966, pp. 549ff; Hatcher and Miller, *Medieval England* (n. 4 above), pp. 27ff.

18 M. Bloch, *Les caractères originaux de l'histoire rurale française*, 3rd edn, Paris 1960 (*French Rural History: An Essay on its Basic Characteristics*, London 1966); G. Duby, *L'économie rurale et la vie des campagnes dans l'Occident médiévale*, 2 vols, Paris, 1962, vol. 1, pp. 139ff (*Rural Economy and Country Life in the Medieval West*, Columbia, SC, 1968, pp. 65ff.); C. Higounet, *Paysages et villages neufs du Moyen Age*, Bordeaux, 1975; Fossier, *La terre et les hommes en Picardie*, Paris, 1968.

19 See D. Claude, 'Die Anfänge der Wiederbesiedlung Innerspaniens', in Schlesinger, *Ostsiedlung*, pp. 607ff; L. S. Fernändez, 'Spanien vom 11. bis 14. Jahrhundert', in Kellenbenz (ed.), *Handbuch*, vol. 2 (n. 8 above), pp. 350ff.

20 A. Dopsch, *Bauern in den Alpenländern*, Oslo, 1930, pp. 129ff.

21 See ch. 15.

22 See W. Abel, *Die Wüstungen des ausgehenden Mittelalters*, Stuttgart, 1976, pp. 98ff; D. Weber, *Die Wüstungen in Württemberg*, 1927, p. 207.

23 See W. Abel, *Geschichte der deutschen Landwirtschaft*, Stuttgart, 1976, pp. 93ff; F.-W. Henning, *Landwirtschaft und ländliche Gesellschaft in Deutschland*, vol. 1, Paderborn, 1979, p. 131.

24 The use of woodland in agriculture is discussed by A. Timm, *Die Waldnutzung in Nordwestdeutschland im Spiegel der Weistümer*, 1960; L. Carlen, 'Allmende', in *Lexikon des Mittelalters*, vol. 1, 1980, cols 439ff.

25 Timm, *Waldnutzung*, p. 69.

26 See Henning, *Landwirtschaft*, pp. 138ff; Duby, 'Medieval Agriculture 900–1500' (n. 6 above), p. 200.

27 For information on the famine of 1315–17 see W. Abel, *Agrarkrisen und Agrarkonjunktur*, Hamburg, 1978, pp. 46ff. (For a translation of Abel's studies see W. Abel, *Agricultural Fluctuations in Europe from the Thirteenth to the Twentieth Centuries*, London/New York, 1980); H. van Werveke, 'La famine de l'an 1316 en Flandre et dans les régions voisines', *Revue du Nord*, 41 (1950), pp. 5ff.

CHAPTER 4 CHANGES IN THE VILLAGE

1 Walter Kempowski, in W. Landzettel (ed.), *Deutsche Dörfer*, 1982, p. 9.

2 For general information on village studies see *Dorferneuerung zwischen Tradition und Fortschritt*, Schriftenreihe für ländliche Sozialfragen 86, 1981; Agrarsoziale Gesellschaft (ed.), *Das erhaltenswerte eigenständige Dorf*, Kleine Reihe 26, 1982; M. Blümcke (ed.), *Abschied von der Dorfidylle?*, 1982; C. H. Hauptmeyer, 'Geschichtswissenschaft und erhaltende Dorferneuerung', *Berichte zur deutschen Landeskunde*, 53 (1979), pp. 61–79; Alan Mayhew, *Rural Settlement and Farming in Germany*, London, 1973 – esp. pp. 37–84.

3 See H. Jäger, 'Das Dorf als Siedlungsform und seine wirtschaftliche Funktion', in H. Jankuhn et al. (eds), *Das Dorf der Eisenzeit und des frühen Mittelalters*, Göttingen, 1977, pp. 62ff.

4 Ibid., p. 71.

5 See K. S. Bader, *Studien zur Rechtsgeschichte des mittelalterlichen Dorfes*, vol. 1: *Das mittelalterliche Dorf als Friedens- und Rechtsbereich*, Weimar, 1957, pp. 21ff.

6 Ibid., p. 21.

7 Ibid., pp. 38ff; vol. 3, p. 5; H. Jänichen, *Beiträge zur Wirtschaftsgeschichte des schwäbischen Dorfes*, Stuttgart, 1970, pp. 109ff.

8 Bader, *Rechtsgeschichte des Dorfes*, vol. 1, p. 46.

9 M. Bronhofer, *Die ausgehende Dreizelgenwirtschaft in der Nordost-Schweiz* (Doctoral Thesis), Zürich, 1956, p. 162.

10 Otto Brunner, 'Europäisches Bauerntum', in Brunner (ed.), *Neue Wege der Verfassungs- und Sozialgeschichte*, 2nd edn, Göttingen, 1968, pp. 199–212, esp. p. 201.

11 For more information on the traditional conception of village development see Bader, *Rechtsgeschichte des Dorfes*, vol. 1, pp. 4. ff.; G. L. von Maurer, *Einleitung zur Geschichte der Mark-, Dorf- und Stadtverfassung und der öffentlichen Gewalt*, 1854 (repr. edn 1966); Mayhew, *Rural Settlement* (n. 2 above), pp. 16–18.

12 For recent studies on the development of the medieval village see K. Kroeschell, 'Dorf', in *HRG*, vol. 1, 1971, cols 764–74; K. H. Schröder and

G. Schwarz, *Ländliche Siedlungsformen*, Bad Godesberg, 1978, pp. 51ff; R. Sablonier, 'Das Dorf im Übergang von Hoch- zum Spätmittelalter. Untersuchungen zum Wandel ländlicher Gemeinschaften im ostschweizerischen Raum', in *Festschrift J. Fleckenstein*, Sigmaringen, 1984, pp. 727ff; Mayhew, *Rural Settlement*, pp. 33–84.

13 See F. Steinbach, 'Gewanndorf und Einzelhof', in H. J. Nitz (ed.), *Historisch-genetische Siedlungsforschung*, Darmstadt, 1974, pp. 42–65; W. Müller-Wille, 'Langstreifenflur und Drubbel', in Nitz (ed.), *Siedlungsforschung*, pp. 247–314; A. Krenzlin, 'Die Entwicklung der Gewannflur als Spiegel kulturlandschaftlicher Vorgänge', in Nitz (ed.), *Siedlungsforschung*, pp. 108–35.

14 See W. A. Boelcke, 'Die frühmittelalterlichen Wurzeln der südwestdeutschen Gewannflur', in Nitz (ed.), *Siedlungsforschung*, pp. 136ff; J. C. Tesdorpf, *Die Entstehung der Kulturlandschaft am westlichen Bodensee*, 1972, pp. 67ff.

15 F. Schwind, 'Beobachtungen zur inneren Struktur des Dorfes in karolingischer Zeit', in Jankuhn (ed.), *Das Dorf der Eisenzeit*, pp. 444–93.

16 See H. Dannenbauer, 'Bevölkerung und Besiedlung Alemanniens in der fränkischen Zeit', *ZWLG* 13 (1954), pp. 12–37.

17 The increase in the number of villages (*Verdorfung*) is discussed by Schröder and Schwarz, *Siedlungsformen*, pp. 54ff; Krenzlin, 'Entwicklung der Gewannflur' (n. 13 above), pp. 108–35; W. Abel, 'Verdorfung und Gutsbildung in Deutschland zu Beginn der Neuzeit', *ZAA* 9 (1961), pp. 39ff.

18 For references on the formation of open fields see H. Ott, *Studien zur spätmittelalterlichen Agrarverfassung im Oberrheingebiet*, Stuttgart, 1970, pp. 86ff; M. Born, *Die Entstehung der deutschen Agrarlandschaft*, Darmstadt, 1974, p. 45.

19 See Born, *Agrarlandschaft*, p. 59; Krenzlin, 'Entwicklung der Gewannflur', p. 117.

20 Krenzlin, 'Entwicklung der Gewannflur', p. 115.

21 See ibid., p. 117; Jänichen, *Wirtschaftsgeschichte*, p. 112; Ott, *Studien*, pp. 87ff.

22 See W. Abel, *Geschichte der deutschen Landwirtschaft*, Stuttgart, 1976, pp. 87ff.

23 G. Schröder-Lembke, 'Wesen und Verbreitung der Zweifelderwirtschaft im Rheingebiet', *ZAA* 7 (1959), pp. 14–31; Ott, *Studien*, pp. 65–109.

24 (Translator's note: For more information on the manorial or *Fronhof* system see ch. 12 n. 13.) See ch. 1 n. 22 for references on the manorial system in the early Middle Ages.

25 On the dissolution of the manorial system see F. Lütge, *Geschichte der deutschen Agrarverfassung*, Stuttgart, 1967, pp. 83ff; A. Dopsch, *Herrschaft und Bauer in der deutschen Kaiserzeit*, Jena, 1939, pp. 129ff; G. Duby, *L'économie rurale*, Paris, 1962, vol. 2, pp. 415ff (*Rural Economy and Country Life in the Medieval West*, Columbia, SC, 1968, pp. 197ff.).

26 (Translator's note: The *ministeriales*, or manorial officials, were responsible for a variety of tasks ranging from the administration of manors to military duties.) See W. Abel, 'Landwirtschaft', in H. Aubin and W. Zorn (eds), *Handbuch der deutschen Wirtschafts- und Sozialgeschichte*, vol. 1, Stuttgart, 1971, pp. 183ff; Lütge, *Agrarverfassung*, pp. 95ff.

27 Jänichen, *Wirtschaftsgeschichte* (n. 7 above), p. 131; V. Ernst, *Die Entstehung des niederen Adels*, 1916, pp. 32ff.

28 See ch. 9.

29 See K. S. Bader, 'Entstehung und Bedeutung der oberdeutschen Dorfgemeinde', *ZWLG* 1 (1937), p. 279.

30 See G. Franz, *Geschichte des deutschen Bauernstandes vom frühen Mittelalter bis zum 19. Jahrhundert*, Stuttgart, 1976, pp. 72ff.

31 H. Grees, *Ländliche Unterschichten und ländliche Siedlung in Ostschwaben*, Tübingen, 1975, pp. 305ff.

32 See Born, *Agrarlandschaft*, p. 47; Bader, *Rechtsgeschichte des Dorfes* (n. 5 above), vol. 1, pp. 230ff.

33 P. Grimm, *Hohenrode, eine mittelalterliche Siedlung im Südharz*, Halle, 1939.

34 For archaeological settlement studies see M. W. Beresford and J. G. Hurst, *Deserted Medieval Villages*, 1971; *Villages désertés et histoire économique, XIᵉ–XVIIIᵉ siècle*, Paris, 1965; P. H. Sawyer (ed.), *Medieval Settlement*, 1976, A. Steensberg, 'Store Valby and Borup: Two Case Studies in the History of Danish Settlement', ibid., p. 94; J. Chapelot and R. Fossier, *The Village and House in the Middle Ages*, Berkeley, Calif., 1985.

35 W. Winkelmann, 'Eine westfälische Siedlung des 8. Jahrhunderts bei Warendorf', *Germania*, 32 (1954), pp. 189–213; W. Winkelman, 'Die Ausgrabungen in der frühmittelalterlichen Siedlung bei Warendorf', in *Neue Ausgrabungen in Deutschland*, 1958, pp. 492–517.

36 E. Ennen and W. Janssen, *Deutsche Agrargeschichte. Vom Neolithikum bis zur Schwelle des Industriezeitalters*, Wiesbaden, 1979, pp. 148ff.

37 Grimm, *Hohenrode* (n. 33 above); G. Buchda, 'Archäologisches zum Sachsenspiegel', *ZRG GA* 72 (1955), pp. 205–15.

38 W. Janssen, *Königshagen, Ein archäologisch-historischer Beitrag zur Siedlungsgeschichte des südwestlichen Harzvorlandes*, Hildesheim, 1965.

39 Ibid., p. 306.

40 For more information on the results of archaeological settlement studies see W. Janssen, 'Dorf und Dorfformen des 7. bis 12. Jahrhunderts im Lichte neuerer Ausgrabungen in Mittel- und Nordeuropa', in Jankuhn et al. (eds), *Dorf der Eisenzeit* (n. 3 above), pp. 285–356 (this work makes particularly good use of recent studies); W. Janssen, 'Mittelalterliche Dorfsiedlungen als archäologisches Problem', *Frühmittelalterliche Studien*, 2 (1968), pp. 305–67; G. P. Fehring, 'Zur archäologischen Erforschung mittelalterlicher Dorfsiedlungen in Südwestdeutschland', *ZAA* 21 (1973), pp. 1–35; D. Zoller, 'Untersuchung von Dorfkernen und Wirtschaftsfluren mit archäologischen Methoden', *Lübecker Schriften zur Archäologie und Kulturgeschichte*, 4 (1980), pp. 207ff; P. Donat, *Haus, Hof und Dorf in Mitteleuropa vom 7. bis 12. Jahrhundert*, Berlin, 1980.

41 Janssen, 'Dorf und Dorfformen', p. 345.

42 M. W. Beresford and J. G. Hurst, 'Wharram Percy: a case study in microtopography', in Sawyer, *Medieval Settlement* (n. 34 above), pp. 114–58; J. G. Hurst, 'Wandlungen des mittelalterlichen Dorfes in England', in *Festschrift W. Abel*, vol. 1, Hanover, 1974, pp. 237–62.

43 Hurst, 'Wandlungen', p. 248.

44 See V. Nekuda. 'Zum Stand der Wüstungsforschung in Mähren', *Zeitschrift für Archäologie des Mittelalters*, 1 (1973), pp. 31–57.

45 V. Nekuda, *Pfaffenschlag*, Brünn, 1975.

46 Ibid., p. 252.

CHAPTER 5 PEASANT HOUSE AND HOLDING

1 For references on the history of medieval peasant houses and farms see M. Heyne, *Fünf Bücher deutscher Hausaltertümer von den ältesten geschichtlichen Zeiten*

bis zum 16. Jahrhundert, Hausaltertümer, vol. 1: *Wohnung,* Leipzig, 1899;
W. Pessler, *Das altsächsische Bauernhaus in seiner geographischen Verbreitung,*
1906; H. Dölling, *Haus und Hof in westgermanischen Volksrechten,* 1958;
T. Gebhard, *Der Bauernhof in Bayern,* 1975; O. Moser, *Das Bauernhaus und
seine landschaftliche und historische Entwicklung in Kärnten,* 1974; R. Weiss,
Häuser und Landschaften der Schweiz, 2nd edn, Erlenbach-Zürich, 1973;
H. Schilli, *Das Schwarzwaldhaus,* 3rd edn, 1977; J. Schepers, *Das Bauernhaus
in Nordwestdeutschland,* 1943; J. Schepers, *Haus und Hof westfälischer
Bauern,* 5th edn, 1980; J. Schepers, *Vier Jahrzehnte Hausforschung,* 1973;
K. Baumgarten, *Das deutsche Bauernhaus,* Berlin, 1980; K. Bedal and
H. Hinz, 'Bauernhaus', in *Lexikon des Mittelalters,* vol. 1, 1980, cols 1606–19
(see this work esp. for recent studies on the subject); J. Chapelot and R. Fossier,
Le village et la maison, Paris, 1980 (*The Village and House in the Middle Ages,*
Berkeley, Calif., 1985); N. Harvey, *A History of Farm Buildings in England and
Wales,* Newton Abbot 1970; B. Schier, *Hauslandschaften und Kulturbewegungen
im östlichen Mitteleuropa,* 2nd edn, 1966; Nekuda, *Pfaffenschlag,* Brünn, 1975.

2 For a survey on the development of studies on peasant housing by specialists in
popular culture (*Volkskunde*) see K. Bedal, *Historische Hausforschung. Eine
Einführung in Arbeitsweise, Begriff und Literatur,* Münster, 1978. See also
J. Hähnel, *Hauskundliche Bibliographie 1961–1970,* 2 vols, 1972/4; G. Eitzen,
'Deutsche Hausforschung in den Jahren 1953–62', *ZAA* 11 (1963), pp. 213–33.

3 For archaeological studies on housing in the Middle Ages see the works by
Janssen, Fehring, Zoller and Donat mentioned in ch. 4 n. 40 and the works by
Beresford and Hurst quoted in ch. 4 n. 42. For further references on the
subject see W. Haarnagel, 'Das eisenzeitliche Dorf "Feddersen Wierde", seine
siedlungsgeschichtliche Entwicklung, seine wirtschaftliche Funktion und die
Wandlung seiner Sozialstruktur', in Jankuhn (ed.), *Das Dorf der Eisenzeit,*
Göttingen, 1977, pp. 253–84; W. Winkelmann, 'Warendorf' (see ch. 4 n. 35).

4 H. Hinz, 'Das mobile Haus. Bemerkungen zur Zeitbestimmung durch die
Dendrochronologie', *Chateau Gaillard,* 7 (1975), pp. 141–5.

5 See R. Wenskus (ed.), *Wort und Begriff 'Bauer',* Göttingen, 1975.

6 See ch. 11.

7 See A. Meitzen, *Das deutsche Haus in seinen volkstümlichen Formen,* 1882;
F. Steinbach, *Studien zur westdeutschen Stammes- und Volksgeschichte,* 1926;
Bedal, *Hausforschung* (n. 2 above), pp. 7ff.

8 It was above all R. Weiss, the Swiss expert on popular culture who developed
this functional approach. Cf. Weiss, *Häuser und Landschaften der Schweiz* (n. 1
above).

9 See J. Schepers, 'Die hausgeschichtliche Stellung des Oberwesergebietes', in
Schepers (ed.), *Vier Jahrzehnte Hausforschung,* pp. 25–9.

10 This has been emphasized especially by Baumgarten, *Bauernhaus,* pp. 41ff;
Chapelot and Fossier, *Le village,* p. 333; Schepers, *Haus und Hof westfälischer
Bauern* (n. 1 above) p. 33.

11 On the shape of early medieval farms see F. Beyerle, 'Das Kulturportrait der
beiden alemannischen Rechtstexte: Pactus und Lex Alamannorum', in W. Müller
(ed.), *Zur Geschichte der Alemannen,* 1975, pp. 126–50; Dölling, *Haus und
Hof* (n. 1 above); Winkelmann, *Warendorf* (see ch. 4 n. 35); F. Garscha et al.,
'Eine Dorfanlage des frühen Mittelalters bei Merdingen', *Badische Fundberichte,*
18 (1948/50), pp. 137–83.

12 See Haarnagel, 'Feddersen Wierde' (n. 3 above) and Schepers, *Haus und Hof*
(n. 1 above), pp. 30ff.

13 See H. Hinz, 'Zur Vorgeschichte der niederdeutschen Halle', *Zeitschrift für Volkskunde*, 60 (1964), pp. 1–22.

14 See D. Zoller, 'Untersuchung von Dorfkernen' (see ch. 4, n. 40); D. Zoller, 'Die Ergebnisse der Grabung Gristede 1960 und 1961', *Nachrichten aus Niedersachsens Urgeschichte*, 31 (1962), pp. 31–57; Hurst, 'Wandlungen' (see ch. 4 n. 42).

15 See H. Hinz, 'Das mobile Haus' (n. 4 above).

16 C. von Schwerin (ed.), *Sachsenspiegel. Landrecht*, Stuttgart, 1977, p. 87 (II. 53).

17 See n. 10 above.

18 Justus Möser. *Osnabrücker Geschichte*, ed. B. R. Abeken, vol. 1: 1843, p. 102.

19 Baumgarten, *Bauernhaus* (n. 1 above, p. 43).

20 For general information on the development of farmhouses in southern Germany see Schilli, *Schwarzwaldhaus* (n. 1 above); Gebhard, *Bauernhof in Bayern* (n. 1 above); K. H. Schröder, 'Zur Entwicklung des bäuerlichen Anwesens im alemannischen Stammesgebiet', *Alemannisches Jahrbuch*, (1970), pp. 209–32.

21 W. Schilli, *Schwarzwaldhaus* (n. 1 above), pp. 72ff.

22 M. Weber et al. (eds), *Das Tennenbacher Güterbuch (1317–41)*, 1969, *passim*.

23 P. Grimm, *Hohenrode*, Halle, 1939, p. 27. See also K. Baumgarten, 'Ethnographische Bemerkungen zum Grabungsbefund Hohenrode', *Ausgrabungen und Funde*, 16 (1971), pp. 49ff.

24 W. Janssen, *Königshagen*, Cologne, 1975, p. 207.

25 T. Gebhard, *Hausforschung in Bayern. Arbeitskreis für deutsche Hausforschung*, 1956, pp. 9ff.

26 G. P. Fehring, 'Dorfsiedlungen in Südwestdeutschland' (see ch. 4 n. 40), p. 20.

27 See K. S. Bader, *Rechtsgeschichte des Dorfes*, vol. 1, Weimar, 1957, pp. 71ff.

28 For information on the houses and farms of the lower peasant classes see Baumgarten, *Bauernhaus*, pp. 117ff; Grees, *Ländliche Unterschichten und Siedlung in Ostschwaben*, Tübingen, 1975, p. 96; Schröder, 'Zur Entwicklung' (n. 20 above), p. 222.

29 See Chapelot and Fossier, *Le Village*, pp. 199ff; Weiss, *Häuser* (n. 1 above), p. 38; J. M. Pesez, 'Une maison villageoise au XIV^c siècle', *Rotterdam Papers*, 2 (1975), pp. 139–50.

30 See J. Schepers, 'Mittelmeerische Einflüsse in der Bau- und Wohnkultur des westlichen Mitteleuropa', in Schepers (ed.), *Vier Jahrzehnte Hausforschung*, 1973, pp. 121–35; Chapelot and Fossier, *Le village*, p. 284; Weiss, *Häuser* (n. 1 above), p. 38.

31 On the development of farm buildings in England see M. W. Beresford and J. G. Hurst, 'Wharram Percy' (see ch. 4 n. 42); J. G. Hurst, 'Wandlungen des Dorfes in England', Hanover, 1974, pp. 244ff; Harvey, *Farm Buildings* (n. 1 above); M. W. Barley, *The English Farmhouse and Cottage*, 3rd edn, London 1972.

32 For more information on farm buildings in Switzerland see Weiss, *Häuser*, passim; J. Hunziker, *Das Schweizerhaus nach seinen landschaftlichen Formen und seiner geschichtlichen Entwicklung*, 8 vols, 1900–14.

33 See P. Donat, *Haus, Hof und Dorf in Mitteleuropa vom 7. bis 12. Jahrhundert*, Berlin, 1980, pp. 26ff.

34 Nekuda, *Pfaffenschlag* (n. 1 above).

35 Ibid., p. 251.

36 On the development of heating ovens and heated parlours (*Stuben*) see J. Hähnel, *Stube. Wort- und sachgeschichtliche Beiträge zur historischen*

Hausforschung, Munich, 1975; E. Meyer-Heisig, *Die deutsche Bauernstube*, 1952; J. Schepers, 'Ofen und Kamin', in Schepers (ed.), *Vier Jahrzehnte Hausforschung*, 1973, pp. 52–74; K. Ilg, 'Die Entwicklung der Stube unter dem Gesichtspunkt bodenständiger Rauchstuben im Südwesten des deutschen Kulturraumes', *Österreichische Zeitschrift für Volkskunde*, 68 (1965), pp. 209–24, Bedal, *Hausforschung*, pp. 119ff; Baumgarten, *Bauernhaus*, pp. 65ff.
37 Neidhart von Reuental, *Lieder* (ed. and tr. from Middle High German into Modern German by H. Lomnitzer), Stuttgart, 1981, p. 35.
38 Ibid., p. 41.
39 See Hähnel, *Stube*, p. 145.
40 H. Kaiser, 'Herdfeuer und Herdgerät im Bauernhaus', in *Jahrbuch für das Oldenburger Münsterland*, 1983, p. 66.
41 See Heyne, *Hausaltertümer* (n. 1 above), vol. 1, p. 121.
42 See Schepers, 'Ofen und Kamin' (n. 36 above).
43 Bedal, *Hausforschung*, p. 119.
44 Grimm, *Hohenrode* (n. 23 above), p. 25.
45 See Heyne, *Hausaltertümer*, vol. 1, pp. 172ff; E. Heinemeyer and H. Ottenjann, *Alte Bauernmöbel aus dem nordwestlichen Niedersachsen*, 2nd edn, 1979; F. Piponnier, 'Une maison villageoise au XIVᵉ siècle: le mobilier', *Rotterdam Papers*, 2 (1975), pp. 151–70.
46 See Baumgarten, *Bauernhaus*, p. 71.

CHAPTER 6 CLOTHING AND FOOD

1 W. Hansen, 'Aufgaben der historischen Kleidungsforschung', in G. Wiegelmann, *Geschichte der Alltagskultur*, Münster, 1980, p. 159.
2 For general information on the history of medieval clothing see D. W. H. Schwarz, *Sachgüter und Lebensformen. Einführung in die materielle Kulturgeschichte des Mittelalters und der Neuzeit*, Berlin, 1970, pp. 98ff; Heyne, *Hausaltertümer*, vol. 2, pp. 207ff; M. von Boehn, *Die Mode*, vol. 1: *Menschen und Moden im Mittelalter*, 6th edn, 1963; A. Schultz, *Das höfische Leben zur Zeit der Minnesinger*, 2 vols, 1889; A. Schultz, *Deutsches Leben im 14. und 15. Jahrhundert*, 2 vols, 1892.
3 The illustrated manuscripts of the Saxon Code (*Sachsenspiegel*) and the illustrated Swiss chronicles (*Schweizer Bilderchroniken*) are particularly helpful in reconstructing the variety of peasant clothing. See W. Koschorreck, *Die Heidelberger Bilderhandschrift des Sachsenspiegels. Kommentar und Faksimile*, 1970; A. A. Schmid (ed.), *Die Schweizer Bilderchronik des Luzerners Diepold Schilling*, 1513 and 1981.
4 Cf. Hansen, 'Aufgaben' (n. 1 above), pp. 149–74; M. Bringemeier, *Mode und Tracht*, 1980.
5 See E. Nienholt, 'Die Volkstracht', in *Handbuch der deutschen Volkskunde*, vol. 3, 1938, pp. 65–139.
6 Cf. M. Heyne, *Fünf Bücher deutscher Hausaltertümer*, vol. 3: *Körperpflege und Kleidung*, Leipzig, 1903, pp. 252ff.
7 *MGH*, ch. 1, no. 52, p. 140, c. 5.
8 See Heyne, *Hausaltertümer*, vol. 3, p. 280.
9 The following works are particularly interesting for the study of the changes in clothing in the high Middle Ages: H. Naumann, *Deutsche Kultur im Zeitalter des Rittertums*, 1938, pp. 116ff; Schwarz, *Sachgüter*, pp. 102ff; F. Pipponnier, 'Le costume nobiliaire dans la France du bas Moyen Age', in

Notes 291

Adelige Sachkultur des Spätmittelalters, Veröffentlichungen des Instituts für mittelalterliche Realienkunde Österreichs 5, Vienna, 1982, pp. 343–63.
10 G. Franz, Der deutsche Bauernkrieg, 10th edn, Darmstadt, 1975, p. 53.
11 See Rösener, 'Bauer und Ritter', (see ch. 1 n. 9). p. 683; A. Hagelstange, Süddeutsches Bauernleben im Mittelalter, Leipzig, 1898, pp. 38ff.
12 G. Franz (ed.), Quellen zur Geschichte des deutschen Bauernstandes im Mittelalter, 2nd edn, Darmstadt, 1974, p. 220, no. 82.
13 MGH, Const. 2, p. 577, col. 71. See W. Schnelbögl, 'Die innere Entwicklung der bayerischen Landfrieden des 13. Jahrhunderts', in Deutschrechtliche Beiträge, 13, 2 (1932), pp. 107ff.
14 E. Wiessner (ed.), Die Lieder Neidharts, Altdeutsche Textbibliothek 44, 1955.
15 K. Speckenbach, Wernher der Gartenaere: Helmbrecht, 1974; H. Brackert, 'Helmbrechts Haube', Zeitschrift für deutsches Altertum und deutsche Literatur, 103 (1974), pp. 166–84.
16 J. Seemüller (ed.), Seifried Helbing, 1886; U. Liebertz-Grün, Seifried Helbing. Satiren contra Habsburg, 1981.
17 Seemüller (ed.), Seifried Helbing, p. 69, lines 70–5.
18 On clothing regulations see L. C. Eisenbart, Kleiderordnungen der deutschen Städte zwischen 1350 und 1700, 1962; G. Hampel-Kallbrunner, Beiträge zur Geschichte der Kleiderordnungen mit besonderer Berücksichtigung Österreichs, 1962.
19 Quoted by Hagelstange, Bauernleben, p. 53.
20 See Schwarz, Sachgüter, pp. 105ff; Heyne, Hausaltertümer, vol. 3, pp. 296ff.
21 See Hagelstange, Bauernleben, p. 51.
22 Quoted ibid., pp. 50ff.
23 Quoted by J. Janssen, Geschichte des deutschen Volkes seit dem Ausgang des Mittelalters, 18th edn, 1897, p. 369.
24 Cf. Hagelstange, Bauernleben, p. 53.
25 For general information on the development of peasant diet see Christopher Dyer, 'English Diet in the Later Middle Ages', in T. H. Aston et al., Social Relations and Ideas: Essays in Honour of R. H. Hilton, Cambridge, 1983, pp. 191–216; G. Wiegelmann, Alltags- und Festspeisen, 1967; M. Wähler, 'Die deutsche Volksnahrung', in Handbuch der deutschen Volkskunde, vol. 3, 1938, pp. 140–55; K. Hintze, Geographie und Geschichte der Ernährung, 1934; E. Schmauderer, Studien zur Geschichte der Lebensmittelwissenschaft, 1975; D. Saalfeld, 'Die Sorge um das tägliche Brot', in J. Blum (ed.), Die bäuerliche Welt, 1982, pp. 109ff (Our Forgotten Past: Seven Centuries of Life on the Land, London, 1982); M. Montanari, 'Rural food in late medieval Italy', in Bäuerliche Sachkultur des Spätmittelalters, Veröffentlichungen des Instituts für mittelalterliche Realienkunde Österreichs, 7, Vienna, 1984.
26 See W. Abel, Stufen der Ernährung, 1981, p. 5.
27 See Schwarz, Sachgüter (n. 2 above), pp. 129ff.
28 See Heyne, Hausaltertümer, vol. 2: Nahrung, Leipzig, 1901, p. 270.
29 See K. S. Bader, Rechtsgeschichte des Dorfes, vol. 3: Rechtsformen und Schichten der Liegenschaftsnutzung im mittelalterlichen Dorf, Vienna, 1973, pp. 36ff.
30 G. Franz (ed.), Quellen zur Geschichte des deutschen Bauernstandes in der Neuzeit, 2nd edn, 1976, pp. 2ff.
31 W. Abel, Strukturen und Krisen der spätmittelalterlichen Wirtschaft, Stuttgart, 1980.
32 See Heyne, Hausaltertümer, vol. 2, pp. 291ff.

33 See W. Abel, *Geschichte der deutscher Landwirtschaft*, Stuttgart, 1976, p. 25.
34 On hunting and fishing see Schwarz, *Sachgüter* (n. 2 above), pp. 142ff; H. Heimpel, 'Fischerei und Bauernkrieg', in *Festschrift P. E. Schramm*, 1964, pp. 353ff; K. Lindner, *Geschichte des deutschen Waidwerks*, vol. 2, 1940.
35 On cattle-breeding see Abel, *Geschichte der deutschen Landwirtschaft*, pp. 93ff.
36 See Heyne, *Hausaltertümer*, vol. 2, pp. 324ff.
37 Ibid., pp. 334ff; H. Huntemann, *Bierproduktion und Bierverbrauch in Deutschland vom 15. bis zum Beginn des 19. Jahrhunderts* (Doctoral Thesis), Göttingen, 1970.
38 On the history of wine in the Middle Ages see Abel, *Strukturen*, pp. 53ff; F. von Bassermann-Jordan, *Geschichte des Weinbaus*, 2 vols, 3rd edn, 1975; R. Dion, *Histoire de la vigne et du vin en France*, 1959.
39 See Abel, *Stufen der Ernährung* (n. 26 above), pp. 65ff; Abel, *Geschichte der deutschen Landwirtschaft*, pp. 23ff.
40 K. A. Eckhardt, 'Leges nationum Germ. 4: Pactus legis Salicae', in *MGH*, Leges Sect. 4 (1962), pp. 20–8.
41 Abel, *Geschichte der deutschen Landwirtschaft*, pp. 26ff.
42 See G. Duby, 'Medieval Agriculture 900–1500', in C. M. Cipolla (ed.), *The Fontana Economic History of Europe*, vol. 1, Brighton, 1976, pp. 191ff; F.-W. Henning, *Landwirtschaft und ländliche Gesellschaft in Deutschland*, vol. 1, Paderborn, 1979, p. 97.
43 See G. Schiedlausky, *Essen und Trinken*, 1959, p. 42.
44 Quoted by Janssen, *Geschichte* (n. 23 above), p. 374.
45 Ibid., p. 374.
46 Abel. *Strukturen*, pp. 41ff; G. Wiegelmann, *Alltags und Festspeisen*, 1967, p. 30.
47 L. Stouff, *Ravitaillement et alimentation en Provence aux XIV^c et XV^c siècles*, 1970, pp. 220ff.
48 On the upper peasant class in south-western Germany see G. Wunder, 'Bäuerliche Oberschicht im alten Wirtemberg', in G. Franz (ed.), *Bauernschaft und Bauernstand 1500–1970*, 1975, pp. 137–51; F. Rapp, 'Die bäuerliche Aristokratie des Kocherberges im ausgehenden Mittelalter und zu Beginn der Neuzeit', in Franz (ed.), *Bauernschaft und Bauernstand*, pp. 89–101.
49 For general information on famines in the Middle Ages see F. Curschmann, *Hungersnöte im Mittelalter*, 1900; H.-J. Schmitz, *Faktoren der Preisbildung für Getreide und Wein in der Zeit von 800 bis 1350*, Stuttgart, 1968, pp. 33ff; W. Abel, *Agrarkrisen und Agrarkonjunktur*, Hamburg, 1978, pp. 35ff; W. Abel, *Massenarmut und Hungerkrisen im vorindustriellen Deutschland*, 1972, pp. 35ff. On the famine of 1437–8 see Abel, *Strukturen*, pp. 85ff.
50 Quoted by Abel, *Strukturen*, pp. 88ff.
51 A. Henne von Sargans (ed.), *Die Klingenberger Chronik*, 1861, p. 222.
52 See ch. 3 n. 3.

CHAPTER 7 AGRICULTURAL IMPLEMENTS,
LAND UTILIZATION AND AGRARIAN DEVELOPMENT

1 G. Duby, 'La révolution agricole médiévale', *Revue de Géographie de Lyon*, 29 (1954), pp. 361–66; L. White, *Medieval Technology and Social Change*, Oxford, 1962; J. Gimpel, 'The agricultural revolution', *The Medieval Machine*, 1977, p. 29.
2 On the history of farming implements in the Middle Ages see K. Hielscher,

'Fragen zu den Arbeitsgeräten der Bauern', *ZAA* 17 (1969), pp. 6–42; U. Bentzien, *Bauernarbeit im Feudalismus*, Berlin, 1980, chs 1–2; K. R. Schultz-Klinken, *Die Entwicklung der ländlichen Handarbeitsgeräte in Südwestdeutschland*, Stuttgart, 1975.

3 For information on the development of agricultural techniques see C. Parain, 'The evolution of agricultural technique', in M. M. Postan (ed.), *The Cambridge Economic History of Europe*, vol. 1, Cambridge, 1966, pp. 125–79; G. Duby, 'Le problème des techniques agricoles', in *Agricoltura e mondo rurale in Occidente nell'alto medievo*, Spoleto, 1966; W. Abel, *Geschichte der deutschen Landwirtschaft*, Stuttgart, 1976, pp. 45ff; A. Steensberg, 'Agrartechnik der Eisenzeit', in H. L. Beck et al. (eds), *Untersuchungen zur eisenzeitlichen und frühmittelalterlichen Flur in Mitteleuropa und ihrer Nutzung*, vol. 2, Göttingen, 1980, pp. 30ff.

4 On the history of the plough see A. G. Haudricourt and M. G. Brunhès-Delamarre, *L'homme et la charrue à travers le monde*, 1955; U. Bentzien, *Haken und Pflug*, 1969; K. R. Schultz-Klinken, *Haken, Pflug und Ackerbau*, 1977.

5 M. Born, 'Acker- und Flurformen des Mittelalters', in Beck et al. (eds), *Flur*, vol. 1, Göttingen, 1979, pp. 310ff.

6 Bentzien, *Bauernarbeit*, p. 25.

7 W. Haarnagel, 'Feddersen Wierde' (see ch. 5 n. 3), pp. 253ff.

8 White, *Medieval Technology*.

9 Cf. Bentzien, *Bauernarbeit*, pp. 65ff; Hielscher, 'Arbeitsgeräte' (n. 2 above), pp. 17ff.

10 Duby, 'Le problème' (n. 3 above), p. 282. Duby emphasized the improvement in ploughing techniques as a decisive factor for the development of agriculture in the high Middle Ages. See also White, *Medieval Technology*. White was misled in the assumption that the widespread application of the wheeled plough goes back as far as Carolingian times.

11 See White, *Medieval Technology*.

12 See Hielscher, 'Arbeitsgeräte', p. 18.

13 Bentzien, *Bauernarbeit*, p. 147.

14 Cf. Schultz-Klinken, *Haken*, p. 5.

15 The following studies focus especially on harnesses: A. G. Haudricourt, 'L'origine de l'attelage moderne', *Annales d'histoire*, 8 (1936), pp. 515ff; W. Jacobeit, 'Zur Geschichte der Pferdeanspannung', *ZAA* 2 (1954), pp. 17–25; Hielscher, 'Arbeitsgeräte', pp. 22ff; White, *Medieval Technology*.

16 Cf. Abel, *Geschichte der deutschen Landwirtschaft*, p. 46.

17 M. Kiem, 'Das Kloster Muri im Kanton Aargau', in *Quellen zur Schweizer Geschichte*, vol. 3, 1883, p. 71.

18 Ibid., p. 61.

19 See e.g. G. Franz (ed.), *Quellen zur Geschichte des deutschen Bauernstandes im Mittelalter*, 2nd edn, Darmstadt, 1974, p. 164, on the manorial law of Münchweier.

20 K. A. Eckhardt (ed.), *Das Landrecht des Sachsenspiegels*, 1955, vol. 3, 51, 1.

21 See Hielscher, 'Arbeitsgeräte', pp. 25ff.

22 Bentzien, *Bauernarbeit*, pp. 71ff; Hielscher, 'Arbeitsgeräte', pp. 19ff.

23 On the history of sickles and scythes see Hielscher, 'Arbeitsgeräte', pp. 28ff; A. Lühning, 'Die schneidenden Erntegeräte', unpublished Doctoral Thesis, Göttingen, 1951; Bentzien, *Bauernarbeit*, pp. 73ff.

24 See K. Ilg, 'Die Sense in ihrer Entwicklung und Bedeutung', in *Festschrift H. Wopfner*, vol. 2, 1948, pp. 179–90.

25 For information on the history of threshing see Hielscher, 'Arbeitsgeräte', pp. 32ff; Bentzien, *Baurnarbeit*, pp. 78ff.

26 Bentzien, *Bauernarbeit*, p. 88.

27 Cf. G. Duby, *Rural Economy and Country Life in the Medieval West*, Columbia, SC, 1968, pp. 107ff.

28 See R. Pleiner, 'Die Technik des Schmiedehandwerks im 13. Jahrhundert im Dorf und in der Stadt', in H. Jankuhn and R. Wenskus (eds), *Geschichtswissenschaft und Archäologie*, VF 22, 1979, pp. 393–402.

29 The following studies include surveys on the history of the three-field system: Abel, *Geschichte der deutschen Landwirtschaft*, pp. 88ff; Duby, *Rural Economy and Country Life*, pp. 90ff; White, *Medieval Technology*. White's study, however, suffers from the fact that it places the development of the three-field system much too early, namely in the eighth century. On the history of the open-field system and their crop rotation see above, ch. 4, and the references given in that chapter.

30 See ch. 4, particularly the section on the combination of the common field economy with the three-field system, i.e. crop rotation within the framework of the open-field system.

31 Cf. M. Born, *Die Entwicklung der deutschen Agrarlandschaft*, Darmstadt, 1974, pp. 45ff; H. Jänichen, *Beiträge zur Wirtschaftsgeschichte des schwäbischen Dorfes*, Stuttgart, 1970, pp. 109ff; Krenzlin, 'Gewannflur' (see ch. 4 n. 13), pp. 108ff.

32 See H. Jäger, 'Bodennutzungssysteme (Feldsysteme) der Frühzeit', in Beck (ed.), *Flur* (n. 3 above), vol. 1, pp. 197–228, esp. the detailed bibliography included in this section; G. Schröder-Lembke, 'Nebenformen der alten Dreifelderwirtschaft in Deutschland', in *Agricoltura* (n. 3 above), pp. 285ff.

33 See Jänichen, *Wirtschaftsgeschichte*, p. 115.

34 See Rösener, 'Brandwirtschaft', in *Lexikon des Mittelalters*, vol. 2, 1983, cols 71f; F. Schneiter, *Agrargeschichte der Brandwirtschaft*, 1970; O. Pickl, 'Brandwirtschaft und Umwelt seit der Besiedlung des Ostalpengebietes', in H. Kellenbenz (ed.), *Wirtschaftsentwicklung und Umweltbeeinflussung*, Stuttgart, 1982, pp. 27–55.

35 Cf. J. Lorsbach, *Hauberg und Hauberggenossenschaften des Siegerlandes*, 1956.

36 For information on ley farming see G. Schröder-Lembke, *Zweifelderwirtschaft* (see ch. 4 n. 23); Ott, *Studien zur spätmittelalterlichen Agrarverfassung im Oberrheingebiet*, Stuttgart, 1970, pp. 65ff.

37 See W. Abel, 'Landwirtschaft', in H. Aubin and W. Zorn (eds), *Handbuch der deutschen Wirtschafts- und Sozialgeschichte*, Stuttgart, 1971, pp. 96ff; White, *Medieval Technology*.

38 Duby, 'Le problème' (n. 3 above), p. 282, estimates that grain yields doubled from the tenth to the twelfth centuries as a result of the modernization of agrarian techniques (ploughs, three-field system etc.), with the relation between seed sown and grain yields increasing from 1:2.5 to 1:4.

39 W. Müller-Wille, 'Langstreifenflur' (see ch. 4 n. 13), p. 306.

40 See F.-W. Henning, *Landwirtschaft und ländliche Gesellschaft in Deutschland*, vol. 1, Paderborn, 1979, pp. 193ff.

41 See n. 1 above.

CHAPTER 8 PEASANT LABOUR AND ECONOMY

1 For the economic situation of the modern peasant family enterprise see T. Bergmann, 'Der bäuerliche Familienbetrieb. Problematik und Entwicklungs- tendenzen', *ZAA 17 (1969), pp. 215–30.*

2 W. H. *Riehl, Die Naturgeschichte des deutschen Volkes,* ed. Ipsen, Leipzig, 1935, pp. 197ff; O. Brunner, 'Das ganze Haus und die alteuropäische Ökonomik', in Brunner, *Neue Wege der Verfassungs- und Sozialgeschichte,* Göttingen, 1968, pp. 103–27.

3 Brunner, 'Das ganze Haus', pp. 107ff.

4 A. V. Chayanov, *The Theory of Peasant Economy,* ed. D. Thorner et al., 1966.

5 Ibid., p. 60.

6 R. Hilton, 'Medieval peasants – any lessons?', *Journal of Peasant Studies,* 1 (1973/4), pp. 207–17; Hilton, 'Die Natur mittelalterlicher Bauernwirtschaft', in L. Kuchenbuch and B. Michael (eds), *Feudalismus. Materialen zur Theorie und Geschichte,* Frankfurt a.M., 1977, pp. 481ff.

7 See Intro. n. 24.

8 Hilton, 'Peasants' (n. 6 above), pp. 207ff.

9 G. Franz (ed.), *Quellen zur Geschichte des deutschen Bauernstandes in der Neuzeit,* 2nd edn, 1976, p. 3.

10 W. Schlesinger, 'Die Hufe im Frankenreich', in H. Beck et al., (eds), *Untersuchungen zur eisenzeitlichen und frühmittelalterlichen Flur,* vol. 1, Göttingen, 1979, pp. 41–70; K. Grinda, 'Die Hide und verwandte Landmasse im Altenglischen', ibid., pp. 92–113; S. Gissel, 'Bol und Bolverfassung in Dänemark', ibid., pp. 134–40. For general information see H. Kellenbenz and G. Philippe, 'Hufe', in *HRG,* vol. 2, 1978, cols 248–51. This essay includes further references.

11 Schlesinger, 'Hufe' (n. 10 above), p. 64.

12 For general information on grain production in the Middle Ages see W. Abel, *Geschichte der deutschen Landwirtschaft,* Stuttgart, 1976, pp. 90ff; G. Duby, *L'économie rurale,* Paris, 1962, vol. 1, pp. 170ff (G. Duby, *Rural Economy and Country Life,* Columbia SC, 1968, pp. 88ff).

13 See H. Jänichen, *Beiträge zur Wirtschaftsgeschichte des schwäbischen Dorfes,* Stuttgart, 1970, p. 97; R. Gradmann, 'Der Dinkel und die Alemannen', *Württ. Jahrbuch für Statistik und Landeskunde* (1901), pp. 103ff.

14 On types of medieval produce see J. A. van Houtte, in Kellenbenz, *Handbuch der europäischen Wirtschafts- und Sozialgeschichte,* vol. 2, Stuttgart, 1980, pp. 31ff; U. Willerding, 'Anbaufrüchte der Eisenzeit und des frühen Mittelalters, ihre Anbauformen, Standortverhältnisse und Erntemethoden', in Beck (ed.), *Flur,* vol. 2, pp. 125–96; U. Willerding, 'Botanische Beiträge zur Kenntnis von Vegetation und Ackerbau im Mittelalter', in H. Jankuhn and R. Wenskus (eds), *Geschichtswissenschaft und Archäologie,* VF 22, 1979, pp. 271–353. This study includes a large reference section.

15 J. Grimm, *Weisthümer,* Darmstadt, 1957, vol. 4, p. 6.

16 M. Weber et al., *Tennenbacher Güterbuch* (ch. 5 n. 22), p. 191.

17 Cf. K.-E. Behre, 'Zur mittelalterlichen Plaggenwirtschaft in Nordwest- deutschland und angrenzenden Gebieten nach botanischen Untersuchungen', in Beck (ed.), *Flur,* vol. 2, pp. 30–44, including references.

18 See ch. 5, pp. 70 ff.

19 For general information on gardening and its history see M. L. Gothein, *Geschichte der Gartenkunst,* 2 vols, 1914; K. S. Bader, *Rechtsgeschichte des*

Dorfes, vol. 3, Vienna, 1973, pp. 52–91; M. Heyne, *Fünf Bücher deutscher Hausaltertümer,* vol. 2: *Nahrung,* Leipzig, 1901, pp. 62ff; A. Hauser, *Bauerngärten der Schweiz,* 1976.

20 Cf. Bader, *Rechtsgeschichte des Dorfes,* vol. 3, pp. 97ff; Jänichen, *Wirtschaftsgeschichte,* p. 118.

21 See H. Ammann, 'Die Anfänge der Leinenindustrie des Bodenseegebiets', *Alemannisches Jahrbuch* (1953), pp. 251ff.

22 P. Jaffé (ed.), 'Descriptio Alsatiae', in *MGH SS* 17, 1861, p. 237.

23 For information on wine production see Abel, *Geschichte der deutschen Landwirtschaft,* pp. 129ff; R. Dion, *Histoire* (see ch. 6 n. 38).

24 On yields in medieval grain production see B. H. Slicher van Bath, 'Landwirtschaftliche Produktivität im vorindustriellen Europa', in Kuchenbuch and Michael (eds), *Feudalismus,* pp. 523ff; B. H. Slicher van Bath, *The Agrarian History of Western Europe 500–1850,* London, 1963, pp. 66ff.

25 G. Duby, 'Un inventaire des profits de la seigneurie clunisienne à la mort de Pierre le Vénérable', in Duby, *Hommes et structures du moyen âge,* Paris, 1973, pp. 87ff (Duby, *The Chivalrous Society*).

26 B. H. Slicher van Bath, *Yield ratios 810–1820,* AAG Bijdragen 10, 1963, pp. 30ff, 112f, 154ff.

27 G. Duby, 'Medieval agriculture' (see ch. 3 n. 6), p. 195.

28 G. Duby, 'Le problème' (see ch. 7 n. 3), p. 282.

29 See H.-J. Schmitz, *Faktoren der Preisbildung für Getreide und Wein,* Stuttgart, 1968, pp. 12ff: Slicher van Bath, *Agrarian History,* pp. 18ff.

30 For general information on medieval livestock production see W. Abel, *Geschichte der deutschen Landwirtschaft,* pp. 94ff; U. Bentzien, *Bauernarbeit im Feudalismus,* Berlin, 1980, pp. 83ff.

31 See Bentzien, *Bauernarbeit,* pp. 82ff; A. Hagelstange, *Süddeutsches Bauernleben,* Leipzig, 1898, pp. 158ff.

32 See Abel, *Geschichte der deutschen Landwirtschaft,* pp. 94ff.

33 A thorough study of the Tyrolean cattle farms has been presented by O. Stolz, *Die Schwaighöfe in Tirol,* 1930.

34 Quoted by Stolz, ibid., p. 31, n. 1.

35 Cf. S. Bökönyi, *History of Domestic Mammals in Central and Eastern Europe,* Budapest, 1974, pp. 136–9.

36 Grimm, *Weisthümer* (n. 15 above), vol. 1, p. 315.

37 Ibid., vol. 2, p. 148.

38 For a detailed study on pig-keeping in the Middle Ages see C. L. ten Cate, *Wan god mast gift . . . Bilder aus der Geschichte der Schweinezucht im Walde,* 1972, pp. 59–136.

39 F. von Weech (ed.), *Code Diplomaticus Salemitanus,* vol. 1, 1883, no. 525, pp. 127ff.

40 *ZGO* 8 (1857), p. 133.

41 Stolz, *Schwaighöfe* (n. 33 above), p. 36.

42 On the economic aspects of sheep-raising in general see W. Jacobeit, *Schafhaltung und Schäfer in Zentraleuropa bis zum Beginn des 20. Jahrhunderts,* 1961, *passim.*

43 E. Le Roy Ladurie, *Montaillou: Cathars and Catholics in a French village 1294–1324,* London, 1978.

44 On the keeping of bees in the Middle Ages see C. Warnke, 'Bienen', in *Lexikon des Mittelalters,* vol. 2, 1983, cols 128–33; E. H. Segschneider, *Imkerei im nordwestlichen Niedersachsen,* 1978.

45 Bader, *Rechtsgeschichte des Dorfes,* vol. 3, p. 4.

46 G. Duby, 'Medieval agriculture' (see ch. 3 n. 6), p. 187.

47 U. Jeggle, *Kiebingen – Eine Heimatgeschichte*, 1977, p. 129.

48 See K. S. Bader, *Rechtsgeschichte des Dorfes*, vol. 1, Weimar, 1957, pp. 49ff; J. Vincke, *Die Lage und Bedeutung der bäuerlichen Wirtschaft im Fürstentum Osnabrück während des späten Mittelalters*, 1928, pp. 11ff, 40.

49 (Translator's Note: For a definition of the term manorial, or *Fronhof*, system see ch. 12 n. 13.) See F. Lütge *Geschichte der deutschen Agrarverfassung*, Stuttgart, 1967, pp. 83ff; W. Rösener, 'Die Spätmittelalterliche Grundherrschaft im südwestdeutschen Raum als Problem der Sozialgeschichte', *ZGO* 127 (1979), pp. 29ff.

50 See W. Rösener, 'Abgaben', in *Lexikon des Mittelalters*, vol. 1, 1980, cols 32ff.

51 K. Lamprecht, *Deutsche Wirtschaft im Mittelalter*, 3 vols, Leipzig, 1885/6, vol. I.1, p. 603; vol. I.2, p. 205.

52 M. M. Postan (ed.), *The Cambridge Economic History of Europe*, vol. 1, Cambridge, 1966, p. 603.

53 Abel, *Geschichte der deutschen Landwirtschaft*, p. 98.

54 Ibid., p. 109.

55 See W. Abel, *Agrarkrisen und Agrarkonjunktur*, Hamburg, 1978, pp. 44ff. For more information in this study see ch. 15.

CHAPTER 9 NEIGHBOURHOOD AND VILLAGE COMMUNITY

1 Cf. U. Jeggle, 'Krise der Gemeinde – Krise der Gemeindeforschung', in Wiegelmann (ed.), *Gemeinde*, 1979, p. 104; K. Bergmann, *Agrarromantik* (see Intro. n. 11).

2 W. H. Riehl, *Die Naturgeschichte des deutschen Volkes*, ed. Ipsen, Leipzig, 1935, p. 108.

3 Ibid., pp. 116ff.

4 See Jeggle, 'Krise' (n. 1 above), p. 105; A. Ilien and U. Jeggle, *Leben auf dem Dorf*, Opladen, 1978; C.-H. Hauptmeyer, 'Dorfgemeinde und Dorfbewohnermentalität aus der Sicht der Geschichtswissenschaft', *Essener Geogr. Arb.*, 2 (1982), pp. 31ff.

5 U. Jeggle, *Kiebingen* (see ch. 8 n. 47), p. 114.

6 See ch. 4.

7 Cf. G. L. von Maurer, *Geschichte der Dorfverfassung in Deutschland*, 2 vols, 1865/66; O. von Gierke, *Das deutsche Genossenschaftsrecht*, vol. 1, 1868, pp. 609ff.

8 Cf. ch. 4.

9 K. S. Bader, *Studien zur Rechtsgeschichte des Dorfes*, vol. 1, Weimar, 1950, p. 7.

10 On the relation between village co-operative and village community see Bader, *Rechtsgeschichte des Dorfes*, vol. 2: *Dorfgenossenschaft und Dorfgemeinde*, Vienna, 1962, pp. 3ff (etymology), pp. 21ff (terminological discussion); K. H. Quirin, *Herrschaft und Gemeinde nach mitteldeutschen Quellen des 12. bis 18. Jahrhunderts*, 1952, pp. 72ff.

11 Bader, *Rechtsgeschichte des Dorfes*, vol. 2, p. 29.

12 The following is a list of important works on the structure and development of the village and the rural community: Bader, *Rechtsgeschichte des Dorfes*, 3 vols, 1957/73; K. S. Bader, 'Entstehung und Bedeutung der Dorfgemeinde', *ZWLG* 1 (1937); K. S. Bader, 'Dorf und Dorfgemeinde in der Sicht des Rechtshistorikers', *ZAA* 12 (1964), pp. 10–20; T. Mayer (ed.) *Die Anfänge der Landgemeinde und ihr Wesen*, 2 vols, Konstanz, 1964 (this work includes a

number of detailed studies on the constitutional history of rural communities
in Europe); K. Bosl, 'Eine Geschichte der deutschen Landgemeinde', *ZAA* 9
(1961), pp. 129–42; Genicot, *Le XIIIe siècle européen*, Paris, 1968, pp. 72ff;
R. H. Hilton, *A Medieval Society*, London, 1966, pp. 149ff; K. Kroeschell,
'Dorf', in *HRG*, vol. 1, 1971, cols 764–74; M. Nikolay-Panter, *Entstehung
und Entwicklung der Landgemeinde im Trierer Raum*, 1976; M. Mitterauer,
'Pfarre und ländliche Gemeinde in den österreichischen Ländern', *Blätter für
deutsche Landesgeschichte*, 109 (1973), pp. 1–30; P. Blickle, *Deutsche
Untertanen*, 1981, pp. 37ff; R. Sablonier, 'Das Dorf im Übergang vom Hoch-
zum Spätmittelalter', in *Festschrift J. Fleckenstein*, 1984, Sigmaringen, 1984,
pp. 727–45.

13 F. Steinbach, 'Ursprung und Wesen der Landgemeinde nach rheinischen
Quellen', in Mayer, *Landgemeinde*, vol. 1, pp. 245–88.

14 Ibid., p. 285.

15 A. Dopsch, *Herrschaft und Bauer in der deutschen Kaiserzeit*, Jena, 1939, see
esp. pp. 99–114.

16 Cf. n. 12 above.

17 Bader, *Rechtsgeschichte des Dorfes*, vol. 2, pp. 88ff.

18 Ibid., p. 92.

19 Ibid., p. 37.

20 Cf. T. Mayer, 'Vom Wesen und Werden der Landgemeinde', in Mayer (ed.),
Landgemeinde, vol. 2, pp. 465ff.

21 Cf. K.-S. Kramer, *Die Nachbarschaft als bäuerliche Gemeinschaft*, Munich,
1954, p. 75; O. G. Oexle, 'Die mittelalterlichen Gilden: Ihre Selbstdeutung
und ihr Beitrag zur Formung sozialer Strukturen', in *Soziale Ordnungen im
Selbstverständnis des Mittelalters*, Berlin, 1979, pp. 203ff.

22 See Mayer, 'Wesen' (n. 20 above), p. 477; H. Dannenbauer, 'Hundertschaft,
Centena und Huntari', *HJb* 63/69 (1949), pp. 155ff.

23 Cf. K. Bosl, 'Landgemeinde' (n. 12 above), p. 129.

24 Cf. T. Mayer, 'Wesen' (n. 20 above), p. 466.

25 Cf. Bader, 'Dorfgemeinde' (n. 12 above), p. 276; Bader, *Rechtsgeschichte des
Dorfes*, vol. 2, pp. 90ff. On the territorialization of political rule see T. Mayer,
'Der Staat der Herzöge von Zähringen', in Mayer, *Mittelalterliche Studien*,
1959, pp. 350ff; H. Patze (ed.), *Der deutsche Territorialstaat im 14.
Jahrhundert*, 2 vols, Sigmaringen, 1970.

26 Cf. U. Stutz, 'Zur Herkunft von Zwing und Bann', *ZRG GA* 57 (1937), pp. 289–
354; H. Rennefahrt, 'Twing und Bann', *Schweizer Beiträge zur Allgemeinen
Geschichte*, 10 (1952), pp. 22–87; Bader, *Rechtsgeschichte des Dorfes*, vol. 2,
pp. 90ff.

27 The following section on the development of the village community is
essentially based on Mayer, *Landgemeinde*, vols 1 and 2 (n. 12 above).

28 Cf. A. Verhulst, 'Binnenkolonisation' (see ch. 3 n. 9), pp. 447ff.

29 Cf. F. Petri, 'Marschenkolonisation' (see ch. 3 n. 9), pp. 695ff.

30 On the development of the rural community in the newly settled territories
east of the Rivers Elbe and Saal see esp. W. Schlesinger, 'Bäuerliche
Gemeindebildung in den mittelelbischen Landen im Zeitalter der mittelalterlichen
deutschen Ostbewegung', in Mayer (ed.), *Landgemeinde*, vol. 2, pp. 27–87.
See also, for further references, W. Schlesinger (ed.), *Die deutsche Ostsiedlung
des Mittelalters*, Sigmaringen, 1975.

31 For information on the history of the village community in Italy see
I. Imberciadori, 'Italien', in H. Kellenbenz (ed.), *Handbuch der Europäische
Wirtschafts- und Sozialgeschichte*, vol. 2, Stuttgart, 1980, pp. 438ff.

32 Cf. W. Maas, 'Loi de Beaumont und Jus Teutonicum', *VSWG* 32 (1939), pp. 209–27; O. A. Kielmeyer, *Die Dorfbefreiung auf deutschem Sprachgebiet* (Doctoral Thesis), Bonn, 1931.

33 Cf. F. Uhlhorn, 'Beobachtungen über die Ausdehnung des sogenannten Frankfurter Stadtrechtskreises', *Hessisches Jahrbuch für Landesgeschichte*, 5 (1955), pp. 124ff.

34 See E. Ennen, *The Medieval Town* (see ch. 2 n. 12), pp. 95ff; *Les libertés urbaines et rurales du XIe au XIVe siècle*, 1966, Colloque international, Spa, 1968.

35 Cf. E. Hering, *Befestigte Dörfer in südwestdeutschen Landschaften* (Doctoral Thesis), Frankfurt a.M., 1934.

36 Cf. Bader, *Rechtsgeschichte des Dorfes*, vol. 1, pp. 74ff.

37 For general information see J. Grimm (ed.), *Weisthümer*, 7 vols, 1840–78; repr. Darmstadt, 1957; H. Wiessner, *Sachinhalt und wirtschaftliche Bedeutung der Weistümer im deutschen Kulturgebiet*, 1934; K. Kollnig, 'Probleme der Weistumsforschung' (1957), in G. Franz (ed.), *Deutsches Bauerntum*, Darmstadt, 1976, pp. 394ff; P. Blickle (ed.), *Deutsche Ländliche Rechtsquellen*, 1977 (this volume contains a fine selection of both older and more recent studies).

38 Cf. D. Werkmüller, *Über Aufkommen und Verbreitung der Weistümer*, Berlin, 1972.

39 For general references see K.-S. Kramer, 'Nachbar, Nachbarschaft', in *HRG*, vol. 3, 1981, cols 813ff; Kramer, *Nachbarschaft* (n. 21 above); Bader, *Rechtsgeschichte des Dorfes*, vol. 2, pp. 38ff.

40 R. Schmidt-Wiegand, 'Nachbar' (an etymological and semantic study), in *HRG*, vol. 3, 1981, cols 812ff.

41 C. von Schwerin *Sachsenspiegel* (ch. 5 n. 16), pp. 55ff. See also G. Buchda, 'Die Dorfgemeinde im Sachsenspiegel', in Mayer, *Landgemeinde*, vol. 2, p. 12.

42 Von Schwerin, *Sachsenspiegel*, p. 86 (II. 52, 2).

43 Ibid., p. 96 (II. 52, 1).

44 Ibid., p. 80 (II. 38).

45 Cf. Kramer, *Nachbarschaft*, pp. 47ff, 67ff.

46 Cf. A. Hagelstange, *Süddeutsches Bauernleben*, Leipzig, 1898, p. 241.

47 L. Bechstein (ed.), *Der Ring von Heinrich Wittenweiler*, Bibl. des Lit. Vereins 23, 1851, pp. 148–65.

48 Cf. Kramer, *Nachbarschaft*, p. 10.

49 Quirin, *Gemeinde* (n. 10 above), p. 74.

50 See ch. 4, esp. pp. 50ff.

51 Bader, *Rechtsgeschichte des Dorfes*, vol. 2, p. 56.

52 Ibid., p. 59.

53 Cf. H. E. Feine, 'Kirche und Gemeindebildung', in Mayer (ed.), *Landgemeinde*, vol. 1, pp. 53ff; M. Erbe (ed.), *Pfarrkirche und Dorf*, Texte zur Kirchen- und Theologiegeschichte 19, 1973.

54 Bader, *Rechtsgeschichte des Dorfes*, vol. 2, p. 61.

55 Ibid., pp. 266ff; Quirin, *Gemeinde* (n. 10 above), pp. 55ff; G. Franz, *Geschichte des deutschen Bauernstandes*, Stuttgart, 1976, pp. 55ff.

56 Cf. Buchda, 'Dorfgemeinde' (n. 41 above); B. Schwineköper, 'Die mittelalterliche Dorfgemeinde in Elbostfalen und in den benachbarten Markengebieten', in Mayer (ed.), *Landgemeinde*, vol. 2, pp. 15–48; Von Schwerin, *Sachsenspiegel* (see ch. 5 n. 16).

57 The high medieval German formula was: 'Waz der burmeister schaffet des dorfes vromen mit wilkore der meren menige der gebure, des en mag daz minre teil nicht widerkomen.' *Sachsenspiegel*, p. 88 (II. 55).

58 Cf. Schwineköper, 'Dorfgemeinde' (n. 56 above), p. 130.
59 Buchda, 'Dorfgemeinde' (n. 41 above), p. 24.

CHAPTER 10 PEASANT FAMILY AND KINSHIP

1 Special mention must be made of the following recent studies on the history of the family: H. Rosenbaum (ed.), *Familie und Gesellschaftsstruktur*, 1974; H. Rosenbaum, *Familie und Sozialstruktur*, 1977; I. Weber-Kellermann, *Die Familie, Geschichte, Geschichten und Bilder*, 1976; P. Laslett, *The World We Have Lost*, London, 1965; P. Laslett (ed.), *Household and Family in Past Time*, Cambridge 1974; K. Hausen, 'Familie als Gegenstand Historischer Sozialwissenschaft', *Geschichte und Gesellschaft*, 1 (1975), pp. 171ff; M. Mitterauer and R. Sieder, *Vom Patriarchiat zur Partnerschaft*, 1977; H. Reif (ed.), *Die Familie in der Geschichte*, 1982.
2 Cf. U. Planck, *Der bäuerliche Familienbetrieb zwischen Patriarchiat und Partnerschaft*, 1964; G. Ipsen, *Die Landfamilie in Wirtschaft und Gesellschaft*, 1953; H. Linde, 'Persönlichkeitsbildung in der Landfamilie', in Rosenbaum (ed.), *Familie* (n. 1 above), pp. 194ff.
3 Planck, in Rosenbaum (ed.), *Familie* (n. 1 above), pp. 182ff.
4 Cf. P. Steinbach, 'Wilhelm Heinrich Riehl', in H.-U. Wehler (ed.), *Deutsche Historiker*, vol. 6, 1980, pp. 37–54.
5 W. H. Riehl, *Die Naturgeschichte des deutschen Volkes*, ed. Ipsen, Leipzig, 1935, p. 202.
6 Ibid., p. 211.
7 Cf. Mitterauer and Sieder, *Patriarchiat* (n. 1 above), p. 39; Weber-Kellermann, *Familie* (n. 1 above), p. 69.
8 See ch. 8.
9 Cf. O. Brunner, 'Das "ganze Haus" und die alteuropäische Ökonomik', in Brunner (ed.), *Neue Wege der Verfassungs- und Sozialgeschichte*, Göttingen, 1968, pp. 103ff.
10 Konrad von Mengenberg, *Ökonomik*, vol. 1, ed. S. Krüger, *MGH* Staatsschriften des späteren Mittelalters 3, 5, 1973.
11 Cf. E. R. Wolf, *Peasants*, Englewood Cliffs, NJ, pp. 65ff.
12 (Translator's note: Many researchers, such as Maurice Keen, Lawrence Stone and others use 'kinship' or 'kindred' to describe what Rösener means by the term *Sippe* in the German original. Max Weber, on the other hand, has chosen the Gaelic word 'clan' as the most accurate rendition for the functions of this complex phenomenon. The present translation employs the Gaelic and the English terms interchangeably: 'The Gaelic word clan means "blood kindred", and like the corresponding German word "Sippe" is identical with the Latin "proles" . . . the agnatic clan is most important . . . Its functions are, first to perform the duty of blood vengeance against outsiders; second, the division of fines within the group; third, it is the unit for land allotment.' – Max Weber, *General Economic History*, tr. F. H. Knight, London, 1927, pp. 43–4.) For more information on kinship see Weber-Kellermann, *Familie*, pp. 13ff; F. Genzmer, 'Die germanische Sippe als Rechtsgebilde', *ZRG GA* 67 (1950), pp. 34–49.
13 Cf. K. Kroeschell, 'Die Sippe im germanischen Recht', *ZRG GA* 77 (1960), pp. 1ff.
14 Cf. Rösener, 'Zur Problematik des spätmittelalterlichen Raubrittertums', in

Festschrift B. Schwineköper, Sigmaringen, 1982, pp. 469–88; O. Brunner, *Land und Herrschaft*, Vienna 1965, pp. 1–110.

15 W. Preiser, 'Blutrache', in *HRG*, vol. 1, 1971, cols 459ff; H. Aubin, 'Zur Entwicklung der freien Landgemeinden im Mittelalter, Fehde, Landfrieden, Schiedsgericht', in G. Franz (ed.), *Deutsches Bauerntum*, Darmstadt, 1976, pp. 191–218; P. Frauenstädt, *Blutrache und Todschlagssühne im deutschen Mittelalter*, 1881; H. Fehr, 'Das Waffenrecht der Bauern im Mittelalter', *ZRG GA* 35 (1914), pp. 111ff.

16 Cf. E. Kaufmann, 'Fehde', in *HRG, vol. 1, 1971, cols 1083–93; R. His, Das Strafrecht des deutschen Mittelalters*, vols. 1, 1920, p. 266.

17 Aubin, 'Landgemeinden' (n. 15 above), p. 198.

18 His, *Strafrecht* (n. 16 above), p. 295.

19 Aubin, 'Landgemeinden', p. 197.

20 Frauenstädt, *Blutrache* (n. 15 above), pp. 13ff.

21 Cf. Aubin, 'Landgemeinden', pp. 198ff.

22 Frauenstädt, *Blutrache*, pp. 10ff.

23 J. Strange (ed.), *Caesarii Heisterbacensis monachi ordinis Cisterciensis dialogus miraculorum*, vol. 2, 1851 (XI. 56).

24 His, *Strafrecht*, p. 295.

25 E. Osenbrüggen, *Das alemannische Strafrecht im deutschen Mittelalter*, 1860, pp. 25ff; A. Hauser, 'Zur soziologischen Struktur eidgenössischen Bauerntums im Spätmittelalter', in G. Franz (ed.), *Bauernschaft und Bauernstand*, 1975, pp. 65–8.

26 Frauenstädt, *Blutrache* (n. 15 above), p. 26.

27 L. Kuchenbuch, *Bäuerliche Gesellschaft und Klosterherrschaft im 9. Jahrhundert*, Wiesbaden, 1978, pp. 76ff.

28 Cf. C. I. Hammer, 'Family and *familia* in early medieval Bavaria', in P. Laslett (ed.), *Family Forms in Historic Europe*, Cambridge 1983, p. 243; R. R. Ring, 'Early medieval peasant households in central Italy', *Journal of Family History*, 4 (1979), pp. 2–21.

29 Cf. Mitterauer and Siedler, *Patriarchiat* (n. 1 above), p. 57.

30 E. Le Roy Ladurie, *The Peasants of Languedoc*, tr. J. Day, Urbana Ill., 1974, p. 36; G. Duby, Medieval Agriculture' (see ch. 3 n. 6), p. 184.

31 See article on 'Zadruga', in *Reallexikon der Vorgeschichte*, vol. 14, 1939, pp. 458ff.

32 For more information on the historical development of marriage and weddings see P. Mikat, 'Ehe', in *HRG*, vol. 1, 1971, cols 909–33 (the essay includes further recent references on the subject-matter); R. Köstler, 'Raub-, Kauf- und Friedelehe bei den Germanen', *ZRG GA* 63, (1943), pp. 92–136; K. Fröhlich, 'Die Eheschliessung des deutschen Frühmittelalters im Lichte der neuen rechtsgeschichtlichen Forschung', *Hess. Blätter für Volkskunde*, 27 (1928), pp. 144–94.

33 Wernher der Gärtner, *Peasant Life in Old German Epics: Meier Helmbrecht and Der arme Heinrich*, tr. from Middle High German by Clair Hayden Bell, New York, 1931, pp. 77–8, verses 1503–34 (for the German original see *Meier Helmbrecht*, Stuttgart, 1980, p. 46, verses 1337–66).

34 Weber-Kellermann, *Familie* (n. 1 above), p. 15.

35 On the influence of the church on marriage regulations see R. Sohm, *Das Recht der Eheschliessung aus dem deutschen und canonischen Recht geschichtlich entwickelt*, 1875; A. Spamer, 'Sitte und Brauch', in *Handbuch der deutschen Volkskunde*, vol. 2, 1935, p. 172; W. M. Plöchl, *Geschichte des Kirchenrechts*, vol. 2, 1962, pp. 305ff.

36 On the influence of the manorial and servile lords on peasant marriage see W. Müller, *Entwicklung und Spätformen der Leibeigenschaft am Beispiel der Heiratsbeschränkungen*, Sigmaringen, 1974, *passim*; O. Ulbrich, *Leibherrschaft am Oberrhein im Spätmittelalter*, Göttingen, 1979, pp. 261ff.

37 H. Ott, *Studien zur spätmittelalterlichen Agrarverfassung*, Stuttgart, 1970, p. 131.

38 G. Franz (ed.), *Quellen zur Geschichte des deutschen Bauernstandes im Mittelalter*, Darmstadt, 1974, p. 130, no. 51.

39 Müller, *Heiratsbeschränkungen*, pp. 28ff.

40 On marriage fines see P. Dollinger, *L'évolution des classes rurales en Bavière*, Paris, 1949; Müller, *Heiratsbeschränkungen*, pp. 9ff; E. Searle, 'Seigneurial control of women's marriage', *Past and Present*, 82 (1979), pp. 3ff.

41 G. Droege, 'Bedemund', in *Lexikon des Mittelalters*, vol. 1, 1980, col. 1781; H. Wiessner, *Sachinhalt* (see ch. 9 n. 37), pp. 155ff.

42 K. Schmidt, *Jus primae noctis. Eine geschichtliche Untersuchung*, 1881; Müller, *Heiratsbeschränkungen*, p. 10.

43 H. Fehr, *Die Rechtstellung der Frau und der Kinder in dem Weistümern*, Jena, 1966, p. 2.

44 J. Grimm (ed.), *Weisthümer*, Darmstadt, 1957, vol. 3, p. 311.

45 Ibid., p. 48.

46 Cf. Fehr, *Rechtsstellung*, pp. 4ff.

47 Ibid., pp. 52ff.

48 Ibid., p. 52.

49 E. Le Roy Ladurie, *Montaillou*, Paris, 1976; London, 1978, *passim*.

50 Fehr, *Rechtsstellung*, p. 59.

51 J.-L. Flandrin, *Familien. Soziologie-Ökonomie-Sexualität*, 1978, p. 146.

52 Ibid., p. 147.

53 Cf. J. C. Russel, 'Population' (see ch. 2 n. 6), p. 26; K. Arnold, *Kind und Gesellschaft in Mittelalter und Renaissance*, 1980, pp. 29ff.

54 M. M. Postan and J. Z. Titow, 'Heriots and prices on Winchester manors', in Postan (ed.), *Essays on Medieval Agriculture*, Cambridge, 1973, pp. 159ff, 180ff.

55 For more information on the social position of women in the Middle Ages see particularly the following recent studies: S. M. Stuard (ed.), *Women in Medieval Society*, Philadelphia 1976; S. Shahar, *The Fourth Estate: A History of Women in the Middle Ages*, tr. Chaya Galai, London, 1983; P. Ketsch, *Frauen im Mittelalter*, 1983 (this work contains many further references).

56 A number of studies are in particular concerned with the position of the medieval peasant woman in the family, household, and agriculture: J. Barchewitz, *Beiträge zur Wirtschaftstätigkeit der Frau* (Doctoral Thesis), Breslau, 1937; Huppertz, *Räume und Schichten bäuerlicher Kulturformen in Deutschland*, Bonn, 1939, pp. 304ff; G. Wiegelmann, 'Zum Problem der bäuerlichen Arbeitsteilung in Mitteleuropa', in *Franz Steinbach zum 65. Geburtstag, 1960*, pp. 637ff; R. H. Hilton, *The English Peasantry in the Later Middle Ages*, London, 1983, pp. 95ff; Shahar *Fourth Estate* (n. 55 above), pp. 191ff; H. Wunder, 'Zur Stellung der Frau im Arbeitsleben und in der Gesellschaft des 15.–18. Jahrhunderts', *Geschichtsdidaktik*, 6 (1981), pp. 239ff.

57 Cf. ch. 7.

58 Cf. S. Epperlein, *Der Bauer im Bild des Mittelalters*, Leipzig, 1975, *passim*; S. Epperlein, 'Bäuerliche Arbeitsdarstellungen auf mittelalterlichen Bildzeugnissen', in *Jahrbuch für Wirtschaftsgeschichte*, vol. 1, 1976, pp. 181–208.

59 Hilton, *Peasantry*, p. 103.

60 For general information on the social status of children in medieval society see

K. Arnold, *Kind und Gesellschaft*, 1980; P. Ariès, *Centuries of Childhood: A Social History of Family Life*, tr. Robert Baldick, New York, 1962; M. M. McLaughlin, 'Survivors and surrogates: children and parents from the ninth to the thirteenth centuries', in Lloyd deMause (ed.), *The History of Childhood*, New York, 1974, pp. 101–83.

61 McLaughlin, 'Survivors' (n. 60 above).

62 For more information on peasant inheritance customs see W. Bungenstock, 'Anerbenrecht', in *HRG*, vol. 1 (1971), cols 163–6 (this essay includes references to recent studies); T. Mayer-Edenhauser, *Untersuchungen über Anerbenrecht und Güterschluss in Kurhessen*, 1942; M. Sering, *Erbrecht und Agrarverfassung in Schleswig-Holstein auf geschichtlicher Grundlage*, 1908; H. Röhm, *Die Vererbung des landwirtschaftlichen Grundeigentums in Baden-Württemberg*, 1957; J. Goody et al. (eds), *Family and Inheritance*, Cambridge 1976; W. Rösener, 'Spätmittelalterliche Grundherrschaft' (see ch. 8 n. 49), pp. 59ff.

63 For a helpful discussion of the divergent views on the origin of the various inheritance customs see Röhm, *Vererbung* (n. 62 above), pp. 66ff.

64 In the Black Forest and in upper Swabia, for instance, inheritance customs changed in the course of the late Middle Ages, cf. E. Gothein, 'Die Hofverfassung auf dem Schwarzwald dargestellt an der Geschichte des Gebiets von St. Peter', *ZGO* 40 (1886), pp. 257ff; D. Sabean, 'Probleme der deutschen Agrarverfassung zu Beginn des 16. Jahrhunderts', in P. Blickle (ed.), *Revolte und Revolution in Europa*, Munich, 1975, p. 141.

65 Huppertz, *Räume* (n. 56 above), p. 49.

66 This part of the farmhouse was called *Ausgedinge* or *Leibzucht* in some German sources. On the problems of peasant retirement see Mitterauer and Sieder, *Patriarchiat* (n. 1 above), pp. 193ff; D. Gaunt, 'The property and kin relation of retired farmers in northern and central Europe', in P. Laslett et al. (eds), *Family Forms in Historic Europe*, pp. 249–79.

67 Cf. C. Schott, *Der 'Träger' als Treuhandform*, 1975.

68 Cf. Fehr, *Rechtsstellung*, pp. 147ff.

69 Cf. Sabean, 'Probleme' (n. 64 above), p. 143.

CHAPTER 11 THE SOCIAL STRATIFICATION OF THE PEASANT POPULATION

1 Theoretical aspects of the study of the social stratification of the medieval peasantry are in particular discussed by M. Mitterauer, 'Probleme der Stratifikation in mittelalterlichen Gesellschaftssystemen', *Geschichte und Gesellschaft*, special issue 3 (1977), pp. 13–43; K. Bosl, 'Kasten, Stände, Klassen', *ZBLG* 32 (1969), pp. 477–94; E. Münch, 'Bauernschaft und bäuerliche Schichten im vollentfalteten Feudalismus', *Jb. für Wirtschaftsgeschichte*, 3 (1980), pp. 75–85.

2 For more information on this problem see T. B. Bottomore, 'Soziale Schichtung', in *Handbuch der empirischen Sozialforschung*, vol. 5, 2nd edn, 1976, pp. 1–39 (this essay contains many further references).

3 The following studies treat the problem of the social stratification of peasant population in the Middle Ages: B. H. Slicher van Bath, *The Agrarian History of Western Europe*, London, 1963, pp. 310ff; R. H. Hilton, *Bond Men Made Free*, London, 1973, pp. 33ff; K. Blaschke, *Bevölkerungsgeschichte von Sachsen bis zur Industriellen Revolution*, Weimar, 1967, pp. 142ff; W. A. Boelke, 'Wandlungen der dörflichen Sozialstruktur während Mittelalter und

Neuzeit', in *Festschrift G. Franz*, Frankfurt a.M., 1967, pp. 80ff; K. Helleiner, 'Ländliches Mindervolk in niederösterreichischen Weistümern', *ZAA* 25 (1977), pp. 12ff; L. Genicot, 'Sur le nombre des pauvres dans les campagnes médiévales. L'exemple du Namurois', *RH* 257 (1977), pp. 273ff; H. Grees, *Ländliche Unterschichten und Siedlung in Ostschwaben*, Tübingen, 1975; W. Rösener, 'Bauer und Ritter im Hochmittelalter' (see ch. 1 n. 9), pp. 681ff.

4 K. Bosl, 'Die "familia" als Grundstruktur der mittelalterlichen Gesellschaft', *ZBLG* 38 (1975), pp. 402–24, esp. p. 411; K. Bosl, 'Freiheit und Unfreiheit. Zur Entwicklung der Unterschichten in Deutschland und Frankreich während des Mittelalters', in G. Franz (ed.), *Deutsches Bauerntum*, Darmstadt, 1976, pp. 75–104; cf. H. Dopsch, 'Freiheit und Unfreiheit', in C. A. Lückerath and U. Uffelmann (eds), *Geschichte des Mittelalters*, 1982, pp. 23–54.

5 For more information on the social structure of the *familia* on the manors between the ninth and the twelfth centuries see L. Kuchenbuch, *Bäuerliche Gesellschaft*, Wiesbaden, 1978, pp. 59ff; Dollinger, *Bauernstand*, pp. 59ff. G. Duby, *L'économie rurale*, Paris, 1962, vol. 1, pp. 100ff. (G. Duby, *Rural Economy and Country Life in the Medieval West*, Columbia, SC, 1968, p. 37); M. Bloch, *Feudal Society* (see ch. 1 n. 21), p. 255ff; K. H. Ganahl, *Studien* (see ch. 1 n. 34), pp. 83ff; E. Linck, *Sozialer Wandel in klösterlichen Grundherrschaften des 11. bis 13. Jahrhundert*, Göttingen, 1979, pp. 252ff.

6 Cf. K. Schulz, 'Zum Problem der Zensualität im Hochmittelalter', in *Festschrift H. Helbig*, 1976, pp. 86–127.

7 G. Franz (ed.), *Quellen zur Geschichte des deutschen Bauernstandes im Mittelalter*, Darmstadt, 1974, p. 126, no. 51.

8 'Chronicon Eberheimense' in *MGH SS* no. 23, p. 433.

9 E. König and K. O. Müller (eds), *Die Zwiefaltener Chroniken Ortliebs und Bertholds*, Schwäbische Chroniken der Stauferzeit 2, 1941, pp. 45ff; Rösener, 'Bauer und Ritter', pp. 670ff.

10 A. Longnon (ed.), *Polyptyque* (see ch. 1 n. 26); Cf. F. L. Ganshof, 'Das Fränkische Reich' (see ch. 1 n. 18), pp.177ff.

11 Cf. Kuchenbuch, *Bäuerliche Gesellschaft*, pp. 59ff.

12 Cf. K. Stackmann, 'Bezeichnungen für "Bauer" im frühmittelhochdeutschen Quellen', in R. Wenskus et al. (eds), *Bauer*, Göttingen, 1975, pp. 159ff; see also ch. 1.

13 Changes in the manorial system in the high Middle Ages are discussed by F. Lütge, *Geschichte der deutschen Agrarverfassung*, Stuttgart, 1967, pp. 83ff; Linck, *Sozialer Wandel* (n. 5 above). See ch. 1 for more information on the forces which stimulated the formation of a distinct peasant estate before the eleventh century.

14 See ch. 4.

15 Cf. K. S. Bader, 'Bauernrecht und Bauernfreiheit im späteren Mittelalter', *HJb* 61 (1941), pp. 53ff; T. Mayer, 'Bemerkungen', (see ch. 2 n. 13), pp. 46ff; Lütge, *Agrarverfassung*, pp. 63ff.

16 P. Dollinger, *L'évolution des classes rurales en Bavière*, Paris, 1949.

17 Ibid.

18 M. Bloch, *Les caractères originaux de l'histoire rurale française*, Paris, 1960, p. 94 (Bloch, *French Rural History*, London, 1966); Dollinger, *Évolution des classes rurales*, C.-E. Perrin, 'Le servage en France et en Allemagne', in X. Congresso Internazionale di Scienze Storiche, *Relazioni*, vol. 3, Rome, 1955.

19 Weber et al. (eds), *Tennenbacher Güterbuch* (see ch. 5 n. 22); Rösener, 'Bauer und Ritter', pp. 681ff; H. Ott, *Studien zur spätmittelalterlichen Agrarverfassung*,

Stuttgart, 1970, pp. 8ff; E. Schillinger, 'Studien zu den sozialen Verhältnissen in Mundingen und umliegenden Siedlungen im ausgehenden Mittelalter', *Alemannisches Jahrbuch* (1976–8), pp. 73ff.

20 Cf. L. Fenske, 'Soziale Genese und Aufstiegsformen kleiner niederadliger Geschlechter im südöstlichen Niedersachsen', in *Festschrift J. Fleckenstein*, Sigmaringen, 1984, pp. 713ff.

21 J. Schulze (ed.), *Das Landbuch der Mark Brandenburg von 1375*, 1940; E. Müller-Mertens, 'Hufenbauern und Herrschaftsverhältnisse in brandenburgischen Dörfern nach dem Landbuch Karls IV. von 1375', *Wiss. Zs. der Humboldt-Universität Berlin*, (1951–2), pp. 35–79.

22 E. Engel, 'Lehnbürger, Bauer und Feudalherren in der Altmark um 1375', in E. Engel an d B. Zientara, *Feudalstruktur, Lehnbürgertum und Fernhandel im spätmittelalterlichen Brandenburg*, Weimar, 1967, p. 76.

23 Cf. H. Helbig, *Gesellschaft und Wirtschaft der Mark Brandenburg im Mittelalter*, Berlin, 1973, pp. 10ff; E. O. Schulze, *Die Kolonisierung und Germanisierung der Gebiete zwischen Elbe und Saale*, pp. 166ff.

24 W. Ribbe, 'Zur rechtlichen, wirtschaftlichen und ethnischen Stellung der Kossäten', in W. Fritze (ed.), *Germania Slavica*, vol. 2, 1981, pp. 21–40.

25 For general information on rural servants see O. Könnecke, *Rechtsgeschichte des Gesindes in West- und Süddeutschland*, 1912; H. Firnberg, *Lohnarbeiter und freie Lohnarbeit im Mittelalter und zu Beginn der Neuzeit*, 1935.

26 Cf. A. E. Verhulst, 'Die Niederlande im Hoch- und Spätmittelater', in H. Kellenbenz (ed.), *Handbuch der europäischen Wirtschaft- und Sozialgeschichte*, vol. 2, Stuttgart, 1980, p. 279. On the general development of agriculture in Belgium see L. Genicot, *L'économie rurale namuroise au bas Moyen Age (1199–1429)*, 2 vols, Louvain, 1974/5; G. Sivery, *Structures agraires et vie rurale dans le Hainaut à la fin du Moyen Age*, 1973.

27 L. Genicot, 'Sur le nombre des pauvres' (n. 3 above), p. 279.

28 On the development of the rural population in France in the high and late Middle Ages see R. Fossier, *La terre et les hommes en Picardie*, Paris, 1968, pp. 439ff; G. Fourquin, *Les campagnes de la région parisienne à la fin du Moyen Age*, 1964; G. Duby, 'La seigneurie et l'économie paysanne. Alpes du Sud 1338', in G. Duby, *Hommes et structures du moyen âge*, Paris, 1973, pp. 167ff (also in English in Duby, *The Chivalrous Society*); G. Bois, *The Crisis of Feudalism*, Cambridge, 1989; J. Favier, 'Frankreich im Hoch- und Spätmittelalter', in Kellenbenz (ed.), *Handbuch*, vol. 2, pp. 279ff.

29 G. Duby, 'Medieval agriculture' (see ch. 3 n. 6), p. 187.

30 For general information on the history of the rural population in England see R. Lennard, *Rural England 1068–1135*, Oxford, 1959; R. H. Hilton, *A Medieval Society*, London, 1966; Hilton, *The English Peasantry in the Later Middle Ages*, Oxford, 1975; J. Hatcher and E. Miller, *Medieval England*, 1978 (see Intro. n. 23); A. J. Raftis, *Tenure and Mobility*, Toronto, 1964; J. Z. Titow, *English Rural Society 1200–1350*, London, 1969; E. Britton, *The Community of the Ville*, Toronto, 1977; C. Dyer, *Lords and Peasants in a Changing Society*, Cambridge, 1980; Z. Razi, *Life, Marriage and Death in a Medieval Parish*, Cambridge, 1980.

31 E. A. Kosminsky, *Studies in the Agrarian History of England in the Thirteenth Century*, Oxford, 1956, pp. 216, 223; E. Miller, in Kellenbenz, *Handbuch*, vol. 2, p. 238.

32 M. M. Postan, 'England', in Postan (ed.), *Cambridge Economic History*, 2nd edn, Cambridge, 1966, vol. 1, p. 619.

33 Cf. A.-M. Dubler and J. J. Siegrist, *Wohlen, Geschichte von Recht, Wirtschaft und Bevölkerung einer frühindustrialisierten Gemeinde im Aargau*, Aarven, 1975, p. 393.
34 On the upper layers of the peasantry see G. Franz (ed.), *Bauernschaft und Bauernstand*, 1975, esp. the studies by Hauser and Rapp on wealthy peasants in Alsace and Switzerland during the later Middle Ages.
35 K. S. Bader, 'Dorfpatriziate', in *ZGO* 101 (1953), pp. 269–74; K. S. Bader, *Rechtsgeschichte des Dorfes*, vol. 2, Vienna, 1962, pp. 282ff.
36 K. Speckenbach (ed.), *Wernher der Gartenaere: Helmbrecht*, 1974; G. Schindele, 'Helmbrecht. Bäuerlicher Aufstieg und landesherrliche Gewalt', in D. Richter (ed.), *Literatur im Feudalismus*, 1975, pp. 131–211.
37 Cf. L. Genicot, *Le XIIIᵉ siècle européen*, Paris, 1968, p. 87.
38 On the lower layers of the peasantry see Grees, *Ländliche Unterschichten* (n. 3 above); Helleiner, 'Mindervolk' (n. 3 above); Blaschke, *Bevölkerungsgeschichte* (n. 3 above), pp. 182ff.
39 Grees, *Unterschichten*, pp. 24ff.
40 Cf. Ott, 'Studien' (n. 19 above), pp. 11ff; Dubler and Siegrist, *Wohlen* (n. 33 above), p. 393.
41 Genicot, 'Sur le nombre des pauvres' (n. 3 above), pp. 273ff.
42 Cf. B. H. Slicher van Bath, 'Landwirtschaftliche Produktivität' (see ch. 8 n. 24), p. 553; R. H. Hilton, 'Reasons for inequality among medieval peasants', *Journal of Peasant Studies*, 5 (1978), p. 279.

CHAPTER 12 MANORIAL DEPENDENCE

1 Max Weber, *General Economic History*, tr. F. H. Knight, London, 1927, p. 65.
2 For general information on the manorial regime in the Middle Ages see ch. 1 n. 18, and C.-E. Perrin, 'Le servage' (see ch. 11 n. 18); A. Dopsch, 'Die Grundherrschaft im Mittelalter', in G. Franz, *Deutsches Bauerntum*, Darmstadt, 1976, pp. 281–97; M. Bloch, *Seigneurie française et manoir anglais*, 2nd edn, 1967.
3 Cf. F. Lütge, *Deutsche Sozial- und Wirtschaftsgeschichte*, 3rd edn, 1966, p. 55.
4 O. Brunner, *Land und Herrschaft*, Vienna, 1965, p. 263.
5 Quoted by Brunner, ibid., p. 263.
6 K. Borchardt, *Grundriss der deutschen Wirtschaftsgeschichte*, 1978, p. 16.
7 See ch. 1, esp. pp. 16ff.
8 Cf. A. Verhulst, 'La genèse du régime domaniale' (see ch. 1 n. 22); A. Verhulst, 'La diversité du régime domanial entre Loire et Rhin à l'époque carolingienne', in W. Janssen and D. Lohrmann (eds), *Villa-curtis-grangia. Landwirtschaft zwischen Loire und Rhein von der Römerzeit zum Hochmittelalter*, Munich, 1983, pp. 133–48; L. Kuchenbuch, *Bäuerliche Gesellschaft*, Wiesbaden, 1978; F. Lütge, *Geschichte der deutschen Agrarverfassung*, pp. 51ff; R. Kötzschke, *Allgemeine Wirtschaftsgeschichte des Mittelalters*, 1924, pp. 227ff.
9 For general information on labour service see O. Siebeck, *Der Frondienst als Arbeitssystem*, 1904.
10 Cf. W. Rösener, 'Abgaben', in *Lexikon des Mittelalters*, vol. 1, 1980, cols 32ff.
11 Cf. W. Müller, *Die Abgaben des Todes wegen in der Abtei St. Gallen*, 1961.
12 Cf. ch. 10.
13 (Translator's note: One of the first descriptions of the *Villikationen*, or *Fronhöfe*, i.e. the fully developed manorial system, was supplied by Max Weber, *General Economic History* (n. 1 above), pp. 73, 75.) For the source

itself see G. Franz (ed.), *Quellen zur Geschichte des deutschen Bauernstandes im Mittelalter*, Darmstadt, 1974, pp. 110–14. Discussions of this source have been provided by R. Kötschke, *Studien . . . Werden*, Leipzig, 1901, pp. 8ff; E. Wisplinghoff, 'Bäuerliches Leben am Niederrhein im Rahmen der benediktinischen Grundherrschaft', in Janssen and Lohrmann, *Villa-curtisgrangia* (n. 8 above), pp. 149ff.

14 Cf. Kötzschke, *Werden*, pp. 52ff.

15 For more information on the dissolution of the great estates and the old type of the manor see Lütge, *Agrarverfassung*, pp. 83ff; W. Wittich, *Die Grundherrschaft in Nordwestdeutschland*, Leipzig, 1896, pp. 301ff; A. Dopsch, *Herrschaft und Bauer in der deutschen Kaiserzeit*, Jena, 1939, pp. 129ff. (Dopsch underestimates the extent of this structural change in the high Middle Ages.) See also *III*. ch. 2, pp. 27ff.

16 Cf. C.-E. Perrin, *Recherches sur la seigneurie rurale en Lorraine*, Paris, 1935, pp. 626ff.

17 Kötzschke, *Werden*, pp. 25ff.

18 P. Dollinger, *L'évolution des classes rurales en Bavière depuis la fin de l'époque carolingienne jusqu'au milieu du XIIIe siècle*, Paris, 1949.

19 On the rise of the unfree knights and administrators known as *ministeriales* (*Ministeriale*) see K. Bosl, *Die Reichsministerialität der Salier und Staufer*, 2 vols, 1950–1, *passim*.

20 Cf. J. A. van Houtte in H. Kellenbenz (ed.), *Handbuch der europäischen Wirtschafts- und Sozialgeschichte*, vol. 2, Stuttgart, 1980, p. 112; H. Mottek, *Wirtschaftsgeschichte Deutschlands*, 5th edn, 1976, p. 117; R. H. Hilton, *The Decline of Serfdom in Medieval England*, 2nd edn, London, 1983.

21 Cf. ch. 3.

22 For more information on the manorial system in its late medieval form see H. Patze (ed.), *Die Grundherrschaft im späten Mittelalter*, 2 vols, Sigmaringen, 1983; W. Rösener, 'Die spätmittelalterliche Grundherrschaft' (see ch. 8 n. 49), pp. 17ff; Lütge, *Agrarverfassung*, pp. 159ff.

23 See ch. 15.

24 Mottek, *Wirtschaftsgeschichte* (n. 20 above), vol. 1, pp. 289ff.

25 Cf. Blickle, 'Agrarkrise und Leibeigenschaft im spätmittelalterlichen deutschen Südwesten', in H. Kellenbenz (ed.), *Agrarisches Nebengewerbe und Formen der Reagrarisierung im Spätmittelalter und 19./20. Jahrhunderte*, Stuttgart, 1975, pp. 39ff.

26 I. Imberciadori, 'Italien', in Kellenbenz (ed.), *Handbuch*, vol. 2, p. 443; Lütge, *Agrarverfassung*, p. 191.

CHAPTER 13 PEASANT FREEDOM AND
INDEPENDENT PEASANT COMMUNITIES

1 For general information on peasant freedom in the Middle Ages see W. Rösener, 'Bauernfreiheit', in *Lexikon des Mittelalters*, vol. 1, 1980, cols 1605ff.

2 Cf. O. Brunner, 'Die Freiheitsrechte in der altständischen Gesellschaft', in Brunner, *Neue Wege der Verfassungs- und Sozialgeschichte*, Göttingen, 1968, p. 187ff; G. Dilcher, 'Freiheit', in *HRG*, vol. 1, 1971, cols 1227ff.

3 On the problem of defining the medieval conception of freedom see H. Grundmann, 'Freiheit als religiöses, politisches und persönliches Postulat im Mittelalter', *HZ 183 (1956), pp. 23ff; R. von Keller, Freiheitsgarantien für*

Person und Eigentum im Mittelalter, 1933; H. Fehr, 'Die Lehre vom mittelalterlichen Freiheitsbegriff', *MIÖG* 47 (1933), pp. 290ff.

4 This view was for example promoted by H. Rennefarth, *Die Freiheit der Landleute im Berner Oberland*, 1939; F. Wernli, *Die mittelalterliche Bauernfreiheit*, 1959.

5 This view has above all been set forth by T. Mayer, 'Bemerkungen' (see ch. 2 n. 13), pp. 46ff; T. Mayer, 'Die Entstehung des "modernen" Staates im Mittelalter und die freien Bauern', *ZRG GA* 57 (1937), pp. 210ff; K. Weller, 'Die freien Bauern in Schwaben', *ZRG GA* 54 (1934), pp. 178ff; K. Bader, 'Bauernrecht' (see ch. 11 n. 15), pp. 49ff.

6 See T. Mayer, 'Königtum und Gemeinfreiheit im frühen Mittelalter', *DA* 6 (1943), pp. 329–62, T. Mayer, 'Die Königsfreien und der Staat des frühen Mittelalters', in *Das Problem der Freiheit*, Sigmaringen, 1955, pp. 7ff; H. Dannenbauer, 'Die Freien im karolingischen Heer', in *Festschrift T. Mayer*, vol. 1, 1954, pp. 49–64.

7 Mayer, 'Die Königsfreien', p. 19.

8 See H. Kämpf, *Herrschaft und Staat im Mittelalter*, Darmstadt, 1956, esp. the essays by O. Brunner, H. Dannenbauer, W. Schlesinger and T. Mayer.

9 Criticism of the argument concerning the royal freemen in Germany was in particular raised by F. Lütge, 'Das Problem der Freiheit in der frühen deutschen Agrarverfassung' (1963), in Franz (ed.), *Deutsches Bauerntum*, Darmstadt, 1976, pp. 23–74; E. Müller-Mertens, *Karl der Grosse, Ludwig der Fromme und die Freien*, Berlin, 1963; H. Krause, 'Die liberi der lex Baiuvariorum', in *Festschrift M. Spindler*, 1969, pp. 41–73.

10 H. K. Schulze, 'Rodungsfreiheit und Königsfreiheit. Zu Genesis und Kritik neuerer verfassungsgeschichtlicher Theorien', *HZ* 219 (1974), p. 549.

11 The following works focus particularly on the privileged peasants in the high Middle Ages: Weller, 'Die freien Bauern' (n. 5 above); Mayer, 'Bemerkungen' (n. 5 above); Mayer, 'Entstehung' (n. 5 above); K. S. Bader, *Das Freiamt im Breisgau und die freien Bauern am Oberrhein*, 1936; K. S. Bader, 'Bauernrecht' (see ch. 11 n. 15); Rennefarth, *Freiheit* (n. 4 above); Wernli, *Bauernfreiheit* (n. 4 above); B. Meyer, 'Freiheit und Unfreiheit in der alten Eidgenossenschaft', in *Das Problem der Freiheit*, VF 2, 1955, pp. 123ff; H. H. Hofmann, 'Freibauern, Freidörfer, Schutz und Schirm im Fürstentum Ansbach', *ZBLG* 23 (1960), pp. 195ff; B. H. Slicher van Bath, 'Boerenvrijheid', in *Economisch-historische herdruken*, Economisch-historisch Archief, 1964, pp. 272ff; H. Schmidt, 'Studien zur Geschichte der friesischen Freiheit im Mittelalter', *Jb. der Gesellschaft für bildende Kunst*, (Emden), 43, (1963); J. Asch, 'Grundherrschaft und Freiheit' (see ch. 3 n. 12), pp. 107ff.

12 See ch. 3.

13 Cf. F. Petri, 'Marschenkolonisation', (see ch. 3 n. 9), pp. 728ff.

14 F. Molitor, 'Verbreitung und Bedeutung des Hägerrechts', in Mayer (ed.), *Adel und Bauern im deutschen Staat des Mittelalters*, Leipzig, 1943, pp. 331–45.

15 Some of the best documents on settlement privileges were compiled by H. Helbig and L. Weinreich (eds), *Urkunden und erzählende Quellen zur deutschen Ostsiedlung im Mittelalter*, vol. 1, 2nd edn, 1968.

16 See Schulze, 'Rodungsfreiheit' (n. 10 above), pp. 529ff.

17 A collection of relevant essays on this particular aspect was published by W. Schlesinger (ed.), *Die deutsche Ostsiedlung*, Sigmaringen, 1975.

18 See A. E. Hofmeister, *Besiedlung und Verfassung der Stader Elbmarschen im Mittelalter*, vol. 2, 1981, pp. 93ff.

19 On the privileges granted to townspeople in the high Middle Ages see H. Strahm, 'Stadtluft macht frei', in *Das Problem der Freiheit*, VF 2, 1955, pp. 103ff.

20 See Bader, 'Bauernrecht' (n. 11 above), pp. 70ff; H. Mitteis, 'Über den Rechtsgrund des Satzes "Stadtluft macht frei"' (1952), in C. Haase (ed.), *Die Stadt des Mittelalters*, vol. 2, 1976, pp. 182–202; K. A. Kroeschell, 'Rodungssiedlung und Stadtgründung' (see ch. 2 n. 13), pp. 53ff.

21 For general information on free peasants in northern Germany see E. Molitor, 'Über Freibauern in Norddeutschland', in Mayer (ed.), *Adel und Bauern* (n. 14 above), pp. 312–30; T. Mayer, *Die Pfleghaften des Sachsenspiegels*, 1941.

22 See Petri, 'Marschenkolonisation' (n. 13 above), pp. 695ff.

23 Hofmeister, *Besiedlung* (n. 18 above), *passim*.

24 (Translator's note: The *Stedinger* were the peasant inhabitants of marshlands south of Bremen and also the descendants of Dutch and Frisian pioneer settlers. In the twelfth century they defended their independence against the territorial claims of the archbishops of Bremen and the counts of Oldenburg, as a result of which the church called for a crusade against them and only defeated them after a series of extremely violent battles.) Cf. ch. 14.

25 Free peasant communities in southern Germany have been studied by T. Mayer, K. S. Bader and K. Weller (cf. n. 11 above). For further information see K. Weller, 'Die freien Bauern des Spätmittelalters im heutigen Württemberg', *ZWLG* 1 (1937), pp. 47–67; A. Diehl, 'Die Freien auf der Leutkircher Heide', *ZWLG* 4 (1940), pp. 257–341; K. R. Kollnig, 'Freiheit und freie Bauern in elsässischen Weistümern', in *Elsass–Lothringisches Jahrbuch*, 19 (1941), pp. 108–28; H. Büttner, 'Anfänge des Walserrechtes im Wallis', in *Das Problem der Freiheit*, VF 2, 1955, pp. 89–102.

26 See Mayer, 'Entstehung des "modernen" Staates' (n. 5 above), pp. 210–88.

27 O. Stolz, 'Bauer und Landesfürst in Tirol und Vorarlberg', in Mayer (ed.), *Adel und Bauern* (n. 14 above), pp. 170–212; O. Stolz, *Rechtsgeschichte des Bauernstandes und der Landwirtschaft in Tirol und Vorarlberg*, Bozen, 1949, pp. 12ff.

28 For the status of the peasantry in the colonization areas in the east of the Empire see W. Schlesinger (ed.), *Ostsiedlung* (n. 17 above); R. Kötzschke, 'Staat und Bauerntum im thüringisch-obersächsischen Raum', in Mayer (ed.), *Adel und Bauern*, pp. 267–311; F. Lütge, *Geschichte der deutschen Agrarverfassung*, Stuttgart, 1967, pp. 111ff.

29 Kötzschke, 'Staat' (n. 28 above), pp. 283ff; Helbig and Weinreich, *Urkunden* (n. 15 above), pp. 64ff, nos 9–15.

30 See Petri, 'Marschenkolonisation', pp. 705ff; A. Verhulst, 'Die Binnenkolonisation und die Anfänge der Landgemeinde in Seeflandern', in T. Mayer (ed.), *Die Anfänge der Landgemeine und ihr Wesen*, Konstanz, 1964, vol. 1, pp. 447ff.

31 C. Higounet, 'Zur Siedlungsgeschichte Südwestfrankreichs vom 11. bis zum 14. Jahrhundert', in Schlesinger (ed.), *Ostsiedlung* (n. 17 above), pp. 657–94, esp. pp. 674 and 688.

32 See ch. 9.

33 See W. Rösener, 'Bauernstaaten', in *Lexikon des Mittelalters*, vol. 1, 1980, cols 1622ff.

34 See Bader, 'Bauernrecht' (n. 11 above), pp. 81ff; Bader, 'Staat und Bauerntum im deutschen Mittelalter', in Mayer (ed.), *Adel und Bauern*, pp. 109ff; P. Blickle, *Landschaften im Alten Reich*, Munich, 1973, pp. 35ff.

35 Cf. T. Mayer, 'Über die Freiheit der Bauern in Tirol und in der Schweizer Eidgenossenschaft' (1959), in Franz (ed.), *Bauerntum* (n. 9 above), pp. 185ff.

36 Cf. Aubin, 'Landgemeinden' (see ch. 10 n. 15), pp. 191ff; H. Schmidt, 'Adel

und Bauern im friesischen Mittelalter', *Niedersächsisches Jahrbuch für Landesgeschichte*, 45 (1973), pp. 45ff; B. U. Hucker, 'Adel und Bauern zwischen unterer Weser und Elbe im Mittelalter', in *Nierdersächsisches Jahrbuch für Landesgeschichte*, 45 (1973), pp. 97ff.

37 On the development of the Swiss Confederation see T. Mayer, 'Freiheit' (n. 35 above), pp. 181ff; B. Meyer, *Die Bildung der Eidgenossenschaft im 14. Jahrhundert*, 1972; K. Haff, 'Der freie Bergbauer als Staatsgründer', *ZRG GA* 67 (1950), pp. 394ff; K. S. Bader, *Der deutsche Südwesten und seine territorialstaatliche Entwicklung*, 1950, pp. 177ff; H. C. Peyer, in *Handbuch der Schweizer Geschichte*, vol. 1, 1972, p. 163ff.

38 For general information on the history of Dithmarschen see H. Stoob, *Die dithmarsischen Geschlechterverbände*, 1951; H. Stoob, 'Landausbau und Gemeindebildung an der Nordseeküste im Mittelalter', in Mayer (ed.), *Landgemeinde* (n. 30 above), vol. 1, pp. 365–422; R. Chalybaeus, *Geschichte Dithmarschens bis zur Eroberung des Landes im Jahre 1559*, 1888 (repr. 1973); G. Franz, *Geschichte des deutschen Bauernstandes*, Stuttgart, 1976, pp. 92ff.

39 W. Lammers, *Die Schlacht bei Hemmingstedt*, 1954.

CHAPTER 14 PEASANT REVOLTS AND RESISTANCE, 1000–1400

1 M. Bloch, *Les caractères originaux de l'histoire rurale française*, Paris, 1960 (*French Rural History: An Essay on its Basic Characteristics*, London, 1966).

2 Cf. P. Blickle, 'Bäuerliche Erhebungen im spätmittelalterlichen deutschen Reich', *ZAA* 27 (1979), p. 208.

3 O. Brunner, *Land und Herrschaft. Grundfragen der territorialen Verfassungsgeschichte Österreichs im Mittelalter*, Vienna, 1965, p. 346.

4 F. L. A. Lassberg (ed.), *Schwabenspiegel*, 1840 (repr. 1961), p. 133.

5 Cf. Brunner, *Land und Herrschaft*, pp. 265ff.

6 For general information on peasant resistance see W. Schulze, *Bäuerlicher Widerstand und Empörung? Studien zum bäuerlichen Widerstand im Alten Reich*, Munich, 1980 (this study contains an excellent bibliography); P. Blickle (ed.), *Aufruhr und feudale Herrschaft in der frühen Neuzeit*, Stuttgart, 1980; G. Heitz and G. Vogler, 'Bauernbewegungen in Europa vom 16. bis zum 18. Jahrhundert'. *ZfG* 28 (1980), pp. 442–54; W. Schulze (ed.), *Aufstände, Revolten, Prozesse. Beiträge zu bäuerlichen Widerstandsbewegungen im frühneuzeitlichen Europa*, 1983. The following studies concentrate on peasant resistance in the Middle Ages: S. Epperlein, *Bauernbedrückung und Bauernwiderstand im hohen Mittelalter*, Berlin, 1960; M. Mollat and P. Wolff, *Ongles bleus, Jacques et Ciompi. Les révolutions populaires en Europe aux XIVᵉ–XVᵉ siècles*, Paris, 1970; G. Fourquin, *Les soulèvements populaires à la fin du Moyen Age*, Paris, 1982; R. H. Hilton, *Bond Men Made Free*, London, 1973; W. Eggert, 'Rebelliones servorum. Bewaffnete Klassenkämpfe im Früh- und frühen Hochmittelalter und ihre Darstellung in zeitgenössischen erzählenden Quellen', *ZfG* 23 (1975), pp. 1147–64; A. N. Čistozvonow, 'Die europäischen Bauern im Kampf um Land und Freiheit' [fourteenth and fifteenth centuries], in G. Brendler and A. Laube (eds), *Der deutsche Bauernkrieg 1524/5*, 1977, pp. 37–56; B. Töpfer, 'Volksbewegungen und gesellschaftlicher Fortschritt im 14. und 15. Jahrhundert in West- und Mitteleuropa', *ZfG* 26 (1978), pp. 713–29; Blickle, 'Erhebungen' (n. 2 above); E. V. Gutnowa, 'Hauptetappen' (see Bibliography); S. Hoyer and E. Münch, 'Wandlungen feudaler Herrschafts- und Ausbeutungsverhältnisse auf dem Lande', *ZfG* 30 (1982), pp. 920–31;

E. Münch, 'Agrarverfassung, bäuerliche Klassenstruktur und bäuerlicher Widerstand im entwickelten Feudalismus', *ZfG* 31 (1983), pp. 908–16.
7 B. F. Porshnew, 'Formen und Wege des bäuerlichen Kampfes gegen die feudale Ausbeutung', *Sowjetwissenschaft, Gesellschaftswiss. Abteilung* (1952), pp. 440–59.
8 E.g. J. A. Kosminsky, 'Das Problem des Klassenkampfes in der Epoche des Feudalismus', *Sowjetwissenschaft. Gesellschaftswiss. Abteilung* (1952), pp. 460–82.
9 See J. Petran, 'Typologie der Bauernbewegungen in Mitteleuropa unter dem Aspekt des Übergangs vom Feudalismus zum Kapitalismus', in G. Heitz et al. (eds), *Der Bauer im Klassenkampf*, 1975, pp. 449ff; Schulze, *Widerstand* (n. 6 above), pp. 89ff.
10 See P. Bierbrauer, 'Bäuerliche Revolten im Alten Reich', in Blickle (ed.), *Aufruhr*, pp. 16ff.
11 Cf. ch. 12.
12 See n. 6 above.
13 G. Franz, *Der deutsche Bauernkrieg*, Stuttgart, 1976, pp. 1ff.
14 Blickle, 'Erhebungen', p. 208.
15 On peasant resistance in the early Middle Ages see S. Epperlein, 'Herrschaft und Volk im karolingischen Imperium', *Forschungen zur mittelalterlich Geschichte*, 14 (1969); Eggert, 'Rebelliones' (n. 6 above); G. Franz, *Geschichte des deutschen Bauernstandes*, Stuttgart, 1976, pp. 21ff; A. I. Njeussychin, *Die Entstehung der abhängigen Bauernschaft als Klasse*, Berlin, 1961, *passim*.
16 Gregor von Tours, *Zehn Bücher Geschichten*, vol. 1, ed. R. Buchner, 4th edn, 1955, pp. 334ff.
17 For more information on the Stellinga movement see H. J. Schulze, *Der Aufstand der Stellinga in Sachsen und sein Einfluss auf den Vertrag von Verdun* (Doctoral Thesis), Berlin, 1955; E. Müller-Mertens, 'Der Stellingaaufstand. Seine Träger und die Frage der politischen Macht', *ZfG* 20 (1972), pp. 818–42.
18 For more information on peasant resistance during the high Middle Ages see Epperlein, *Bauernbedrückung* (n. 6 above); B. H. Slicher van Bath, *The Agrarian History of Western Europe*, London, 1963, pp. 189ff; Hilton, *Bond Men*, pp. 63ff; Münch, 'Agrarverfassung' (n. 6 above), pp. 908ff.
19 *UB* of the bishopric of Hildesheim, vol. 1, 1896, no. 237, pp. 216ff.
20 See A. Dopsch, *Herrschaft und Bauer in der deutschen Kaiserzeit*, Jena, 1939, p. 126.
21 R. Kötzschke (ed.), *Die Urbare der Abtei Werden an der Ruhr*, 1906, pp. 174ff.
22 See ch. 2, pp. 27ff.
23 See H. Strahm, 'Stadtluft macht frei' (ch. 13 n. 19), pp. 103ff.
24 T. J. Lacomblet (ed.), *UB für die Geschichte des Niederrheins*, vol. 1, 1840, no. 344, pp. 232ff.
25 H. Wopfner (ed.), *Urkunden zur deutschen Agrargeschichte*, 1928, no. 95, pp. 145ff.
26 *MGH*, Const. 2, 73, pp. 89ff; ibid., Const. 2, 171, pp. 211ff; G. Franz (ed.), *Quellen zur Geschichte des deutschen Bauernstandes im Mittelalter*, Darmstadt, 1974, no. 112, p. 298ff (this compilation of historical documents contains the imperial decree mentioned which prohibited the free towns and cities of the Holy Roman Empire to grant citizenship to bonded peasants).
27 W. Rösener, *Reichsabtei Salem*, 1974, p. 106.
28 W. Rösener, 'Bauernlegen durch klösterliche Grundherren im Hochmittelalter', *ZAA* 27 (1979), p. 77.
29 See ch. 13.

30 See Slicher van Bath, *Agrarian History*, pp. 189ff.
31 For more information on the Stedinger rebellion see H. A. Schumacher, *Die Stedinger*, 1865; C. Woebcken, 'Die Schlacht bei Altenesch am 27. Mai 1234 und ihre Vorgeschichte', *Oldenburger Jahrbuch*, 37 (1933), pp. 5–35; H. Stephan, 'Zur Geschichte der Stedinger', *Oldenburger Jahrbuch*, 46/47 (1942/43), pp. 43–66; L. Deike, *Die Entstehung der Grundherrschaft in den Hollerkolonien an der Niederweser*, 1959; H. Gericke, *Universitas Stedingorum* (Doctoral Thesis), Halle, 1960; R. Köhn, 'Die Verketzerung der Stedinger durch die Bremer Fastensynode', *Bremisches Jahrbuch*, 57 (1979), pp. 15–85; R. Köhn, 'Die Teilnehmer an den Kreuzzügen gegen die Stedinger', *Niedersächsisches Jahrbuch für Landesgeschichte*, 53 (1981), pp. 139–206.
32 Ch. 3, pp. 38ff.
33 'Annales Stadenses', in *MGH* SS 16, p. 361.
34 Cf. the final pages of ch. 13.
35 See G. Franz, 'Ausserdeutsche Bauernkriege im ausgehenden Mittelalter' (1930), in Franz (ed.), *Persönlichkeit und Geschichte*, 1977, pp. 78–96; F. W. N. Hugenholtz, *Die boerenopstanden uit de veertiende eeuw*, Haarlem, 1949; Mollat and Wolff, *Ongles bleus*, (n. 6 above); Čistozvonow, 'Bauern im Kampf' (n. 6 above).
36 For general information on the *jacquerie* of 1358 see Mollat and Wolff, *Ongles bleus*, pp. 116–31; Fourquin, *Soulèvements* (n. 6 above), pp. 176–83; A. Coville, *Les premiers Valois et la guerre de Cent ans*, 1911, pp. 131ff.
37 The English peasant revolt of 1381 is analysed in detail in Hilton, *Bond Men*, pp. 137ff; R. H. Hilton and H. Fagan, 'Soziale Programme im englischen Aufstand von 1381', in P. Blickle (ed.), Revolte und Revolution in Europa, Munich, 1975, pp. 31–46. See also R. H. Hilton, *The English Rising of 1381*, Cambridge; and R. H. Hilton, *Class Conflict and the Crisis of Feudalism. Essays in Medieval Social History*, London, 1985.
38 On the peasant insurrection in Flanders (1323–8) see H. Pirenne, *Geschichte Belgiens*, vol. 2, 1902, pp. 96ff; H. Pirenne, *Le soulèvement de la Flandre maritime de 1323–28*, 1900; Fourquin, *Soulèvements*, pp. 174ff.
39 See ch. 15 and F. Graus, 'Vom "Schwarzen Tod" zur Reformation. Der krisenhafte Charakter des europäischen Spätmittelalters', in Blickle (ed.), *Revolte* (n. 37 above), pp. 10ff.
40 For surveys on peasant revolts in the Empire during the late Middle Ages see Franz, *Bauernkrieg* (n. 13 above), pp. 1ff; P. Blickle, 'Erhebungen' (n. 2 above); A. Laube, 'Die Volksbewegungen in Deutschland von 1470 bis 1517', in Blickle, *Revolte* (n. 37 above), pp. 84–98; K. Arnold, *Niklashausen 1476. Quellen und Untersuchungen zur sozialreligiösen Bewegung des Hans Behem und zur Agrarstruktur eines spätmittelalterlichen Dorfes*, Baden-Baden, 1980.
41 See Bierbrauer, 'Revolten' (n. 10 above), pp. 62ff.
42 Cf. S. Hoyer, 'Die Armlederbewegung – ein Bauernaufstand 1336/1339', *ZfG* 13 (1965), pp. 74ff; K. Arnold, 'Die Armlederbewegung in Franken 1336', *Mainfränkisches Jahrbuch für Geschichte und Kunst*, 26 (1974), pp. 35ff.
43 See F. Seibt, 'Die hussitische Revolution und der deutsche Bauernkrieg', in Blickle (ed.), *Revolte* (n. 37 above), p. 47f; P. Blickle, *Hussitica*, 1964; H. Kaminsky, *A History of the Hussite Revolution*, 1967.
44 (Translator's note: The *Bund ob dem See* was an association of village communities and towns near Lake Constance which from 1405 to 1408 struggled against the nobility of southern Germany. These activities finally led to the independence of the Swiss canton of Appenzell.) B. Bilgeri, *Der Bund ob dem See. Vorarlberg im Appenzeller Krieg*, Stuttgart, 1968.

CHAPTER 15 THE PEASANTS AND THE AGRARIAN CRISIS

1 Special mention must be made of the following studies on deserted settlements: W. Abel, *Die Wüstungen des ausgehenden Mittelalters*, 3rd edn, Stuttgart, 1976; W. Abel (ed.), 'Wüstungen in Deutschland', *ZAA*, special issue 2 (1967) (for an English translation of the important work of Wilhelm Abel see W. Abel, *Agricultural fluctuations in Europe from the Thirteenth to the Twentieth Centuries*, London/New York, 1980); *Villages désertés et histoire économique, XIe–XVIIIe siècle*, Paris, 1965; M. W. Beresford and J. G. Hurst, *Deserted Medieval Villages*, London, 1971; H. Pohlendt, *Die Verbreitung der mittelalterlichen Wüstungen in Deutschland*, 1950; M. Born, *Die Entwicklung der deutschen Agrarlandschaft*, Darmstadt, 1974, pp. 67ff (this survey includes a bibliography of recent studies); H. Jäger, 'Wüstungsforschung in geographischer und historischer Sicht', in H. Jankuhn and R. Wenskus (eds), *Geschichtswissen schaft und Archäologie*, VF 22, 1979, pp. 193–240; G. Mangelsdorf, 'Zum Stand der Wüstungsforschung in der DDR', *Jahrbuch für Wirtschaftsgeschichte*, 2 (1982), pp. 73–101.
2 Abel, *Wüstungen*, p. 11.
3 For a map on the desertion of settlements in Germany see ibid., p. 10 (fig. 40 in this study).
4 Abel, *Wüstungen*, pp. 103ff (with references); W. Abel, *Strukturen*, 1980, p. 7f; H. Kellenbenz, *Deutsche Wirtschaftsgeschichte*, vol. 1, 1977, pp. 144ff; L. Genicot, 'Crisis from the Middle Ages to modern times', in M. M. Postan (ed.), *Cambridge Economic History*, 2nd edn, Cambridge 1966, vol. 1, pp. 660ff; E. Pitz, 'Die Wirtschaftskrise des Spätmittelalters', *VSWG* 52 (1965), pp. 347–67; R. H. Hilton, 'A crisis of feudalism', *Past and Present*, 80 (1978), pp. 3–19; P. Kriedte, 'Spätmittelalterliche Agrarkrise oder Krise des Feudalismus?', *Geschichte und Gesellschaft*, 7 (1981), pp. 42–68.
5 On plagues, see N. Bulst, 'Der Schwarzer Tod. Demographische, wirtschafts- und kulturgeschichtliche Aspekte', *Saeculum*, 30 (1979), pp. 45ff; (this study contains a bibliography of recent studies on this subject). On the demographic situation in the late Middle Ages see J. C. Russell, 'Population in Europe' (see ch. 2 n. 6), pp. 41ff; W. Abel, *Agrarkrisen und Agrarkonjunktur*, Hamburg, 1978, pp. 57ff; Abel, *Agricultural Fluctuations* (n. 1 above); K. Helleiner, 'Europas Bevölkerung und Wirtschaft im späten Mittelalter', *MIÖG* 62 (1954), pp. 254ff; Hatcher, *Plagues, Population and the English Economy 1348–1530*, London, 1977.
6 F. Lütge, 'Das 14./15. Jahrhundert in der Sozial- und Wirtschaftsgeschichte', in Lütge, *Studien zur Sozial- und Wirtschaftsgeschichte*, Stuttgart, 1963, p. 286.
7 See W. Abel, 'Landwirtschaft', in H. Aubin and W. Zorn (eds), *Handbuch der deutschen Wirtschafts- und Sozialgeschichte*, vol. 1, Stuttgart, 1971, p. 305.
8 On the development of agricultural prices in the late Middle Ages see Abel, *Agrarkrisen*, pp. 57ff.
9 Ibid., p. 57.
10 Cf. Abel, 'Landwirtschaft', pp. 315ff; F.-W. Henning, *Landwirtschaft und ländliche Gesellschaft in Deutschland*, vol. 1, Paderborn, 1979, pp. 160ff.
11 See ch. 8.
12 On the position of the lords in the late Middle Ages see Abel, 'Wüstungen', pp. 138ff; W. Rösener, 'Grundherrschaften des Hochadels', in H. Patze (ed.), *Die Grundherrschaft im späten Mittelalter*, Sigmaringen, 1983, vol. 2, pp. 87–

176; T. Zotz, 'Zur Grundherrschaft der Grafen von Leiningen', in Patze (ed.), *Grundherrschaft*, vol. 2, pp. 177–228.

13 H. Rubner, 'Die Landwirtschaft der Münchener Ebene und ihre Notlage im 14. Jahrhundert', *VSGW* 51 (1964), p. 441.

14 Cf. G. Bois, 'Noblesse et crise des revenues seigneuriaux en France aux XIVe et XVe siècles', in P. Contamine (ed.), *La noblesse au moyen âge, 1976, pp. 219– 33; R. Sablonier, Adel im Wandel*, 1979, pp. 224ff; R. Sablonier, 'Zurwirtschafflichen Situation des Adels im Spätmittelalter', in *Adelige Sachkultur des Spätmittelalters* (Veröffentlichungen des Iustituts für mittelalterliche Realienkunde Österreichs 5) 1982, pp. 9ff.

15 See ch. 3.

16 H. P. Sattler, 'Die Ritterschaft der Ortenau in der spätmittelalterlichen Wirtschaftskrise', *Ortenau*, 42 (1962), pp. 220–58, see also ibid., 44 (1964), pp. 22–39, ibid., 45 (1965), pp. 32–42.

17 G. Bois, *Crise du féodalisme*, Paris, 1976 (*The Crisis of Feudalism*, Cambridge, 1984).

18 See Kriedte, 'Agrarkrise', pp. 42ff.

19 Cf. Rösener, 'Raubrittertum', pp. 469ff; H. Patze, 'Grundherrschaft und Fehde', in Patze (ed.), *Grundherrschaft*, vol. 1, 1983, pp. 263ff.

20 J. Vincke, *Bäuerliche Wirtschaft* (see ch. 8 n. 48), p. 23.

21 Ibid.

22 Ibid.

23 Franz, *Quellen zur Geschichte des deutschen Bauernstandes im Mittelalter*, Darmstadt, 1974, pp. 476ff, no. 185.

24 Ibid., pp. 523ff, no. 207.

25 G. Kirchner, 'Probleme der spätmittelalterlichen Klostergrundherrschaft in Bayern: Landflucht und bäuerliches Erbrecht', *ZBLG* 19 (1956), pp. 1ff.

26 G. Aubin, *Zur Geschichte der gutsherrlich–bäuerlichen Verhältnisse in Ostpreussen*, 1910, pp. 86ff.

27 Franz, *Quellen*, p. 448, no. 180.

28 The relationship between the agrarian crisis and the intensification of serfdom in the south-west of Germany was in particular analysed by P. Blickle, 'Agrarkrise' (see ch. 12 n. 25), pp. 39ff; C. Ulbrich, *Leibherrschaft am Oberrhein im Spätmittelalter*, Göttingen, 1979, pp. 264ff.

29 See Blickle, 'Agrarkrise', pp. 44ff.

30 Rösener, 'Grundherrschaften des Hochadels' (n. 12 above), p. 153.

31 Ibid., p. 150.

32 Kirchner, 'Probleme', pp. 1ff; I. Bog, 'Geistliche Herrschaft und Bauer in Bayern und die spätmittelalterliche Agrarkrise', *VSWG* 45 (1958), pp. 62–75.

33 H. H. Hofmann, 'Bauer und Herrschaft in Franken', *ZAA* 14 (1966), pp. 1–29, M. Tischler, *Die Leibeigenschaft im Hochstift Würzburg vom 13. bis zum beginnenden 19. Jahrhundert*, 1963, pp. 88ff.

34 Cf. J. Kulischer, *Allgemeine Wirtschaftsgeschichte des Mittelalters und der Neuzeit*, vol. 1, 2nd edn, 1958, pp. 147ff; H. Pirenne, *Sozial- und Wirtschaftsgeschichte Europas im Mittelalter*, 3rd edn, Munich, 1974, pp. 186ff.

35 On the position of the English peasantry in the late Middle Ages see Kulischer, *Wirtschaftsgeschichte*, vol. 1, pp. 144ff; R. H. Hilton, *The Decline of Serfdom*, London, 1983; R. H. Hilton, *The English Peasantry in the Later Middle Ages*, Oxford, 1975, *passim*.

36 See F. Lütge, *Geschichte der deutschen Agrarverfassung*, Stuttgart, 1967, pp. 119ff; Henning, *Landwirtschaft*, vol. 1, pp. 165ff.

37 H. Helbig, *Gesellschaft und Wirtschaft der Mark Brandenburg im Mittelalter*, Berlin, 1973, pp. 77ff.
38 K. Lamprecht, *Deutsche Geschichte*, vol. 5.1, 3rd edn, 1904, pp. 100ff.
39 G. von Below, *Probleme der Wirtschaftsgeschichte*, 2nd edn, 1926, pp. 73ff.
40 See W. Rösener, 'Zur sozialökonomischen Lage der bäuerlichen Bevölkerung im Spätmittelalter', in *Bäuerliche Sachkultur des Spätmittelalters*, Veröffentlichungen des Instituts für mittelalterliche Realienkunde Österreichs 7, 1984, pp. 9ff.
41 Cf. Abel, 'Landwirtschaft', p. 331.
42 On the social standing of the peasantry in late medieval society see G. Franz, *Geschichte des deutschen Bauernstandes*, Stuttgart, 1976, pp. 125ff; W. Schwer, *Stand und Ständeordnung im Weltbild des Mittelalters*, Paderborn, 1952, pp. 27ff.
43 Abel, 'Landwirtschaft', p. 331.
44 On the origin of the territorial state in the late Middle Ages see H. Patze (ed.), *Der deutsche Territorialstaat im 14. Jahrhundert*, 2nd edn, 1982; K. S. Bader, 'Territorialbildung und Landeshoheit', *Blätter für deutsche Landesgeschichte*, 90 (1953), pp. 109–31.
45 Cf. ch. 14.
46 F. Graus, 'Vom "Schwarzen Tod" zur Reformation' (see ch. 14 n. 39), p. 14. See also F. Graus, *Das Spätmittelalter als Krisenzeit*, Prague 1969; H. Heimpel, 'Das Wesen des deutschen Spätmittelalters', *Archiv für Kulturgeschichte*, 35 (1953), pp. 29ff; E. Meuthen, *Das 15. Jahrhundert*, Grundriss der Geschichte 9, 1980, pp. 118ff.
47 See Abel, *Agrarkrisen*, pp. 104ff.

SELECT BIBLIOGRAPHY

The following selection of source and reference material is far from being complete, as this study is not intended to be a work of reference. In addition to the works cited in the text and notes, particularly recent studies have been included, as well as works in the English language. For abbreviations used, see beginning of Notes section, p. 276

Abel, W., 'Landwirtschaft', in H. Aubin and W. Zorn (eds), *Handbuch der deutschen Wirtschafts- und Sozialgeschichte*, vol. 1, Stuttgart, 1971, pp. 83–108, 169–201, 300–33.
—— *Die Wüstungen des ausgehenden Mittelalters*, QFA 32, 3rd edn, Stuttgart, 1976.
—— *Geschichte der deutschen Landwirtschaft vom frühen Mittelalter bis zum 19. Jahrhundert*, DA 2, 3rd edn, Stuttgart, 1978.
—— *Agrarkrisen und Agrarkonjunktur*, 3rd edn, Hamburg, 1978.
—— *Strukturen und Krisen der spätmittelalterlichen Wirtschaft*, QFA 32, Stuttgart, 1980.
—— *Agricultural Fluctuations in Europe from the Thirteenth to the Twentieth Centuries*, London/New York, 1980.
Achilles, W., 'Überlegungen zum Einkommen der Bauern im späten Mittelalter', ZAA 31 (1983), pp. 5–26.
Arnold, B., *German Knighthood, 1050–1300*, Oxford, 1985.
Arnold, K., *Niklashausen 1476. Quellen und Untersuchungen zur sozialreligiösen Bewegung des Hans Behem und zur Agrarstruktur eines spätmittelalterlichen Dorfes*, Baden-Baden, 1980.
Bader, K. S., 'Entstehung und Bedeutung der oberdeutschen Dorfgemeinde', ZWLG 1 (1937), pp. 265–95.
—— 'Bauernrecht und Bauernfreiheit im späteren Mittelalter', HJb 61 (1941), pp. 51–87.
—— *Studien zur Rechtsgeschichte des mittelalterlichen Dorfes*,
  1: *Das mittelalterliche Dorf als Friedens- und Rechtsbereich*, Weimar, 1957;
  2 *Dorfgenossenschaft und Dorfgemeinde*, Vienna, 1962;
  3 *Rechtsformen und Schichten der Liegenschaftsnutzung im mittelalterlichen Dorf*, Vienna, 1973.
Bartels, A., *Der Bauer in der deutschen Vergangenheit*, 2nd edn, Leipzig, 1924.

—— *Bäuerliche Sachkultur des Spätmittelalters*, Veröffentlichungen des Instituts für mittelalterliche Realienkunde Österreichs 7, Vienna, 1984.

Baumgarten, K., *Das deutsche Bauernhaus*, Berlin, 1980.

Beck, H. et al. (eds), *Untersuchungen zur eisenzeitlichen und frühmittelalterlichen Flur in Mitteleuropa und ihrer Nutzung*, Abhandlungen der Akademie der Wissenschaften in Göttingen, Phil.-Hist. Kl. 3, 115, 2 vols, Göttingen, 1979/80.

Becker-Dillingen, J., *Quellen und Urkunden zur Geschichte des deutschen Bauern*, Berlin, 1935.

Bedal, K., *Historische Hausforschung. Eine Einführung in Arbeitsweise, Begriff und Literatur*, Beiträge zur Volkskultur in Nordwestdeutschland 8, Münster, 1978.

Bentzien, U., *Bauernarbeit im Feudalismus. Landwirtschaftliche Arbeitsgeräte und -verfahren in Deutschland von der Mitte des ersten Jahrtausends u.Z. bis um 1800*, Veröffentlichungen zur Volkskunde und Kulturgeschichte 67, Berlin, 1980.

Beresford, M. W., and Hurst, J. G., *Deserted Medieval Villages*, London, 1971.

Berman, C. H., *Medieval Agriculture, the Southern French Countryside, and the Early Cistercians*, Philadelphia, 1986.

Berthold, R., 'Die Agrarkrisen im Feudalismus', *Jb. für Wirtschaftsgeschichte*, 1 (1979), pp. 179–98.

Bilgeri, B., *Der Bund ob dem See. Vorarlberg im Appenzeller Krieg*, Stuttgart, 1968.

Blaschke, K., *Bevölkerungsgeschichte von Sachsen bis zur Industriellen Revolution*, Weimar, 1967.

Blickle, P., *Landschaften im Alten Reich*, Munich, 1973.

—— (ed.), *Revolte und Revolution in Europa*, *HZ* Beiheft 4, Munich, 1975.

—— 'Agrarkrise und Leibeigenschaft im spätmittelalterlichen deutschen Südwesten', in H. Kellenbenz (ed.), *Agrarisches Nebengewerbe und Formen der Reagrarisierung im Spätmittelalter und 19./20. Jahrhunderte*, Stuttgart, 1975, pp. 39–55.

—— 'Bäuerliche Erhebungen im spätmittelalterlichen deutschen Reich', *ZAA* 27 (1979), pp. 208–31.

—— (ed.), *Aufruhr und Empörung? Studien zum bäuerlichen Widerstand im Alten Reich*, Munich, 1980.

—— *Die Revolutionen von 1525*, 2nd edn, Munich, 1981. In English: *The Revolution of 1525: The German Peasants' War from a New Perspective*, tr. T. A. Brady and H. C. E. Midelfort, Baltimore, 1981.

Bloch, M., *Les caractères originaux de l'histoire rurale française*, 3rd edn, Paris, 1960. In English: *French Rural History: an Essay on its Basic Characteristics*, tr. J. Sondheimer, London, 1966.

—— *Feudal Society*, tr. L. A. Manyon, London 1961/2, 2 vols.

Blum, J. (ed.), *Our Forgotten Past: Seven Centuries of Life on the Land*, London, 1982.

Bökönyi, S., *History of Domestic Mammals in Central and Eastern Europe*, Budapest, 1974.

Boelcke, W. A., 'Die frühmittelalterlichen Wurzeln der südwestdeutschen Gewannflur', *ZAA* 12 (1964), pp. 131–63.

—— 'Wandlungen der dörflichen Sozialstruktur während Mittelalter und Neuzeit', in *Festschrift G. Franz*, Frankfurt a.M., 1967, pp. 80–103.

Bog, I., 'Geistliche Herrschaft und Bauer in Bayern und die spätmittelalterliche Agrarkrise', *VSWG* 45 (1958), pp. 62–75.

Bois, G., *Crise du féodalisme. Economie rurale et démographique en Normandie du debut du 14ᵉ siècle au milieu du 16ᵉ siècle*, Paris, 1976. In English: *The Crisis of Feudalism*.

Born, M., *Die Entwicklung der deutschen Agrarlandschaft*, Darmstadt, 1974.

Borst, A., *Lebensformen im Mittelalter*, Frankfurt a.M., 1973.

Bosl, K., *Frühformen der Gesellschaft im mittelaltlichen Europa*, Munich, 1964.

Brenner, R., 'Agrarian class structure and economic development in pre-industrial Europe', *Past and Present*, 70 (1976), pp. 30–75.

Britton, E., *The Community of the Vill*, Toronto, 1977.

Brunner, O., *Land und Herrschaft. Grundfragen der territorialen Verfassungsgeschichte Österreichs im Mittelalter*, 5th edn, Vienna, 1965.

—— Neue Wege der Verfassungs- und Sozialgeschichte, 2nd edn, Göttingen, 1968.

Bulst, N., 'Der Schwarzer Tod. Demographische, wirtschafts- und kulturgeschichtliche Aspekte der Pestkatastrophe von 1347–1352', *Saeculum*, 30 (1979), pp. 45–67.

Chapelot, J., and Fossier, R., *Le village et la maison au Moyen Age*, Paris, 1980. In English: *The Village and House in the Middle Ages*, Berkeley, Calif., 1985.

Chayanov, A. V., *The Theory of Peasant Economy*, ed. D. Thorner et al., Homewood, Ill., 1966.

Coulton, G. G., *The Medieval Village*, Cambridge, 1925.

Dollinger, P., *L'évolution des classes rurales en Bavière depuis la fin de l'époque carolingienne jusqu'au milieu du XIIIe siècle*, Paris, 1949.

Donat, P., *Haus, Hof und Dorf in Mitteleuropa vom 7. bis 12. Jahrhundert*, Schriften zur Ur- und Frühgeschichte 33, Berlin, 1980.

Dopsch, A., *Die ältere Wirtschafts- und Sozialgeschichte der Bauern in den Alpenländern Österreichs*, Oslo, 1930.

—— *Herrschaft und Bauer in der deutschen Kaiserzeit. Untersuchungen zur Agrar- und Sozialgeschichte des hohen Mittelalters mit besonderer Berücksichtigung des südostdeutschen Raumes*, Jena, 1939.

Dubled, H., 'Servitude et liberté en Alsace au moyen âge', *VSWG* 50 (1963), pp. 164–203, 289–328.

Duby, G., *L'économie rurale et la vie des campagnes dans l'Occident médiévale*, 2 vols, Paris, 1962. In English: *Rural Economy and Country Life in the Medieval West*, tr. C. Postan, Columbia, SC, 1968.

—— *Hommes et structures du moyen âge*, Paris, 1973.

—— *Guerriers et paysans, VIIe–XIIe siècle. Premier essor de l'économie européenne*, Paris, 1973. In English: *The Early Growth of the European Economy: Warriors and Peasants from the Seventh to the Twelfth Century*, tr. H. B. Clarke, Ithaca, NY, 1974.

—— *Les trois ordres ou l'imaginaire du féodalisme*, Paris, 1979. In English: *The Three Orders: Feudal Society Imagined*, tr. A. Goldhammer, Chicago, 1980.

Dyer, C., *Standard of Living in the Later Middle Ages: Social Change in England c.1200–1520*, Cambridge, 1989.

Engel, E., and Zientara, B., *Feudalstruktur, Lehnbürgertum und Fernhandel im spätmittelalterlichen Brandenburg*, Abhandlungen zur Handels- und Sozialgeschichte 7, Weimar, 1967.

Ennen, E., and Janssen, W., *Deutsche Agrargeschichte. Vom Neolithikum bis zur Schwelle des Industriezeitalters*, Wiesbaden, 1979.

Epperlein, S., *Bauernbedrückung und Bauernwiderstand im hohen Mittelalter*, Forschungen zur mittelalterliche Geschichte 6, Berlin, 1960.

—— *Der Bauer im Bild des Mittelalters*, Leipzig, 1975.

Fehn, K., *Siedlungsgeschichtliche Grundlagen der Herrschafts- und Gesellschafts-

entwicklung in Mittelschwaben. Aufgezeichnet am Beispiel der spätmittelalterlichen Rodungssiedlungen, Augsburg, 1966.

Fehr, H., *Die Rechtsstellung der Frau und der Kinder in den Weistümern*, Jena, 1912.

—— 'Das Waffenrecht der Bauern im Mittelalter', *ZRG GA* 35 (1914), pp. 111–211, and 38 (1917), pp. 1–114.

Fehring, G. P., 'Zur archäologischen Erforschung mittelalterlicher Dorfsiedlungen in Südwestdeutschland', *ZAA* 21 (1973), pp. 1–35.

Fleckenstein, J., 'Zur Frage der Abgrenzung von Bauer und Ritter', in R. Wenskus et al. (eds), *Wort und Begriff 'Bauer'*, Göttingen, 1975, pp. 246–53.

Fossier, R., *La terre et les hommes en Picardie jusqu'à la fin du XIIIe siècle*, 2 vols, Paris, 1968.

—— *Enfance de l'Europe. Aspects économiques et sociaux*, Nouvelle Clio 17, 2 vols, Paris, 1982.

—— *Paysans d'Occident (XIe–XIVe siècles)*, Paris, 1984.

Fourquin, G., *Les campagnes de la région parisiennes à la fin du Moyen Age*, Paris, 1964.

—— *Les soulevements populaires au Moyen Age*, Paris, 1972.

—— *Le paysan d'Occident au Moyen Age*, Paris, 1972.

Franz, G. (ed.), *Quellen zur Geschichte des deutschen Bauernstandes im Mittelalter*, 2nd edn, Darmstadt, 1974.

—— *Der deutsche Bauernkrieg*, 10th edn, Darmstadt, 1975.

—— *Geschichte des deutschen Bauernstandes vom frühen Mittelalter bis zum 19. Jahrhundert*, Deutsche Agrargeschichte 4, 2nd edn, Stuttgart, 1976.

—— (ed.), *Deutsches Bauerntum im Mittelalter*, WdF 416, Darmstadt, 1976.

Fritze, K., *Bürger und Bauern zur Hansezeit*, Abhandlungen zur Handels- und Sozialgeschichte 16, Weimar, 1976.

Ganshof, F. L., and Verhulst, A., 'Medieval agrarian society in its prime: France, The Low Countries and western Germany', in M. M. Postan (ed.), *The Cambridge Economic History of Europe*, 2nd edn, vol. 1, Cambridge, 1966, pp. 291–339.

Genicot, L., *L'économie rurale namuroise au bas Moyen Age (1199–1429)*, 2 vols, Louvain, 1974/5.

—— *Le XIIIe siècle européen*, Nouvelle Clio 18, Paris, 1968.

—— 'Sur le nombre des pauvres dans les campagnes mediévales. L'exemple du Namurois', *RH* 257 (1977), pp. 273–88.

Gille, B., 'Recherches sur les instruments du labour au Moyen Age', *Bibliothèque de l'Ecole des Chartes*, 120 (1967), pp. 5–38.

Goody, J., *The Development of the Family and Marriage in Europe*, Cambridge, 1982.

—— et al. (eds), *Family and Inheritance: Rural Society in Western Europe, 1200–1800*, Cambridge, 1976.

Gothein, E., 'Die Lage des Bauernstandes am Ende des Mittelalters', *Westdeutsche Zs. für Geschichte und Kunst*, 4 (1885), pp. 1–22.

—— 'Die Hofverfassung auf dem Schwarzwald dargestellt an der Geschichte des Gebiets von St Peter', *ZGO* 40 (1886), pp. 257–316.

Graus, F., *Das Spätmittelalter als Krisenzeit*, Mediaevalia Bohemica, Supplementum 1, Prague, 1969.

—— 'Vom "Schwarzen Tod" zur Reformation. Der krisenhafte Charakter des europäischen Spätmittelalters', in P. Blickle (ed.), *Revolte und Revolution in Europa*, Munich, 1975, pp. 10–30.

Grees, H., *Ländliche Unterschichten und ländliche Siedlung in Ostschwaben*, Tübinger Geogr. Studien 58, Tübingen, 1975.

Grimm, J. (ed.), *Weisthümer*, 7 vols, 1840–78; reprint edn: Darmstadt, 1957.

Grimm, P., *Hohenrode, eine mittelalterliche Siedlung im Südharz*, Halle, 1939.

Gutnowa, E. V., 'Hauptetappen und -typen des Kampfes der westeuropäischen Bauernschaft gegen die Feudalordnung in der Periode des vollentfalteten Feudalismus (11. bis 15. Jahrhundert)', *Jb. für Geschichte des Feudalismus*, 4 (1980), pp. 37–58.

Hähnel, J., *Stube. Wort- und sachgeschichtliche Beiträge zur historischen Hausforschung*, Munich, 1975.

Hagelstange, A., *Süddeutsches Bauernleben im Mittelalter*, Leipzig, 1898.

Harnisch, H., *Die Herrschaft Boitzenburg. Untersuchungen zur Entwicklung der sozialökonomischen Struktur ländlicher Gebiete in der Mark Brandenburg vom 14. bis zum 19. Jahrhundert*, Weimar, 1968.

Harvey, P. D. A., 'The English inflation of 1180–1220', *Past and Present*, 61 (1973), pp. 3–30.

Hatcher, J., and Miller, E., *Medieval England: Rural Society and Economic Change 1086–1348*, London, 1978.

Helbig, H., *Gesellschaft und Wirtschaft der Mark Brandenburg im Mittelalter*, Veröffentlichungen der Historischen Kommission zu Berlin 41, Berlin, 1973.

Helleiner, K., 'Europas Bevölkerung und Wirtschaft im späten Mittelalter', *MIÖG* 62 (1954), pp. 254–69.

—— 'Ländliches Mindervolk in niederösterreichischen Weistümern', *ZAA* 25 (1977), pp. 12–34.

Henning, F.-W., *Landwirtschaft und ländliche Gesellschaft in Deutschland*, vol. 1, Paderborn, 1979; vol. 2, 1978.

Herlihy, D., *Medieval Households*, Cambridge, 1985.

Heyne, M., *Fünf Bücher deutscher Hausaltertümer von den ältesten geschichtlichen Zeiten bis zum 16. Jahrhundert*, vol. 1: *Wohnung*, Leipzig, 1899; vol. 2: *Nahrung*, Leipzig, 1901; vol. 3: *Körperpflege und Kleidung*, Leipzig, 1903.

Hielscher, K., 'Fragen zu den Arbeitsgeräten der Bauern im Mittelalter', *ZAA* 17 (1969), pp. 6–43.

Higounet, C., *Paysages et villages neufs du Moyen Age*, Bordeaux, 1975.

Hilton, R. H., *A Medieval Soceity: The West Midlands at the End of the Thirteenth Century*, London, 1966.

—— *Bond Men Made Free: Medieval Peasant Movements and the English Rising of 1381*, London, 1973.

—— *The English Peasantry in the Later Middle Ages*, Oxford, 1975.

—— *The Decline of Serfdom in Medieval England*, 2nd edn, London, 1983.

—— *Class Conflict and the Crisis of Feudalism: Essays in Medieval Social History*, London, 1985.

Hobsbawm, E. J., et al. (eds), *Peasants in History: Essays in Honour of D. Thorner*, Oxford, 1980.

Hoffman, R. C., *Land, Liberties, and Lordship in a Late Medieval Countryside: Agrarian Structures and Change in the Duchy of Wrocław*, Philadelphia, 1989.

Höffner, J., *Bauer und Kirche im deutschen Mittelalter*, Freiburg i.Br., 1938.

Hömberg, A. K., 'Münsterländer Bauerntum im Hochmittelalter', *Westfälische Forschung*, 15 (1962), pp. 29–42.

Hoskins, W. G., *The Midland Peasant: The Economic and Social History of a Leicestershire Village*, London, 1965.

Hügli, H., *Der deutsche Bauer im Mittelalter nach den deutschen literarischen Quellen vom 11.–15. Jahrhundert*, Sprache und Dichtung 42, Berne, 1929.

Hugenholtz, F. W, N., *Die boerenopstanden uit de veertiende eeuw*, Haarlem, 1949.

Huppertz, B., *Räume und Schichten bäuerlicher Kulturformen in Deutschland*, Bonn, 1939.

Hurst, J. G., 'Wandlungen des mittelalterlichen Dorfes in England', in *Festschrift W. Abel*, vol. 1, Hanover, 1974, pp. 237–62.

Ilien, A., and Jeggle, U., *Leben auf dem Dorf. Zur Sozialgeschichte des Dorfes und zur Sozialpsychologie seiner Bewohner*, Opladen, 1978.

Irsigler, F., 'Divites und pauperes in der Vita Meinwerci', *VSWG* 57 (1970), pp. 449–99.

Jacobeit, W., *Bäuerliche Arbeit und Wirtschaft*, Berlin, 1965.

Jäger, H., *Die Entwicklung der Kulturlandschaft im Kreise Hofgeismar*, Göttingen Geogr. Abhandlungen 8, Göttingen, 1951.

Jänichen, H., *Beiträge zur Wirtschaftsgeschichte des schwäbischen Dorfes*, Veröffentlichungen der Kommission für geschichtliche Landeskunde in Baden-Württemberg 60, Stuttgart, 1970.

Jankuhn, H., *Vor- und Frühgeschichte vom Neolithikum bis zur Völkerwanderungszeit*, Deutsche Agrargeschichte 1, Stuttgart, 1969.

—— et al. (eds), *Das Dorf der Eisenzeit und des frühen Mittelalters. Siedlungsform – wirtschaftliche Funktion – soziale Struktur*, Abhandlungen der Akademie der Wissenschaften in Göttingen, Phil. Hist. Kl. 3, 101, Göttingen, 1977.

Janssen, W., *Königshagen. Ein archäologisch-historischer Beitrag zur Siedlungsgeschichte des südwestlichen Harzvorlandes*, Hildesheim, 1965.

—— *Studien zur Wüstungsfrage im fränkischen Altsiedelland zwischen Rhein, Mosel und Eifelnordrand*, 2 vols, Cologne, 1975.

—— 'Dorf und Dorfformen des 7. bis 12. Jahrhunderts im Lichte neuer Ausgrabungen in Mittel- und Nordeuropa', in H. Jankuhn et al. (eds), *Das Dorf der Eisenzeit und des frühen Mittelalters*, Göttingen, 1977, pp. 285–356.

—— and Lohrmann, D. (eds), *Villa-curtis-grangia. Landwirtschaft zwischen Loire und Rhein von der Römerzeit zum Hochmittelalter*, Francia Beihefte 11, Munich, 1983.

Kämpf, H. (ed.), *Herrschaft und Staat im Mittelalter*, WdF 2, Darmstadt. 1956.

Kellenbenz, H. (ed.), *Handbuch der europäischen Wirtschafts- und Sozialgeschichte*, vol. 2: *Europäische Wirtschafts- und Sozialgeschichte im Mittelalter*, Stuttgart, 1980.

—— (ed.), *Wirtschaftsentwicklung und Umweltbeeinflussung (14.–20. Jahrhundert)*, Beiträge zur Wirtschafts- und Sozialgeschichte 20, Stuttgart, 1982.

Knapp, T., *Gesammelte Beiträge zur Rechts- und Wirtschaftsgeschichte vornehmlich des deutschen Bauernstandes*, Tübingen, 1902.

Kosminsky, E. A., *Studies in the Agrarian History of England in the Thirteenth Century*, Oxford, 1956.

Kötzschke, R., *Studien zur Verwaltungsgeschichte der Grossgrundherrschaft Werden an der Ruhr*, Leipzig, 1901.

—— *Salhof und Siedelhof im älteren deutschen Agrarwesen*, Berlin, 1953.

Kramer, K.-S., *Die Nachbarschaft als bäuerliche Gemeinschaft*, Bayrische Heimatforschung 9, Munich, 1954.

Kriedte, P., 'Spätmittelalterliche Agrarkrise oder Krise des Feudalismus?', *Geschichte und Gesellschaft*, 7 (1981), pp. 42–68.

Kroeschell, K. A., 'Rodungssiedlung und Stadtgründung. Ländliches und städtisches Hagenrecht', *Blätter für deutsche Landesgeschichte*, 91 (1954), pp. 53–73.

Kuchenbuch, L., *Bäuerliche Gesellschaft und Klosterherrschaft im 9. Jahrhundert: Studien zur Sozialstruktur der Familia der Abtei Prüm*, VSWG Beiheft 66, Wiesbaden, 1978.

Kuchenbuch, L. and Michael, B. (eds), *Feudalismus. Materialien zur Theorie und Geschichte*, Frankfurt a.M., 1977.

Lamprecht, K., *Deutsches Wirtschaftsleben im Mittelalter*, 3 vols, Leipzig, 1885/6.

Langdon, J., *Horses, Oxen and Technological Innovation: the Use of Draught Animals in English Farming from 1066 to 1500*, Cambridge, 1986.

Laslett, P., *The World We Have Lost*, London, 1965.

Le Goff, J., *Das Hochmittelalter*, Frankfurt a.M., 1965.

—— *Kultur des europäischen Mittelalters*, Frankfurt a.M., 1970.

Le Roy Ladurie, E., *Les paysans de Languedoc*, 2 vols, Paris, 1966. In English: *The Peasants of Languedoc*, tr. J. Day, Urbana, Ill., 1974; tr. B. Bray, London, 1978.

—— *Times of Feast, Times of Famine: A History of Climate since the year 1000*, New York, 1971.

—— *Montaillou, village occitan de 1294 à 1324*, Paris, 1976. In English: *Montaillou: Cathars and Catholics in a French Village, 1294–1324*, tr. B. Bray, London, 1978.

Linck, E., *Sozialer Wandel in klösterlichen Grundherrschaften des 11. bis 13. Jahrhunderts*, Veröffentlichungen des Max-Planck-Instituts für Geschichte 57, Göttingen, 1979.

Lütge, F., 'Das 14./15. Jahrhundert in der Sozial- und Wirtschaftsgeschichte', in id., *Studien zur Sozial- und Wirtschaftsgeschichte*, Stuttgart, 1963, pp. 281–335.

—— *Geschichte der deutschen Agrarverfassung vom frühen Mittelalter bis zum 19. Jahrhundert*, Deutsche Agrargeschichte 3, 2nd edn, Stuttgart, 1967.

Martini, F., *Das Bauerntum im deutschen Schrifttum von den Anfängen bis zum 16. Jahrhundert*, Halle, 1944.

Mayer, T., 'Die Entstehung des "modernen" Staates im Mittelalter und die freien Bauern', ZRG GA 57 (1937), pp. 210–88.

—— (ed.), *Adel und Bauern im deutschen Staat des Mittelalters*, Leipzig, 1943.

—— 'Die Königsfreien und der Staat des frühen Mittelalters', in *Das Problem der Freiheit*, VF 2, Sigmaringen, 1955, pp. 7–56.

—— (ed.), *Die Anfänge der Landgemeinde und ihr Wesen*, VF 7/8, 2 vols, Konstanz, 1964.

Mendras, H., *Sociétés paysannes. Eléments pour une theorie de la paysannerie*, Paris, 1976.

Metz, W., 'Die Agrarwirtschaft im karolingischen Reiche', in *Karl der Grosse. Lebenswerk und Nachleben*, vol. 1, Düseldorf, 1965, pp. 489–500.

Mitterauer, M., *Grundtypen alteuropäischer Sozialformen*, Stuttgart, 1979.

—— and Sieder, R., *Von Patriarchat zur Partnerschaft. Zum Strukturwandel der Familie*, Munich, 1977.

Mollat, M., and Wolff, P., *Ongles bleues, Jacques et Ciompi. Les révolutions populaires en Europe aux XIVe et XVe siècles*, Paris, 1970.

Müller, W., *Entwicklung und Spätformen der Leibeigenschaft am Beispiel der Heiratsbeschränkungen*, VF Sonderband 14, Sigmaringen, 1974.

Müller-Mertens, E., *Karl der Grosse, Ludwig der Fromme und die Freien*, Berlin, 1963.

—— 'Der Stellingaufstand. Seine Träger und die Frage der politischen Macht', ZfG 20 (1972), pp. 818–42.

Nekuda, V., *Pfaffenschlag*, Studia Musei Moraviae, Brünn, 1975.

Nitz, H.-J. (ed.), *Historisch-genetische Siedlungsforschung. Genese und Typen ländlicher Siedlungen und Flurformen*, WdF 300, Darmstadt, 1974.

Njeussychin, A. I., *Die Entstehung der abhängigen Bauernschaft als Klasse der frühfeudalen Gesellschaft in Westeuropa vom 6. bis 8. Jahrhundert*, Berlin, 1961.

Oexle, O. G., 'Die mittelalterlichen Gilden: Ihre Selbstdeutung und ihr Beitrag zur Formung sozialer Strukturen', in *Soziale Ordnungen im Selbstverständnis des Mittelalters*, Miscellanea Medievalia, 12, 1, Berlin, 1979, pp. 203–26.

Ott, H., *Studien zur spätmittelalterlichen Agrarverfassung im Oberrheingebiet*, QFA 23, Stuttgart, 1970.

Patze, H. (ed.), *Der deutsche Territorialstaat im 14. Jahrhundert*, VF 13/14, 2 vols, Sigmaringen, 1970.

—— (ed.), *Die Grundherrschaft im späten Mittelalter*, VF 27, 2 vols, Sigmaringen, 1983.

Perrin, C.-E., *Recherches sur la seigneurie rurale en Lorraine d'après les plus anciens censiers (IXᵉ–XIIᵉ siècle)*, Paris, 1935.

—— 'Le servage en France et en Allemagne', in X. Congresso Internazionale di Scienze Storiche, *Relazioni*, vol. 3, Rome 1955, pp. 213–45.

Petri, F., 'Entstehung und Verbreitung der niederländischen Marschenkolonisation in Europa', in W. Schlesinger (ed.), *Die deutsche Ostsiedlung des Mittelalters als Problem der europäischen Geschichte*, VF 18, Sigmaringen, 1975, pp. 695–754.

Pirenne, H., *Sozial- und Wirtschaftsgeschichte Europas im Mittelalter*, 3rd edn, Munich, 1974.

Porschnew, B. F., 'Formen und Wege des bäuerlichen Kampfes gegen die feudale Ausbeutung', *Sowjetwissenschaft, Gesellschaftswiss. Abteilung*, 1952, pp. 440–59.

Postan, M. M. (ed.), *The Cambridge Economic History of Europe*, vol. 1: *The Agrarian Life of the Middle Ages*, 2nd edn, Cambridge, 1966.

—— *Essays on Medieval Agriculture and General Problems of the Medieval Economy*, Cambridge, 1973.

Radbruch, R. M., and Radbruch, G., *Der deutsche Bauernstand zwischen Mittelalter und Neuzeit*, 2nd edn, Göttingen, 1961.

Raftis, A. J., *The Estates of Ramsey Abbey: A Study in Economic Growth and Organisation*, Toronto, 1957.

—— *Tenure and Mobility: Studies in the Social History of the Medieval English Village*, Toronto, 1964.

—— (ed.), *Pathways to Medieval Peasants*, Toronto, 1981.

Razi, Z., *Life, Marriage and Death in a Medieval Parish: Economy, Society and Demography in Halesowen 1270–1400*, Cambridge, 1980.

Redfield, R., *Peasant Society and Culture*, Chicago, 1963.

Riehl, W. H., *Die Naturgeschichte des deutschen Volkes*, ed. G. Ipsen, Leipzig, 1935.

Ring, R. R., 'Early medieval peasant households in central Italy', *Journal of Family History*, 4 (1979), pp. 2–21.

Rösener, W., 'Die spätmittelalterliche Grundherrschaft im südwestdeutschen Raum als Problem der Sozialgeschichte', *ZGO* 127 (1979), pp. 17–69.

—— 'Strukturformen der älteren Agrarverfassung im sächsischen Raum', *Niedersäch. Jb. für Landesgeschichte*, 52 (1980), pp. 107–43.

—— 'Zur Problematik des spätmittelalterlichen Raubrittertums', in *Festschrift B. Schwineköper*, Sigmaringen, 1982, pp. 469–88.

—— 'Grundherrschaften des Hochadels in Südwestdeutschland im Spätmittelalter', in H. Patze (ed.), *Die Grundherrschaft im späten Mittelalter*, VF 27, Sigmaringen, 1983, vol. 2, pp. 87–176.

—— 'Bauer und Ritter im Hochmittelalter. Aspekte ihrer Lebensform, Standesbildung und sozialen Differenzierung im 12. und 13. Jahrhundert', in *Festschrift J. Fleckenstein*, Sigmaringen, 1984, pp. 665–92.

—— (ed.), *Strukturen der Grundherrschaft im frühen Mittelalter*, Veröffentlichungen des Max-Planck-Instituts für Geschichte 92, Göttingen, 1989.

Rubner, H., 'Die Landwirtschaft der Münchener Ebene und ihre Notlage im 14. Jahrhundert', *VSGW* 51 (1964), pp. 433–53.

Sabean, D. W., *Landbesitz und Gesellschaft am Vorabend des Bauernkriegs*, QFA 26, Stuttgart, 1972.

—— *Power in the Blood: Popular Culture and Village Discourse in Early Modern Germany*, Cambridge, 1984.

Sablonier, R., 'Zur wirtschaftlichen Situation des Adels im Spätmittelalter', in *Adelige Sachkultur des Spätmittelalters*, Veröffentlichungen des Instituts für mittelalterliche Realienkunde Österreichs 5, Vienna, 1982, pp. 9–34.

—— 'Das Dorf im Übergang vom Hoch- zum Spätmittelalter. Untersuchungen zum Wandel ländlicher Gemeinschaftsformen im ostschweizerischen Raum', in *Festschrift J. Fleckenstein*, Sigmaringen, 1984, pp. 727–45.

Schlesinger, W., 'Die Hufe im Frankenreich', in H. Beck et al. (eds), *Untersuchungen zur eisenzeitlichen und frühmittelalterlichen Flur in Mitteleuropa und ihrer Nutzung*, vol. 1. Göttingen, 1979, pp. 41–70.

—— (ed.), *Die deutsche Ostsiedlung des Mittelalters als Problem der europäischen Geschichte*, VF 18, Sigmaringen, 1975.

Schmitz, H.-J., *Faktoren der Preisbildung für Getreide und Wein in der Zeit von 800 bis 1350*, QFA 20, Stuttgart, 1968.

Schröder, K. H., and Schwarz, G., *Die ländlichen Siedlungsformen in Mitteleuropa*, Forschungen zur deutschen Landeskunde 175, 2nd edn, Bad Godesberg, 1978.

Schulz-Klinken, K.-R., *Die Entwicklung der ländlichen Handarbeitsgeräte in Südwestdeutschland*, Der Museumsfreund 14/15, Stuttgart, 1975.

Schulze, H. K., 'Rodungsfreiheit und Königsfreiheit. Zu Genesis und Kritik neuerer verfassungsgeschichtlicher Theorien', *HZ* 219 (1974), pp. 529–50.

Schulze, W., *Bäuerlicher Widerstand und feudale Herrschaft in der frühen Neuzeit*, Stuttgart, 1980.

Schwarz, D. W. H., *Sachgüter und Lebensformen. Einführung in die materielle Kulturgeschichte des Mittelalters und der Neuzeit*, Grundlagen der Germanistik 11, Berlin, 1970.

Schwer, W., *Stand und Ständeordnung im Weltbild des Mittelalters*, 2nd edn, Paderborn, 1952.

Scott, T., *Freiburg and the Breisgau: Town–Country Relations in the Age of Reformation and Peasants' War*, Oxford, 1986.

Seeliger, G., *Die soziale und politische Bedeutung der Grundherrschaft im frühen Mittelalter*, Leipzig, 1903.

Shanin, T. (ed.), *Peasants and Peasant Societies*, Harmondsworth, 1971.

Skazkin, S. D., *Der Bauer in Westeuropa während der Epoche des Feudalismus*, Berlin, 1976.

Slicher van Bath, B. H., *The Agrarian History of Western Europe (500–1850)*, London, 1963.

Spiess, K.-H., 'Zur Landflucht im Mittelalter', in H. Patze (ed.), *Die Grundherrschaft im späten Mittelalter*, VF 27, vol. 1, Sigmaringen, 1983, pp. 157–204.

Störmer, W., 'Probleme der spätmittelalterlichen Grundherrschaft und Agrarstruktur in Franken', *ZBLG* 30 (1967), pp. 118–60.

Stolz, O., *Rechtsgeschichte des Bauernstandes und der Landwirtschaft in Tirol und Vorarlberg*, Bozen, 1949.

Titow, J. Z., *English Rural Society 1200–1350*, London, 1969.

Tschajanow, A. V., *Die Lehre von der bäuerlichen Wirtschaft. Versuch einer Theorie der Familienwirtschaft im Landbau*, Berlin, 1923 (see also English translation ed. by D. Thorner listed under A. V. Chayanov).

Ulbrich, C., *Leibherrschaft am Oberrhein im Spätmittelalter*, Veröffentlichungen des Max-Planck-Instituts für Geschichte 58, Göttingen, 1979.

Verhulst, A., *L'économie rurale de la Flandre et la dépression économique du bas moyen âge'*, *Etudes rurales*, 10 (1963), pp. 68–80.

—— 'La genèse du regime domanial classique en France au haut moyen âge', in *Agricoltura e mondo rurale in Occidente nell'alto medioevo*, Spoleto, 1966, pp. 135–60.

Villages désertés et histoire économique, XIᵉ–XVIIIᵉ siècle, Paris, 1965.

Weber-Kellermann, I., *Die Familie. Geschichte, Geschichten und Bilder*, Munich, 1976.

Weiss, R., *Häuser und Landschaften der Schweiz*, 2nd edn, Erlenbach-Zürich, 1973.

Wenskus, R. (ed.), *Wort und Begriff 'Bauer'*, Abhandlungen der Akademie der Wissenschaften in Göttingen, Phil.-Hist. Kl. 3, 89, Göttingen, 1975.

Werkmüller, D., *Über Aufkommen und Verbreitung der Weistümer*, Berlin, 1972.

White, L., *Medieval Technology and Social Change*, Oxford, 1968.

Wiegelmann, G. et al., *Volkskunde*, Grundlagen der Germanistik 12, Berlin, 1977.

—— (ed.), *Geschichte der Alltagskultur*, Beiträge zur Volkskultur in Nordwestdeutschland 21, Münster, 1980.

Wittich, W. *Die Grundherrschaft in Nordwestdeutschland*, Leipzig, 1896.

Wolf, E. R. *Peasants*, Englewood Cliffs, NJ, 1966.

—— and Cole, J. W., *The Hidden Frontier: Ecology and Ethnicity in an Alpine Valley*, New York, 1974.

Wunder, H. (ed.), *Feudalismus. Zehn Aufsätze*. Munich, 1974.

—— 'Serfdom in later medieval and early modern Germany', in *Essays in Honour of R. H. Hilton*, Cambridge, 1983, pp. 249–72.

GLOSSARY

bondage: see serfdom

colonate system: dependence of peasants (*coloni*) in the later Roman Empire preceding the manorial, or seigniorial, system

common: pasture and woodland within the village bounds open to use by all village members

customal, or *Weistum*: written collection of the customs and laws of a manor or village which has traditionally been found and spoken by legal experts and thus an important part of the oral tradition of a community

demesne, or domain: farm and farmland of a feudal lord

Etter: village fence separating peasant houses from fields and pasture

***familia*, or *Hofgenossenschaft*:** community of dependants living on the demesne of a lord of the manor or on a socage farm (*Fronhof*) whose members are legal subjects of this lord

feud, or vendetta: frequently violent dispute legal in the Middle Ages between the clans of two freemen because of such crimes as manslaughter or adultery

feudal system: see pp. 16ff. and ch. 12.

***Flurzwang*:** compulsory use of collectively held land, or even the entire farmland of the peasant community, which was introduced in the high Middle Ages to optimize yield ratios, to facilitate sowing and harvesting works and thus to prevent famines as well as an overexhaustion of the soil (see three-field system)

***formariage*, or *forismaritagium*:** illegal marriage between dependants of different lordships or personal overlords (*Ungenossame* in German)

***Fronhof*, or seigniorial system:** classical type of the manorial system with the demesne farm (*Fronhof*, or socage farm) at its centre which was farmed by two types of dependants: the serfs of the manorial lord who lived on his demesne farm and his bondsmen who had to farm the holdings (*mansi*, *Hufen*) within the lord's territory and pay him dues

gavelkind: chiefly Kentish land tenure and inheritance custom by which a tenant's land was divided equally among his sons

Häger communities: planned clearance settlements in northern Germany from the high Middle Ages enjoying special privileges (*Hagenrecht*) in exchange for the initial clearing labour

heriot: due payable to the lord of the manor or the personal lord on the death of a dependant; as a rule this due consisted of the best live beast (*Besthaupt*) or the finest piece of clothes (*Bestkleid*)

hide: a measure of land (about 120 acres) and standard holding of a bonded peasant which was furnished with farmland, farm buildings, agricultural implements and usage rights (usufructs) to the commons

impartible inheritance (*Anerbenrecht*):   inheritance custom according to which a holding is passed undivided to a single heir

locator: settlement contractor in the land clearings of the high Middle Ages who was appointed by lay and ecclesiastical lords to recruit peasant settlers, to supervise the clearing and allocate the available farmland among them

manorial system: lordship over land and its occupants exerted by the king, the nobility and the Church especially in the Middle Ages which also included jurisdictional rights over the dependants of the manor

merchet: marriage fee paid by bondsman or bondswoman to the lord of the manor

Munt: in Teutonic and Germanic law the sovereign authority of the head of a household over his wife, children and servants

partible inheritance (*Realteilung*):   inheritance custom according to which a holding is divided equally among the sons on the death of a peasant landholder

serfdom: generally the dependent status of a farm labourer in feudal society who owed his lord a variety of personal and agricultural services and was transferred with the land he worked if its ownership changed hands. Serfdom, the rulership over land and jurisdictional rights over dependants were the cardinal aspects of the manorial regime

tithe: recurrent due of a tenth of farm produce (grain, wine, kitchen crops, cattle or sheep) to ecclesiastical or secular holders of this privilege

three-field system: method according to which the arable of a village was divided into open fields (*Gewanne*) for rotation between summer crops, winter crops and fallow which facilitated agricultural labour, increased yield ratios and prevented an overexhaustion of the soil. The arable, which was fragmented into strips held by the individual peasants, was farmed collectively according to the cropping schedule devised by the community (see *Flurzwang*)

Urbar: register of the dues and land of a manor

Urwechselwirtschaft: primitive cropping method which uses the land for only a few years and then abandons it to be overgrown and thus regenerated by wild plants

wergeld: compensation fee for a slain man payable to the clan of the victim by the murderer or his relatives

Zwing und Bann: term used in south-west Germany and Switzerland for what are essentially lower jurisdictional rights of a manorial lord in the medieval village

Index

Note: Most references are to peasants in Germany, except where otherwise indicated. Page references to illustrations are *italicized*.